THE USBORNE BOOK OF
FAMOUS LIVES

❦ CONTENTS ❦

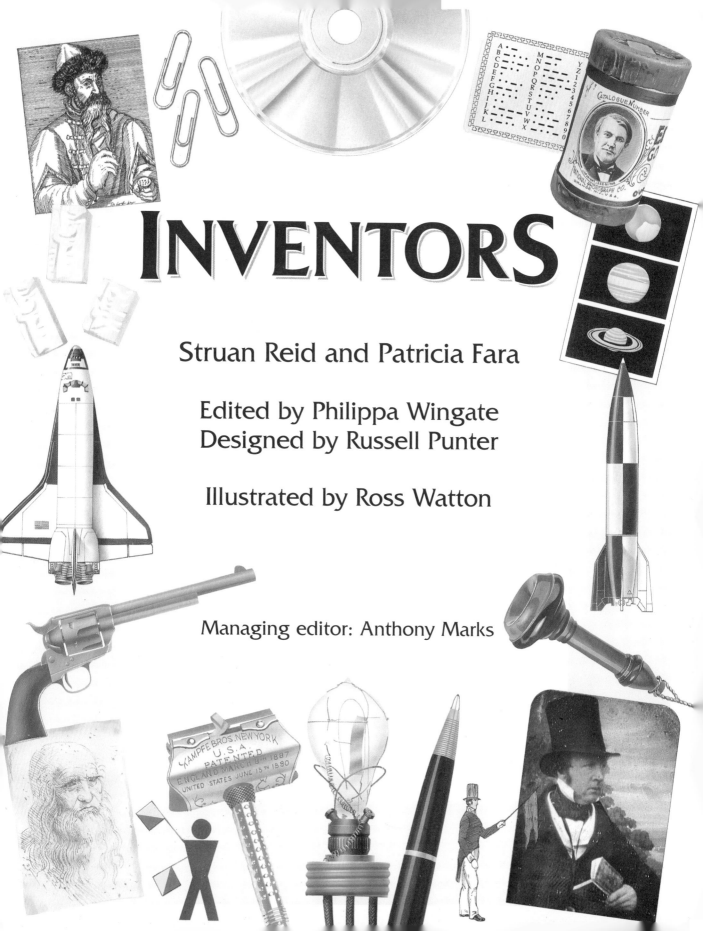

INVENTORS

Struan Reid and Patricia Fara

Edited by Philippa Wingate
Designed by Russell Punter

Illustrated by Ross Watton

Managing editor: Anthony Marks

Contents

Introduction

Inventors and inventions

An inventor is someone who discovers or produces a useful object or process that did not exist before. This section of the book is about the lives and work of the people who invented many of the things we take for granted today.

Many inventions enable people to do things they could not do before; others help them to work more efficiently. Some inventions, like the telephone or television, have had a dramatic effect on the way people live. But while others may seem less revolutionary, they have had equally important consequences. For example, the invention of the harness for horses changed the course of history, because it allowed people to use horses for long journeys and to pull heavy loads.

A "Candlestick" telephone (1905)

Modern invention

Modern inventions are rarely the product of a single inventor's efforts. For example, no single individual can claim that he or she alone invented the silicon chip. Thousands of people have played a useful role in its development and manufacture, and many thousands more have improved its design.

A silicon chip

Many companies employ teams of people to work on new ideas. For example, the managing director of the Japanese company Sony wanted a device which would allow him to listen to music while he played golf. As a result, a team of company technicians developed the Sony Walkman, the first personal stereo.

A personal stereo

Continuous invention

Many inventions have taken several centuries to develop into their modern forms, so it is impossible to give a precise date for their creation. The history of the invention of the piano, for example, lasts more than 2,000 years. Experts have calculated that more than 2,000 separate inventions and developments have contributed to the construction of modern pianos.

A dulcimer, one of the forerunners of the piano, shown in a 16th-century tapestry

Patenting inventions

When an inventor produces a new device, he or she usually applies for a patent. This is a document which gives the inventor the exclusive right to make and sell the invention.

Some people died rich and famous having made a fortune from selling their inventions, others died in poverty, unrecognized for their achievements. In this section of the book, you can read about the lives of both the successful and the unsuccessful inventors.

Whitcomb Judson's 1893 patent for the zip fastener

A stone carving showing a chariot pulled by horses in harness (7th century BC)

Dates

Some of the dates in this book are from the period before the birth of Christ. They are indicated by the letters BC. Early dates in the period after Christ's birth are indicated by the letters AD. Some dates are preceded by the abbreviation *c*, which stands for "*circa*", the Latin for "about". It is used by historians to show they are unsure exactly when a particular event took place.

About *Inventors*

Each chapter in this section of the book is a history of inventors and inventions in a particular field, such as medicine, communications and transport. On pages 46-47 a chart outlines the main developments described in this section.

Beside the title of each chapter in this section, there is a small picture or cartoon relating to an invention on those pages. You could try guessing what they are. The answers are given on page 245.

Early inventions

As soon as the first people appeared on the Earth, about half a million years ago, they started to use materials like stone and wood to make their lives more comfortable. These people were the first inventors.

It is difficult to find information about early inventors. We can often only guess at how early people accomplished many of the things they did. For example, we are still unsure exactly how the Ancient Egyptians built their pyramids so accurately.

Some historians think that workers must have pulled huge stone blocks up ramps to make the Great Pyramid.

A sloping ramp leading to the top of the pyramid

Isolated inventions

Before roads and ocean-going ships were built, many communities were isolated. Individual inventors devised their own solutions to common problems, such as how to build solid houses, kill animals or prepare food.

Certain solutions appeared independently in different places around the world, like China, South America and Egypt. But some inventions used by one group of people simply did not exist anywhere else. For centuries the use of gunpowder and the manufacture of silk were only known in China. Inventions only became more universal when people began to travel, trading goods and exchanging ideas.

Early building

The earliest stone buildings were constructed with flat roofs supported by stone beams on upright posts. Roman builders, using new inventions like arches and concrete, were able to build larger, stronger buildings like the one shown here. Many of these buildings still survive today.

Building a Roman villa

Pillars

An arch under construction

The wheel

No one knows exactly when or where the wheel first appeared. Most scholars believe that it was first used by potters in about 3500BC, either in Mesopotamia (modern Iraq) or in the central or eastern parts of Europe. The first known transport wheel appears in a Mesopotamian picture dated to c.3200BC. The picture shows a cart with solid wheels held together by metal brackets.

Wheeled transport was not used in America before the arrival of European explorers at the end of the 15th century. This may have been because there was a lack of suitable domesticated animals for pulling carts.

The development of the wheel

Mosaic of 3200BC showing wheels held together by brackets

| Wheel in three sections, fixed by brackets | Lighter spoked wheel from Egypt, 1500BC | Greek eight-spoked wheel, c.400BC | A Roman wheel of c.AD100 | Wheel designed by Leonardo da Vinci, late 15th century | An early motor car wheel |

The arch

An arch is made of wedge-shaped stones, held together by pressure. Arches which date from c.3000BC have been found at Ur, in Iraq. The Assyrians and Babylonians also used arches. The 6th-century Ishtar Gate of Babylon is made of sun-dried bricks. The Romans used arches to construct tall buildings like amphitheatres or aqueducts.

Constructing an arch

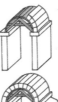

A wooden frame in the shape of an arch was constructed between stone columns.

Wedge-shaped stones were then built on the frame. The weight of the stones held them in place.

Arches were very heavy, so supports called buttresses were used to take the strain.

Strong walls were formed from two brick walls filled with concrete.

Once the concrete had dried, another wall could be built on top in the same way.

Tiles and gutters of baked clay were stamped with the name of the factory at which they were produced.

Central heating

The Romans were masters of home comforts and devised a central heating system in the 1st century AD. It was called the hypocaust and was mainly used to heat public baths, but in cold climates it was also used to heat houses. This Roman invention was forgotten in the West when the Roman Empire collapsed in the 5th century.

A Roman hypocaust

A furnace built underneath the floors produced heat.

Hot air flowed into channels called hypocausts formed by pillars. The pillars themselves also conducted heat.

Hot air and smoke were directed up inside the walls of the house through flues.

Writing

In about 3200BC, the Sumerians of Mesopotamia were the first people to write. Their script used pictures to represent words and is known as "pictographic writing"

Some early pictographic symbols and their meanings.

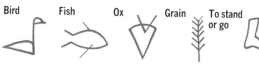

Bird   Fish   Ox   Grain   To stand or go

A stone tablet carved with pictographic writing (c.3000BC)

Five hundred years later, nearby people, like the Babylonians, Persians and Assyrians, had adapted this kind of writing into a type known as cuneiform (meaning "wedge-shaped"). They used a reed with a triangular-shaped end to make inscriptions in clay.

How to make clay tablets with cuneiform inscriptions

The cuneiform symbols for ox and grain

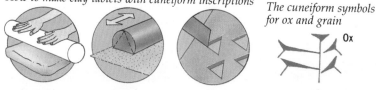

Roll a piece of clay into a pancake and then cut it into small squares.

Using sandpaper, shape the end of a stick into a triangular point.

Press the reed into the surface of the clay to form the symbols.

Ox

Grain

By about 1300BC, at Ugarit in Syria, the first alphabet had evolved from cuneiform. It contained 32 letters, each representing a single sound, which could be joined together to form a word. The Greeks adopted this system, which is the ancestor of the European alphabet.

In Egypt, in 3000BC, a writing system known as hieroglyphs was introduced. This used symbols to represent words, sounds or letters.

These Egyptian hieroglyphs spell out the name of the Egyptian queen Cleopatra

C L E O P A T R A

Money

Throughout history, many different things have been used for barter and exchange, such as copper bars, precious stones, shells and cattle. But as trade between nations increased, a standard, easy form of exchange was needed. The invention of money enabled deals to be carried out quickly using coins of an agreed value.

The first proper coinage was introduced in 700BC by King Gyges of Lydia (now in Turkey). The Lydian coins were made of a metal called electrum (a natural mixture of gold and silver) and were stamped with the king's emblem.

The king's emblem was a lion and a bull.

A mark was imprinted on the coin.

Two sides of a coin issued in about 550BC by King Croesus of Lydia

People have always attempted to measure quantities such as length, weight and time. Countless inventors, many of them now unknown or forgotten, have gradually improved the design of measuring instruments. Today, there are even devices that can measure things which are not visible to the naked eye, such as subatomic particles.

Early clocks

Sundials were the first method of charting the passing of time. In ancient times, water clocks and candles were employed, but they were never very accurate.

A 13th-century water clock, built for an Arab sultan

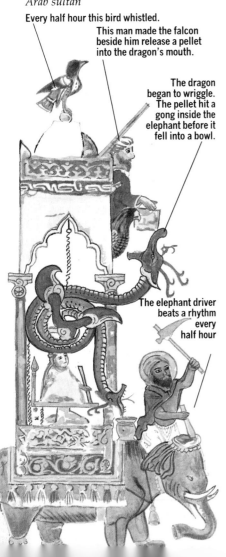

Every half hour this bird whistled.

This man made the falcon beside him release a pellet into the dragon's mouth.

The dragon began to wriggle. The pellet hit a gong inside the elephant before it fell into a bowl.

The elephant driver beats a rhythm every half hour

A new way of measuring time

The first mechanical clock, driven by weights, was made by Gerbert, a French monk who in 999 became Pope Sylvester II. Many further changes were introduced until, in 1300, fairly accurate mechanical clocks were used in Europe. A device called a verge escapement turned the hands.

The verge escapement of a mechanical clock

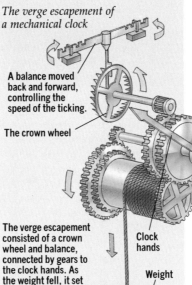

A balance moved back and forward, controlling the speed of the ticking.

The crown wheel

The verge escapement consisted of a crown wheel and balance, connected by gears to the clock hands. As the weight fell, it set the crown wheel moving around in jerks or ticks. This made the clock hands move around too.

Clock hands

Weight

Pendulums

In 1656, Christian Huygens (1629-95), a Dutch physicist, invented the first accurate pendulum clock. Its design was based on an idea suggested by Galileo Galilei (1564-1642; see page 8). Galileo had observed that pendulums always swing back and forward at regular intervals. Huygens developed a way of keeping a pendulum swinging while linking its movement to the hands of a clock dial through a series of toothed wheels.

A reconstruction of Galileo's pendulum escapement

Pivoted lever

Forked arm

Toothed wheel

Cog wheels

The swing of the pendulum made the pivoted lever and the forked arm turn the toothed wheel.

The movement of the toothed wheel turned the cog wheels.

The pendulum always took an identical period of time to swing backward and forward.

A new kind of map

A map is a two-dimensional representation of the Earth's surface. But the Earth is spherical, which means that the shapes on early maps are distorted. In 1569, Gerardus Mercator (1512-94), a Flemish geographer and mapmaker, introduced a more accurate way of drawing maps than had previously been used. He drew the world as though it was a cylinder divided up by parallel horizontal and vertical lines, called lines of latitude and longitude. In 1585, Mercator published an atlas of maps drawn using his new system. His method is still used in atlases today.

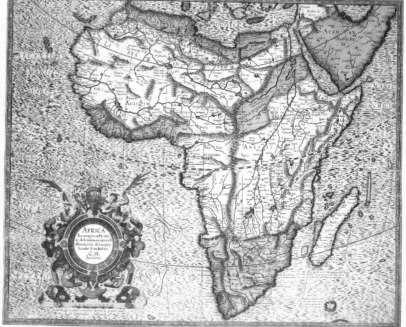

A map of Africa from Mercator's Atlas

Under pressure

Evangelista Torricelli (1608-47), was the son of an Italian textile worker. He experimented with vacuums and pressure. In 1643, he produced a device, now known as a mercury barometer, which is used to measure atmospheric pressure.

How Torricelli's barometer worked

A bowl was half-filled with mercury. The open end of a test tube full of mercury was placed under the surface of the mercury in the bowl.

Some of the mercury in the tube ran out into the bowl. As a result the level of the mercury in the tube fell.

The height of the column of mercury in the tube was directly affected by the magnitude of atmospheric pressure. It could, therefore, be used to measure atmospheric pressure.

Torricelli and his barometer

Measuring temperature

For thousands of years, people measured temperature by noting the expansion of a liquid as it is heated. But by the 17th century there were over 30 scales of measurement, so comparing readings from different thermometers was difficult. In 1742, Anders Celsius (1701-44), a Swedish astronomer devised a standard scale for the measurement of temperature. It is called the Celsius scale and contains a hundred degrees. Each degree is one hundredth of the temperature difference between the boiling and freezing points of water.

One of the first thermometers to use the Celsius scale

Absolute zero

Jacques Charles (1746-1823), a French physicist noticed that when a gas cooled, its volume contracted by 1/273 for every fall of one degree Celsius in its temperature. William Thomson (1824-1907), another physicist, suggested that at –273°C, the energy of motion of gas molecules must have reached zero. Thomson, who was awarded the title Baron Kelvin of Largs for his achievements, devised a new temperature scale in which 0°K (which is called absolute zero) is the equivalent of –273°C. Known today as the Kelvin scale, it helps scientists measure very low temperatures.

Detecting radiation

In 1908, German-born physicist Hans Geiger (1882-1945), invented a hand-held machine used to detect radiation in the air. It is now called the Geiger counter. When radiation is present, the machine makes a clicking noise. The level of radiation is counted and shown on a dial.

An early Geiger counter

Low pressure gas in a copper cylinder

Wire inside the counter

When radioactive particles entered the tube, an electric pulse passed between the wire and the cylinder's walls. The pulses were detected by a counter.

Instruments of observation

People have always wanted to see things more closely than is possible with the naked eye. The first magnifying lenses were made about 700BC in the Middle East. Since that time, developments have helped people to see the world in greater detail. Today, the electron microscope can even make the invisible visible.

An astronomical lens

One of the first people to make a practical telescope was Hans Lippershey (c.1570-1619), a Dutch optician. It consisted of a long tube with a magnifying lens at each end. The combined effect of two lenses enabled him to see distant objects in greater detail than with the naked eye.

A controversial view

Galileo Galilei (1564-1642), born in Pisa, Italy, studied medicine and became a university lecturer. In 1592, he built a telescope which magnified objects about 30 times. He used it to examine the Moon and the movement of the planets.

Galileo using his telescope

In 1632, Galileo wrote *Dialogue Concerning the Two Chief World Systems*. He supported the views of Copernicus, a Polish monk, who claimed that the Earth revolved around the Sun. This idea clashed with the teachings of the Roman Catholic Church, which said that the planets revolved around the Earth. Galileo was convicted for holding a view contrary to the teachings of the Church.

Eyepiece

Galileo's telescope of c.1609

Reflecting telescopes

In 1668, an English scientist named Isaac Newton (1642-1727) built a new kind of telescope, using mirrors as well as lenses to direct the rays of light from an object onto the observer's eye. This reduced the blurring which had previously been caused by imperfections in the lenses. This is known as a reflecting telescope.

Newton's design was improved by William Herschel (1738-1822), a German astronomer, who studied astronomy in England. He incorporated giant mirrors with diameters of 1.2m (4ft), which collected more light and enabled him to see very distant objects. With this powerful new telescope, Herschel and his sister Caroline (1750-1848) studied the skies. They discovered the planet Uranus and many new stars and comets.

Newton's reflecting telescope (1668)

Herschel's giant reflecting telescope

Light rays from the object were collected by a mirror at the base of the telescope.

Eyepiece

This mirror directed the light to the eyepiece

The telescope was mounted on a wooden ball so that it could be swivelled.

Telescope tube made of iron

The observer stood at the top of the telescope and communicated observations to an assistant in a hut at the base through a speaking tube.

Galileo made sketches of his observations of the Moon. They showed the mountains and "seas" that he had seen.

Examining small objects

The first microscope was probably invented by Hans Janssen, a Dutchman, at the end of the 16th century. It contained one lens that produced a magnified image of an object, and a second lens that enlarged the magnified image.

A prolific inventor of scientific instruments, the Englishman Robert Hooke (1635-1703), built an instrument that produced clearer images than Janssen's device. In 1665, Hooke published a book called the *Micrographia*, which contained beautiful engraved plates of his drawings of objects seen through his microscope.

Herschel's
drawings
(top to bottom):
a moon of
Jupiter;
Jupiter
and Saturn

Hut where
an assistant
recorded
observations

The telescope
could be
moved around
on wheels.

Winches were used to
move the telescope
tube up or down.

Hooke's compound microscope

Glass bulb with
oil for flame

Water-filled
bulb focused
the flame onto
the lens.

Flame

Lens

Focusing
screw

Specimen
placed here

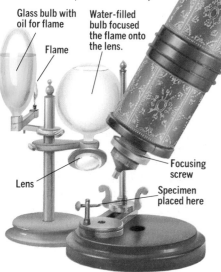

The electron microscope

All matter is made of atoms which are so tiny that they cannot be seen under ordinary microscopes. In 1933, two German scientists, Max Kroll and Ernst Ruska, developed an electron microscope which could produce an image of an atom. When tiny particles of atoms, called electrons, are fired at a specimen, it too emits electrons. These produce a three-dimensional image of the specimen on a screen.

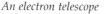
An electron telescope

Electron emitter

Beam of electrons

Magnets focus the
electrons

Bacteria cells
magnified 5,000
times

Electrons emitted by
the specimen produce
a magnified image on
this screen.

Eyepiece

Radar

Robert Watson-Watt (1892-1973), a Scottish physicist, first developed a system called radar (Radio Detecting and Ranging). The system sends out radio waves, and any object they meet reflects them back. The pattern of reflections indicates how far away the object is, its speed and direction.

Watson-Watt first used radio waves to detect storms which were endangering aircraft. In 1935, he built a long-range radar system which could detect aircraft up to 64km (40 miles) away. The system was vital in helping Britain to defend itself from air attack during World War II.

*A radar image
of a hurricane
near Mexico*

*A radar station built on
the British coast
during World
War II*

Spectacles and contact lenses

In 1280, an Italian physicist named Salvino degli Armati (1245-1317) is thought to have made the first pair of glasses. These contained two convex lenses, which magnified objects so that people could see them more easily.

Leonardo da Vinci (see page 45) experimented with the idea of contact lenses. In *Codex on the Eye*, he described a water-filled tube sealed with a lens which could correct eye defects. Da Vinci's idea was tested in the 18th century by Thomas Young and John Herschel (son of William Herschel). A layer of transparent gel was put on Herschel's eye to correct his eye defect.

*Contact lenses made
in about 1930*

*An illustration of hand-
held spectacles (1493)*

Manufacturing and automation

By the end of the 18th century, more people were starting to work in huge factories, manufacturing a variety of goods. The introduction of new inventions led to great increases in the production of cloth, iron, pottery and coal. This period of rapid technological change is called the Industrial Revolution.

Increasing output

Cloth making was the first manufacturing process to be greatly altered by new inventions. In 1733, John Kay (1704-c.1764), an English weaver, mechanized weaving when he invented the "flying shuttle". It doubled the amount of cloth a person could produce in one day.

In 1764, another English weaver named James Hargreaves (c.1722-78) invented the Spinning Jenny.

The Spinning Jenny

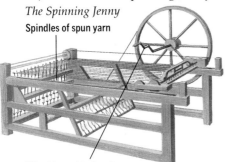

Spindles of spun yarn

Wheel turned by hand

Eight spindles could be worked by a hand-turned wheel, so a single operator could spin eight threads. In 1771, Richard Arkwright (1732-92) built a water-powered spinning machine that produced stronger thread than the Spinning Jenny.

Arkwright's spinning machine

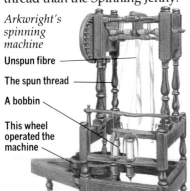

Unspun fibre

The spun thread

A bobbin

This wheel operated the machine

A steam-driven toy

The use of steam as a source of power can be traced back as far as the 1st century AD, to a Greek engineer named Hero of Alexandria. He designed a toy consisting of a metal sphere filled with water. The sphere was heated over a fire. When the water inside it boiled, steam began to escape from two holes on opposite sides of the sphere. This produced a force that caused the sphere to rotate.

Hero considered his invention no more than a clever toy.

Steam engines

In the 18th century, giant steam engines were used to power machinery. The first was made in 1698, by Thomas Savery (c.1650-1715), an English engineer. Inside the engine, steam from a boiler passed into the cylinder. A plunger, called a piston, was forced out of the cylinder by the pressure of the steam. Cold water was sprayed onto the cylinder to cool and condense the steam. This produced a much lower pressure inside the cylinder, causing the piston to fall again. His engine was used to pump water out of flooded mines.

Later, Thomas Newcomen (1663-1729), another Englishman, improved Savery's machine, which often broke down. In Newcomen's machine the piston was chained to one end of a wooden crossbeam. The pumping machinery was attached to the other end.

Newcomen's steam engine

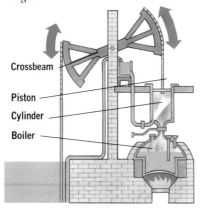

Crossbeam

Piston

Cylinder

Boiler

In 1777, an engineer named James Watt (1736-1819) designed an engine with a separate condenser, into which steam from the cylinder was passed and cooled. This allowed the engine to be kept hot, reducing fuel consumption and saving time.

Watt's steam engine became the main source of power in Britain's textile mills.

Coal was burned in a furnace to heat the water in the boiler.

A steam-pipe carried steam from the boiler to the cylinder.

Boiler

The cylinder contained a piston. The piston was driven up and down by changes in pressure inside the cylinder.

Here in the condensing system, exhaust steam from the cylinder was turned back into water. The water was then lifted into a separate tank, and pumped back to the boiler.

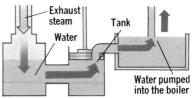

Exhaust steam

Water

Tank

Water pumped into the boiler

Sewing machines

The first sewing machine was designed in 1830, by a French tailor named Barthélemy Thimonnier. A wheel, powered by a foot pedal, raised and lowered a needle. It could sew 200 stitches in a minute, compared to the 30 stitches of a tailor. But many tailors feared they would lose their jobs, and an angry mob destroyed 80 of the machines.

Elias Howe (1819-67), an American engineer, also developed a sewing machine. But to support his family he was forced to sell his invention for a small sum of money. Later he found that Isaac Singer (1811-76) was selling sewing machines based on his original design. In 1854, Howe launched a law case against Singer, in which he won the right to receive payment for all sewing machines sold in the USA.

Needle thread

Connecting belt

Needle

Presser foot

Bobbin hook

A cutaway picture of a modern sewing machine

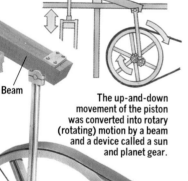

Thimonnier using his sewing machine, patented in 1830

An early sewing machine

Needle

How a sewing machine makes a stitch

The needle pierces the cloth.

A hook on the bobbin catches the needle thread.

The needle thread is looped around the bobbin.

The needle rises and pulls the stitch tight.

Robots

A robot is a machine that can be instructed to perform tasks. One of the first robotic devices was the automatic pilot, invented in 1913, by an American named Elmer Sperry (1860-1930). He developed instruments that were sensitive to a plane's movements. If the plane veered off a certain flight path, the automatic pilot adjusted the controls to correct its direction.

In the 1940s, mechanical arms were used to handle dangerous chemicals behind protective screens. Today increasingly precise robots are being built. Some can be given verbal commands and respond to their surroundings.

A cutaway picture of a robotic arm used for welding

Beam

The up-and-down movement of the piston was converted into rotary (rotating) motion by a beam and a device called a sun and planet gear.

Sun and planet gear

Flywheel

This belt transferred the movement of the fly wheel to power machinery

This pump supplied cold water to the condensing system.

These hoses supply water, air and electricity to the welding gun.

The welding gun is attached to the robotic arm.

These wires supply electricity to the robot.

This joint called the "elbow" allows the arm to rotate.

This joint allows the arm to move up and down.

This is "Wabot", a Japanese-made robot with two legs. It was built to study how robots can walk and balance.

Motor cars

T he first horseless road vehicles, built at the end of the 18th century, were huge steam-powered carriages. In 1860, the invention of the internal combustion engine (see below) made smaller, fuel-driven vehicles a possibility. Since then thousands of inventions have contributed to the development of faster, cheaper, readily available motor cars. It is estimated that there are almost 500 million motor cars on the road today.

A steam-driven carriage built in 1770 by French army engineer Nicolas Cugnot

Horseless carriages

The first lightweight engine was built in 1860 by Étienne Lenoir (1822-1900), a Belgian engineer. It is called an internal combustion engine because a mixture of air and coal gas was burned in a tube (called a cylinder) inside the engine. The power produced by the burning gases moved a piston which, in turn, rotated the wheels. Lenoir attached his engine to an old cart and drove down a dirt track in a wood.

In 1876, Nikolaus Otto (1832-91), a German engineer, produced a "four-stroke" engine, which takes its name from the four movements made by the piston inside the engine (see panel). Most modern motor car engines are based on Otto's design.

Lenoir's gas engine

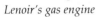

A four-stroke cycle

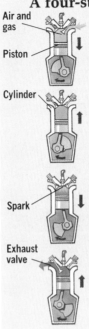

Air and gas

Piston

1) The "induction" stroke – A piston descends, sucking a mixture of air and gas into the cylinder.

Cylinder

2) The "compression" stroke – The piston is pushed back up, compressing the gas in the top of the cylinder.

Spark

3) The "power" stroke – An electric spark ignites the gas at the top of the cylinder. It explodes, pushing the piston down.

Exhaust valve

4) The "exhaust" stroke – The piston rises again, forcing the burned gases out through an exhaust valve.

Benz

The first motor car ever sold was produced by Karl Benz (1844-1929). He developed an internal combustion engine which ran on gasoline. The vehicle he attached it to had three wheels and a horseshoe-shaped steel frame. Benz tested his vehicle in 1885, and it reached a speed of 14.5km/h (9mph).

Benz's gasoline-driven car

A steering handle turned the front wheel.

Leather seat for driver and passenger

Seat spring

Hand brake

Fuel tank

Wheels with solid rubber tires

The engine was attached behind the seat.

A chain transmitted power from the engine to the back wheels.

Daimler

In 1885, Gottlieb Daimler (1834-1900) and Wilhelm Maybach (1846-1929), two German engineers, developed a lightweight, high speed engine to run on gasoline. They attached it to a wooden bicycle, and created the first motorbike. By 1889, they had produced the first four-wheeled motor car. Its wheels were turned by a belt-drive mechanism.

Daimler's car

It had a steering column and a four-speed gearbox. Daimler also developed the carburetor, which mixes the air and gasoline vapor that ignites in the cylinders, making an engine run more efficiently. Daimler set up the Daimler Motor Company in 1890, which he then merged with the Benz Company in 1926 to form Mercedes–Benz. (Mercedes was the name of the daughter of one of Daimler's backers.)

Mass production

At the beginning of the 20th century, cars were still extremely expensive because they were built by hand for individual customers. Henry Ford (1863-1947), born into a farming family in Michigan, believed that reducing the price of cars would greatly increase public demand for them. In 1903, he set up his own business called the Ford Motor Company. He standardized the components from which cars were constructed and introduced the idea of a moving assembly-line to build his cars. A car was moved from one worker to the next, each of whom performed a simple task in its construction.

The first mass-produced car, the Ford Model T, rolled off the production line in 1908. By 1913, 1,000 cars were being produced each day.

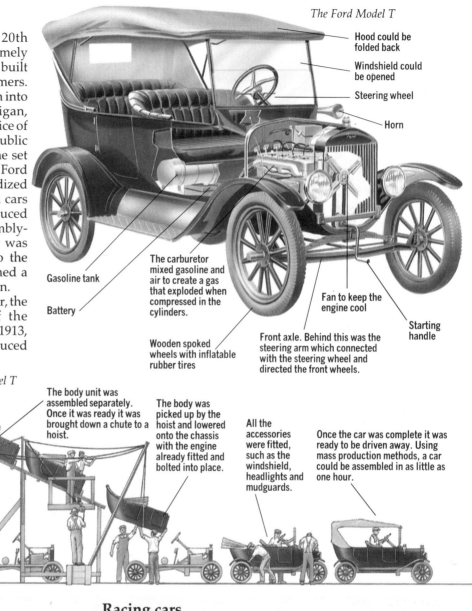

The Ford Model T

Hood could be folded back

Windshield could be opened

Steering wheel

Horn

Fan to keep the engine cool

Starting handle

Front axle. Behind this was the steering arm which connected with the steering wheel and directed the front wheels.

Wooden spoked wheels with inflatable rubber tires

The carburetor mixed gasoline and air to create a gas that exploded when compressed in the cylinders.

Battery

Gasoline tank

The assembly line of the Ford Model T

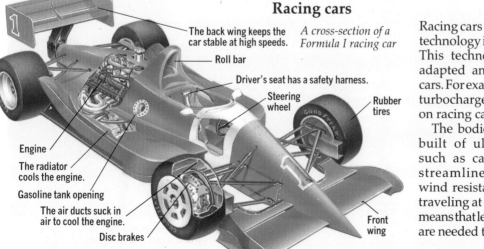

The chassis was a strong steel frame on which the major parts of the car - the wheels, engine and mechanical parts - were attached.

The body unit was assembled separately. Once it was ready it was brought down a chute to a hoist.

The body was picked up by the hoist and lowered onto the chassis with the engine already fitted and bolted into place.

All the accessories were fitted, such as the windshield, headlights and mudguards.

Once the car was complete it was ready to be driven away. Using mass production methods, a car could be assembled in as little as one hour.

Racing cars

The back wing keeps the car stable at high speeds.

Roll bar

Driver's seat has a safety harness.

Steering wheel

Rubber tires

A cross-section of a Formula I racing car

Engine

The radiator cools the engine.

Gasoline tank opening

The air ducts suck in air to cool the engine.

Disc brakes

Front wing

Racing cars incorporate the latest technology in the motor industry. This technology is often later adapted and used in ordinary cars. For example, disc brakes and turbochargers were first tested on racing cars.

The bodies of racing cars are built of ultra light materials such as carbon fiber. A low, streamlined design reduces wind resistance when the car is traveling at high speed. This also means that less power and gasoline are needed to drive the car.

Trains and railways

The age of railways began at the end of the 18th century, with the invention of the steam engine and the introduction of cast iron rails. At that time, many people believed that it was dangerous to travel faster than the speed of a galloping horse, and opposed the development of locomotives.

Rail tracks were first used in mines to transport coal.

The first steam locomotive

An English mining engineer named Richard Trevithick (1771-1833) realized that steam engines could be used to propel vehicles along tracks. In 1804, he introduced the *New Castle*, the first steam locomotive ever to run on rails. It pulled wagons containing 70 passengers, and ten freight

The Catch Me Who Can, a locomotive built in 1808 by Trevithick

containers, along a track almost 16km (10 miles) long. It could travel at a top speed of 8km/h (5mph).

A new railway age

One of the most famous early railway engineers was George Stephenson (1781-1848), an Englishman. He was a fireman in a coal mine and a very skilled mechanic. The owner of the mine where he worked asked him to build a locomotive to carry coal.

In 1814, he produced the *Blucher*, a steam engine that could pull a weight of 30.5 tonnes (30 tons) at a speed of 6.5km/h (4mph). But it took a long time for the engine to build up enough power to move.

George Stephenson's Locomotion

Stephenson worked hard on improving both locomotives and the rails they ran on. In 1825, he built the first public railway to carry steam trains. He also designed the *Locomotion*, the steam engine which pulled the world's first public passenger train.

Stephenson's Rocket

Locomotives quickly became an important means of transportation. In 1829, the directors of the Liverpool and Manchester Railway offered a prize for the best steam locomotive. Stephenson and his son, Robert (1803-59) won the competition with an engine called the *Rocket*, capable of speeds of up to 48 km/h (30mph). to 48km/h (30mph).

Stephenson's Rocket pulling a passenger wagon.

Passenger wagons

The wheels were made of wood with metal rims.

The tender carried coal for the fire and a barrel of water for making the steam.

The advantages of electricity

Some inventors investigated the possibility of building trains powered by electricity. In 1879, Ernst von Siemens (1816-92), a German electrical engineer, exhibited a train that ran on a 274m (300yd) long electrified track. Electric trains are quieter, safer and cause less pollution than steam trains.

Soon Germany and Britain had built tramways. Carriages called trams ran along tracks, powered by electricity. The use of electric railways gradually spread worldwide.

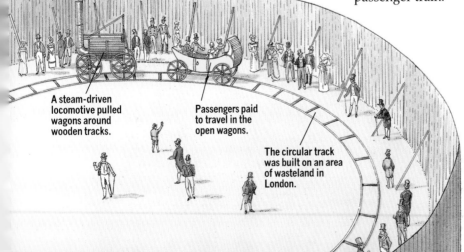

A steam-driven locomotive pulled wagons around wooden tracks.

Passengers paid to travel in the open wagons.

The circular track was built on an area of wasteland in London.

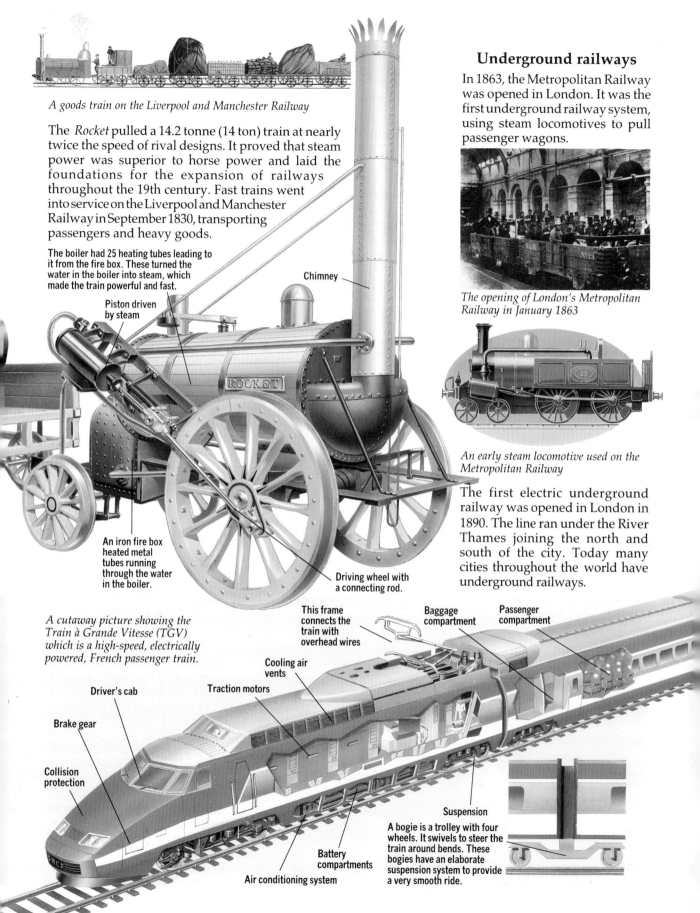

A goods train on the Liverpool and Manchester Railway

The *Rocket* pulled a 14.2 tonne (14 ton) train at nearly twice the speed of rival designs. It proved that steam power was superior to horse power and laid the foundations for the expansion of railways throughout the 19th century. Fast trains went into service on the Liverpool and Manchester Railway in September 1830, transporting passengers and heavy goods.

The boiler had 25 heating tubes leading to it from the fire box. These turned the water in the boiler into steam, which made the train powerful and fast.

Piston driven by steam

Chimney

ROCKET

An iron fire box heated metal tubes running through the water in the boiler.

Driving wheel with a connecting rod.

Underground railways

In 1863, the Metropolitan Railway was opened in London. It was the first underground railway system, using steam locomotives to pull passenger wagons.

The opening of London's Metropolitan Railway in January 1863

An early steam locomotive used on the Metropolitan Railway

The first electric underground railway was opened in London in 1890. The line ran under the River Thames joining the north and south of the city. Today many cities throughout the world have underground railways.

A cutaway picture showing the Train à Grande Vitesse (TGV) which is a high-speed, electrically powered, French passenger train.

This frame connects the train with overhead wires

Baggage compartment

Passenger compartment

Cooling air vents

Traction motors

Driver's cab

Brake gear

Collision protection

Battery compartments

Air conditioning system

Suspension

A bogie is a trolley with four wheels. It swivels to steer the train around bends. These bogies have an elaborate suspension system to provide a very smooth ride.

Sea transport

The first sailors used trees, grass and animal skins to build rafts and canoes. But as sea transport became essential for communication and trade, stronger and faster ships were needed. In time, wooden sailing ships were replaced by vessels made of iron and later of steel. The invention of the steam engine (see page 10) meant that ships no longer had to rely on oars, wind or tides for power.

Steam power

Frenchman Claude Marquis de Jouffroy d'Abbans (1751-1832) built the first steamboat, called the *Pyroscape*, in 1783. The boat had a steam engine which turned its paddle wheels.

In 1836, an English farmer named Francis Pettit Smith (1803-74) designed a screw propeller. It had curved blades which propelled a boat forward by pushing water backward. Unlike a paddle wheel, a propeller stayed under water and was less easily damaged.

The Pyroscape, built in 1783

The Great Eastern was launched in 1858.
Both paddles and engines powered the ship.

Revolutionary ship design

Isambard Kingdom Brunel (1806-59), an English engineer, revolutionized ship design. In 1837, he designed the *Great Western*, the largest wooden ship of its time and the first steamship to sail across the Atlantic regularly.

Brunel's next vessel, the *Great Britain*, was driven by a huge screw propeller and built of iron, making it very strong.

Brunel's largest ship was the *Great Eastern*. It was designed to transport 4,000 passengers in great luxury and carry enough coal to sail from England to Australia and back. It was launched in 1858, but there was an explosion on board, and it proved too expensive to run. Brunel died soon after the launch, overworked and financially ruined. The *Great Eastern* was sold for scrap 30 years later.

Isambard Kingdom Brunel

Submarines

In the 17th century, one of the first boats to travel under water was built for King James I of England by Cornelius Van Drebbel (c.1572-1633), a Dutchman.

The Nautilus was built in 1800. It was driven under water by a hand-cranked propeller and above water by a sail.

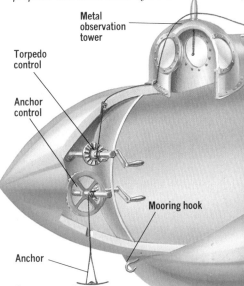

Metal observation tower
Torpedo control
Anchor control
Mooring hook
Anchor

Later, an American engineer and inventor named Robert Fulton (1765-1815) designed the *Nautilus* for Emperor Napoleon I of France. This submarine could carry four passengers and remain submersed for three hours.

The first naval submarine was designed by an Irish engineer named John Holland (1840-1914). In 1900, he made the *Holland VI*, which had an internal combustion engine for travel above water and an electric motor for moving underwater.

A cutaway diagram of the Ben Franklin, a modern research submarine

Surface radio antenna
TV camera
Surface lookout
Hatch
Control panel
Ballast tank
Propulsion motor
Viewing ports

The sail could be folded when the submarine submerged.

A handle was used to turn the sail when sailing above water.

The pilot turned the propeller using handles and gears.

The torpedo could be released under enemy ships.

A propeller drove the submarine underwater.

Rudders directed the submarine up or down when it was in the water.

Pumps to expel water

Deep-sea divers

Deep-sea divers are affected by water pressure. Breathing air that is not at the same pressure as the surrounding water can be extremely dangerous.

In 1819, a German mechanic named Augustus Siebe (d.1872) designed a diving suit that solved this problem. It was made of waterproof canvas and had a screw-on helmet. A pipe supplied air from the surface, and a pressure pump in the pipe kept the air at the same pressure as the water around the diver. The suit enabled people to dive safely to depths of up to 100m (328ft) so that they could build and repair under water structures.

Siebe's diving suit

Hovercraft

The hovercraft was invented in 1959, by a British engineer named Christopher Cockerell (b.1910). He designed a vessel with a long, flexible skirt hanging down beneath it. Large fans on the deck sucked in air. The air was pumped down through the vessel in powerful streams called "peripheral jets". The high-pressure air was captured by the skirt, creating a cushion which lifted up the craft, allowing it to hover above smooth surfaces such as water or ice.

Cockerell carried out an experiment to demonstrate the principle of peripheral jets.

Cockerell testing a model of one of his hovercraft designs

Cockerell's early experiment

Hairdryer

Tin cans

Tin cans

Kitchen scales

A cross-section of a hovercraft

Air blown into cans where it is forced to the edges

Propellers suck in air

Air inflates the flexible skirt, forming an air cushion

He used two tin cans, a hairdryer and kitchen scales. He pumped air into the cans, which lay one inside the other. This created high-pressure air jets which lifted the cans above the kitchen scales.

By 1968, regular hovercraft services were operating between England and France.

A cutaway diagram of a modern SR-N4 hovercraft

Fins and rudders

Propeller

Fan intake

Lift fan

Control cabin

Outer trunk

Engines

Transmission shaft

Buoyancy tanks

Transmission main gearbox

Air transport

The idea of being able to fly has captured people's imagination from the earliest times. In Greek mythology, a man called Icarus tried to fly to the Sun with wings made of feathers and wax. But hot air balloons, the first successful way of flying, were not built until the 18th century. Aircraft were invented in the 20th century and soon revolutionized both transport and warfare.

Balloon flight

Balloons filled with hot air float because hot air is lighter than cold air. The first successful hot air balloon was built in France in 1783 by the Montgolfier brothers, Joseph (1740-1810) and Étienne (1745-99).

The balloon was made from paper pasted onto linen.

A sheep, a duck and a cockerel were among the first passengers. They flew for about eight minutes, covering only a short distance. The first balloon flight with human passengers lasted about 25 minutes and covered a distance of 8km (5 miles).

Later, instead of hot air, balloons were filled with gases that are lighter than air, such as hydrogen. Ballooning became a very popular sport. But when one of the first balloons crash landed, the people who found it thought it was a monster and tried to kill it.

Long-distance balloons

Balloons were very difficult to steer. They often blew a long way off course, or climbed so high above the Earth's surface that pilots had difficulty breathing. In 1852, Frenchman Henri Giffard (1825-82) designed an "airship", a balloon 44m (144ft) in length and pointed at each end. It was steered by a propeller, and driven by a steam engine.

In 1898, Ferdinand von Zeppelin (1838-1917) built an airship with a rigid frame inside made of a lightweight metal. After this, huge airships were built for passenger trips. One, the *Graf Zeppelin*, made 144 transatlantic flights. But in 1937, 35 people were killed when the world's largest balloon, the *Hindenburg*, caught fire. Airships were taken out of service shortly after this.

Wooden struts supported the wings.

Twin rudders at the rear gave directional control.

Gun platform

Observation platform

Winch platform

Bow cabins

Control car

Observation and gun platform

Aircraft compartment

Helium gas cell

Metal frames

An American airship. In Europe, airships were converted into bombers in World War I and carried out air-raids, dropping bombs on London.

A pioneer of flight

A flying machine which successfully imitated a bird's flight was built by a rich English landowner, Sir George Cayley (1771-1857). In 1853 he launched a glider, piloted by his coachman, from a hilltop on his estate in Yorkshire.

Otto Lilienthal (1849-96), a German engineer, made over a thousand flights in monoplane (single-wing) and biplane (double-wing) gliders that he had designed and built. But he was eventually killed when one of his gliders crashed.

The pilot hung below the glider and moved his body and legs to control the direction of flight.

Otto Lilienthal's glider

The Wright brothers' Flyer I was powered by an engine and two propellers.

Wooden propeller

Flexible but strong wooden frame

The pilot had simple handles to control the plane's movement.

The plane was powered by a four-cylinder engine. The power was transmitted from the engine to the propellers by a bicycle chain.

The wings were covered in a cotton fabric.

Thin wires were used to twist the wings to lift one side or the other. This meant that the plane could not only fly level but also bank to either side to make turns.

The first aircraft flights

Orville (1871-1948) and Wilbur (1867-1912) Wright were the sons of an American bishop. They designed an extremely lightweight engine and fitted it to their first aircraft, *Flyer I*.

On December 17, 1903, Orville Wright piloted the first powered and controlled aircraft flight. He made four flights that day. The longest lasted 59 seconds and covered a distance of 260m (852ft). *Flyer III*, built in 1905, was the first efficient plane. It could fly for over half an hour, and was easy to steer and control. In 1909, the American army recognized the importance of the Wright brothers' achievement and ordered a military version of the plane.

Wilbur Wright in Flyer III

From aircraft to helicopters

Igor Sikorsky (1889-1972) was an engineer who emigrated to America from Russia. In 1939, he built the first modern helicopter, *Sikorsky VS-300*. Like helicopters today, it had a single main propeller called a rotor and a small tail propeller. It was able to take off and land vertically, fly backwards and sideways, and hover.

The Sikorsky VS-300

Defying gravity

In the 17th century, the British scientist Isaac Newton (1642-1727) predicted that it would be possible to launch an object into space. Two hundred years later Konstantin Tsiolkovsky (1857-1933), a Russian school teacher, calculated that a

rocket would have to travel at about 40,250km/h (25,000mph) to leave the Earth's atmosphere. He realized that if certain liquid fuels were mixed and ignited, the explosion could propel a rocket into space at such a speed. In 1926, the first liquid fuel rocket was launched by an American named Robert Goddard (1882-1945).

Space travel was made possible by the work of a German engineer, Baron Wernher von Braun (1912-77). During World War II, he designed a number of rockets, including the V-2 missile. It could travel at a speed of 1.6km (1 mile) per second, to a target over 322km (200 miles) away (see page 41).

After the war, von Braun worked on the American space project. In 1958, he built a system called *Jupiter* which launched the USA's first satellite (see page 29).

The Space Shuttle, launched in 1977, was the first reusable spacecraft.

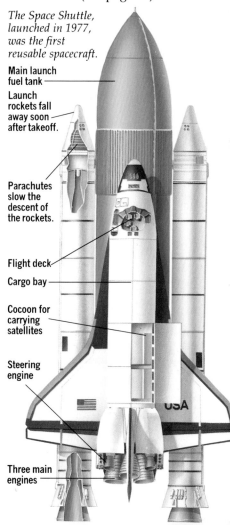

Main launch fuel tank

Launch rockets fall away soon after takeoff.

Parachutes slow the descent of the rockets.

Flight deck

Cargo bay

Cocoon for carrying satellites

Steering engine

Three main engines

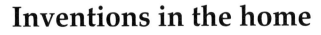

Inventions in the home

In the 20th century, many inventions have transformed life in the home. Standards of hygiene have risen with the introduction of new ways of storing and preserving food. Exhausting tasks which had previously been performed by hand are now quickly completed using a variety of electrical devices.

Electric irons

The first irons were metal pans, filled with hot charcoal. They were used in the 8th century by the Chinese to smooth silk. In the 17th century, pieces of cast iron fitted with handles were heated on a fire or stove. In 1882, Henry Seely, an American, made an iron that had an electric element.

An early electric iron

Electric element

High-powered cleaning

Up until the 19th century, people had to clean their carpets by beating or washing them. The first mechanical carpet cleaners were sweepers with rotating brushes, or devices fitted with bellows to suck up dust.

The first successful vacuum cleaner was invented by Hubert Booth (1871-1955), a British engineer, who set up the British Vacuum Company in 1901. His fuel-driven machine, known as the "Puffing Billy", was taken from house to house by a horse-drawn van. Uniformed employees put hoses through windows to clean people's carpets. Booth's machine was such a success that he was asked to clean the ceremonial carpet at Westminster Abbey, London, before the coronation of King Edward VII of England.

In 1908, an American named Murray Spangler patented a new lightweight vacuum cleaner. His design was eventually made and marketed by a firm owned by William Hoover.

An early Hoover "bag and stick" vacuum cleaner

An electric motor turned a large fan, creating a vacuum inside the Hoover. The vacuum sucked in dirt and dust off the carpet, which was collected in a large bag at the back.

A brush at the front picked up and pushed back dirt.

On/off switch

Keeping cool

Food which is kept cool lasts longer than food left at room temperature. People often used ice to preserve things until Karl von Linde (1842-1934), a German inventor, made the first domestic refrigerator. It was powered by a steam motor which pumped a gas called freon into pipes behind a food cabinet. Inside the pipes the gas condensed into a liquid. As this happened, the temperature of the freon dropped, cooling down the food cabinet.

The first electric refrigerator was designed in 1923 by two Swedish inventors, Balzer von Platen and Carl Munters.

A cutaway of a modern refrigerator

Evaporator absorbs heat from the air

Freezer compartment

Cooled air at the top sinks to the bottom; warmer air rises to be cooled.

Compressor

Condenser

A compressor pumps freon gas around the refrigerator inside pipes. When it reaches the condenser it is condensed into a liquid. Its temperature drops, cooling the refrigerator.

A close shave

The first safety razor, in which only the edge of the blade touched the skin, was made in 1771, by Jean-Jacques Perret, a Frenchman. Before this, blades were unshielded, making shaving dangerous. King Camp Gillette (1855-1932), an American salesman, had the idea of a razor blade which was thrown away when blunt. With an inventor, William Nickerson, he patented the disposable safety razor in 1901. In 1908, 300,000 razors and 13 million blades were sold.

An early disposable razor

The head of the razor could be taken apart and a new blade fitted.

Electric toaster

In 1909, the General Electric Company of the USA produced the first electric toaster. A slice of bread was placed on a mesh of wires heated by an electric current. The bread had to be turned over when one side was done, to toast the other side.

An American named Charles Strite designed the first pop-up toaster in 1927. It had heating elements to toast both sides of the bread at once. A clockwork timer turned off the electricity and, at the same time, released a spring which ejected the toast.

An electric toaster, dating from 1938

Coiled wires glowed red hot when the electricity was switched on.

The bread was placed here and pushed into the toaster.

Washing machines

The world's first electric washing machine was built in 1906 by an American, named Alva Fisher. Dirty clothes were placed in a horizontally-mounted metal drum, which was rotated by an electric motor. As the clothes tumbled they gradually became clean. The first combined electric washer and tumble dryer was introduced in 1924 by the Savage Arms Co. of the USA.

A modern tumble dryer

Heating element

Drum

Hot air is pumped into the rotating drum. This heats the water held in the clothes causing it to evaporate.

An electric motor turns the drum

A condenser unit dries the moisture in the air inside the drum.

Pump

Electric kettles

The first electric kettles contained wires in separate compartments beneath their bases. The water did not come into contact with the wire and therefore took a long time to heat up. In 1923, Arthur Large made a breakthrough. He developed a copper tube containing a wire that could safely be covered by water in a kettle. It heated water quickly.

An electric kettle made in about 1920

Electric element

Canned food

Food preserved in tin canisters was introduced by an Englishman named Peter Durand. His idea was bought by a company called Donkin, Hall and Gamble. They set up a canning factory in 1811 and canned foods were sold in London shops by 1830.

This can of roast veal was taken on an expedition to the Arctic in 1824. When scientists opened it 114 years later, the meat was in perfect condition.

Microwave ovens

In 1945, the idea of making an oven which used radio waves to heat up food was patented by an American inventor named Percy Spencer. In a microwave oven, food is bombarded with radio waves, called microwaves. These make the molecules inside the food vibrate, producing heat which cooks the food quickly.

A modern microwave oven

The microwaves are directed onto a fan. This spins around and spreads the waves throughout the oven.

A special metal mesh across the oven door prevents the microwaves from escaping, but allows the food to be viewed safely.

A turntable rotates so that the food will be cooked evenly.

The microwaves are generated in a vacuum tube called a magnetron.

Control panel

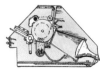

A revolution in the office

With the mass-production of a selection of tiny electronic components, many sophisticated devices have become commonplace in offices. Word processors, photocopiers and facsimile machines have simplified business transactions all over the world. This new equipment also enables more and more people to work from home.

Mechanical writing

The first practical typewriter was designed in 1867, by Christopher Sholes (1819-90), an American newspaper editor and politician. He spent much of his spare time inventing. With his friend, Carlos Glidden, he invented a numbering machine, which they later decided to convert into a lettering machine.

Sholes built about 30 different machines and designed a keyboard layout similar to that used today. But he did not make money out of his invention. He sold it to a company named Remington and Sons, who sold their first typewriter in 1874. Typewriters soon became very popular. The author Mark Twain, an early enthusiast, typed his own manuscripts.

An early Sholes typewriter

Drum carrying paper

Small hammers with inked letters strike the paper.

Cutaway showing rods connecting the keys with the letters.

Christopher Sholes with one of his typewriters

Keyboard

Personal computers

In 1964, a US company called IBM produced the first word processor. It was a typewriter with a computer memory that could store text on magnetic tapes. When a tape was played back, the typewriter printed out the text. In 1978, another US company, called Qyx, introduced a machine which used magnetic disks to store text. These disks could store more information than the tapes, and allowed the user to retrieve stored information quickly.

In the 1980s, personal computers running special word processing programs began to replace typewriters. Today computers can be used to produce many types of publications, such as this book, to keep accounts and to store and organize huge amounts of office information of all kinds.

A modern personal computer

Monitor

System unit, inside which are the workings of the computer

Floppy disk drive into which floppy disks can be inserted.

Hard disk drive

Graphics card

Keyboard

Mouse

Paper clips

The paper clip was invented in 1900 by Johann Vaaler of Norway. The design, which has remained almost the same ever since, consisted of a simple double loop of wire which could hold sheets of paper tightly together. Before, loose pieces of paper had to be pinned together.

Sticky tape

In 1928, Richard Drew an American, produced a general-purpose sticky tape. It was known as "Scotch tape", but in Europe it was sold under the name "Sellotape". It consisted of a strip of clear plastic called cellulose, with glue on one side.

Photocopying

In 1938, an American inventor named Chester Carlson (1906-68) invented the xerographic copier, now known as the photocopier. Modern photocopiers work in the following way:

1. An image of the page to be copied is projected onto a metal plate using a light source and lenses. The plate is electrically charged, creating positive and negative charges on its surface.

2. Light areas of the image destroy the positive charges on the plate. Where the image is dark, the positive charges remain. The plate is then coated with toner powder.

3. The toner powder sticks to the positively charged areas of the metal plate. It is then transferred onto a sheet of paper which comes from the feed tray.

4. The toner powder is then sealed onto the sheet of paper as it passes between two heated fusing rollers.

Mirrors

Fusing rollers seal the toner powder onto the paper.

Photo-receptor drum

Toner powder

Paper feed tray

Photographic exposure lamp

Photographic lens

Chester Carlson with his invention

The picture above shows a cutaway of a modern photocopier

Facsimile transmission

A facsimile (fax) machine can transmit text and photographs by telephone to a receiving machine a few seconds later. The first fax machine appeared in 1843. It consisted of a pendulum which scanned raised lettering and sent out electrical pulses. Modern machines use diodes (see page 32) which detect light reflected from the document being sent.

In 1922, Arthur Korn, a German physicist, sent photographs by radio transmission across the Atlantic. The first fax service was set up in 1926.

How a modern fax machine works

1. The document to be faxed is fed in here.

2. A fluorescent tube bounces light off the document, reflecting its image onto a lens.

3. The lens passes the light to a microprocessor. This breaks the image down into a series of lines.

4. The lines are then changed by another microprocessor into white and black dots. These are converted into a number code - "1" for white and "0" for black.

5. Another microprocessor converts this information into signals which are sent down a telephone line.

6. At the receiving fax machine, the telephone message is converted back to a number code.

7. The code is sent to a printer, which contains a line of dots which heat up or cool down according to the electrical current supplied by the number code.

8. An image of black dots is formed on a piece of paper, matching the information given by the code.

The ballpoint pen

In 1938, a design for the first ballpoint pen was patented by Lazlo Biro (1900-85) a Hungarian artist and journalist, and his brother Georg, a chemist. They called their pen the biro. Ink from a reservoir inside the pen flowed onto a free-moving steel ball.

A special ink was invented for use in ballpoint pens. It dried instantly when it was exposed to air. The pen was first used by the British Royal Air Force, because it did not leak at high altitudes.

A ballpoint pen, 1940s

Ink in a plastic tube

Ink flows onto a small metal ball.

Construction and buildings

In the 18th and 19th centuries, millions of people left rural areas to work in the world's growing industrial cities. Many traditional building methods had to change in order to provide accommodation for the new urban population. The work of many inventors enabled architects to design and construct much bigger, brighter and safer buildings.

Cranes

The earliest description of a crane appears in a handbook written in about 10BC by the Roman architect Vitruvius. It consisted of a pole held in position by ropes, with a pulley at the top. A rope running through the pulley was attached to heavy loads such as building materials or ships' cargoes. The loads were then lifted by slaves in a treadmill.

The crane described by Vitruvius

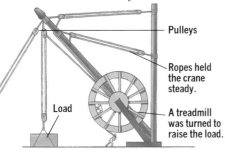

Pulleys

Ropes held the crane steady.

Load

A treadmill was turned to raise the load.

A more efficient crane, known as the derrick crane, was designed in Italy during the 15th century. Steam-powered cranes were built in the 19th century by a Scots engineer named John Rennie (1761-1821).

Building the Tower of Babel – an illustration of the mythical tower, from an English book published in 1425

A bucket being raised with ropes and pulleys

Elevators for high-rise buildings

During the 19th century, architects designed such tall buildings that machinery was needed to transport people and goods up and down them. Elisha Otis (1811-61) was an engineer from Vermont. In 1852 he took a job in a factory in New York, where he designed a steam-powered safety elevator. It included a spring operated safety mechanism to hold the passenger platform securely if the elevator cables broke. Otis demonstrated his new invention to the public. He was lifted high up in the air in an elevator and then its cables were cut. In 1857, the first safety elevator was installed in a New York department store.

Elevators were installed at the Eiffel Tower in Paris in 1889.

Ticket collector

Passengers going up a leg of the Eiffel Tower.

A driver controlled the speed.

Elevator controls

One of the elevators carried sightseers up 160m (146ft) to a viewing platform.

The elevator was hydraulically powered, which means the car was pushed up rails using a liquid under pressure.

Moving staircases

In 1894, the world's first escalator was installed as a tourist attraction on a pier at Coney Island, New York. It was named the "inclined elevator" and was designed by Jesse Reno, a businessman from New York. A conveyor belt pulled around a sloping ramp. But the ramp sloped at an angle of about 30 degrees to the ground, which made it dangerous for passengers. So Reno replaced the ramp with a set of rotating steps.

In the early 1980s, a Japanese company named Mitsubishi built the first spiral escalator. It was installed in a department store.

Toilets

As the population in cities increased, a hygienic way of disposing of sewage was urgently needed. In 1778, Joseph Bramah (1748-1814), an English cabinet maker whose job was fitting water closets (an early kind of toilet), designed and patented a new toilet. A valve shut the toilet off from the main sewer pipes when it was not in use. This stopped poisonous gases from seeping into houses.

Lifting this handle opened two flaps. One flushed water into the bowl, and the other let it drain away.

Bramah's toilet

Locks

Bramah also invented a complex lock. He offered a reward to anyone who could open it. 75 years later, at London's Great Exhibition of 1851 (a fair at which the world's newest technology was shown), a visitor finally picked it open; even then it took 51 hours.

Locks were first used in Ancient Egypt. They were made of wood and were opened using a key. The key had cylindrical pins of different lengths which fitted into grooves in the lock. Inspired by the Egyptian ideas, Linus Yale (1821-68) produced a modern pin lock, known as a Yale lock.

Bramah's original lock of 1787

How a Yale lock works

- Springs
- Plug
- Tumblers
- Key
- Cylinder

The lock consists of a brass cylinder with a central plug, both with a row of holes. In each hole is a moveable pin made in two pieces called a tumbler. Springs hold down the tumblers.

The key has a serrated top edge. When it is inserted, it pushes up each tumbler against its spring so the holes in the tumbler align with the edge of the central plug.

When the key is turned, the central plug also turns. A lever attached to the central plug draws in a bolt and the lock opens.

Gas lamps

Mantle

Most early gas lamps were simply holes in gas pipes. When lit, the escaping gas gave off a very weak light. In 1885, an Austrian chemist, Carl Auer (1858-1929), designed a new kind of gas lamp. It contained a device known as a mantle, which consisted of a mesh of carbonized cotton that glowed brightly when heated in a gas flame.

Auer's gas mantle of 1885

Electric lighting

In 1878, an English scientist named Joseph Swan (1828-1914) invented an electric light bulb. It consisted of a glass bulb containing a filament made of carbonized cotton. He removed air from the bulb, because without air the filament would never burn away.

The following year, Thomas Edison (1847-1931), a prolific inventor from the USA, also produced a light bulb. After experimenting with filaments of carbonized thread, he used carbonized paper filaments. In 1880, he began manufacturing light bulbs that were safe to use in houses, and sold them for $2.50 each. Eventually Thomas Edison combined forces with Swan to form the Edison and Swan United Electric Light Company.

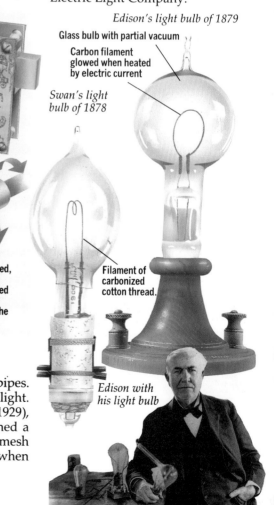

Edison's light bulb of 1879

Glass bulb with partial vacuum

Carbon filament glowed when heated by electric current

Swan's light bulb of 1878

Filament of carbonized cotton thread.

Edison with his light bulb

Printing

Before printing was invented, texts had to be copied out by people called scribes. Only a small number of books could be produced, which made them very expensive. In one day, a printer could produce the amount of material that a scribe took a whole year to complete. Books and pamphlets became widely available, and knowledge and new ideas spread more quickly.

Blocks and types

The first printed pages were prayer sheets, produced in Japan in the 8th century. They were made from blocks of wood, carved with raised characters or pictures. But each block took a long time to make, and could only be used for one page.

The Diamond Sutra, the oldest known printed book, AD868

In about 1045, Pi Cheng, a member of the royal court of China, invented movable type. He used baked clay to make single Chinese characters, which were then fitted into an iron frame ready for printing. The characters could be used again to make up new pages.

Early blocks of reusable Turkish type

Printing in Europe

In the 15th century, Johannes Gutenberg (c.1400-68), a German printer, who was unaware of the techniques used in China, developed his own version of movable type. He made individual letter blocks from metal. The letters required for each page of text were arranged in a wooden frame and fitted into a press. They were then inked and paper was pressed onto them. Thousands of copies could be printed and the type could then be rearranged for a new page.

A reconstruction of Gutenberg's press

An engraving of Johannes Gutenberg, and a page from his Bible

Conflict and loss

Gutenberg's work won him the support of Johannes Fust, a businessman. Fust was impatient for financial success. In 1455, he successfully sued Gutenberg and seized all the printing equipment.

He set up a printing business with his son-in-law, who had trained as one of Gutenberg's apprentices.

Before his death in 1468, Gutenberg saw his invention used throughout Europe and watched other people making rich profits. By 1500 there were 100 German presses in Italy, and 30 in Spain.

A wooden screw enabled the press to be raised and lowered.

Metal letters were arranged into pages in a metal frame called a forme. They were then covered in ink by a hand roller.

Padded wooden hammers were used to make all the letters level.

Paper was placed in a frame called a tympan.

The tympan hinged over the forme and both were slid under the press.

The press was screwed down so that the inked letters printed clearly onto the paper.

The steam press

By the end of the 18th century, newspapers and books had become so popular that hand-worked presses could not keep up with demand. Friedrich König (1774-1833), a printer and engineer from Saxony (now part of Germany), and his partner Andreas Bauer designed a steam-driven press. It printed 1,000 sheets an hour, four times the speed of a hand-worked press.

König's machine, produced in 1814, contained two large cylinders on which paper was placed. After one sheet had been printed on each, the cylinders rotated, bringing new blank sheets into position. The plate holding the type was automatically re-inked when necessary.

König's printing press of 1814

The press had two cylinders, so that two copies of each sheet could be printed with every backward-and-forward motion.

LONDON 1814

Feeding board

Feeding board

Sheet of paper placed here

Paper carried around printing cylinders

Inking rollers

Delivery table receives printed sheets

The invention of Linotype

In 1886, Ottmar Mergenthaler (1854-99), a German watchmaker, invented a way of setting type mechanically, called the Linotype system. Text was typed on a keyboard like a typewriter. The machine produced complete lines of type, with each letter and word correctly spaced, at four times the speed that was previously possible.

Mergenthaler using a Linotype machine

Computer typesetting

In 1965, a computer-controlled method of setting type, called Digiset, was developed in Germany. Text was typed on a keyboard and stored in a computer's memory. The text was then scanned by a laser and an image of the letters projected onto photographic paper, which was developed. The Digitek system of computer typesetting shown below was developed in the 1980s. Text stored in a computer's memory is scanned and converted into a code of pulses of light. An image of the text is projected onto photographic paper by the exposure head.

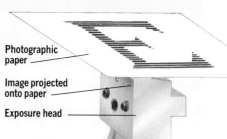

Photographic paper

Image projected onto paper

Exposure head

The Digitek system of typesetting

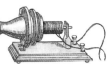

Communication machines

Before message-sending machines were invented in the 19th century, communication was a very slow and difficult process. People could only send letters by messengers, or signals using drums, smoke, fires, church bells and flashing mirrors. Most of these methods were only effective over a short distance, and correspondence over long distances was a very time-consuming operation. Even with the invention of steamships, it took months for a letter sent from Europe to arrive in Australia.

Communication towers

Claude Chappe (1763-1805), a Frenchman, introduced a system called the telegraph, which means "writing at a distance". A network of towers was built on hilltops. Each tower housed a machine with two long pointers that could be set in 49 different positions. Each of the positions corresponded to a letter or number. Operators could send messages from one tower to the next. The system was very successful. By the mid-19th century, the network of towers stretched at least 4,828km (3,000 miles) throughout France.

One of Chappe's towers

Messages along wires

The first electric telegraph machine was produced in 1837 by the British inventors William Cooke (1806-79) and Charles Wheatstone (1802-75). Electrical currents were sent along a wire to a receiving device. The currents then moved several needles that were mounted on a dial on the receiver. The needles pointed to letters, spelling out the message.

A later version of Cooke and Wheatstone's telegraph machine

Morse code

In 1843, an American artist by the name of Samuel Morse (1791-1872) designed a new telegraph code which replaced the one used by Cooke and Wheatstone. He gave every letter of the alphabet a coded equivalent of dots and dashes. When messages were transmitted, long electrical pulses stood for dashes and short pulses for dots. Morse code, as it is known, is still used today.

Morse publicized his code by erecting a telegraph wire 60km (37 miles) long, which stretched from Baltimore to Washington. He used this to transmit news of the presidential election.

In 1858, Charles Wheatstone devised a system in which an operator punched messages in Morse code onto long paper tapes which were fed through a telegraph transmitter. At the other end of the wire, a pen drew the code on to another tape, which was read and translated.

Eventually, the pen was replaced with a "sounder", which converted the dots and dashes into long and short sounds. Operators could listen to the coded message and write down the translation.

A	.-
B	-...
C	-.-.
D	-..
E	.
F	..-.
G	--.
H	....
I	..
J	.---
K	-.-
L	.-..
M	--
N	-.
O	---
P	.--.
Q	--.-
R	.-.
S	...
T	-
U	..-
V	...-
W	.--
X	-..-
Y	-.--
Z	--..

The alphabet and its equivalent in Morse code

Morse's telegraph machine printed the dots and dashes of Morse code.

Roller pulled tape along

Clockwork motor

Clockwork key to wind up receiver

Paper tape fed out from a reel in the drawer

Electromagnet

A message was tapped out with this key.

An alphabet called semaphore, invented in 1812

A B C D E F G   H I J   K L M   N   O P Q R   S T U   V W X   Y Z

Spoken messages

Some inventors concentrated on producing a device that would enable people to talk over very long distances. A breakthrough was made by Alexander Graham Bell (1847-1922), a Scotsman who lived in Boston, Massachusetts. He ran a school for the deaf, and later went on to work at the city's university.

He and Thomas Watson (1854-1934), an electrical engineer, made an instrument consisting of a transmitter (or mouthpiece) and a receiver (or earpiece). The transmitter turned voice sounds into a varying electric current. This was sent along a wire to the earpiece, where it was changed back into voice sounds.

Bell's telephone - the mouthpiece and earpiece were identical devices.

Used as a mouthpiece – the speaker's voice vibrated a diaphragm, causing an electric current passing through it to vary in strength.

Diaphragm

Used as an earpiece – the varying current passed along the wire to the earpiece, which also contained a diaphragm. The electric current made the diaphragm vibrate, reproducing the voice sounds.

Bell made the first telephone call ever on March 10, 1876. He had spilled acid on his trousers and spoke to his colleague, "Mr Watson, can you come at once, I want you." The world's first telephone exchange opened in Connecticut in 1877. Operators had to connect the lines between one caller and another by hand. New York and Boston were linked by telephone in 1883.

The mouthpiece and earpiece of a Bell telephone in use

Telephones through the ages

Over the last century, the design of the telephone has undergone many changes.

A selection of different styles of telephones

An Edison receiver, 1879 – the user turned the handle while listening.

A Crossley telephone, 1880 – the user spoke into the top of the box and listened through the receiver.

A Gower-Bell telephone, 1880s

A design introduced in the 1890s – the speaker turned the handle to call the operator.

A 'Candlestick' telephone, 1905 – the operator was called by lifting the receiver.

A 'cradle' telephone, 1930

A portable phone – these can be used without a cable.

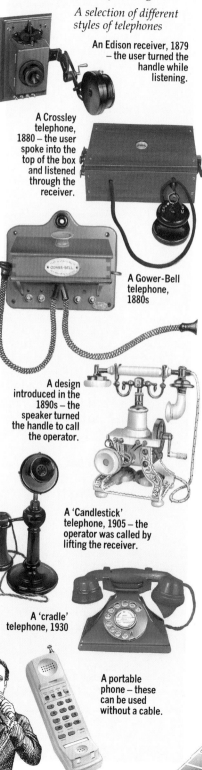

Satellite communications

Satellites are unmanned spacecraft that orbit the Earth. They can transmit telephone calls and television pictures across the world. They can also send information about weather and navigation conditions. In 1957, the USSR launched *Sputnik I*, the first man-made object to orbit the Earth.

Sputnik I

In 1960, the USA launched the *Courier* and *Echo* satellites. They relayed the first satellite telephone calls between the USA and Europe. In 1962, the USA launched *Telstar*, the first satellite to relay live television shows as well as telephone calls. It could transmit 60 calls or a single television channel at any one time.

The Telstar satellite

Today, an elaborate network of satellites links areas all over the globe. Companies can now buy private satellites for their own communication needs.

A modern communications satellite

Solar panels power the communications system.

Communications antennae send out and receive messages.

Units for telephone and television transmissions

Photography and film

People have been drawing and painting the world around them since the first cave paintings. During the 10th century, Arab astronomers used an early camera obscura (see box below) to look at images of the Sun without damaging their eyes. From the 15th century, this idea was used by artists to project images onto canvases to help them draw accurately. But only the invention of the camera in the 19th century has enabled people to produce exact replicas of the things we see.

The camera obscura

The camera obscura is a box or darkened room into which light passes through a tiny pin-hole, forming an image on the opposite inside wall. You can make your own camera obscura.

How to make a camera obscura

Make a box out of black cardboard which does not let in any light. Cut a square window into one side.

Cover the window with paper to make a screen. Make a tiny hole in the side of the box opposite the screen.

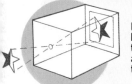

Light rays from a bright object will pass through the pinhole and form an image on the paper screen.

The first photographs

By the 18th century, people began to realize that certain chemicals are affected and changed by light. They discovered that materials coated with these substances would record patterns of light which fell across them. The world's first photograph was taken in 1826, by a French physicist named Joseph Niepce (1765-1833). He used a camera obscura to project an image onto special sheets of pewter, called plates. These had been coated with a light-sensitive substance called bitumen. It took eight hours for a blurred image to form. The length of time that light is allowed to fall on photographic plates or film is called the exposure time.

A conical camera of 1841

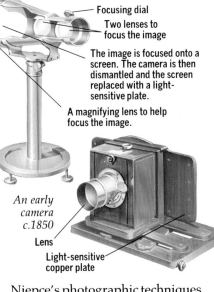

Focusing dial

Two lenses to focus the image

The image is focused onto a screen. The camera is then dismantled and the screen replaced with a light-sensitive plate.

A magnifying lens to help focus the image.

An early camera c.1850

Lens

Light-sensitive copper plate

Niepce's photographic techniques were improved by his partner Louis Daguerre (1789-1851). By 1839, Daguerre was obtaining clear photographs after an exposure time of only 20 minutes. His pictures were known as daguerreotypes and were very popular, particularly for portraits. But people sitting for a portrait had to have clamps around their heads to stop them from moving. The metal plates were very expensive and the pictures could not be copied.

Photography comes of age

William Fox Talbot (1800-77), an English scientist, invented a new method of developing pictures. He soaked paper in light-sensitive chemicals. When an image was projected onto the paper, the brightest areas turned it black, and the darkest parts left it white. This version of the image is called a negative. Fox Talbot then shone light through the negative onto another sheet of light-sensitive paper. This produced positive prints which he called calotypes, from the Ancient Greek words meaning "beautiful pictures".

William Fox Talbot

Photography for all

George Eastman (1854-1932), an American inventor, realized the commercial potential of making photography available to ordinary people. He produced a simple, hand-held camera called the Kodak no. 1, which was sold already fitted with a roll of film.

George Eastman's Kodak camera of 1888

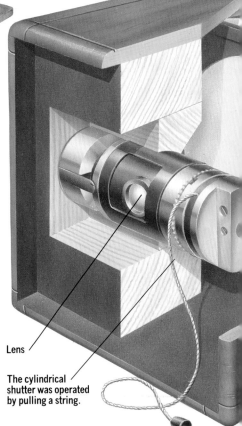

Lens

The cylindrical shutter was operated by pulling a string.

After taking one picture, the user wound the film on, ready for the next shot. When the film was finished, the camera was returned to the Eastman factory where the pictures were developed. Eastman's company motto was "You press the button, we do the rest".

Arrangement of film roll holders seen from above

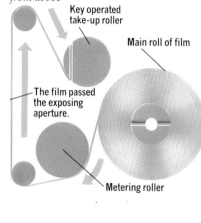

Key operated take-up roller

Main roll of film

The film passed the exposing aperture.

Metering roller

The Polaroid camera

The Polaroid camera was invented in 1947, by an American, Edwin Land (1909-91). It contained a tiny processing laboratory which produced positive black and white prints in less than one minute. The first Polaroid cameras that could take color photographs became available in 1963. Today, Polaroid cameras can develop prints in a few seconds.

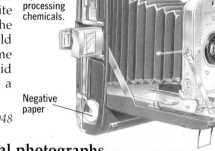

Print paper

Rollers broke open a pod of processing chemicals.

Negative paper

Edwin Land's Polaroid camera of 1948

Sequential photographs

In 1872, Eadweard Muybridge (1830-1904), a British photographer, was hired by a Californian horse owner. To settle a bet, Muybridge was asked to discover whether a galloping horse lifts all its hooves off the ground at once. He set up 48 cameras on a racing track and rigged them to be triggered by clockwork or by threads which were broken as the horse passed. He produced the sequence of photographs shown here, which settled the bet.

Photographs from Muybridge's famous experiment

The birth of moving pictures

Any image produced in our eyes takes a moment to fade. So if many pictures of an object which is changing position are viewed in rapid succession, the brain perceives the object to be in motion. This phenomenon is called "persistent vision". It is the principle on which motion pictures work.

In 1894, two French brothers, Auguste (1862-1954) and Louis (1864-1948) Lumière, heard about the Kinetoscope, a machine invented by Thomas Edison (see page 34). It was a box containing a strip of moving photographs. When the viewer looked into the box, the objects in the pictures appeared to be moving. The brothers built a similar machine called a *Cinématographe* which projected images onto a screen. In 1895, they showed 10 films.

The first Cinématographe used in Britain

Far right: Stills from an early film of a man sneezing

The take-up roller was turned by a key.

The main roller carried the film.

The film was fed past a circular exposing aperture.

A metering roller controlled the amount of film being wound on.

Radio and television

Unlike the telephone or telegraph, radio and television do not need cables or wires for signals to be transmitted. Today sounds and images can be sent rapidly via satellites from one side of the world to the other. This has dramatically affected communications as events can be reported around the world as soon as they happen.

Making waves

In the 19th century, scientists began to suspect that electrical and magnetic effects were transmitted in waves, like light. Heinrich Hertz (1857-94) a German scientist, proved this in 1885. He showed that the waves emitted by an electric spark on one side of his laboratory could be detected by a loop of wire on the other.

Messages without wires

Guglielmo Marconi (1874-1937), an Italian inventor, discovered a way in which waves could be used to send messages from one place to another without wires or cables. At the age of 20, having read about Hertz's work with electromagnetic waves, he began to carry out his own experiments. In 1894, he successfully sounded a buzzer 9m (30ft) away from where he stood.

Guglielmo Marconi with his wireless telegraph.

He pressed a key which was not connected by wire to the bell. The electromagnetic waves that made this happen are called radio waves.

Marconi moved to London, where he patented his ideas and demonstrated his equipment to the British Post Office, who decided to

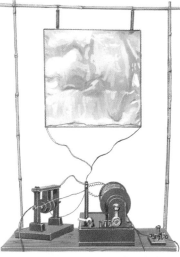

A "Marconiphone" patented in 1896

finance his work. After improving his equipment, Marconi was able to send a message in Morse code (see page 28) from England to a radio receiver 50km (31 miles) away in France.

In 1902, Marconi sent a radio signal across the Atlantic – the letter 's' in Morse code. Five years later, a Canadian scientist, Reginald Fessenden, transmitted a human voice by radio for the first time.

The Marconiphone broadcaster-receiver wireless sets (1922)

Diodes

An important contribution to the development of radio and television was made in 1904 by a British engineer named John Fleming (1849-1945), who designed the diode. Diodes are used to convert radio waves into electrical signals which can be transmitted over long distances.

Spinning discs

In 1884, Paul Nipkow (1860-1940), a German engineer, developed a disc with a spiral pattern of square holes. When the disc was rotated in front of an object, each hole captured the light from a small area of the object. These fragments could be transmitted through another disc which reformed them as a whole image on a screen. The Nipkow disc was an important step in the invention of television.

A diagram demonstrating the principle of the Nipkow disc

Light from the object passes through a spinning Nipkow disc to a photoelectric cell.

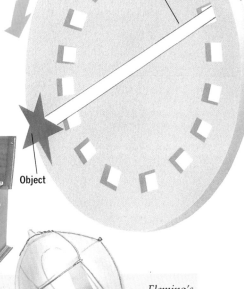

Object

Fleming's diode of 1904

Glass bulb containing a vacuum

Negative electrode

Positive electrode

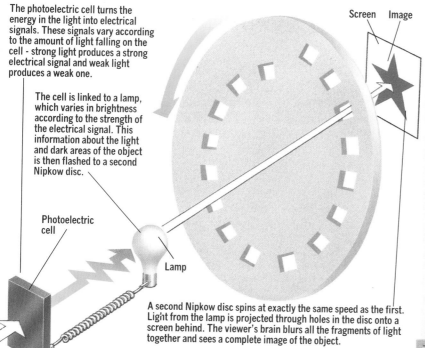

The photoelectric cell turns the energy in the light into electrical signals. These signals vary according to the amount of light falling on the cell - strong light produces a strong electrical signal and weak light produces a weak one.

The cell is linked to a lamp, which varies in brightness according to the strength of the electrical signal. This information about the light and dark areas of the object is then flashed to a second Nipkow disc.

Photoelectric cell

Lamp

Screen   Image

A second Nipkow disc spins at exactly the same speed as the first. Light from the lamp is projected through holes in the disc onto a screen behind. The viewer's brain blurs all the fragments of light together and sees a complete image of the object.

Live television

In 1926, John Logie Baird (1888-1946), a Scottish inventor, made the first television transmission of a human face. His apparatus included an old box, a cake tin, knitting needles, a bicycle lamp and a cardboard Nipkow disc. In his laboratory, he transmitted a blurred image of the face of a boy named William Taynton. As Baird improved his equipment, the pictures he produced became less distorted. Later that year he gave the first public demonstration of television.

After this breakthrough, many television systems were developed. The British Broadcasting Corporation (BBC) began operating a black and white television service from London in 1936, and by 1939 there were television receivers in 20,000 homes. In the USA in 1953, the first successful transmission of color television was made.

A television picture of a face was achieved in 1926

Baird's transmitting equipment of 1926

Nipkow disc

Slotted disc for scanning

Photoelectric cell

Spiral disc for scanning

A motor for turning the discs

Images of this puppet's head are transmitted.

A motorized wheel turned the discs.

Hi-tech television

High definition television (HDTV) was first broadcast on June 25, 1990. It was a transmission of the football match between Italy and Uruquay in the 1990 World Cup. HDTV was developed by a group of companies called Eureka 95. Television pictures are made up of lines and tiny dots called pixels. On an ordinary television set there are 625 lines and 120,000 pixels. On a HDTV there are 1,250 lines and 480,000 pixels giving the picture greater detail and clarity.

HDTV produces very realistic images.

The large number of pixels makes the image on an HDTV clear and detailed

HDTV screens can be much larger than normal TV screens.

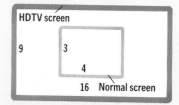

HDTV screen

9

3

4

16   Normal screen

The height/width ratio of a normal TV screen is 3:4, while that of an HDTV screen is 9:16.

HDTV viewing conditions

Range of vision

The best viewing distance for HDTV is three times the height of the screen, compared with seven times for normal televisions.

Recording sound

fter the invention of the telephone in 1876, many scientists began to research the possibilities of saving or storing sound. Once this had been achieved, inventors continually tried to improve methods of recording sound and playing it back. The machinery has become more and more sophisticated and the sound quality better and better.

A prolific inventor

During his lifetime an American-born inventor named Thomas Edison (1847-1931) registered 1,093 patents. In 1876, he set up the world's first industrial research laboratory, which he called his "invention factory". However, some inventors accused Edison of stealing their ideas.

In 1877, he produced the phonograph, one of his most famous inventions. This machine could record sounds and play them back. At first it was sold as a toy, but before long Edison and other inventors had improved its design so that it could be used to record music.

Edison's phonograph of 1877

A horn focused sound onto a metal diaphragm which touched a steel needle, called a stylus.

Sound made the diaphragm vibrate, causing the stylus to make indentations of different depths in tin foil wrapped around a wax cylinder.

Horn

Cylinder wrapped in tin foil

When the cylinder was played back, the indentations in the foil made the stylus vibrate. The vibrations were changed into sound by the diaphragm.

Tin foil
Stylus
Diaphragm
Cylinder

The gramophone

Émile Berliner (1851-1929) was a German scientist who emigrated to the USA to seek his fortune. He set up a laboratory where he researched into acoustics (the science of sound) and electricity.

In 1887, he patented a new device which he called the gramophone, after the Greek for "recorded voice". Instead of the cylinders used by Edison, Berliner stored sound in grooves on flat discs made of a substance called shellac (a resin produced by insects). The discs were played back using a needle which vibrated between the walls of the groove on the disc. The recording was played back through a loudspeaker. Berliner's discs produced a much clearer sound than Edison's cylinders.

Berliner's gramophone of 1895

Horn
Needle
Disc

Recording an early Berliner disc

This man is speaking into a mouthpiece and his voice is recorded on a disc.

Mastering

In 1891, Berliner introduced "mastering", a system used to produce many copies of a disc. A glass disc coated with shellac (called a negative) was used to engrave a recording pattern onto flat metal discs (positives). Later, he developed a system in which shellac positives were pressed from a nickel-plated negative. By 1908, Berliner's German factory was producing over six million discs a year. For the first time, people were able to listen at home to music recorded in concert halls.

Mastering a modern vinyl disc

1. Grooves are cut into a master disc made of a very hard plastic called lacquer.

2. The master disc is coated with nickel which is peeled off to be used as a negative.

3. Hot plastic is pressed between two negatives, to produce a positive.

Handle

Tape recording

The forerunner of modern tape recorders was designed in 1898, by Valdemar Poulsen (1869-1942), a Dane. He developed a machine called the telegraphone, which converted sound waves into magnetic patterns stored on a wire. To play back the sound, the wire was wound past a magnet. It generated tiny electric pulses which corresponded to the sound originally recorded. These pulses were converted back into sound waves, heard through headphones.

This 1903 Poulsen telegraphone recorded sounds on wire.

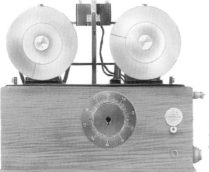

The invention of plastic tape turned the tape recorder into a commercial success. It was introduced in 1935 by AEG, a German company. The tape was coated with magnetic particles. It was light and compact, and enabled people to make longer recordings than on discs.

Today, recordings can be made on small audio cassette tapes.

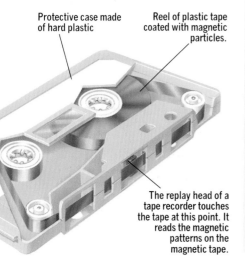

Protective case made of hard plastic

Reel of plastic tape coated with magnetic particles.

The replay head of a tape recorder touches the tape at this point. It reads the magnetic patterns on the magnetic tape.

Compact discs

In 1982, a Dutch company called Philips, and the Japanese firm Sony, introduced the first compact discs. On a compact disc, sound is stored as digital information in tiny pits on the surface. A laser beam scans the pits, and the information is converted into electrical signals and then into vibrations. There is no contact between the laser scanner and the disc, so compact discs do not wear out. They are also unaffected by scratches and dust. A compact disc can store about an hour of music.

A compact disc scanned by a laser

Microscopic pits

Laser beam

Instead of a stylus there is a laser beam. It scans the disc and "reads" the pattern of pits.

Digital audio tapes

Digital audio tapes (DAT) were introduced in 1987. They are half the size of previous audio cassette tapes, yet they can record two hours of music. Sound is recorded onto these tapes as a numbered code.

Recording sound on to digital audio tapes

A digital audio cassette

Number code

To record music onto DAT, sound is converted into a code of numbers. Inside a DAT recorder this code is converted into a magnetic pattern.

The magnetic pattern is recorded onto the DAT.

To play back the music on a DAT, this process happens in reverse. The magnetic patterns on the tape are converted into sound signals reproducing the original music.

Movie soundtracks

In 1889, Thomas Edison's assistant Charles Batchelor experimented with combining moving pictures and sound. Over the next 40 years other inventors, many of them associated with the new motion picture industry, developed methods for synchronizing film and speech.

Diagram showing how a film's soundtrack works

1. A stripe along the edge of a movie film carries the soundtrack. The width of this sound stripe varies according to the sound signals produced during the recording.

2. A light is shone through the sound stripe toward a photoelectric cell. The varying width of the stripe varies the amounts of light reaching the photoelectric cell.

3. The photoelectric cell converts the light into sound signals, which are the same as those of the original.

4. The sound signals travel down a cable to the cinema loudspeakers, where they are converted into sound waves.

Lifesavers

Life in the home and at work has always been fraught with dangers. Inventions and technological advances, such as motor cars or aircraft, create new dangers for the people using them. Inventors have had to develop safety devices to compensate for these hazards.

A miner's lamp

Working in mines has always been dangerous. Before the beginning of the 19th century, many miners were killed or injured by explosions when the candles they carried underground ignited pockets of gas. In 1815, an Englishman named Humphry Davy (1778-1829), produced a lamp in which the flame was enclosed by fine wire mesh. This stopped the lamp's flame from igniting gas in the air. The number of gas explosions in mines fell dramatically soon after the lamp was introduced.

A cutaway of Davy's safety lamp

The wire mesh absorbed the heat of the flame before it could come into contact with the gas in the air.

Wick in oil

Extinguishing fires

In 1816, an English inventor named George Manby, designed a fire extinguisher. It consisted of a metal cylinder containing water. The water was forced out of the cylinder by compressed air.

Alexander Laurent, a Russian inventor, designed the first chemical fire extinguisher in 1905. Foam which smothered flames was pumped by hand out of a metal container.

A modern fire extinguisher uses carbon dioxide gas. When the handle is pressed, a valve opens. This releases the pressure inside, and allows the carbon dioxide to turn into a gas which shoots out of the nozzle.

Handle

Valve

Carbon dioxide gas

Carbon dioxide liquid

Nozzle

Carbon dioxide gas can be directed at the flames with the nozzle.

Hidden points

Brooches made of bronze and of a similar design to modern safety pins were used to fasten cloaks in western Europe in the 12th century BC. The modern safety pin itself was designed in 1849, by Walter Hunt of New York.

Hunt's 1849 patent for the safety pin

Today's safety pins look very similar to Hunt's originals.

Jumping safely

There is a design for a parachute among the drawings of Leonardo da Vinci (see page 45). However, it is not until 1783 that a parachute was used. A Frenchman named Louis Lenormand used one to jump from a high tower. Many early parachutes looked like umbrellas.

Silk parachutes which fold away were introduced in the USA in about 1880. The first parachute with a ripcord was used in the USA in 1908.

Leonardo da Vinci's design for a parachute

In 1797, a Frenchman named André-Jaques Garnerin used a parachute to jump from a hydrogen balloon.

Green for go

In 1868, a traffic signal arm used to indicate stop and go was first used in London. It had red and green gas lamps for use at night. But the signal was abandoned after an incident in which a gas lamp exploded, killing a policeman.

In 1914, the first electrical traffic light, hand-operated and using red and green lights only, was installed in Cleveland, Ohio. The first automatic traffic lights with red, green and amber lights were installed in London in 1925.

The first traffic signal, installed in London in 1868

Arms lowered meant "go"

Arms extended meant "stop"

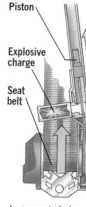

Martin-Baker Mk16 ejection seat

Parachute container

Ejection guns unit

Auxiliary oxygen handle

A pilot ejector seat

In 1921, James Martin (1893-1981), an Irish engineer, set up a company to build lightweight monoplanes. During World War II, he designed a fighter aircraft. It included a device that ejected the canopy of the cockpit, allowing the pilot to escape quickly if the plane caught fire.

After the war, Martin tackled the problem of getting pilots out of fast-moving aircraft, and he produced the ejection seat. The pilot pulled a handle above his head, and a seat powered by a compressed spring shot him out of the cockpit. Once the seat was clear of the aircraft, a mini parachute reduced its speed and a large chute allowed the pilot to descend safely. Ejection seats became standard in jet fighters from the 1950s.

The ejection sequence of a Mk16 ejection seat

3. A mini parachute, called a drogue, opens to slow the seat down.

1. The pilot pulls a handle which triggers the ejection seat.

2. Guns attached to the ejection seat fire, and all locks and connections to the chair are automatically released.

4. The seat descends with the pilot still in a sitting position.

5. The drogue is released and the lines connecting it to the seat are cut.

6. A large parachute inflates. The pilot is pulled out of the ejection seat, which is then abandoned.

7. The pilot descends on the parachute. A life-raft is automatically inflated, in case of a landing in water.

Saved by a cat

An Englishman named Percy Shaw (1890-1976) made a fortune from one simple invention. One foggy night in 1933, he almost drove his car off the edge of a cliff. He was only saved by seeing his headlights reflected in the eyes of a cat sitting at the side of the road. Inspired by this incident, Shaw invented reflecting devices that he called "cat's eyes". They were soon fitted on roads in many countries.

How a cat's eye works

A glass stud is mounted in a rubber case with a metal surround. The mounting is raised above the level of the road.

When a car passes over it, the stud descends into its rubber casing. This reduces obstruction to the car's wheel.

Once the car has passed, the stud rises again and the glass is wiped clean by a rubber pad.

Strapped down for safety

Many inventions have attempted to make people's chances of surviving a car collision greater. In 1903, Gustave Liebau, a Frenchman, patented a design for protective braces, used in cars and aircraft. This formed the basis of the modern seat belt. The Swedish car manufacturer Volvo first fitted seat belts to their cars in 1963.

In 1988, the Japanese car manufacturer Toyota fitted an electrical system in some of its cars that automatically fastens the belt. The following year, Kim Nag-Hyun of South Korea developed a system that, in the event of a collision, automatically releases the belt 30 seconds after impact.

Piston

Explosive charge

Seat belt

Automatic belt tensioners – On impact, the piston is pushed up by an explosive charge, tightening the belt.

Stages in a head-on collision of a car and a wall

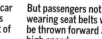

Head-on collisions cause deceleration from running speed to zero in an instant.

As the front of the car crumples it absorbs some of the impact of the collision.

But passengers not wearing seat belts will be thrown forward at high speed.

Stages in the activation of an airbag safety system.

An airbag system contained in the driver's steering wheel is activated on impact.

The airbag inflates to further absorb the energy of sudden deceleration.

When the driver is thrown forward the airbag protects him or her from serious injury.

Medical inventions

Many important inventions have helped doctors to diagnose and treat diseases. Some devices have been developed by doctors themselves, others have been produced as a result of technological advances in other fields which have then been applied to medicine.

Helping nature

Forceps are a surgical instrument used to help in the delivery of babies. They were invented by an English doctor named Peter Chamberlen (d.1631). For many years they remained a well-kept family secret, until Chamberlen's nephew, also named Peter Chamberlen (1601-83), inherited them. His use of forceps made him internationally famous in the field of childbirth.

Chamberlen's original forceps. They were like large pincers, operated by hand.

Ambulances

Dominique Larrey (1766-1842) was a French surgeon who received a gold medal for inventing a curved surgical needle. He is also famous for the invention of the ambulance. In 1792, France was at war with Prussia and Austria. Larrey saw that heavy wagons could not get to the battle front to collect wounded soldiers. He designed a light-weight carriage to transport people to hospitals quickly.

Larrey's ambulance carriage of the 1790s

Patients were placed on a thin mattress

Listening to the body

While out walking in Paris in 1816, a French doctor named René Laënnec (1781-1826) saw two children playing. One child held a stick to his ear, while the other child tapped the opposite end with a pin. The sound of the blows was transmitted along the wood. Later, Laënnec rolled up a sheet of paper and tied it with string. When he placed the tube on a patient's chest he could hear a heartbeat. He called his instrument a stethoscope, after the Greek word *stethos* meaning chest.

Try making a stethoscope of your own.

Laënnec's wooden stethoscope

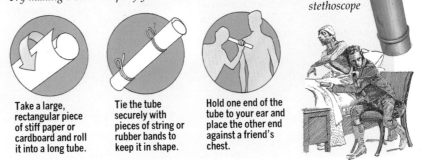

Take a large, rectangular piece of stiff paper or cardboard and roll it into a long tube.

Tie the tube securely with pieces of string or rubber bands to keep it in shape.

Hold one end of the tube to your ear and place the other end against a friend's chest.

Painless operations

An anesthetic is a drug that causes a temporary loss of feeling in a part of the body. Before anesthetics were invented, patients had to be held down by force during painful operations.

The pain-numbing effects of nitrous oxide were first noticed in 1799 by Humphry Davy (1778-1829), an English scientist. In 1846, an American dentist, William Orton, used a powerful anesthetic called ether to perform an operation on a patient's jaw. The following year, a Scottish doctor used a liquid called chloroform to reduce the pain of childbirth. In 1853, chloroform was given to Queen Victoria of England during the birth of one of her children.

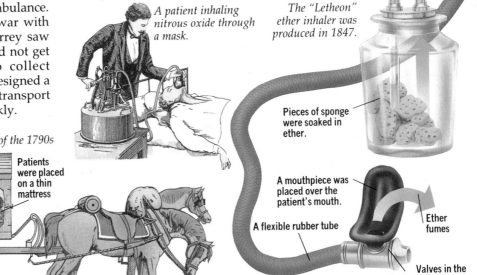

A patient inhaling nitrous oxide through a mask.

The "Letheon" ether inhaler was produced in 1847.

Pieces of sponge were soaked in ether.

A mouthpiece was placed over the patient's mouth.

A flexible rubber tube

Ether fumes

Valves in the mouthpiece enabled the patient to breathe in and out.

Injecting beneath the skin

The hypodermic syringe, used to inject drugs into blood vessels or muscles, was invented in 1853 by Frenchman Charles Pravaz.

In 1987, another French doctor, Jean-Louis Brunet, patented a device which is attached to syringes when taking blood samples. The device automatically seals the needle as soon as it is withdrawn from the patient. This reduces the risk of doctors and nurses becoming contaminated by blood infected with dangerous viruses such as AIDS or hepatitis.

A selection of syringes

19th-century syringes

Needle

Scale

In this modern syringe fluid is forced out through the needle by a plunger.

Monitoring the heart

In 1903, Willem Einthoven (1860-1927) a Dutch doctor, invented the electrocardiograph (ECG) machine. It measures and records the electrical impulses produced by the heart's activity and is used to detect irregularities which can indicate heart disease. In 1924, Einthoven was awarded a Nobel Prize for his invention. An electrocardiograph machine produces a photographic chart of the heart's pulses, which is known as an electrocardiogram.

Einthoven demonstrating equipment which monitored the heartbeat of a dog.

From submarines to babies

By 1918, French scientists led by Pierre Langevin (1872-1946) had developed the sonar (sound navigation and ranging) system. The system sends out beams of sound waves and any object they meet reflects them back. The pattern of reflections forms a picture of the object. Sonar was installed in submarines and ships to detect other vessels. The principle was used in medicine in the 1950s by Ian Donald, a Scottish doctor. He discovered he was able to study the shape of an unborn baby's body and internal organs by passing pulses of sound through its mother's abdomen. This process, called ultrasound scanning, is used to check the health of unborn children.

Ultrasound image of a human fetus in the womb

Assisted breathing

In 1929, Philip Drinker, an American engineer, designed a device called a respirator, or iron lung, which helps people with breathing difficulties. It consists of an airtight box enclosing the patient's body from the neck down. Changes of pressure inside the box force air in and out of the lungs.

Early respirator of the 1930s

A 1950s respirator

The patient lies with his or her head outside the airtight box.

Tube to the air pump

A pump created a vacuum inside the airtight box.

Each time a vacuum is created inside the box, the pressure of the atmosphere outside forces air into the patient's lungs. The air is forced out of the lungs when there is no vacuum.

Surgery using lasers

Doctors often use technology developed for non-medical purposes. Lasers, for example, were first used in industry for drilling, welding and engraving. They are now used in surgical operations to cut through flesh and seal off tiny blood vessels to reduce bleeding. The theory of laser light was suggested in 1958 by Charles Townes (b.1915) and Arthur Schawlow (b.1921), American physicists. The first laser was built in 1960 by Theodore Maiman (b.1927).

How a ruby laser works

A rod of ruby inside a spiral shaped flash lamp.

Mirror

The ruby crystal absorbs white light from the flash lamp.

It re-emits the energy as a strong red beam which can travel great distances without becoming spread out or weak.

The laser beam increases in strength as it bounces between the mirrors.

Flash lamp

Weapons and warfare

Weapons are among man's earliest inventions. The first warriors made spears and axes by tying bones and flints to sticks. The Romans used sophisticated mechanical weapons, and by AD1000 the Chinese were making gunpowder for fireworks and sending signals. In the 13th century, Europeans began using gunpowder to fire cannons and hand-held guns.

A 16th-century machine gun. Each barrel had a bullet and was fired by hand.

Today, science and warfare are very closely linked. New and increasingly deadly weapons have been invented by both chemists and physicists.

A fast-firing revolver

Early handguns were very difficult to fire. Before each shot, a gun had to be loaded with gunpowder and pellets, and a fuse lit to ignite it. A more efficient gun was patented in 1836, by Samuel Colt (1814-62) who was born in Connecticut. His gun designs included one called a revolver which could fire six shots before it needed to be reloaded. At first, revolvers were considered very complicated, but later they were extensively used in the American Civil War (1861-65) and by settlers making their way westward across the USA.

This man with two fast-firing revolvers is thought to be Black Jack Ketcham, an outlaw.

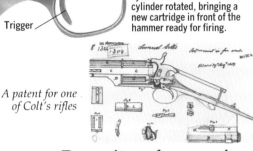

A Colt revolver

The hammer was cocked (pulled back) by hand.

When the gun was fired, the hammer struck a firing pin on the cartridge. This detonated an explosive charge and shot the bullet out of the gun barrel.

Cartridge containing a bullet

Barrel

Cartridges were placed in the cylinder. After each shot the cylinder rotated, bringing a new cartridge in front of the hammer ready for firing.

Trigger

A patent for one of Colt's rifles

A quick killing

Richard Gatling (1818-1903) was an inventor from North Carolina. After the outbreak of the American Civil War in 1861, he designed a gun, called a machine gun, which could be fired rapidly. It had ten barrels arranged as a cylinder around the central shaft. The cylinder was rotated using a hand crank. A cartridge on top of the gun dropped bullets into position for firing. The multiple barrels enabled the gun to be fired many times without overheating. It could fire 350 bullets in a minute.

Gatling's design was improved by Hiram Maxim (1840-1916) who introduced the first fully automatic machine gun in 1884.

A cutaway of a Maxim machine gun

Dynamite and peace prizes

Alfred Nobel (1833-96), a Swedish chemist, owned a factory that made an explosive called nitroglycerin. When the factory blew up in 1865, killing several people, Nobel began to look for a way to make explosives safer to handle

By mixing nitroglycerin with a chemical called *kieselguhr*, he produced a more stable substance. He sold the mixture in tubes of waxed cardboard and called it "dynamite", after the Greek word *dynamis* meaning power.

Though Nobel made his fortune manufacturing explosives, he was a dedicated pacifist. He left the bulk of his large fortune to fund the Nobel Prizes, awarded annually to people who make major contributions in the fields of literature, chemistry, physics, medicine and world peace.

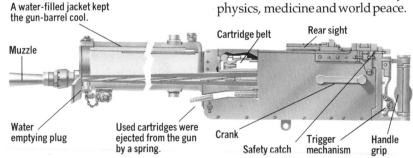

A water-filled jacket kept the gun-barrel cool.

Cartridge belt

Rear sight

Muzzle

Water emptying plug

Used cartridges were ejected from the gun by a spring.

Crank

Safety catch

Trigger mechanism

Handle grip

Chemical warfare

Fritz Haber (1868-1934) was a German chemist. His early studies involved converting nitrogen (a gas found in air) into ammonia, a substance used in crop fertilizers. He won the Nobel Prize for chemistry in 1918 for this work. But many people objected to the award because Haber had been involved in developing poisonous gases for use in warfare. He produced chlorine gas, which attacks the lining of the nose, throat and lungs. During World War I, both sides used poisonous gases.

Haber also devised a gas mask to protect both civilians and soldiers from harmful gases.

Gas masks were introduced in 1915.

Tight-fitting mask made of cotton pads soaked in chemicals

Connecting pipe

A box containing charcoal and lime-permanganate granules filtered the poisoned air.

War rockets

In 1942, a long-range rocket called the V-2 was launched (see page 19). Designed by Wernher von Braun (1912-77), it flew at several times the speed of sound, giving no warning of its approach. It had a range of 320km (200 miles). It had a warhead that weighed about 1.02 tonnes (1 ton) and was packed with explosives.

Today, many missiles are guided to their targets by electronic devices. Some have a range of 9,600km (6,000 miles), and can strike within 30.5m (100ft) of their target.

Nose fuse
Warhead
Fuse conduit
Guidance chamber
Radio control
Nitrogen bottles

A V-2 rocket

This fuel tank contains a mixture of ethyl alcohol and water.

This fuel tank contains liquid oxygen to speed up burning of fuel.

The two fuels are forced by pumps into the combustion chamber. The mixture is then ignited by gunpowder.

The exhaust fumes escape at supersonic speed.

Steerable rudder

Nuclear warfare

By the outbreak of World War II, scientists realized that if the nucleus of an atom was split in two, a huge amount of energy would be released. If this energy was uncontrolled there would be a massive explosion. A bomb based on this principle is called an "atomic bomb".

In 1942, Enrico Fermi (1901-54), an Italian scientist, built a nuclear reactor, in which he produced controlled nuclear energy. The first atomic bomb was developed under the supervision of American physicist Robert Oppenheimer (1904-67). He was in charge of the Los Alamos Science Laboratory, in New Mexico, when the atomic bomb was tested in 1945. The USA was at war with Japan and later that year they dropped two atomic bombs on the Japanese cities of Hiroshima and Nagasaki, killing many thousands of civilians. When they saw the huge destruction the bomb caused, many scientists spoke out against American plans to build another more powerful bomb, known as the hydrogen bomb or "H" bomb.

Oppenheimer (left) at a bomb testing site

This atomic bomb, called "Fat Man", was dropped on Nagasaki, Japan.

Inside the bomb was a substance called plutonium. All the atoms in the plutonium split, releasing huge amounts of uncontrolled energy.

Stabilizing fin

Nose fuse

The nuclear explosion was detonated by charges inside the bomb.

Calculators and computers

Counting and calculating systems have been needed for as long as people have bought and sold goods. One of the earliest adding machines, the abacus, was invented about 5,000 years ago, in Babylonia (now the area occupied by Iran and Iraq).

A 19th-century engraving of an abacus being used in China

Special numbers

In 1614, John Napier (1550-1617), a Scottish mathematician, invented logarithm tables. The principle of the tables was that every number had an equivalent special number called a logarithm. Logarithms made mathematical division and multiplication quick and easy. For example, to multiply two numbers their logarithms were simply added together. The resulting logarithm was looked up in the tables to find its corresponding number.

An early calculator

Blaise Pascal (1623-62) was a French mathematician. In 1642, he designed an adding machine to help his father, a tax inspector, whose job involved carrying out many complicated calculations.

Pascal's mechanical adding machine

Cogwheels turned dials next to each other in a mechanical gear system

Numbers appeared in these windows.

Dials representing units

Convinced that the machine would make their fortunes, father and son invested a lot of money in it. But their work was opposed both by clerks who feared they would lose their jobs, and by employers who preferred to pay low wages rather than buy Pascal's expensive machine.

Cogs for calculating

Charles Babbage (1792-1871), the son of a rich banker from Devon, England, was a very talented mathematician. He was concerned about errors in Napier's logarithm tables. In 1821, he began to design a "difference engine", a very large and complicated machine, designed to calculate logarithms automatically. But it was difficult to make the machine's parts accurate enough to prevent errors in its calculations.

For about ten years the British government poured money into Charles Babbage's project. But, finally, they lost patience and stopped.

Next, Babbage began to design an "analytical engine", which could carry out many different types of calculation. Working with him was mathematician Ada Lovelace (1815-52). She devised several computer programs for the engine, which were coded on cards with holes punched in them.

A modern reconstruction of Babbage's analytical engine. It was designed to be driven by steam.

Numbers were stored in columns by wheels which could be put in any of ten positions corresponding to the digits 0 to 9.

Punched program cards

Babbage devoted the last 37 years of his life to building the analytical engine. He refined his design again and again, and applied for extra funds to pay for the work. He became increasingly frustrated by what he considered a lack of public recognition and support for his work. In 1871, he died before he had completed the machine. In fact, his engine was well beyond the technology of the time and it is unlikely that it would ever have been finished.

Lady Ada Lovelace became the first computer programmer.

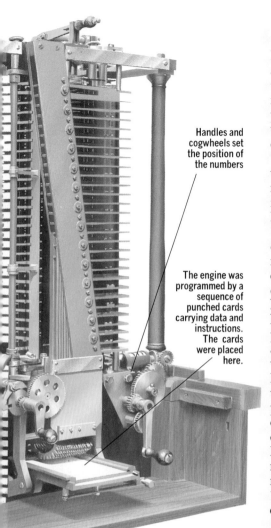

Handles and cogwheels set the position of the numbers

The engine was programmed by a sequence of punched cards carrying data and instructions. The cards were placed here.

Census collection

In the USA during the 19th century, a census of the population was taken every ten years. This became increasingly complicated as the population grew. In 1887, officials were still struggling to compile the results of the 1880 census. A competition was held to find a quicker method of analysing the figures. It was won by Herman Hollerith (1860-1929), an engineer who designed an electric counting machine. Information about each citizen was stored on a card as a series of punched holes. The position of the holes corresponded to particular characteristics, such as age or marital status. The cards were inserted into the machine. Inside, a set of wires was pushed up against them. When a wire passed through a hole, an electric circuit was completed, making a counter advance by one unit. Hollerith's invention sped up methods of processing data so much that the results of the 1890 census were compiled in only six weeks.

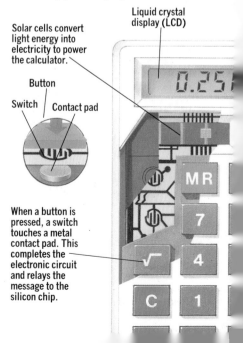

The Hollerith tabulator used to compute the results of the 1890 census.

A card used in the 1900 USA census

Electronic computers

An early electronic computer was ENIAC (Electronic Numerical Integrator and Calculator). It was developed by John Mauchly (1907-80) and John Eckert (b.1919) for the American army. Compared with modern computers it was huge, filling an entire large room. Yet it could perform fewer tasks than a modern desk-top computer.

As technology has advanced, computers have become smaller and smaller,

Eckert (right) holding one of ENIAC's components

yet they are capable of performing an increasing number of tasks.

In 1948, the glass valves, called diodes, used in the first computers (see page 32), were replaced by minute electronic devices called transistors. They were invented by three scientists: John Bardeen (b.1908), Walter Brattain (1902-87) and William Shockley (1910-89), who were jointly awarded the Nobel Prize for physics in 1956. Today, pocket calculators and computers contain tiny electrical circuit boards (called silicon chips) which include thousands of transistors.

Today, computers are used for many tasks, from composing music and creating graphics, to guiding aircraft and milking cows. You can find out more about computers and the tasks they perform on page 22.

A cutaway picture of a pocket calculator

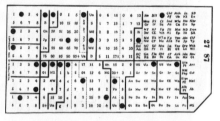

Liquid crystal display (LCD)

Solar cells convert light energy into electricity to power the calculator.

Button

Switch   Contact pad

When a button is pressed, a switch touches a metal contact pad. This completes the electronic circuit and relays the message to the silicon chip.

The power of the imagination

Throughout the centuries, inventors have imagined machines that were beyond the technological capabilities of their time. Other inventors imagined machines which we now know are beyond the realms of possibility. Some of these inventions never went further than the drawing board; others were built, tested and rapidly forgotten.

Wishful thinking

Some of the machines that inventors have believed possible in the past may seem ridiculous to us today. For example, some people believed that it was possible to build a machine which would go on working forever, without an outside power source. This was known as a perpetual motion machine. In 1618, an English doctor named Robert Fludd (1574-1637) designed a perpetual motion watermill. He believed that once the machine was moving it would continue forever. We now know that it is impossible to achieve perpetual motion. The moving parts of a machine rub together and produce friction. This wastes energy and slows the machine down.

Science fiction

Science fiction writers create imaginary worlds, filled with weird inventions. Sometimes the creators believe that in the future, with new materials and greater scientific knowledge, their vision may become reality.

A century before men walked on the Moon, the French author Jules Verne (1828-1905) wrote about space travel. Perhaps writers today, when they describe imaginary worlds are predicting how we will live in the future.

A propeller-driven skating outfit designed by William Heath Robinson

Some writers have made fun of science and invention, by dreaming up machines which could not possibly be built. The writer Jonathan Swift's book *Gulliver's Travels* is full of mock inventions, including a magnetic flying island.

Flights of fancy

In 1867, two English inventors, Edmund Edwards and James Butler, designed an aircraft based on the shape of a paper dart. It was fitted with a rudder for side-to-side control and flaps for up-and-down control. But it was powered by a steam engine and needed a furnace and boiler that would have been so heavy that the machine could never have flown.

A steam-powered aircraft designed by Edwards and Butler

Landing springs

Star wars

Archimedes (287-212 BC) was a mathematician born in Sicily. He invented many very efficient devices. He also tried to design a weapon which used giant mirrors to capture and focus the Sun's rays to destroy enemy ships. We now know that Archimedes' idea would not have worked; but even today scientists sometimes attempt projects which are beyond the capabilities of modern technology. In the 1980s the USA announced plans to build the Strategic Defense Initiative (SDI), known as "Star Wars", which involved a system of satellites used to shoot down enemy missiles with lasers. Some scientists believe the system will never work successfully.

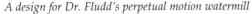

A design for Dr. Fludd's perpetual motion watermill

A channel carried the water back to the water-wheel

The water-wheel was perpetually driven around by the circulating water.

A rotating screw inside a hollow tube raised water from a tank to the channel.

Millstones for grinding corn were turned by an axle connected to the water-wheel.

The propeller was turned by steam jets on the end of each blade.

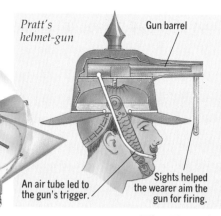

Pratt's helmet-gun

Gun barrel

A helmet gun

In 1917, Albert Pratt, an American inventor, patented a helmet fitted with a gun. To fire it, the wearer blew through a tube leading to a bulb beside the trigger. The bulb expanded, squeezing the trigger. It could also be turned upside-down and used as a cooking pot. In reality, the recoil of the gun when it was fired would have broken the wearer's neck.

An air tube led to the gun's trigger.

Sights helped the wearer aim the gun for firing.

Rudders were used to move the aircraft from side to side.

A water tank was heated by a furnace to produce the steam needed for power.

The pilot's compartment contained a furnace and boiler. It would also take one passenger.

Wires provided support

Wooden frame

Anchor for docking

The Renaissance man

Leonardo da Vinci (1452-1519), born near Florence in Italy, was one of the world's greatest artists, as well as being a talented musician and sculptor. He was also a prolific inventor. Throughout his life, he filled notebooks with drawings of many things: the human body, birds in flight and the strange machines he had invented.

Da Vinci's inventions included a flying machine with wings like a bird, vessels to travel under water, a giant crossbow, a spinning wheel, a helicopter and powerful guns. Some of these were built; but many others could not have worked and remained hidden away in his sketch books for centuries.

Leonardo's design for a tank. He was also a military engineer, designing war machines and fortifications.

Viewing turret

Wheel driven by hand cranks

A portrait of Leonardo da Vinci shortly before his death

Gun barrels

A design for a missile-detecting satellite system

Solar panels provide power

Infrared telescope

This shield protects the telescope from radiated heat.

Superfluid helium cooling system

Infrared grid locates and monitors aircraft and missiles.

A reconstruction of a giant crossbow sketched in Leonardo da Vinci's notebook

A lever was pulled and a rope holding the arrow was released. The arrow flew off.

A soldier operated a gear mechanism which pulled back the arrow.

The crossbow could be moved into position on three pairs of wheels.

Key dates in the history of invention

Dates BC

4241BC The first year in which events can be precisely dated. This is made possible by the introduction of the Egyptian calendar.

c3200BC The Sumerians in Mesopotamia are the first people to use writing and to draw a picture showing a wheel.

c3000BC The Babylonians invent the abacus, the first adding machine.

c1300BC The Syrians develop their own alphabet.

700BC Coins are used in Lydia (Turkey) for buying and selling goods.

287BC The birth of Archimedes, who invents many valuable mechanical devices using screws and levers.

c10BC The Roman architect Vitruvius describes a crane.

Dates AD

999 The first mechanical clock is invented by a monk.

c1000 The Chinese use gunpowder for fireworks and sending signals.

c1045 In China, Pi Cheng invents movable type.

1280 The first pair of glasses is made in Italy.

1450s Johannes Gutenberg's printing presses revolutionize the production of books. This, in turn, speeds up the spread of information about new inventions.

1452 The birth of Leonardo da Vinci, an artist who invents numerous machines.

1569 Mercator, a Flemish mapmaker, introduces a new method of drawing maps.

1592 Galileo builds a telescope which magnifies things 30 times.

1614 John Napier, a Scottish mathematician, invents his logarithm tables.

1642 Blaise Pascal designs an adding machine to speed up his father's tax calculations.

1643 Evangelista Torricelli makes a device now known as the mercury barometer for measuring air pressure.

1656 Christian Huygens designs an accurate pendulum clock, based on Galileo's ideas.

1665 The illustrations in Robert Hooke's *Micrographia* reveal the power of new microscopes.

1668 Isaac Newton builds a reflecting telescope.

1698 The first steam engine, built by Thomas Savery, is used for pumping water out of flooded mines.

1733 The flying shuttle, invented by an English weaver, doubles the amount of cloth a person can produce in one day.

1771 Richard Arkwright's water-powered spinning machine produces much stronger cotton thread than was previously possible.

1778 Household sanitation is greatly improved by the introduction of Joseph Bramah's new toilets.

1783 The Marquis de Jouffroy d'Abbans launches the first steamboat.

1783 The Montgolfier brothers successfully fly a hot air balloon.

1797 The value of parachutes is demonstrated by a Frenchman jumping from a hot air balloon.

1801 The *Nautilus*, an early submarine, completes its maiden voyage.

1804 Richard Trevithick builds the first steam locomotive to run on rails.

1814 Friedrich König develops the steam-driven press, which works far more quickly than hand-operated printing machinery.

1815 Humphry Davy invents a miner's lamp, which makes it far safer to work in mines.

1819 Augustus Siebe designs a pressurized diving suit enabling people to dive to greater depths.

1821 Charles Babbage starts work on his difference engine, designed to draw up complicated mathematical tables automatically.

1826 Joseph Niepce, a French physicist, takes the world's first photograph.

1829 George Stephenson wins a competition to design and build the best steam locomotive. He produces a locomotive called the *Rocket*.

1830 The first sewing machine is designed by Thimonnier, a French tailor.

1836 Samuel Colt patents his fast-firing revolver.

1837 Isambard Kingdom Brunel launches the first transatlantic steamship.

1837 Two British inventors named William Cooke and Charles Wheatstone make the first electric telegraph machine.

1839 Louis Daguerre invents daguerreotype photographs, which become very fashionable for portraits.

1843 Samuel Morse designs his famous dot-dash code for use when sending telegraphic messages.

1846 An American dentist uses ether to numb pain during a jaw operation.

1848 The first escalator is opened in New York as a tourist attraction.

1849 The safety pin is invented.

1857 A New York store becomes the first shop to have a safety elevator.

1860 The Belgian Étienne Lenoir builds the first internal combustion engine.

1863 The first underground railway line opens in London.

1868 A newspaper editor, Christopher Sholes, builds the first practical typewriter.

1872 Photographer Eadweard Muybridge takes the first set of sequential photographs.

1876 Alexander Graham Bell sends the first telephone message.

1876 America's most prolific inventor, Thomas Edison, sets up his invention factory.

1877 Edison produces the musical phonograph.

1878 Joseph Swan invents the electric light bulb.

1879 Ernst von Siemens demonstrates the first train to run on electrified tracks.

1881 Émile Berliner patents a gramophone using flat discs.

1884 Hiram Maxim introduces an automatic machine gun.

1885 Physicist Heinrich Hertz demonstrates the existence of electromagnetic waves.

1885 An Austrian chemist named Carl Auer invents a gas mantle, which is easier and safer to use than candles.

1886 Linotype machines enable the text for printed books and newspapers to be produced far more quickly.

1888 George Eastman produces the Kodak No.1 camera and develops customers' films.

1889 Edison's assistant Charles Batchelor experiments with the idea of movie soundtracks.

1890 The Daimler Motor Company starts to manufacture four-wheel, fuel-driven cars.

1890 The American census is rapidly completed with Herman Hollerith's electric counting machine.

1895 In Paris, the Lumière brothers put on a show with ten moving films.

1898 Valdemar Poulsen designs the forerunner of the modern tape recorder.

1900 King Camp Gillette patents the disposable safety razor blade.

1902 Italian Guglielmo Marconi transmits a radio message across the English Channel.

1903 The American Wright brothers make the first powered aircraft flight.

1903 Henry Ford introduces mass-production techniques at his new car factory.

1903 Willem Einthoven invents the electrocardiograph machine to record the heart's activity.

1904 John Fleming's glass diodes become an essential part of radio equipment.

1908 The Geiger counter, named after its inventor, is used for detecting and measuring radiation.

1909 The General Electric Company introduces the electric toaster.

1923 Two Swedish engineers design the first refrigerator.

1925 Traffic lights are installed in London.

1926 John Logie Baird successfully transmits the first television image of a human face.

1926 Robert Goddard launches the first liquid fuel rocket.

1928 The American invention "Sellotape" becomes an everyday item.

1929 Philip Drinker invents the iron lung to help sick people breathe.

1933 Two German scientists named Max Kroll and Ernst Ruska introduce the electron microscope.

1933 Percy Shaw, inspired by seeing his headlights reflected in an animal's eyes, invents "cat's eyes" for marking roads.

1935 The German company AEG introduces magnetic plastic tape for recording sound.

1937 People begin to stop using airships after the *Hindenburg* catches fire and passengers are killed.

1938 A Hungarian inventor, Lazlo Biro, introduces the first ballpoint pen, called a biro.

1938 An American, Chester Carlson, invents the first photocopying machine.

1939 The first helicopter is built by a Russian engineer named Igor Sikorsky.

1942 Wernher von Braun launches the first long-range V2 rocket.

1942 In Chicago, USA, controlled nuclear energy is successfully produced.

1945 An American inventor named Percy Spencer patents his design for the first microwave oven.

1945 The USA drops two atomic bombs on Japanese cities.

1946 ENIAC, America's first electronic computer, is publicly demonstrated.

1947 Edwin Land's Polaroid camera produces black and white photographs in under one minute.

1948 Three American scientists named John Bardeen, Walter Brattain and William Shockley miniaturize electronic circuitry by inventing a device named the transistor, and win a Nobel Prize for their work.

1957 The Russian *Sputnik 1* is the first artificial object to orbit the Earth.

1959 The hovercraft, designed by Christopher Cockerell, is publicly demonstrated.

1960 Theodore Maiman builds the world's first laser.

1962 *Telstar* is launched, the first satellite to relay live TV as well as telephone calls.

1977 America launches the Space Shuttle, the world's first reusable spacecraft.

1982 Philips and Sony introduce compact discs.

1987 Digital audio cassettes are introduced.

1990 The first transmission of high definition television.

The *Inventors* quiz

The answers to all the following questions can be found between pages 3 and 45 of this book. You will also find the answers upside down at the bottom of this page.

1. What is the name of the central heating system invented by the Romans?

2. Name of the 16th century map maker whose methods are still used in atlases today.

3. Name one of the universally accepted scales of temperature measurement.

4. Which planet did William and Caroline Herschel discover?

5. Who first experimented with the idea of contact lenses?

6. Why did an angry mob destroy 80 sewing machines designed by Barthelmey Thimonnier?

7. Who produced the first motor car to be sold?

8. In what city was the first underground railway opened?

9. Can you identify the following inventors?

a)   b)   c)

10. Which ship, designed by Isambard Kingdom Brunel, carried enough coal to sail from England to Australia and back?

11. What equipment did Christopher Cockerell first use to demonstrate the principle of peripheral jets?

12. Which of the two Wright brothers piloted the first powered and controlled aircraft flight?

13. What was the name given to Hubert Booth's first fuel-driven vacuum cleaner?

14. Why did Christopher Sholes, the inventor of the typewriter, not make any money out of his invention?

15. Identify these inventions and name their creators.

a)   b)

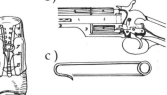

c)

16. Why was the first ballpoint pen so useful to the British Air Force?

17. How did Elisha Otis demonstrate the spring-operated safety mechanism in his elevator?

18. What happened to Johannes Gutenberg's printing equipment in 1455?

19. How many sheets of paper could Friedrich König's machine print in an hour?

20. What does the word "telegraph" mean?

21. Who took the world's first photograph?

22. What bet did photographer Eadweard Muybridge settle?

23. What was the first radio signal sent across the Atlantic Ocean?

24. Who made the first television transmission of a human face?

25. Which important invention designed by Thomas Edison in 1877 was first sold as a toy?

26. Émile Berliner's discs were made of shellac. What is shellac?

27. Why were the first gas-powered traffic signals abandoned?

28. What animal saved Percy Shaw's life in 1933?

29. Name the process used to check the health of unborn babies which has its origins in a device used by submarines and ships.

30. How many bullets could the Maxim machine gun fire in a minute?

31. Who invented the explosive called dynamite, yet left much of his fortune to fund a series of prizes including one for world peace?

32. In 1642 Blaise Pascal invented an adding machine. Why was it particularly useful for his father?

33. An early electronic computer was called ENIAC. What does ENIAC stand for?

34. Can you recognize the inventions from these close-ups?

a)   b)   c)

35. Name one of the reasons why the aircraft designed by Edwards' and Butler would not have been able to fly.

Answers

1. Hypocaust
2. Gerardus Mercator
3. Centigrade, Fahrenheit or Kelvin
4. Uranus
5. Leonardo da Vinci
6. The mob was made up of tailors who feared that they would lose their jobs because of the machines.
7. Karl Benz
8. London
9. a) Thimonnier; b) Mergenthaler; c) Ada Lovelace
10. The *Great Eastern*
11. Two tin cans, a hairdryer and kitchen scales

12. Orville
13. "Puffing Billy"
14. He sold his invention to a company named Remington
15. a) Zip fastened boots by Whitcomb Judson; b) Rifle by Colt; c) Safety pin by Hunt
16. Because it did not leak at high altitudes.
17. He was lifted high up into the air in an elevator and the cables were then cut.
18. It was seized by businessman Johannes Fust.
19. 1,000
20. "Writing at a distance"
21. Joseph Niépce
22. Whether a trotting horse lifted all its hooves off the ground at once
23. The letter 's' in Morse code

24. John Logie Baird
25. The phonograph
26. A resin produced by insects
27. A gas lamp exploded, killing a policeman
28. A cat
29. Ultrasound
30. 350
31. Alfred Nobel
32. His father was a tax inspector and had to make complicated calculations.
33. Electronic Numerical Integrator and Calculator
34. a) A photocopier; b) A cassette tape c) König's Printing Press
35. The engine needed to power it would have been too heavy for the plane to get off the ground.

48

SCIENTISTS

Struan Reid and Patricia Fara

Designed by Russell Punter

Illustrated by Stephen Conlin
and Peter Dennis

Managing editor: Anthony Marks

With thanks to Tom Petersen and Jane Chisholm

Contents

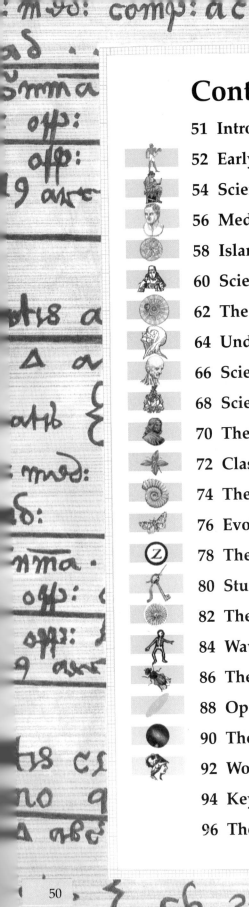

Introduction

This section of the book is about the lives and work of some of the world's greatest scientists, from the earliest observations of the skies to modern theories of the universe. It is not a comprehensive history of science, but it describes in detail the breakthroughs and discoveries that have had the greatest impact on the lives of people through the ages.

What is a scientist?

Scientists are people who gather knowledge about the world and how it works. To do this they ask questions, then try to answer them by using observation and experiment. Today there are many different types of scientist, but until about 200 years ago people did not distinguish between the scientific disciplines. In fact, the word "scientist" was not invented before 1830.

For thousands of years most people believed that the earth lay at the middle of the universe, as this 16th-century engraving shows.

How science began

Science began as a search for knowledge that arose out of a need for survival. For example, early hunters studied the habits and variety of animals they hunted. They discovered the uses of plants and herbs as food and medicine, and worked out how to make use of natural substances such as metals and minerals. By experimenting with these materials, people developed ways to improve the quality of their lives.

16th-century illustration showing liquids being heated and collected in bottles

Today we depend upon science for many of the things we take for granted, for comfort, health and entertainment. This section of the book is about the people who made these scientific developments possible.

Expanding frontiers

Scientific knowledge is always expanding, and the scientific truths of one age are often questioned by people of the next. Scientists today generally accept that their theories will be revised in the future. New inventions and discoveries also change the way we look at the world. For example, many 15th-century Europeans believed that the sky was made up of crystal spheres which carried the stars and planets around the earth. But discoveries such as those made possible by the invention of the telescope forced people to reject that idea. They began to regard the universe as larger than had previously been thought. This in turn altered people's ideas of their own position in the universe.

A map of our galaxy formed from radio waves

Historical arrangement

This section of the book is arranged historically, beginning with the earliest scientific ideas and medical skills used in the ancient world. It then considers medieval Arab thinkers and the vital role they played in preserving and developing classical learning and passing it on to Renaissance Europe. From this point on, the development of science into the individual disciplines familiar to us today is revealed. It discusses the changing relationship between science and religion, and the difficulties that many earlier scientists faced. There are also pages on scientific societies and the very important but underrated role of women scientists. A chart on pages 94-95 outlines the main events described in this section of the book.

Dates

Some of the dates are from the period before the birth of Christ. They are indicated by the letters B.C. Early dates in the period after Christ's birth are indicated by the letters A.D. Some of the dates begin with the abbreviation "c". This stands for *circa*, the Latin for "about". It is used when historians are unsure exactly when an event took place.

Early scientific ideas

Science is the process of gathering knowledge and answering questions about the world and how it works. Today, science is divided into different branches, such as chemistry and biology. But in ancient times people did not make the distinction between science and other forms of investigation. Many questions that we would now regard as scientific were then given religious or philosophical explanations. Very few early "scientists" are known by name, but we do have evidence of their ideas.

The Ancient Egyptians

One of the first civilizations in the history of the world was that of Ancient Egypt. It began over 5000 years ago and lasted for more than 3000 years. The Egyptians were very practical, and were especially skilled as builders and craftspeople. But they were also great thinkers, with theories and ideas about the world around them.

This wall painting shows an Egyptian surveyor taking measurements.

Egyptian priest-astronomers used the position of the Moon and stars like a giant clock, to work out the timing of their religious festivals. This enabled them to calculate when the River Nile would flood each year. This was the most important event in the agricultural year. They also used their knowledge of the stars to work out several calendars. The first calendar to divide the year into 365 days may have been

This Egyptian painting depicts the constellations (groups of stars) as gods.

introduced by an Egyptian man called Imhotep (see page 56).

The Mesopotamians

The region of Mesopotamia (now in modern Iraq) was the site of several ancient civilizations, including those of Sumer and Babylon. The Sumerians flourished from about 4000B.C. They were skilled astronomers and mathematicians, and built huge temples called ziggurats.

The Sumerians also devised a system of writing known as cuneiform ("wedge-shaped"). This was the first form of writing in which abstract signs, rather than pictures of objects, were used to represent sounds. The Sumerians also used two counting systems. One was a decimal system based on units of ten. The other was based on units of sixty.

The Babylonian civilization flourished in Mesopotamia for over 1300 years from 1900B.C. Babylonian astronomers made many observations of eclipses, the Moon and the planets Venus and Mercury. They named the constellations after their gods and divided the skies into areas. This later formed the basis for Greek astrology.

The Babylonians were able to predict future movements of the planets by consulting detailed lists

of planetary motions which they had compiled over many years. The purpose of this work was not to explain the motions, but rather to put together calendars and to make predictions about the future. The Babylonians saw the world as a flat disc floating on the seas. Babylon was ringed by mountains.

A Babylonian stone map of the world, c.600B.C.

Central America

From about 2000B.C., several civilizations grew up in Meso-America (Mexico and parts of Central America). One of the greatest was that of the Mayans (300B.C. to A.D.900). Later civilizations included the Toltecs and Aztecs.

Mayan observatory at Chichen Itza, Mexico

This Aztec stone depicts the stars and planets. The Aztecs (c.1300-1521) adopted the Mayan calendar.

Thales of Miletus (c.624-546B.C.)

A mathematician and astronomer, he taught that water was the main ingredient of all things and that the earth was a disc floating on water. The work of Thales is very significant because he tried to give natural explanations to puzzling phenomena. For example, he said that earthquakes were not caused by the anger of the gods, but by eruptions of hot water in the oceans.

Pythagoras

Pythagoras was born on the island of Samos and became one of the most highly respected of the early Greek philosophers. As a young man he visited Egypt and Babylon, and was greatly influenced by many of the ideas he found there. He became an important religious leader whose followers were known as the Pythagorean Order.

Pythagoras' ideas about the universe were based on his emphasis on the importance of particular numbers and symmetry in everything. Because of their love of beauty and order, he and his followers believed that the planets moved in circles, and that the heavens and earth were spherical. These ideas were still extremely influential 2000 years later.

An Athenian coin depicting Pythagoras (c.560-480B.C.)

The Mayans divided the world into four "directions", or sections, each associated with a tree and a bird. They believed the world was made up from the back of a giant crocodile lying in a pond.

This is part of a Mayan calendar. The Mayans used dots, dashes and curved lines to indicate dates.

The earliest Greek science

Scholars in Ancient Greece were known as philosophers, which means "lovers of knowledge". Apart from the subject we now know as philosophy (the study of ideas), they also studied scientific subjects such as mathematics, biology, astronomy and geography. They carefully collected as much information as possible to help their studies.

Thales of Miletus

The first important place of Greek learning was based in the eastern Mediterranean. One of the most influential philosophers there was Thales, who came from the port of Miletus, which is now in Turkey.

Pythagoras worked out how the size of bells relates to the sounds they make.

PYTACORA

53

Science in Ancient Greece

The people of Ancient Greece used stories about their gods to explain things they found puzzling. For example, the god of the sea, called Poseidon, was also known as "the earth-shaker" because he was thought to cause earthquakes when he was angry. But from the 6th century B.C. some people started to look for more practical explanations of how and why things look and behave as they do. In order to obtain this knowledge, they asked lots of questions and made many observations and calculations about all sorts of things in the world around them.

Greek coin showing Poseidon

The Academy at Athens

Plato is regarded as the founder of western philosophy. He was born in Athens and later studied under another famous philosopher called Socrates. When he was in his thirties, Plato decided to travel abroad. He visited many of the lands bordering the Mediterranean Sea and met other philosophers.

By the time he returned to Athens in 388B.C., Plato had decided to become a teacher. The following year he founded a school called the Academy which became famous throughout the Greek world. It lasted for over 900 years until it was closed by the Roman emperor Justinian in A.D.529.

Mosaic showing philosophers at the Academy

Plato's work and influence

Plato developed a set of teachings known as the Doctrine of Ideas, which were handed down to us via the Arabs. They were very important for later thinkers because they linked scientific thought with religion and philosophy. Plato argued that everything we detect with our five senses (sight, hearing, taste, smell and touch) is only an outward appearance. He believed that reality is something that we can never observe but only contemplate with our minds. This became one of the foundations of later western thought. Although Plato had a great influence on later philosophers and scientists, today his views are often regarded as a hindrance to modern experimental science. This is because Plato did not encourage experiment, thinking that observation only confused the search for pure theoretical knowledge. For

Plato
(427-347B.C.)

example, he believed that the movements of the planets are best understood by the mind, not by accurate observations. He emphasized mathematics as the key to all knowledge but, unlike Archimedes (see below), was not interested in its practical use.

Tutor to Alexander

Aristotle (384-322B.C.) was born in Macedonia in northeastern Greece. His parents died when he was a boy and he was sent by his guardian to study at Plato's Academy. On Plato's death, he left Athens and journeyed for twelve years in Greece and Asia Minor. He returned to Macedonia in 343B.C., and for three years he served as tutor to the young Prince Alexander of Macedonia (later Alexander the Great). After Alexander succeeded his father as king,

This fragment of a mosaic shows Alexander in battle.

Aristotle moved back to Athens and set up his own school, the Lyceum.

Illustration from a Greek cup showing students at work

After Alexander's death in 323B.C., Aristotle left Athens for the last time and retired to his estate at Chalcis on the island of Euboea where he died.

Teaching at the Lyceum

Aristotle's beliefs were very different from Plato's. Unlike Plato, he thought it was necessary to gather as much information as possible. His writings, passed down to us through the ages via the Arabs, laid many of the foundations of modern scientific study.

According to Aristotle, the gods had given a fixed position to every object in the sky above and the earth below. He believed that nothing could change by itself without displacing everything else in the system. Aristotle devised a "Ladder of Nature", with living things placed above inanimate matter such as stones. Human beings were placed above the animals and the gods ruled over them all.

A medieval illustration showing Aristotle's Ladder of Nature

Aristotle believed that the universe consisted of a series of spheres fitting one inside the other, arranged around a spherical earth. Immediately around the earth was the sphere of the atmosphere, followed by spheres containing earth, water, air and fire. Beyond the fire sphere lay a region containing a substance he called the *aether* (from the Greek for "shining"). Farther out

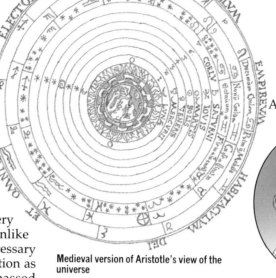

Medieval version of Aristotle's view of the universe

still were spheres carrying planets and stars, and finally, around them all, lay a sphere which controlled the movement of the whole system.

Aristotle's influence

Aristotle's main contribution to science was his emphasis on careful observation and very detailed classification. His ideas were highly influential in Europe for about 1500 years. It was not until the Renaissance that they were questioned, most notably by Galileo (see page 66).

Aristotle's system was not in itself rigid. But it was used by many people in the Middle Ages to justify and maintain the feudal system, a strict social order by which kings ruled over lords, who in turn ruled over peasants.

This illustration shows the three main occupations in the Middle Ages: priests, warriors and peasants.

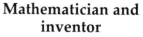

Mathematician and inventor

Archimedes was born in the Greek colony of Syracuse in Sicily. He was a brilliant mathematician and studied at a famous school of learning in Alexandria in Egypt called the Museum. He was killed in 212B.C. when the Romans captured Syracuse.

Archimedes (287-212B.C.)

He is best known for a law called Archimedes' Principle. This states that when an object is immersed in a fluid it is subject to an upward force equal to the weight of the fluid displaced. It is said that Archimedes shouted *Eureka* ("I have found it") when he saw that his body displaced the water as he climbed into his bath.

Medieval picture of Archimedes in his bath

Practical mathematics

Archimedes used geometry to measure curves and the areas and volumes of solids. He designed leverage systems such as the Archimedean screw for removing water from flooded ships. This principle is still used to raise water from one level to another.

Mosaic showing the murder of Archimedes by a Roman soldier.

Medicine in the ancient world

People have always had to deal with illness, disease and death, but explanations and treatments have varied from area to area throughout history. In many places, illness was seen either as the invasion of the body by some poison or spell, or it was attributed to angry gods who had stolen the person's soul. Early physicians were part doctors and part priests. They believed that medical treatment could relieve the illness, but that the main cause could only be removed by praying to the gods and offering them sacrifices.

Egyptian medicine

The Ancient Egyptians were extremely good surgeons and used a variety of drugs and surgical techniques. Their knowledge of human anatomy was excellent because of their practice of embalming (the preservation of the dead). They believed that the dead person's spirit, or *Ka*, would die if the body rotted away. In order to provide a home for the spirit, the body was preserved as carefully as possible.

This Egyptian wall painting shows part of the embalming process.

First the corpse was cleaned, then the brain and internal organs (such as heart, liver, lungs) were removed and washed in wine. They were then stored in special jars, called canopic jars, with preserving herbs. The body was next

A brightly painted Egyptian canopic jar

stuffed with perfumes and sweet-smelling resins and sewn up. It was covered with natron (a mixture of sodium salts that absorbed moisture) and dried for about 35 days. Finally it was coated with resin, wrapped in linen and placed in an airtight coffin. The most famous Egyptian doctor was called Imhotep (lived c. 2650B.C). He was also an architect and high priest.

Imhotep

Indian medicine

The best-known ancient Indian medical text is the *Ayurveda*, originally compiled in India around 700B.C. In it, disease is seen as an imbalance of substances in the body. Doctors used medicines to drive out harmful substances, and replace them with ones that were more in tune with the body. The *Ayurveda* also shows that Hindu doctors had a good understanding of diet and the digestive system.

The Ancient Indians excelled in surgical treatment, and the *Ayurveda* describes many different types of surgical instrument. Their doctors knew how to perform many operations, especially on the stomach and bladder. They could also remove cataracts (clouded lenses) from eyes, and were famous for their plastic surgery (rebuilding wounded parts of the body). They used hairs to stitch up torn lips.

An Indian illustration showing a type of plastic surgery of the nose.

Chinese medicine

In the 6th century B.C., a Chinese philosopher called Confucius (551-479B.C.) taught that people are closely linked to a universe dominated by two opposing types of force known as *yin* and *yang*. *Yin* was regarded as a negative force, while *yang* was positive. He claimed that the harmony of the universe and the health of people depended on keeping a balance between the two forces. Today, many Chinese believe that these two forces circulate around the body in the form of spirits or fluids.

Chinese illustration showing how to take a patient's pulse

By inserting needles at specified points on the body, the correct flow of the two spirits can be maintained. This technique, known as acupuncture, is used to ease the pain of surgical operations instead of drugs. Today in China, and increasingly in the West, acupuncture and other alternative medicines are used with drugs and surgery.

A 17th-century Chinese wooden acupuncture figure

Greek medicine

In the 5th century B.C. a medical school on the small Greek island of Cos became very influential. The physicians at Cos were good at treating bone injuries but knew little about internal organs. They believed that disease was caused by a lack of balance in the body between four fluids - which consisted of blood, black bile, yellow bile and phlegm - and four related qualities - heat, cold, dryness and dampness.

The island was the home of Hippocrates, a doctor who is often known as "the father of medicine". Like modern doctors, he insisted on keeping medical records, noting when treatments failed, as well as when they were successful.

A 14th-century portrait of Hippocrates (c.450-370B.C.)

Hippocrates emphasized the importance of letting the body heal naturally, so he used few drugs, instead recommending treatments such as warm relaxing baths and a simple diet. At that time many people thought that an illness such as epilepsy was a punishment from the gods. But Hippocrates rejected

This medieval illustration shows a Greek patient being treated for a dislocated arm.

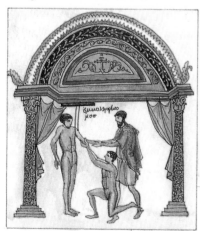

A selection of 2nd-century B.C. Greek surgical instruments

this, and suggested instead that it had natural causes.

Greek medicine was very influential in medieval and Renaissance Europe. Hippocrates' teachings were gathered by Greek scholars to form a massive medical work called the Hippocratic Collection. Parts of it were still being used as textbooks in European medical schools as late as the 19th century. Today, doctors make a promise to work for the benefit of the patient at all times. It is known as the Hippocratic Oath, after Hippocrates.

Roman medicine

The most famous of all doctors in Roman times was Galen. He was born at Pergamum in Asia Minor (now in Turkey) the son of a Greek architect. In A.D.161 he moved to Rome, where he spent nearly all his active life. He set up a medical practice and became so successful that he was eventually appointed physician to the emperor's family.

Galen's work dominated medieval medical thought in the Arabic world and Europe. He did important research into the physical structure and functions of the body. He could not learn anatomy by cutting up dead humans, as this was illegal, and had to use carcasses of apes and pigs. But because animals are different from humans, his anatomical theories contained many errors which were accepted until the work of Vesalius in the 16th century (see page 64).

Bust of Galen (c.A.D.129-200)

Galen's system was wrong in several ways. He put veins (carrying blood to the heart) on the right side of the body and arteries (carrying blood from the heart to various parts of the body) on the left. He believed that blood seeped through pores in the septum (internal wall) of the heart.

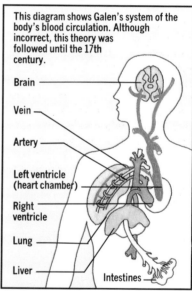

This diagram shows Galen's system of the body's blood circulation. Although incorrect, this theory was followed until the 17th century.

Brain

Vein

Artery

Left ventricle (heart chamber)

Right ventricle

Lung

Liver

Intestines

Galen taught that the heart pumped blood through the arteries mixed with something he called "pneuma" (a sort of spirit which the lungs obtain when air is breathed in). He proposed that the blood was sent to the organs that needed it, but not in a circulatory motion. This theory is incorrect, but it was not until the 17th century that an English doctor called William Harvey (see page 65) correctly worked out how the blood circulates continuously all the way around the body.

Islamic science

In Arabia in the 7th century A.D., the Prophet Mohammed founded a new religion called Islam. Within a century of his death in 632, his followers (known as Muslims) had conquered a huge empire that stretched from Spain to the borders of China. The arts and sciences flourished in the Arab world, particularly between 900 and 1200. As well as making their own contributions to science, the Arabs absorbed scientific ideas from many different parts of their great empire, particularly from the Greeks and Persians. In this way Islamic thinkers helped to transmit the ideas of the ancient world to medieval Europeans. Without them, much of this information would have been lost.

This Islamic illustration shows the Greek philosopher Aristotle (see page 54) with a student.

A great thinker

Ibn Sina, known in Europe as Avicenna, was an extremely learned and versatile man who wrote about 270 books on a huge range of subjects. He was born at Bokhara in Iran. At the age of only 16 he was working in medicine. At various times during his life he was a lawyer and teacher of science. He was also involved in politics and acted as adviser to the Iranian ruler. He died of colic

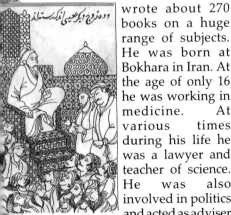

Ibn Sina (980-1037) teaching a class of students

An Islamic manuscript showing a dentist extracting a tooth

(inflammation of the abdomen), but there were suspicions that he may have been poisoned.

Ibn Sina wrote the *Canon*, a huge book about medicine. This work influenced medical teaching in Europe until the 17th century. Islamic law forbade the dissection of the human body, so the book was mainly about how to recognize and treat diseases, and how to prepare drugs. Another of ibn Sina's major works was a large encyclopedia entitled *The Cure*, which covered a wide range of subjects from philosophy to mathematics and physics.

The master of alchemy

Alchemy was a very important part of Arabic thinking. Alchemists mainly looked for a way of changing non precious metals such as iron into gold. Alchemical studies were important because although they used magic and spells, they also involved the use of experiment. This laid the foundations for several modern sciences, including chemistry and mineralogy (the study of minerals).

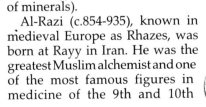

An alembic, a vessel used in distillation

Al-Razi (c.854-935), known in medieval Europe as Rhazes, was born at Rayy in Iran. He was the greatest Muslim alchemist and one of the most famous figures in medicine of the 9th and 10th centuries. But al-Razi also questioned religious teachings, and so made himself unpopular with the powerful clergy.

Al-Razi devoted the first part of his life to alchemy. He rejected much of the magic and spells performed by alchemists and concentrated more on their experimental ideas. He was very interested in the use of chemical substances and clearly described some of the techniques used in alchemy, such as distillation (boiling a liquid until it becomes gaseous, then cooling it back into a liquid again).

These brass instruments were used in geomancy, a method of prophesying the future.

He also made some of the earliest suggestions for equipping a laboratory, listing some of the instruments.

Al-Razi was appointed director of the hospital in Rayy and then moved to become director of the hospital in Baghdad. He was one of the first of the Muslim writers on medicine, producing over a hundred works on the subject. His most famous publication was the huge *Comprehensive Book* which covered the whole of medical practice known at that time, including Greek, Indian and Chinese medical knowledge.

Islamic surgical instruments

Islamic astrological signs. From left to right: Aries, Taurus, Gemini, Cancer, Leo, Virgo.

Astronomer and courtier

Abu Rayhan al-Biruni (973-c.1050) was born in Khwarazm, Armenia. He began his scientific studies while still very young and by the age of 17 had designed and made an instrument for observing the sun. But in 995 a civil war forced him to flee abroad.

The observatory at Samarkand, c.1420

Al-Biruni returned home two years later and held a number of official positions at royal courts. He continued his scientific studies and astronomical observations, and designed and built many instruments for observing the sun, the moon and the stars.

This Turkish astronomer is observing a meteor with an instrument called a quadrant.

But al-Biruni's interests and studies were not limited to astronomy. In all, he wrote about 13,000 pages of highly technical material about geography, mathematics, optics (the study of light and the eye), medicines and drugs, precious stones and astrology. His interest in alchemy also led him to study the composition of minerals and metals, and his writings in this field later proved very influential as the science of chemistry developed. He also wrote a huge work on mineralogy called *The Book of the Multitude of Knowledge of Precious Stones*. Although he was ill for many years, by the time of his death at the age of 80 he had written over 140 books on many different subjects.

A page from an Islamic book about mineralogy

Lenses and light

Ibn al-Haytham (965-c.1040) was the greatest of all the Islamic physicists. He was born at Basra in Iraq and became known in Europe as Alhazen. He moved to Cairo where he worked at a school called the Academy during the reign of the Caliph al-Hakim (996-1020).

Al-Haytham wrote on a range of subjects, including optics, astronomy and mathematics. His work on optics was so extensive and detailed that it formed the basis of many later European studies of the subject. In his book called *The Treasury of Optics* he rejected an earlier Greek idea that the eye sends out rays of light to the object it is looking at. Instead he suggested that rays of light come from the object to the eye.

A 16th-century illustration of al-Haytham's study of the structure of the eye

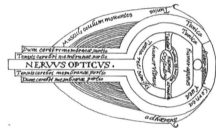

Al-Haytham also examined the effect of light through lenses. He concluded that the refraction (bending) of light is caused by light rays moving at different speeds through different materials, such as air, glass and water. This idea was used in the 17th century by Kepler (see page 63) and Descartes (page 67). Al-Haytham was also the first person to develop the *camera obscura*, a box in which images from outside are projected onto a wall. He used a hole in a wall to reproduce the image of the sun during an eclipse.

A 19th-century English camera obscura, based on al-Haytham's principles.

Islamic astrological signs. From left to right: Libra, Scorpio, Sagittarius, Capricorn, Aquarius, Pisces.

Science in medieval Europe

The period from about A.D.400 to 1400 in Europe is often known as the medieval age. For much of this time the Christian Church was very powerful and ruled all aspects of life. As most scholars were Christian monks, they had to follow the teachings of the Church. People who contradicted the Church's views were often persecuted.

Pope Innocent III (1198-1216), a very powerful Church leader

From the end of the 11th century, many ancient Greek, Roman and Arab books reached northern Europe through Muslim Spain (see page 58). Bishops feared that the new knowledge contained in these books would make people question the Bible's account of the creation of the world. Over the years, however, much science and philosophy from the classical and Arab worlds was slowly reconciled with Christian teachings.

Religion and philosophy

Thomas Aquinas was an Italian monk. In 1264 he wrote a book, *Summa contra gentiles*, in which he stated that while everything was created by God, knowledge and truth could also come from other sources. He said that on religious questions the Church and the Bible were the only authorities, but that in scientific matters the work of the Greeks and Arabs could also help to explain the world that God had created. These ideas enabled the Church to come to terms with the teachings of the ancient world.

Thomas Aquinas (1225-74)

The rise of new learning

From the late 12th century, places of learning called universities were founded all over Europe. The most important were those at Bologna, Oxford, Cambridge and Paris. Many of the people who taught and studied there were associated with the Church, so the universities became important in developing ideas about religious matters.

Illustration showing man at the middle of the universe which is embraced by God

Robert Grosseteste (c.1168-1253) was born in Sussex, England. He became a leading figure in scientific studies in the first half of the 13th century. He studied at Oxford University and then, from 1209, taught at the University of Paris. In 1214 he returned to Oxford, where he acted as tutor to some of the students, including a community of monks.

A class in progress at the new university at Bologna in Italy.

A supporter of Aristotle

Grosseteste always stressed the great importance of testing all scientific propositions. In this he was a supporter of Aristotle who recommended the use of careful observation and analysis. He wrote on a wide range of subjects, including astronomy and music. His most famous work was on optics and how light behaves, and in this he was influenced by the work of the Arabic scientist ibn al-Haytham (see page 59).

Grosseteste's drawing of light passing through a lens

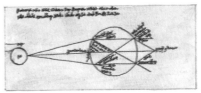

Grosseteste's pupil

Roger Bacon (c.1214-c.1294) was born in Somerset, England. He studied at Oxford University and in 1241 moved to Paris. In 1247 he returned to Oxford where he was one of Grosseteste's pupils. He taught for the rest of his life in England and France.

Bacon did not experiment himself, but he did carry out some research into optics and the eye. He described ibn al-Haytham's account of the eye as a device for forming images. He also understood the causes of the refraction (bending) of light and was one of the first people to suggest that lenses could be used as spectacles for magnification.

This illustration of 1352 is the earliest known picture of lenses being used as spectacles.

Conflict with the Church

When he was almost 40, Bacon became a Franciscan monk. He had an argumentative nature and had many disputes over astronomy and astrology with John of Fidanza (later Saint Bonaventure), the head of the Franciscans.

In 1267, at the invitation of his friend Pope Clement IV, Bacon wrote a work called *Opus majus*, an important volume of papers covering all areas of knowledge. In addition, it condemned the teaching methods of both the Franciscans and the Dominicans, claiming that they were out of date and narrow-minded. This made him still more unpopular with the authorities and even the Pope was outraged. In 1277 Bacon was put on trial and sent to prison in Paris for several years. The charge was that he regarded reason and philosophy as more important than the established teachings of the Christian Church.

Science supporting religion

Bacon is a major figure in the history of science, not because he challenged the authority of the Church, but because of his scientific approach. He believed that the study and advancement of science could complement and support religion. He thought that scientific study would enable people to understand all aspects of the world. In this way, he argued, they would gain a better knowledge of God and his works.

This medieval illustration shows the Church (at the top) controlling the different areas of knowledge (below).

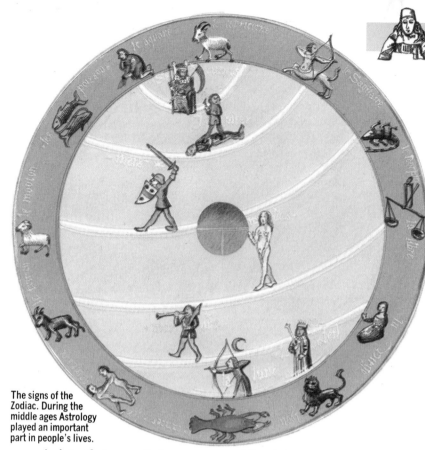

The signs of the Zodiac. During the middle ages Astrology played an important part in people's lives.

Aristotle's work is questioned

By the 14th century scholars had adopted many ancient ideas, especially Aristotle's. But they interpreted these rigidly, taking them to mean that the universe was unchanging and perfect, with the earth fixed at the middle.

Jean Buridan (c.1300-85), a teacher at Paris University, adopted a Greek idea called the "impetus theory". His version stated that God had set the planets and stars moving around the earth at a speed that would continue forever. This was an important step toward a physical explanation of planetary motion, because it rejected supernatural causes. Buridan was afraid to publish his work because it contradicted Aristotle's teaching that divine beings pushed the planets along.

The friend of princes

Nicolas Oresme (c.1320-82) was born in Normandy in France and became Bishop of Lisieux. From about 1340 he studied in Paris under Buridan. Oresme went much further than Buridan in questioning Aristotle's work. He suggested that the earth might not be fixed but might actually rotate daily on its own axis. He also used mathematics to work out planetary movements. Oresme's ideas helped later scientists to formulate new ideas about the structure of the universe. This eventually led to the overthrow of the Aristotelian system by Galileo and others in the 17th century (see page 66).

This medieval engraving depicts a mathematics class.

The earth and the sun

From the earliest times, people have wanted to understand the mystery of the stars and planets. Early civilizations charted the movements of the sun and the moon to construct calendars.

This picture shows Nut, Egyptian goddess of the sky, bending over gods of the earth and air.

The Ancient Egyptians arranged the stars into groups called constellations, which they often gave religious significance. The science of astronomy developed as people gradually learned more about the world beyond them. Astronomers examine the skies in order to answer questions about space and the movements of the planets and stars.

The Ptolemaic system

In about A.D.150 Ptolemy, a Greek astronomer living in Alexandria in Egypt, wrote an important textbook now known as the *Almagest* (Arabic for "the greatest work"). In this, he described a system of the universe in which the earth lay stationary and the moon, the sun, and the planets all moved around it in circular paths called orbits. All the stars were fixed to the surface of a rotating sphere. This idea, which was based on the work of Aristotle (see page 54), is known as the geocentric (from the Greek for earth) theory. It

This brass sphere, based on Ptolemy's ideas, was used to work out the positions of the stars.

became the accepted view of the universe for nearly 1400 years. But as new and more efficient instruments were invented to examine the skies, the findings of astronomers became more and more accurate. The new evidence began to contradict Ptolemy's geocentric theory.

Ptolemy (c.A.D.90-170) as shown in this medieval engraving

Doubts are raised

Niklas Kopernik was a Polish monk more commonly known by his latinized name of Copernicus. He studied mathematics, medicine and law in Poland and Italy and became a canon at Frauenburg Cathedral in Poland. There he became interested in astronomy, and he began to doubt that the earth lay at the middle of the universe. Instead, he suggested a system with the sun lying at the middle and the planets, including the earth, orbiting around it in circles. This is known as the heliocentric (from the Greek for sun) theory.

Copernicus (1473-1543)

Copernicus recorded this theory in a book called *De revolutionibus orbium caelestium* ("Concerning the revolutions of the heavenly spheres"). The Church, however, taught that the earth was the heart of the universe, which was the view that had been presented in the Bible. Because

he was a clergyman, Copernicus decided not to publish his book for fear of being criticized and punished by the Church.

In 1543, shortly before he died, Copernicus was finally persuaded to publish his book. But without his knowledge, the publishers added a preface in order to protect themselves from criticism by the Church. It stated that Copernicus' scheme was not a real picture of the universe, but only a theory. This reduced the impact of the book when it came out. But while his book contained many ideas we now know to be incorrect, it provided a structure for the work of such later astronomers as Kepler (see opposite) and Galileo.

Engraving of the Copernican, heliocentric system of the universe

A new star appears

Tycho Brahe was born in Skåne, then in Denmark but now Sweden. He was a very quarrelsome man and had most of his nose cut off in a duel. While studying at Copenhagen University, he became very interested in astronomy.

In 1572 astronomers noticed that a new star had appeared in the sky. (It was probably an exploding object now known as a supernova.) Brahe calculated that the new star lay beyond the moon. This conflicted with the Aristotelian theory that only the skies between the earth and the moon could change.

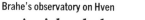

A contemporary drawing of the 1572 supernova

Brahe's observatory on Hven

An island observatory

In 1574 Brahe set up an observatory on Hven, an island in the Baltic Sea given to him by King Frederick II of Denmark. His observations of a comet (see page 71) in 1577 showed that it moved among the planets lying beyond the moon. This again proved that changes did occur in the skies. Although his findings contradicted Aristotle's view of the universe on several fundamental points, Brahe would not accept Copernicus' view because it opposed the teachings of the Church. Instead he proposed a compromise, a system in which the planets orbited the sun, and the sun orbited the earth, which lay still at the heart of the universe.

When Frederick died in 1588, the Danish royal family withdrew the money used for the upkeep of the Hven observatory. The following year Brahe moved to Prague. He remained there for the rest of his life, continuing his work as an astronomer.

Tycho Brahe (1546-1601)

Medallion commemorating the great comet of 1577

New theories

Johannes Kepler was born in Germany. He taught mathematics at Graz in Austria, then moved to Prague to become Brahe's assistant. When Brahe died he left his astronomical findings to Kepler, instructing him to use them to disprove Copernicus' theories.

Kepler worked for years on the orbits of the planets, but the information he had collected did not fit with the theories of either Brahe or Copernicus. He worked out that although the planets did indeed move around the sun, they moved not in perfect circles but in extended circular paths called ellipses. He also realized that the speed of the planets varies as they travel, according to their distance from the sun. These ideas are the basis of Kepler's three laws of planetary movement. He also understood that the sun has a very strong influence on the movement of the planets.

Johannes Kepler (1571-1630)

Kepler published many of his theories in his books *The New Astronomy* (1609) and *Epitome of Copernican Astronomy* (1621). At the time most people did not realize the significance of his ideas, but his writings influenced many later scientists. Newton used Kepler's laws when he formulated his theories of gravity (see page 70).

Understanding the human body

During the Middle Ages medical knowledge in Europe remained based on the work of Galen and other early doctors (see pages 56-57). In the 12th century, however, new ideas began reaching western Europe, as Greek and Arab medical texts were translated into Latin. Doctors and medical scientists began to question ancient theories and later to replace them with new ones of their own.

A flamboyant personality

Aureolus Philippus Theophrastus Bombastus von Hohenheim, otherwise known as Paracelsus, was born near Zürich in Switzerland. He studied at the University of Ferrara in Italy, then worked as a surgeon in the army. Paracelsus was a violent man who angered even his closest friends. He charged rich people huge fees, but treated the poor for free. He took the name Paracelsus because he disagreed so much with the Roman physician Celsus and other traditional doctors. (*Para* is the Greek word for "beyond" or "against".)

Paracelsus (1493-1541)

A restless doctor

In 1527 Paracelsus became professor of medicine at Basle University, where he also had a successful doctor's practice. But he had many arguments with the

16th-century illustration showing Paracelsus lecturing

medical authorities and, after publicly burning books by Galen and Avicenna, he had to leave Basle. For the rest of his life he journeyed around Europe, never staying more than two years in one place, and died in Austria.

This picture shows Paracelsus performing a surgical operation.

Paracelsus did not believe in the old Greek idea that disease was caused by an imbalance of the four fluids (see page 57). Instead he thought it was caused by a poison entering the body. He sometimes treated people with drugs that produced symptoms similar to those of the disease they had. This was an early form of homeopathy, a method that claims to heal the body by reinforcing its natural defences.

The great anatomist

Andreas Vesalius was born in Brussels, the son of an apothecary (pharmacist) to the Holy Roman Emperor, Charles V. He first studied at Louvain (now in Belgium), then at the University of Paris, but war forced him back to Louvain. By this time Vesalius was very interested in human anatomy, the science of the structure of the body. In order to study this thoroughly, he needed to dissect (cut up) dead bodies. As this was forbidden by law, he sometimes had to rob graves to get the corpses he required, or take the bodies down from gallows. In 1537 he attended the medical school at Padua in Italy,

one of the most famous in Europe. His knowledge was already so extensive that he was awarded his doctorate after only two days of exams, then appointed lecturer of anatomy. He later became physician to Charles V, but in 1564 he drowned in a shipwreck on his way back to Madrid from a pilgrimage to Jerusalem.

Galen's work is questioned

While he was at Padua, Vesalius carried out as many dissections as possible, using animals as well as human bodies. He did all the dissections himself and used large anatomical diagrams as guides for his students. But these drawings were still based on Galen's theories.

Andreas Vesalius (1514-64)

Vesalius gradually discovered many differences between Galen's ideas and the results of his own dissections. By 1539 he was able to prove that Galen's descriptions fitted an ape's body rather than a human being's. In 1543 he published *The Fabric of the Human Body*, one of the greatest scientific books ever written. It gave anatomy the status of an academic pursuit, and by the 17th century Vesalius' theories were accepted almost everywhere in Europe.

A drawing from *The Fabric of the Human Body*

This illustration from *The Fabric of the Human Body* shows the body's muscles.

A royal physician

William Harvey was born in Folkestone, England. After studying arts and medicine at Cambridge University, he went to Padua to continue his medical training with a famous professor of anatomy called Fabricius. In 1602 he returned to London and set up a medical practice. He was appointed physician at St Bartholomew's Hospital, London in 1609. In 1618, he was made physician to James I in 1618, and later to Charles I, and was a staunch royalist during the English Civil War.

William Harvey
(1578-1657)

A new theory of circulation

In 1628 Harvey published a book, *De motu cordis* ("On the movement of the heart and blood"). It was the product of many observations and set out his theories about how blood travels around the body.

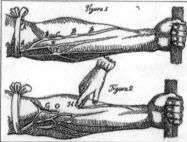

Harvey's diagram showing valves in the veins

At that time, most doctors believed Galen's idea that blood was passed from one side of the heart to the other through small holes. From his own experiments, Harvey introduced the concept of circulation, showing that blood flows away from the heart through the arteries, and back to the heart through veins. Fabricius had found valves in the veins, but had not understood their function.

Harvey realized that the valves in large veins direct the blood back toward the heart, and that the valves of the heart keep the blood flowing around the body in one direction only - to the lungs from the right side, and to the rest of the body from the left. He also realized that the heart acts as a pump to circulate the blood.

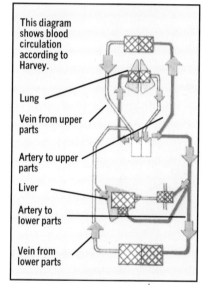

This diagram shows blood circulation according to Harvey.

Lung

Vein from upper parts

Artery to upper parts

Liver

Artery to lower parts

Vein from lower parts

One more puzzle

Harvey's discovery was a brilliant piece of reasoning based on observation. But there was still a final question: how did blood that left the heart through the arteries enter the veins? Harvey guessed that tiny blood vessels must connect the veins and arteries, but he was unable to prove it. In 1661, while examining a frog's lungs under a microscope, an Italian called Marcello Malpighi (1628-94) found the tiny linking vessels (called capillaries) and the puzzle was finally solved.

Science during the Renaissance

I n Europe in the 14th century there began a period of about 200 years that became known as the Renaissance (meaning "rebirth"). During this time people began to rediscover the arts and learning of Ancient Greece and Rome, and to develop new ideas about the world around them. They began to look at things more critically and observation and experiment in all areas became more important. They also challenged the established Aristotelian teachings, which combined Greek and Christian philosophy (see page 60).

The universal man

Many thinkers during the Renaissance believed in the ideal of the "universal man", someone who combined a wide range of talents and interests. Leonardo da Vinci was a painter, sculptor, musician, architect, scientist and an ingenious inventor who typified this ideal.

Leonardo was born near Florence, the son of a legal clerk called Pietro da Vinci. His father noticed Leonardo's artistic talents and sent him to work in the studio of a painter called Andrea del Verrochio. Although he only completed a relatively small number of paintings, Leonardo is now recognized as one of the world's greatest artists. One of his most famous pictures is the *Mona Lisa*, which he painted in 1503.

Leonardo da Vinci (1452-1519)

Leonardo's sketchbooks

Leonardo dissected about 30 human bodies (a practice that was illegal at the time), and produced anatomical drawings that were much more accurate than anything that had been done before. He studied the properties of light and the movement of water, and his sketchbooks are filled with his designs for mechanical devices, including flying machines. We now know that many of these would not have worked, but they demonstrate Leonardo's ability to combine detailed observation with powerful imagination.

Sketches by Leonardo showing various anatomical features

This is a reconstruction of a design by Leonardo for a flying machine. Below are his sketches of a mechanical wing and birds in flight.

Leonardo's later years

From 1483 Leonardo worked in Milan as an inspector of fortifications, and then in Florence as a military engineer. In 1507 he moved to Amboise in France, where he spent the rest of his life.

Despite his enormous range and creativity, Leonardo's work had little influence on the progress of science. His studies were made for his own satisfaction; most of his contemporaries knew nothing of them. His many sketches and notebooks were dispersed after his death and remained largely unknown for centuries.

Copernicus' champion

Galileo Galilei (1564-1642) was born in Pisa in Italy, the son of a composer. He played a vital part in establishing Copernicus' view (see page 62) that the earth rotates around a stationary sun. A pioneer of the experimental approach to science which was developing at this time, he was also a gifted teacher.

At the age of 17, Galileo enrolled as a medical student at the University of Pisa.

While he was attending a service at the cathedral, he noticed that the chandeliers were swinging in a wind, and used his pulse to time their movements. He found that though the swings slowly got smaller they always took the same amount of time. This led him to suggest that pendulums could be used to measure time. This idea was the basis of the first mechanical clocks.

Galileo left Pisa to continue his work in mechanics and mathematics, but he later returned there as professor of mathematics. The results of his experiments at this time provided increasing evidence to contradict many of Aristotle's theories about the organization of the universe (see page 54).

"And yet it moves!"

After hearing about the invention of the telescope in Holland, Galileo designed and built some more powerful models himself. In 1610 he published his observations of the stars and planets in *The Starry Messenger*, a book which became both popular and influential. In it he described mountains on the moon, and dark spots which occasionally move across the face of the sun. He also showed that some planets, like Jupiter, have their own small orbiting planets. Galileo's work demonstrated the uses of the telescope. But more importantly, all his findings supported the view of Copernicus that the earth rotates around the sun.

Two of Galileo's telescopes

In 1632 Galileo published his *Dialogue Concerning the Two Chief World Systems*, which summed up his observations. The work was seen as a masterpiece all over Europe. But in Italy it clashed with the teachings of the Church, which upheld the traditional view of the earth lying in the middle of the solar system.

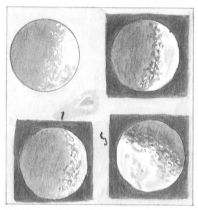

Paintings by Galileo of the surface of the Moon

In 1633 Galileo was charged with heresy (holding a view contrary to the established teaching of the Church). He was brought before a Church court in Rome known as the Inquisition. Having been found guilty, he was threatened with torture unless he publicly denied his claim that the earth moved round the sun. Appearing old and frail, Galileo did as the Inquisition demanded. He was ordered to retire to the countryside for the rest of his life. But it is said that as he was leaving the court he murmured "And yet it moves!" because he still believed in his theory.

Galileo's sketch of the method of measuring the height of mountains on the Moon

The mathematical philosopher

The ideas of René Descartes were very influential in both mathematics and philosophy. He was born in Brittany in France, the son of a lawyer. In 1628 he moved to the Netherlands, where the Protestant Church took a more relaxed view of new ideas. He worked there for the next 20 years.

One of the most important contributions Descartes made to philosophy was his concept of doubt. He did not accept an unquestioning belief in biblical and classical sources of knowledge. He declared that his René Descartes (1596-1650) own existence was the only thing he could be certain about: *Cogito ergo sum* ("I think, therefore I am"). In his major scientific work, *Principles of Philosophy*, he suggested that the movement of the universe could be described in terms of moving particles of various sizes.

Drawing by Descartes which shows the universe as whirlpools of matter

Descartes laid the basis for co-ordinate mathematics, a system that enables different quantities, such as age and height, to be related to each other in graphs or charts. His ideas on the structure of the universe were very influential, though they were later challenged by Newton (see page 70).

Scientific societies

In Europe from the middle of the 17th century, groups of men began to meet regularly in such cities as London, Florence, Oxford and Paris to discuss their scientific experiments and ideas. They were mostly wealthy people who experimented at home and who wanted to share their discoveries. These very informal meetings developed into the first scientific societies. During the following centuries, these societies grew stronger and more influential, often helped by an increasing government interest in science. Partly as a result of their influence, science gradually divided into specialized subjects such as geology and astronomy, and many people began to take up the activity of scientific research as a paid career.

The coat of arms of the Royal Society, the earliest scientific society

would lead to new scientific discoveries and enable people to develop new theories. He suggested that scientists should collect facts and figures on each subject and from as many sources as possible. In 1627 he published *The New Atlantis*, his last book. This described his vision of a world in which scientists were dedicated to improving the lives of everyone in the community.

Although Bacon did not carry out any scientific experiments himself, his ideas remained very influential for many years. During the 17th century, his writings and his philosophy of experiment stimulated people all over Europe to establish new scientific organizations.

A belief in experiment

Francis Bacon was the son of a courtier to King Henry VIII of England. He trained as a lawyer, eventually becoming a politician under Queen Elizabeth I. In 1617 King James I appointed him Lord Chancellor of England, but in 1621 he was convicted of taking bribes, dismissed from office and banished from the royal court.

Bacon wrote about his views on scientific methods in a series of books and essays. He felt that it was important to find the answers to scientific problems by means of experiment. In his book *Novum organum* he argued that careful experiment and observation

Francis Bacon (1561-1626)

The Royal Society

The establishment of the Royal Society in London was extremely important because for the first time it offered a permanent meeting place for the scientific community. Members were no longer isolated individuals but now felt that they belonged together in a social group where they could discuss their latest experiments.

The Society was founded in 1662, at the beginning of the reign of Charles II. It received the personal backing of the king, who granted it a Royal Charter that outlined its purposes and gave it certain rights. The founding members were

This engraving shows Gresham College, a scientific college founded in 1596 which was a forerunner of the Royal Society.

Part of the Charter of the Royal Society, granted by Charles II

mainly doctors, philosophers, and important officials. They included the architect Christopher Wren and the writer Samuel Pepys. The Royal Society is still in existence today and is an important forum for ideas.

This illustration of Louis XIV visiting the Académie Royale des Sciences was issued by the French government in the 17th century.

Académie Royale des Sciences

The Académie Royale des Sciences was founded in Paris in 1666. Although it was based on the Royal Society, it was very different from its counterpart in England. The French king, Louis XIV, was keen to use science to increase his own power and influence, and he took a close interest in the running of the Académie.

Membership was strictly limited to those people who had proved

A giant burning lens made and used by Lavoisier (see page 78) in experiments at the Académie Royale des Sciences.

themselves to be academically excellent and who also had the king's approval. However, unlike the members of the English Royal Society, who never received a salary, the French academicians were paid by the government. This marked the beginning of the age of the salaried scientist.

The Académie produced a lot of excellent scientific work, especially in the second half of the 18th century. But because of its strong links with the monarchy it was abolished during the French Revolution. It was replaced by the Institut de France, which was founded by Napoleon.

Specialist societies in Britain

Until scientific study became common in universities in the second half of the 19th century, scientists tended to discuss their ideas in learned societies. The members included people from a range of backgrounds, including industry, chemistry and medicine. This interaction of people and skills contributed to the Industrial Revolution, which happened earlier

in Britain than in the rest of Europe. From the end of the 18th century, many countries in Europe were transformed into industrial nations.

Specialist societies grew up in London, such as the Linnean Society (biology and natural history) in 1788, the Geology Society in 1807, and the Astronomical Society in 1831. They quickly became professional organizations with their own journals and limited membership.

Germany in the 19th century

Justus von Liebig was one of the greatest chemists of the 19th century. He was born in Germany, the son of a chemist. In 1822 he moved to Paris to study chemistry. He visited laboratories in France and was very impressed by the standards of chemistry he found there. On his return to Germany he set up his own research laboratory in 1824 at the University of Giessen. Here teamwork rather than individual research was encouraged.

Justus von Liebig (1803-73)

Liebig's laboratory was one of the best equipped in Europe. (He invented the Liebig condenser, a cooling device that turns gases into liquids.) His work influenced the development of Germany's industries, particularly those that produced of dyes and drugs. In the 19th century German universities became centres of scientific research that acted as the models for new universities all over the world.

Bottles of artificial dye, produced in Germany in the 19th century

The rise of experiment

Today experimentation is regarded as one of the main activities of scientists, but for many centuries this was not the case. Scientific ideas were often based on religion and philosophy rather than experiment. But at the end of the 17th century scientists began to stress the importance of experiment as a valid way of gaining knowledge. They examined the natural world in a new light, trying out new ideas and instruments. Their methods and achievements were to shape western scientific thinking.

Physicist and mathematician

Isaac Newton, one of the most famous scientists in the world, was born into a farming family in Lincolnshire, England. He went to Cambridge University in 1661 to study mathematics and graduated in 1665, the year of the Great Plague. When the plague spread to Cambridge, the university was closed down and Newton returned to Lincolnshire.

Newton's house in Lincolnshire

Newton went back to Cambridge in 1667 and two years later became professor of mathematics there. He later moved to London, where from 1703 until his death he was President of the Royal Society (see page 68).

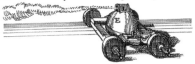

Isaac Newton (1642-1727)

Motion and gravity

Newton's stay in Lincolnshire was very productive, but it was not until 1687 that the material he worked on while he was there was published as a book. The full title, translated from the original Latin, was *The Mathematical Principles of Natural Philosophy*, but it is usually known as the *Principia*.

Pages from Newton's book the *Principia*

The first volume included Newton's three Laws of Motion and his theory of gravitation. He is said to have begun wondering about this when he saw an apple fall. He noted that there is a force between the earth and all objects which pulls them together. The earth pulls things like the apple toward it by force of gravity.

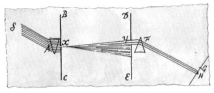

A device designed by Newton to illustrate his Third Law of Motion

With the use of mathematical calculations, Newton was able to solve the age-old problem of how planets move in space. He demonstrated that, in the same way as the apple was pulled to earth, the planets were pulled around the sun by gravitation. This proved Kepler's laws of planetary motion (see page 63), which had been based on observation. Newton brought the whole of the universe - the earth as well as the stars and planets - under one set of mathematical laws, organized under the principle of universal gravitation. This has had a major influence on scientific thinking up to the present day.

Experiments with light

In 1704 Newton published another famous work, entitled *Opticks*. This described his experiments with light. In one, he directed a beam of sunlight through a glass prism in a dark room. He noticed that the light was split into the different shades of the spectrum, ranging from violet to red.

Newton's sketch of his light experiments

Newton's experiment showed that sunlight is not white, but a mixture of violet, indigo, blue, green, yellow, orange and red.

An 18th-century cartoon mocking Newton's Laws of Gravity

Pumps and pressure

Robert Boyle, the fourteenth child of the Earl of Cork, was born at the family's castle in Lismore, Ireland. He went to school in England and then journeyed throughout Europe, accompanied by tutors. There he first read the works of Galileo (see page 66) which had a great influence on him.

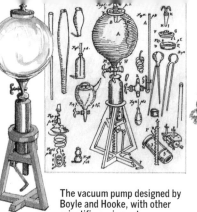

The vacuum pump designed by Boyle and Hooke, with other scientific equipment

In 1654, while at Oxford University, Boyle became interested in investigations being carried out in Europe on the nature of the vacuum. (A vacuum is a closed space from which everything, including air, has been removed.) By 1658, with the help of Robert Hooke (see below), he had designed and built a new kind of air pump. The two scientists used it to create a vacuum by pumping air out of a glass globe. It was used mainly for research into air and air pressure, and to study how animals and plants breathe.

Robert Boyle
(1627-91)

An atomic theory of matter

Boyle's work with air and gases enabled him to formulate a law that describes the relationship between the volume of a gas and its pressure. He showed that if an amount of gas is stored at a constant temperature, and the pressure on it is doubled, its volume reduces by half.

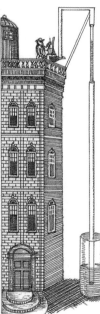

This illustration shows one of Boyle's experiments on the pressure of liquids.

In 1661 Boyle published a book called *The Sceptical Chymist*. One of his conclusions was that if air could be compressed it must be made up of tiny particles. He suggested that everything was made up of "primary particles" that could collect together to form larger "corpuscles". He was in fact describing what scientists now call atoms and molecules, though these terms were not introduced until later by Dalton and others (see page 79).

A mechanical genius

Robert Hooke (1635-1703) was an outstanding experimenter and inventor of new instruments. He was born on the Isle of Wight, off the south coast of England. While at Oxford University he met Robert Boyle, who employed him as an assistant.

Hooke moved to London in 1660, and two years later became the curator of

Hooke's compound microscope

An illustration of a louse from Hooke's *Micrographia*

experiments at the Royal Society. In 1665 he published *Micrographia*, a book containing illustrations of some of the specimens he had viewed under microscopes (instruments which magnify small objects). It also showed several instruments that he had designed. These included the compound microscope which was much more accurate than early microscopes.

The return of a comet

Edmond Halley (1656-1742) was the son of a London businessman. His experimental work in astronomy and magnetism was of great importance. He first became interested in comets (giant balls of ice and dust that move around the solar system) with the appearance of the Great Comet in 1682.

Halley's comet also appeared before the Battle of Hastings in 1066, as shown here (top) in the Bayeux Tapestry.

Applying Newton's theory of gravitation, Halley noted that the orbits of the comets seen in 1531, 1607 and 1682 were very similar and that the comets appeared at regular intervals. He believed that they must all be the same comet and correctly predicted its return in 1758. It is now named after him and its reappearance helped support Newton's picture of the universe.

71

Classifying the natural world

Ever since people first hunted animals and gathered plants, they have been aware of the great variety of living things. From the earliest times people tried to arrange the different types into groups according to their characteristics, in order to understand them better. This is known as classification. Over the years, however, so many new varieties were discovered and identified that new classification systems were needed to accommodate them.

This is a page from an Arabic version of a classification of animals by Aristotle.

Pages from Gesner's *Historiae animalium*, written between 1551 and 1558

Edward Topsell's *The Historie of Foure-footed Beastes* (above) was the English translation of Gesner's work.

An early naturalist

Konrad Gesner (1516-65) was born in Switzerland. In 1537, at the age of only 21, he was appointed professor of Greek at the newly-founded Lausanne Academy. He eventually worked as a physician in Zürich, and died there in a plague epidemic.

Gesner is famous for the huge five-volume work he compiled entitled *Historiae animalium* (History of animals). In it, he listed alphabetically every creature he could find from his own observations and from books.

Although this work included such mythical creatures as the bishop-fish, it was an important step toward a new understanding of animals. It gave many details of the appearance of the animals, what they ate and where they lived.

Classification takes shape

One of the most outstanding developments in classification was made by John Ray in the 17th century. He was born in Essex, England. His mother was a well-known medical herbalist who encouraged her son's interest in botany. Ray lectured on botany at Cambridge University for more than ten years, but had to leave for religious reasons. He then toured Europe with a biologist called Francis Willughby. After returning to England in 1660, Ray produced a botanical catalogue entitled *Plants Growing in the Neighbourhood of Cambridge.*

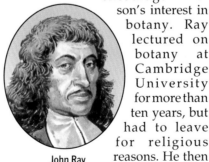

John Ray (1627-1705)

Between 1686 and 1704 Ray wrote an enormous book called *A General Account of Plants* which contained descriptions of 17,000 different types. His system of classification of the plants in this work was organized according to their fruits, flowers and leaves. This was an important advance on Gesner's method of classifying animals, which merely listed particular features. Ray's system, however, detailed different features of the plants and then grouped them according to the characteristics they shared. This gave a clearer idea of how they were related to each other.

An illustration from Ray's *Flora of Britain*

Animals from a 17th-century naturalist's museum

Modern classification

The Swedish botanist Carl von Linné is often known by his latinized name of Linnaeus. He studied medicine at the University of Uppsala in Sweden, but spent much of his time there studying plants in the university gardens.

Linnaeus then settled at Leiden in the Netherlands for three years. While he was there he published a vast number of works, including *Systema naturae* (System of nature). Two years later he wrote *Genera plantarum* (The Genera of plants).

Linnaeus (1707-78)

Linnaeus worked at Uppsala from 1741 until his death in 1778. He was first appointed professor of medicine, but became professor of botany the following year.

A page from *Systema naturæ* by Linnaeus

In 1753 Linnaeus published his *Species plantarum*, which is now regarded as the starting point for the modern system of classification of plants. In it he developed a method of classification called "binomial nomenclature" (two-part naming system), a method which is still used in a modified form today.

Linnaeus' house at Uppsala

The binomial system gives each plant two names. The first indicates the genus, or large family group to which it belongs, and the second gives the species, or smaller specific type within the genus. In this way a lemon tree is named *Citrus limon*, while an orange tree is a *Citrus aurantium*.

The publication of *Species plantarum* made Linnaeus famous throughout Europe and greatly influenced the study of natural history. When Linnaeus died, an English admirer shipped his collection and papers to London.

Although Linnaeus was aware of the differences between wild and domesticated plants, he still claimed that the universe had remained the same since God's creation. He regarded each species of plant and animal as fixed and unchanging. This view was challenged by Buffon.

Evidence of change

Georges-Louis Leclerc, Comte de Buffon, was born into a wealthy family living near Dijon, France. He became very active in scientific circles and studied mathematics and botany. In 1739 he was appointed superintendent of the royal botanical garden in Paris, the Jardin du Roi.

Buffon wrote two major works: the *Mémoires* (1737-52), scientific treatises on a range of topics in mathematics, astronomy and physics; and the 36-volume *Natural History* (1749-88). The second book was a survey of the natural world and a history of the Earth. In it, Buffon suggested that fossils provided evidence of extinct species of animal life.

Georges de Buffon (1707-88)

Researchers at the Jardin du Roi

Contradicting Linnaeus, Buffon claimed that fossils showed that the natural world had not remained unaltered, but had changed over the years. The *Natural History* was very important because it was the first book to propose that species had developed over long periods of time. But much more work was needed before the theory of evolution could be devised (see page 76).

Buffon claimed that fossils showed evidence of change.

73

The age of the earth

Before the 19th century, most theories about the earth and its history were based on biblical accounts. But people gradually began to find evidence that the earth was much older than the Bible suggested. It was discovered that some strata (layers) of rock were older than others, and evidence from fossils indicated many extinct species of plants and animals. Volcanoes and earthquakes showed that the surface of the earth did in fact change. A new science, called geology, developed as people tried to answer questions about how old the earth really is. Geology is the study of the earth's origins, structure and history.

This 16th-century illustration shows God creating the world in six days.

The Neptunist theory

Abraham Werner was born into a wealthy German family with connections in the iron and mining industries. He entered university to study law, but gave this up to study geology. In 1775 at Freiberg in Saxony, Werner founded an institute for studying mining and mineralogy. He worked out the first widely accepted system for classifying types of rock and landscape.

Toward the end of the 18th century many people thought the earth had been shaped by the action of volcanoes and earthquakes. But Werner proposed instead that the earth had once been covered by a huge ocean, created by the flood described in the Bible. This water slowly receded, leaving behind layers of rocks which were formed from minerals in the water. This is known as the "Neptunist" theory, after Neptune, the Roman god of the sea. One of Werner's most important conclusions was that this process must have taken a very long time, as much as one million years. This had a great influence on the work of later geologists.

Abraham Werner (1749-1817)

The Plutonist theory

Although he trained first as a lawyer in Scotland and then qualified as a medical doctor, James Hutton became a famous geologist. In 1795 he published a book called *The Theory of the Earth*. In this he did not include the biblical idea of a flood. Instead he suggested that the earth had changed very slowly over millions of years, and was continuing to do so. According to his theory, the earth's crust was first eroded by natural forces like wind, water, earthquakes and volcanoes. Then the material from this erosion formed a layer and hardened into the earth's surface. Lastly, heat from the middle of the earth caused the movement of rocks, which in turn formed new continents. He suggested that this cycle goes on all the time so that the earth is constantly renewing itself. Hutton's idea is known as the "Plutonist" theory, after Pluto, the Roman god of the underworld. It encouraged a new way of thinking. While Werner's theory had also suggested that the creation of the world took an extremely long time, it could still be related to the flood of the Bible. Hutton's theory, on the other hand, questioned the literal interpretation of the biblical account of the creation.

James Hutton (1726-96) collecting rock samples

This is an early illustration of an eruption of Mt Vesuvius, a volcano in southern Italy.

Fossils

Fossils are the remains of plants and animals preserved in rocks. They are as old as the rocks in which they are found and some were formed more than 500 million years ago. By studying fossils closely, it is possible to build up a picture of life as it was on earth many millions of years ago.

Promicroceras Lower Jurassic

Onnia Ordovician

Vesuvius

Uniform change

Charles Lyell was born in Scotland. He studied law at Oxford University, but became interested in geology at the age of 21. In 1831 he was appointed professor of geology at King's College, London. He helped turn the subject from a hobby for rich amateurs into a science in its own right.

Lyell thought that geological features were caused by natural processes acting over very long periods of time. Winds wore away mountains, glaciers moved huge rocks, volcanoes erupted, valleys were eroded by rivers and cliffs by the sea. This theory is known as "uniformitarianism" because it claims that nature acts uniformly in a set pattern. The theory had first been proposed in a general way by Hutton. But it was much more convincingly argued and illustrated by Lyell who used new information gathered after Hutton's day to support his ideas. In time it became the view of most geologists and remains so today.

Charles Lyell
(1797-1875)

Supercontinents

Alfred Wegener was a German meteorologist (someone who examines weather conditions). He studied at the universities of Berlin, Heidelberg and Innsbruck. In 1910, looking at a map of the world, Wegener noticed that part of the west coast of Africa appeared to fit the shape of the east coast of South America. From this and fossil evidence he suggested that the two continents had once been joined together in one "supercontinent", which he called Pangaea. He then suggested that Pangaea had broken up and that the present continents were formed from the drifting pieces. This is known as the "continental drift" theory.

From 1960 Wegener's ideas were extended to make up the new theory of "plate tectonics". This claims that the earth's crust is not one solid mass, but is cracked into giant pieces (known as "plates") carrying the continents. The theory describes a never-ending process, in which molten rock is forced up between the plates to the earth's surface, where it solidifies. Similarly, the edges of the plates slide down beneath the adjacent ones and become molten again. If this does not happen and two plates collide, earthquakes occur along the point of impact.

Continental drift

These illustrations show the gradual break-up of Pangaea into the continents we see today.

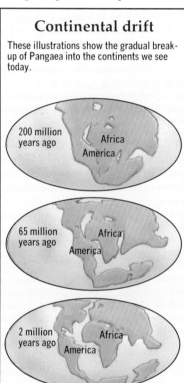

200 million years ago — Africa / America

65 million years ago — Africa / America

2 million years ago — Africa / America

According to the continental drift theory, the continents of the southern hemisphere once fitted together as one giant continent, as did those of the northern hemisphere. Because the earth's crust has drifted, the continents have not always been in the same place, and are still moving. For example, according to the theory, North Africa was once covered in a sheet of ice and was situated where the South Pole is today. The South Pole was once covered with tropical forests.

Lyell's drawings of fossil shells

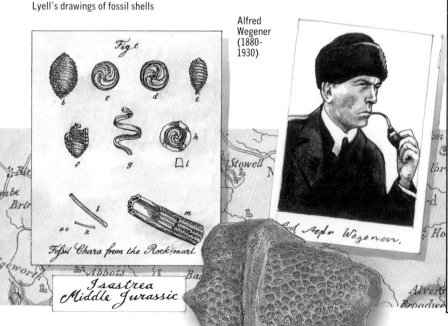

Fig. 1.

Fossil Chara from the Rock-marl.

Isastrea
Middle Jurassic

Alfred Wegener (1880-1930)

Evolution

Until the end of the 17th century, most Europeans believed that everything in nature was exactly the same as it always had been; they thought that plant and animal species were fixed, remaining in the state in which they had originally been created by God. In the 18th century, however, an increasing amount of evidence built up which contradicted this. People started to suggest that the characteristics of plants and animals could have changed over very long periods of time. This is now known as evolution.

Early evolutionary ideas

Jean-Baptiste de Monet, Chevalier de Lamarck, was born in France, the eleventh and youngest child of aristocratic but poor parents. He had a difficult life and died poor and blind, his work forgotten. At the age of 16 he joined the army but he had to leave because of ill health. Lack of money forced him to work in a bank rather than taking up his preferred career in medicine.

Chevalier de Lamarck (1744-1829)

Botanist to the king

In his spare time, Lamarck took up the study of plants and became so good at the subject that eventually, in 1781, he was appointed botanist to the French king. Ten years later, after the French Revolution, he was elected professor of zoology at the new Museum of Natural History in Paris. There he gave lectures, arranged the displays and organized exhibitions.

Noticing the differences between fossils and modern forms of animals, Lamarck became convinced that plant

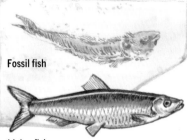

Fossil fish

Living fish

and animal species were not fixed forever, but could change from one generation to the next. His ideas were influenced not only by fossils but also by other geological evidence that suggested that the earth's surface had changed over many years (see page 74).

The Jardin du Roi in Paris where Lamark studied

Lamarck concluded that within their own lifetimes, animals' characteristics could alter in order to cope with their surroundings. He suggested that these changes were then passed on to their offspring. For instance, he argued that the neck of the giraffe would become longer during its lifetime as a result of stretching for leaves in trees, and that this change would then be passed on to the next generation.

This theory is now thought to be incorrect, though aspects of it were used in the theory of evolution presented 50 years later by Darwin and Wallace.

A South American expedition

Charles Darwin was born in Shrewsbury in England, the son of a successful doctor. He attended school in Shrewsbury and went on to study medicine at the University of Edinburgh. But he did not enjoy the subject and, at his father's insistence, moved to Cambridge University to study for the priest-hood. But although he managed to gain a degree, again he was unhappy with the

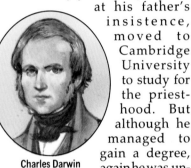

Charles Darwin (1809-82)

subject. However he showed a great interest in botany and entomology (the study of insects). In 1831 a professor of botany called John Henslow noticed his abilities and found him a place as the naturalist on an expedition to South America. Before leaving, Darwin read works by the geologist Charles Lyell (see page 75). These books made a great impression on him and later influenced his own work.

A page from one of Darwin's notebooks

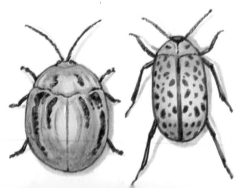

One of the two types of iguana from the Galapagos Islands

Darwin's discoveries

The expedition left in a ship called HMS *Beagle* and was away for five years. During that time it visited Brazil, Argentina, Chile, Peru and the Galapagos Islands, ten rocky islands lying off the coast of Ecuador in the Pacific Ocean, each with different wildlife.

Darwin's drawing of types of finch from the Galapagos Islands

Along the way Darwin built up a huge collection of rocks and fossils as well as samples of plants, birds and animals. He also made very detailed notes of everything he saw on the journey. He later used much of this material, particularly the observations he made on the Galapagos Islands, in the formulation of his theory of evolution.

Beetles collected by Darwin on the expedition

The *Beagle* returned to England in October 1836. Darwin spent the next 20 years writing up his findings. In 1858 he received a manuscript written by Alfred Wallace (1823-1913), a scientist with very similar ideas to his own. Although they presented their ideas together, Darwin's role was seen as more important than Wallace's.

In 1859 Darwin published *On the Origin of the Species by Means of Natural Selection*, which set out his theories on evolution. The book was an immediate success. But it also led to an uproar because it challenged traditional beliefs on the beginning of life on earth. One of the most revolutionary ideas was that all living things had evolved over many millions of years. This rejected the biblical teaching that the world was created in six days and had remained unchanged ever since. Today, most scientists accept a form of the Darwinian theory to explain biological change, although the theory is still being modified. Some people, however, still object to Darwin's ideas on religious grounds.

Cartoon mocking Darwin's idea that humans are descended from apes

Natural selection

Darwin realized that organisms have to compete with each other for food and shelter. He noticed that within each species, some individuals are born with features that by chance make them more able to survive than others. Their offspring inherit these features, which gradually become more common. If other individuals do not have the helpful features, they are more likely to die out. So over many generations the entire species adapts to its environment. This process, called natural selection, can be seen in the way the peppered moth adapted to environmental changes in the 19th century.

At first, the moths were silver and blended with light tree-trunks. But as trees became blackened with pollution, the moths were more visible, and so more likely to be eaten by birds. Some individuals, born slightly darker than the others, were less visible and so survived better. They passed on their darker shading to their offspring, and so the entire species became darker.

Silver peppered moth

Black peppered moths blended into the darker background.

The growth of modern chemistry

Chemistry (the study of the substances that make up the world around us) has its origins in the ancient practice of alchemy (see page 58). But alchemy was closely connected to magic and superstition, and is not currently regarded as a true science. Chemistry also has its roots in industrial processes such as iron-working and the making of drugs for medicine. With the growth of experiment and research, the practice of chemistry devloped into a modern science.

An experiment in a 16th-century laboratory

Studying chemical reactions

In 1756 a Scottish experimenter called Joseph Black (1728-99) made an important study of a chemical reaction (the change that takes place when a new substance is formed). Black discovered that when he heated a substance called magnesium carbonate it lost weight. He then suggested that this was because the substance gave off a gas during the heating process. He named the gas "fixed air"; today we know it as carbon dioxide.

A newly discovered gas

Joseph Priestley was born in Yorkshire, England. He trained as a Church minister but soon became interested in scientific research. His work made him famous, but political pressures forced him to leave England for the USA in 1791. In 1774 Priestley made his most important discovery. He noticed that when he heated a chemical called mercuric oxide, a gas was given off. When he placed a lighted candle in the gas, he saw that the flame burned very brightly. At this time, many scientists believed that when something burned it lost a substance they called phlogiston (from *phlox*, the Greek for "flame"). Priestley called his gas "dephlogisticated air" because it seemed to have lost phlogiston. But in fact he had identified the gas we now know as oxygen.

Joseph Priestley (1733-1804)

A late 18th-century cartoon of "Doctor Phlogiston"

The founder of modern chemistry

Antoine Lavoisier (1743-94) was born in Paris. He trained as a lawyer but became interested in science and worked as a tax collector in order to support his scientific research. Tax collectors were very unpopular with the leaders of the French Revolution and Lavoisier was one of many people to be executed at the end of the revolution.

Arrest of Lavoisier by French revolutionaries

Priestley's microscope

The naming of oxygen

Lavoisier performed a series of experiments designed to examine the process of combustion (burning). He heated a number of different substances in air, carefully weighing them before and after heating. His results showed that, rather than losing weight, the substances often became heavier. He reasoned that they must therefore have absorbed something from the air. He showed that this unknown substance was the same gas as the one that Priestley had identified, and renamed it oxygen.

Apparatus used by Lavoisier to investigate combustion.

By successfully explaining some of the phenomena scientists had observed, Lavoisier's results helped to disprove the phlogiston theory, which had been held for nearly a hundred years. His definition of burning - as the uniting of a substance with oxygen - is still used today. He was the first person to demonstrate that all kinds of burning (including the breathing of animals and plants) involve the addition of oxygen. His work helped to overthrow many of the incorrect ideas inherited from alchemy.

Chemical building blocks

In 1789 Lavoisier published *Methods of Chemical Nomenclature*, which built on the work of Robert Boyle (see page 71). In it he developed the idea of elements (substances that cannot be split into simpler substances) as chemical building blocks. Lavoisier listed 33 elements, arranged to show how they combine to form compounds (substances made of more than one element). The book also introduced a new system of naming substances based on their chemical content. Before, they had often had confusing names, some derived from alchemy.

A modern atomic theory

John Dalton was born in a small village in the north of England and taught himself science. His ideas led to a greater understanding of the most fundamental chemical process: the way elements combine to form compounds. In 1808 he published a book called *A New System of Chemical Philosophy*. It had two main points. One was that all chemical elements are composed of very small particles called atoms, which do not break up during chemical reactions. The other was

John Dalton (1766-1844)

that all chemical reactions are the result of atoms joining together or separating. Another important feature of the book was its proposal that different atoms weigh different amounts.

The relationship between elements

Dmitri Mendeleev was born and brought up in Siberia in Russia, the last in a family of 14 children. He was a brilliant student of science at the University of St Petersburg and later became professor of chemistry there. He studied the relationship between different chemical elements. At this time, a few scientists had noticed that some elements had similarities that related to their atomic weights. The atomic weight of an element is the weight of one of its atoms compared with the weight of a hydrogen atom.

Dmitri Mendeleev (1834-1907) and part of his *Periodic Table*

In 1869 Mendeleev published his Periodic Table of Elements. This grouped the elements into "families" according to their atomic weights, the smallest (hydrogen) on the left, and the largest (lead) on the right. It showed how the elements are related to each other. Mendeleev identified gaps in the periodic table which he claimed represented elements still to be discovered. He was right. Four years later, the first of these, gallium, was discovered. Over a hundred elements have so far been listed.

Some of the equipment used by Dalton

Studying electricity

Electricity plays a very important part in our lives. There are two types: static (not moving) and current (moving). People have known about the effects of electricity since ancient times. But until the end of the 18th century, the only kind they knew how to make was static electricity. The study of electricity became very popular, and during the 19th century people gradually learned more about it and its uses.

Early experiments

In 1705 an English scientist called Francis Hauksbee (c.1666-1713) discovered that if he rubbed a glass globe containing a vacuum (an airless space), it flashed with light. The light was caused by electricity and the globe was acting as an electrical generator.

Hauksbee's static electricity generator

Another man, Stephen Gray (1666-1736), devised experiments which showed that electricity could be conducted (transmitted) through a number of different materials. These included the human body.

An early demonstration of static electricity.

He made electricity travel along a string suspended from cords hung on poles in his orchard.

This French playing card of c.1750 shows a demonstration of static electricity.

Storing static electricity

In 1745 a German priest called Ewald von Kleist (c.1700-48) designed an instrument that could collect and store static electricity. It became known as the Leiden jar, after being used and perfected at the University of Leiden. This was a major development in people's knowledge about electricity. The Leiden jar consisted of a glass jar held in one hand. The inside glass surface was charged (electrified) with static electricity by dipping a brass wire connected to a generator, very similar to Hauksbee's, into the water inside the jar. Once charged, the jar could store the electricity and could also transmit a shock if the wire was touched.

This illustration shows a Leiden jar being charged with static electricity from a generator.

Making electricity useful

One of the first people to study electricity in detail was Benjamin Franklin. He was born in the USA, one of 17 children of a Boston candlemaker. During his long life he had several successful careers: as printer, publisher and politician. At the age of 40 he became interested in electricity, which at that time was mainly used as a form of entertainment in displays. In 1752 Franklin showed that lightning was a form of electricity. He flew a kite fitted with a metal key into a storm cloud. When lightning hit the key, sparks flew off it.

Benjamin Franklin (1706-90)

This experiment was very dangerous and another scientist was later killed doing the same thing. But with it Franklin was able to prove that storm clouds are charged with static electricity. It also showed that lightning is caused by the discharge of that electricity in the form of a very powerful spark. In the same year he fitted the first lightning conductor to the outside wall of a house. This attracted lightning and carried it safely to the ground, preventing damage to the building.

18th-century lady wearing a lightning conductor hat

Animal electricity

Luigi Galvani (1737-98) was professor of anatomy at Bologna University. He realized that an electric ray fish gave a shock similar to that from a Leiden jar. He then wanted to find out whether electricity existed in all forms of life. In 1780, while he was dissecting a dead frog, he noticed that its legs twitched when his scalpel blade touched a nerve. He also noticed that the leg muscles twitched when

Galvani's experiment with frogs' legs

they were in contact with two different metals, in this case brass and iron. Galvani concluded, mistakenly, that the frog's legs produced electricity and that animals must contain electricity in their muscles and nerves.

Electricity from metals

Alessandro Volta (1745-1827) showed that the frog's legs did not contain their own form of electricity and that Galvani's results were in fact due to the contact of the two different metals in a damp atmosphere. Using this information, in 1799 Volta succeeded in building the first electric battery. This became known as a "voltaic pile" and was made up of discs of silver and zinc with damp card between them. It generated a steady current of electricity. The volt, a measurement of electricity, is named after him.

The first battery, known as a voltaic pile

Popular science

Michael Faraday was born near London, the son of a blacksmith. His first job was in a bookshop, but in 1813 he started work as a laboratory assistant at the Royal Institution in London. In 1833 he was made professor of chemistry there. Many people now regard Faraday as the greatest of all experimental physicists. He was one of the first people to try to make science popular with the general public. In 1826 he gave the first lectures about science for children, at the Royal Institution. These are still held every year.

Michael Faraday
(1791-1867)

Electricity and magnetism

Faraday became very interested in the relationship between electricity and magnetism. People had known about magnetism for thousands of years, and many believed that electricity and magnetism were related in some way. Then, in 1820, a Danish scientist called Hans Oersted (1777-1851) noticed that a wire with an electric current running through it acted like a magnet, making the needle move on a compass lying nearby.

Investigating this further, Faraday found that when he charged a coil of wire with electricity, an electric current also flowed in another, separate coil nearby. He reasoned that this second current must have been generated by the magnetic effect of the first one.

Faraday argued that if electricity flowing in a wire could produce a magnetic effect, then the opposite might also be true - a magnetic effect should produce an electric current. He found that when he moved a magnet in and out of a coil of wire, the wire became charged with electricity. This showed that magnets alone could produce an electric current. Faraday had created the first dynamo (a machine that uses mechanical energy to generate electrical energy).

These discoveries had all kinds of far-reaching practical results. Faraday's work led to the invention of the electric motor, and to the development of large-scale systems to generate electricity. This eventually led to the introduction of a public electricity supply.

Faraday produced an electric current from a moving magnet, using this device called a disc dynamo.

81

The fight against disease

During the Renaissance in Europe much progress was made in the understanding of the human body (see page 64). But doctors were still unable to cure a number of diseases, including smallpox and the plague, which killed millions all over the world. Many of these illnesses were caused by viruses (microscopic particles that live off the body's cells). Another problem was that while surgical techniques had improved, many people still died from infections they caught during surgery. From the mid-18th century scientists began to find ways to beat these forms of disease.

This engraving of 1656 shows an Italian doctor wearing special clothing to protect him against the plague.

Early vaccination

Edward Jenner was born in Gloucestershire, England. From the age of 13 he went to work as an apprentice to a surgeon, and then became a medical student at St George's Hospital, London. After two years Jenner returned to his home town and set up a medical practice. At this time smallpox was one of the most serious viral diseases. Jenner had heard that people who had caught a mild disease called cowpox did not catch smallpox. The cowpox had immunized (protected) them against smallpox. In 1796 Jenner scratched some cowpox into the skin of a healthy boy. Two months later he did the same with smallpox. The experiment was a complete success: the boy did not develop smallpox and had therefore become immune to it. Jenner named the process vaccination, from *vacca*, the Latin word for cow. His work was one of the most important advances in medical science ever made. By 1980 there were no more reported cases of smallpox.

Edward Jenner (1749-1823)

The birth of bacteriology

Louis Pasteur was born near Dijon in eastern France. In 1843 he went to Paris to study chemistry, and in 1854 he was appointed professor of chemistry at the University of Lille. In Lille, Pasteur was asked to find out why alcohols such as wine and beer sometimes turn sour. He discovered that this was caused by germs called bacteria, and that heating the liquid to a certain temperature killed the bacteria but left the liquid unchanged. This process is now known as "pasteurization" and is used to treat milk. Pasteur also showed that the bacteria which cause liquids to go sour and meat to rot exist invisibly all around us. Pasteur's most famous work was on rabies, one of the most horrific diseases that can affect a human being. It causes paralysis and eventually kills the victim. In 1885 he injected a weak solution of rabies germs into a boy who had been bitten and infected by a rabid (rabies-infected) dog. After a series of these injections the boy recovered completely.

Louis Pasteur (1822-95)

A statue of Joseph Meister, the boy Pasteur vaccinated against rabies

Normally the rabies germs would have become active a few weeks after the bite, but this did not happen. The injections, prepared from weakened germs, caused a very mild attack of rabies. This stimulated the boy's resistance, making him immune to the germs from the bite. This is the principle behind all vaccination.

Glass flask and microscope used by Pasteur

Robert Koch (1843-1910) was, with Pasteur, the founder of the science of bacteriology. Here Koch is inoculating a patient against tuberculosis.

Jenner used these points to scratch vaccine into the skin.

A 19th-century cartoon showing Jenner's patients turning into cows

Antiseptic operations

Joseph Lister was born in Essex, England, the son of a wine merchant and amateur scientist. In 1848 he enrolled at University College, London to study medicine. He qualified in 1852 and, because his work was so outstanding, he was made a Fellow of the Royal College of Surgeons the same year. In 1853 he moved to Edinburgh to take up the post of assistant to James Syme, a leading surgeon. In 1861 Lister was appointed surgeon at the Glasgow Royal Infirmary.

Joseph Lister
(1827-1912)

In those days, many patients died after surgical operations. Wounds rarely healed cleanly and usually became septic (badly infected). This often led to blood poisoning and other fatal diseases. In 1865 Pasteur published his theory of germ disease, which claimed that bacteria can cause disease and that fermentation and rotting are caused by bacteria which live in the air. When Lister read this, he thought that the rotting of meat and sepsis of wounds might

These machines sterilize instruments by steam-heating them.

Some modern sterilizing units use ultra-violet light and ultrasound to destroy germs.

be caused by the same thing. Shortly after the publication of Pasteur's paper, Lister performed his first operation in which he took care to clean everything that came into contact with the patient's wound with carbolic acid. This method is known as antisepsis and it destroys germs already present.

Lister's antiseptic carbolic spray

As a result of these precautions, the wounds in this and other similar operations healed properly, and the rate of infection fell dramatically. Lister received many awards for his work. His introduction of antisepsis to hospitals was one of the major advances in medicine in the 19th century. It changed general surgery from being highly dangerous into something that saves lives.

This illustration shows Lister directing an antiseptic surgical operation.

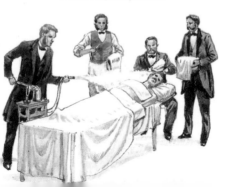

Antibiotic drugs

Alexander Fleming was born in Ayrshire, Scotland. From 1901 he studied medicine at St Mary's Hospital, London. Much later, in 1928, when he was studying the bacteria responsible for blood poisoning, he noticed that a dish of the bacteria had become infected with a growth called *Penicillium notatum*. The bacteria in the area infected by the growth had been killed. The chemical that had caused this is now known as "penicillin".

Alexander Fleming
(1881-1955)

Some years later two scientists called Howard Florey (1898-1968) and Ernst Chain (1906-79) produced the first large quantities of purified penicillin. This was the first of a group of drugs called antibiotics which attack and kill bacteria. Because of the development of antibiotics in the 20th century, bacterial illnesses are no longer a major cause of death.

A dish of *Penicillium notatum*, from which penicillin is made

More obstacles

Though smallpox and other diseases have been eradicated, many more fatal diseases still remain. Scientists are still seeking cures for viral and other diseases. Two of the major ones facing doctors today are cancer and the AIDS virus.

Waves and radiation

People have always been interested in nature and the world about them. From the earliest times they asked questions about why things get hot, how light works and sounds are made. Some of these questions were answered by scholars in the ancient world, but in the 19th century scientists began to study problems like these in more detail. They started to describe light, electricity, and magnetism as the products of different kinds of energy.

Developing Faraday's work

James Maxwell was born and brought up near Edinburgh, Scotland. He was a mathematician and physicist whose most important work was on electricity and magnetism. In 1820 Hans Oersted (see page 81) had shown that an electric current had a magnetic effect on a compass needle. An effect like this is now said to be "electromagnetic". Later, Michael Faraday (see page 81) suggested that electric and magnetic forces spread out in "fields" from their sources.

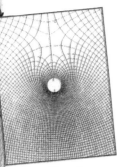

Lines of force in a magnetic field

In 1855 Maxwell developed Faraday's ideas to give a mathematical explanation for the transmission of electromagnetic forces. He devised mathematical equations which showed that the magnetic

James Maxwell (1831-79), with a page of his calculations

field generated by an electric current spreads outward from its source at a constant speed. He calculated that this speed was roughly the same as the speed of light. He suggested that light must therefore be some kind of electromagnetic wave and that the light we can see may be only one of many types of electromagnetic radiation. (Radiation is the emission of rays from a source.)

Radio waves

Heinrich Hertz was born in Hamburg, Germany. He orginally trained to be an engineer but then began studying physics. His experiments showed that electro-magnetic waves emitted by an electrical spark on one side of his laboratory could be detected by a loop of wire some distance away. This proved the existence of radio waves, another form of electromagnetic radiation. It was later shown that, like light, radio waves could be focused and reflected. Hertz's work therefore proved Maxwell's earlier theory that electromagnetic waves behave in the same way as light waves.

Heinrich Hertz (1857-94)

More electromagnetic waves

Wilhelm Röntgen was born in a small village in Germany and studied at Zürich Polytechnic. He became professor of physics at the University of Würzburg where he experimented with gases and expanded Maxwell's work on electromagnetism.

In 1895 Röntgen was researching cathode rays, which are produced when an electric current is passed through a glass tube containing a near-vacuum. The tube glows whenever the rays hit the glass. In order to examine this more closely, Röntgen surrounded the tube with a piece of black paper. He was mystified when some cardboard on the other side of the room started to glow. It was coated with a chemical, known as a fluorescent, which glows when exposed to light.

Wilhelm Röntgen (1845-1923)

Röntgen found that the cardboard still glowed even when he moved it into the next room. It appeared that the tube was emitting another form of radiation which was able to pass through all sorts of materials. He named the new rays X-rays, because of their unknown origin.

An early cathode ray tube

Later Röntgen found that by directing X-rays at a person's hand he could take photographs which showed the bones inside it. The X-rays were stopped by the bones, but passed through the flesh, allowing a photographic image to form.

A 19th-century cartoon of the X-ray effect

STRAND-IDYLL Á LA

An early X-ray machine

Two X-ray photographs: A modern X-ray of the human head, generated in colour by a computer; and one of the first X-rays, taken by Röntgen of his wife's hand

Confirmation of radioactivity

Marya Sklodowska (later Marie Curie) was born in Warsaw, Poland. She left to study chemistry at the Sorbonne in Paris. In 1894 she married another chemist, Pierre Curie (1859-1906).

In their own research into radiation, the Curies discovered that pitchblende, a mineral that contains uranium, is four times as radioactive as pure uranium. They thought that it must therefore contain some other, unknown, radioactive element. The Curies spent several years purifying huge quantities of pitchblende, which became increasingly radioactive. By 1902 they had gathered 0.1 gram of the unknown element, which they gave the name "radium".

Caricature of the Curies

This revolutionized the medical world, particularly the diagnosis and treatment of broken bones.

The beginning of the atomic era

Antoine Becquerel was born into a scientific family and brought up in Paris. He was a physicist who specialized in the study of fluorescence. When he heard of Röntgen's discovery, he wanted to devise an experiment to find out whether fluorescent chemicals, as well as emitting ordinary light rays, would emit X-rays.

Antoine Becquerel (1852-1908)

At that time Becquerel was studying a fluorescent compound that included an element called uranium. He wrapped some of it in metal foil, then placed the parcel on a photographic plate. He reasoned that any ordinary light emitted by the fluorescence in the

substance would not be able to pass through the foil and register on the plate, but that X-rays might. When he developed the plate, it had indeed been blackened, so he was able to confirm that the substance was giving out some type of ray. He later discovered that this only happened with uranium compounds, not with other types of fluorescent chemical.

Becquerel realized that the substance was giving out an extremely strong form of radiation. At first he thought he had found a new form of electromagnetism. But further experiments showed that there were two distinct types of radiation, now known as alpha and beta radiation. These consisted of electrically-charged particles. Later a third type, gamma radiation, was discovered, which was proved to be a form of electromagnetic radiation. These discoveries implied that atoms of radioactive substances were themselves the source of energy. They led scientists to conclude that atoms must therefore have some kind of internal structure that was able to generate this energy. This realization was a very important step, because it marked the beginning of the modern understanding of the atom.

In 1903 the Curies received the Nobel Prize for physics. When Pierre was killed in a car crash three years later, Marie took over as professor in Paris, the first woman to hold such a position. In 1911 she was awarded the Nobel Prize for chemistry, the first person to receive two Nobel prizes.

Radium, used in small doses, became very important in the treatment of cancer. But years of exposure to it damaged Curie's own health, and she died of a blood cancer called leukemia.

A medal of Marie Curie (1867-1934), issued on the centenary of her birth

The science of life

Although by the end of the 19th century Darwin's theory of evolution was accepted by many scientists, there were a few who disagreed with it. They claimed that it did not explain how changes originated in plants and animals, or how characteristics were passed on from one generation to the next. People began to investigate these questions. Their studies led to the foundation of genetics, the science of heredity (how characteristics in plants and animals are inherited).

The birth of genetics

Gregor Mendel grew up in Heinzendorf in Austria. He became a priest at the monastery in Brno in 1847, and was elected abbot there eleven years later.

Mendel was interested in how plants pass on particular features such as height and shape to their offspring. He bred pea plants to find out how this worked, and noticed that characteristics like the shape of their flowers were passed on to the next generation. He also found that some features were more likely to be inherited than others. Those that had a three in four chance of being inherited he called "dominant". Those that only had a one in four chance of being inherited he called "recessive".

Mendel suggested that each characteristic was controlled by a pair of units (now called genes), one from each parent. This is known as Mendel's First

Mendel performed most of his experiments on pea plants.

Law. His discoveries and theories revealed the secret of heredity and formed the basis of modern studies in genetics. However, though he published his work in 1866, its true significance remained unrecognized for nearly forty years.

Gregor Mendel (1822-84)

Experiments with fruit flies

Thomas Morgan (1866-1945) was born in Kentucky, USA. He founded the department of biology at the California Institute of Technology in 1928, and ran it for the rest of his life. At first Morgan was one of the fiercest critics of Mendel's theory of heredity, but he later became its strongest supporter. He wanted to find out whether the kind of changes Mendel had noticed in plants also occurred in animals. In 1908 he began studying fruit flies; this work was very important in establishing Mendel's theories.

Fruit flies normally have red eyes, but Morgan found a white-eyed male in one of the breeding jars. When he bred this male with other members of the same generation, some white-eyed flies appeared again in

Fruit flies (Drosophila melanogaster)

the next generation. They were mostly male, but when one of these white-eyed males mated with females of the first generation, half the males and half the females of their offspring had white eyes. Morgan used Mendel's theory to explain this result by showing that the dominant feature of white eyes was passed on by the male parent's units.

Mapping chromosomes

All organisms (living things) are made up of cells, the basic units of life. Inside each cell is a tiny ball called a nucleus, which in turn contains thread-like forms called chromosomes.

Morgan and his research team discovered that the units suggested by Mendel were indeed actual physical units, placed at definite positions along each chromosome. They named the units "genes", after the Greek word for birth. Using this discovery, they were able to work out the first "chromosome map". This showed the position of the genes on a chromosome. By 1922 they had worked out a map

Magnified human chromosomes

showing the positions of more than 2000 genes on the chromosomes of fruit flies. This enabled them to identify the gene responsible for the white eyes in the flies. In this way they confirmed that Mendel's theories were correct, and provided the evidence to explain them.

Molecular biology

Genes provide a chemical code of instructions to control the way plants and animals look and how their bodies work. A "copy" of these instructions is passed from parents to their offspring. The study of how this happens is part of an important area of scientific research known as molecular biology, which is concerned with the structure of the molecules that make up living animals and plants.

Cross-section of an animal cell, magnified many times

Cell membrane (outer skin)

Nucleus

By the early 20th century scientists knew that plant and animal cells contained a chemical called deoxyribonucleic acid (DNA). By 1950, they thought that DNA molecules acted as the chemical code of instructions responsible for heredity, but they did not know what they looked like or how they worked. A number of scientists were using a variety of approaches to solve the problem.

Building the DNA model

Francis Crick was brought up in London. He studied physics at the University of London and then biology at Cambridge University.

With an American scientist called James Watson (b.1928), he carried out research into the structure of DNA. They also used the results of the work of other scientists, in particular Maurice Wilkins (b.1916) and Rosalind Franklin. Wilkins and Franklin studied DNA using X-ray photographs. Their work was crucial in the eventual discovery of the structure of DNA and how it transmits genetic information from one generation to the following one.

Francis Crick (b.1916)

In 1953, Crick and Watson built a scale model of the DNA molecule from pieces of wire and plastic balls. Its shape was that of a double helix, which looks like a twisted rope ladder. It showed how the DNA molecule divides to form two identical copies of itself.

Rosalind Franklin (1920-58)

When plants and animals reproduce, each of the cells they are made up from divides into two copies. Every time a new cell is made, the DNA is also copied, so that when the cell divides, each of the two new cells has its own copy of the instructions responsible for heredity. In this way the characteristics are passed from parents to their offspring.

Many scientists regard this as one of the most important discoveries of the 20th century. In 1962 Crick, Watson and Wilkins were awarded the Nobel Prize for Medicine. Had she not died very young from cancer, Rosalind Franklin would have shared the prize with them.

This is a computer-generated illustration showing the structure of the DNA molecule.

1. DNA consists of two strands shaped in a double helix, like a twisted rope ladder.

5. Two new identical strands are formed

2. The steps in the ladder are made up of four chemical building blocks, called bases, which are linked in pairs.

3. The two DNA strands separate

4. Spare bases join their matching pairs on the separated strands.

Opening up the atom

At the end of the 19th century, many physicists believed they were close to explaining the construction of the universe. They described matter in terms of the movement of tiny, indivisible particles called atoms. However, new discoveries threatened their confidence. It became apparent that atoms themselves were composed of even smaller particles, and that the way in which they behaved could not be explained by Newton's laws of force and motion (see page 70).

The birth of quantum physics

Max Planck was born in Kiel, now in Germany. He studied physics at Munich University, where he later became a professor. In 1900 he published an article introducing the idea of "quantizing energy". On the basis of Planck's work, Einstein suggested that electromagnetic radiation (see page 84), instead of being made up of waves, is in fact discontinuous and is composed of tiny particles, or "quanta", of energy.

$$E = h\nu$$

Max Planck
(1858-1947)

This equation, formulated by Einstein, includes Planck's constant (h). This relates the mechanical properties of matter to its wave properties.

Although Planck's idea was not seen as revolutionary at the time, it led to the development of quantum mechanics, a new set of laws describing how atomic particles behaved. Unlike Newton's laws, quantum mechanics is based on the idea that matter can behave either as waves or as particles.

From clerk to professor

Albert Einstein is one of the 20th century's most famous scientists. But he was a shy man whose work was very abstract and theoretical. He is best known for his relativity theories and for establishing the idea of the quantization of energy, both of which are important for describing how atoms and atomic particles move and interact.

Einstein was born in Ulm, Germany. His family moved to Switzerland and he studied physics at Zürich Polytechnic. After failing to secure an academic position, he became a clerk in Berne.

Albert Einstein
(1879-1955)

In 1905, Einstein worked in his spare time to produce three papers which re-examined some of the most fundamental ideas in science. His theories were so revolutionary that they were not immediately accepted, but his ability was quickly recognized. In 1909 he became a professor at Zürich University, and then in 1914 moved to the University of Berlin.

The University of Berlin

The relativity theories

The first paper on relativity (known as the Special Theory of Relativity) overturned Newton's view of fixed measurements of time and motion. Einstein showed that all movement is relative; that all we can measure is how fast we are moving in relation to something else. There is a relation between the mass and energy of moving objects, which he expressed in the equation $E=mc^2$. This means that the energy (E) contained in any particle of matter is equal to its mass (m) multiplied by the square of the speed of light (c^2). This formula is at the heart of all methods of obtaining nuclear energy.

A sheet of Einstein's calculations

In 1915 Einstein published a second paper on relativity (the General Theory of Relativity), which dealt with what happens when an object is speeding up or slowing down. It included the idea that light has mass and is therefore affected by gravity. This theory was confirmed when the bending of light by gravity was detected by photographing the light from two stars during a solar eclipse in 1919. Einstein's discoveries caused a sensation and made him internationally famous.

A computer image of a solar eclipse

The heart of the atom

Ernest Rutherford is important for his brilliant experimental and theoretical work on **the nucleus** (core) of the atom, and for his laboratory skills. The son of a New Zealand farmer, Rutherford studied at Christchurch College where he carried out research based on Hertz's study of radio waves (see page 84). He won a scholarship to Cambridge University, England and worked at the Cavendish Laboratory on the recently discovered X-rays and uranium radiation (see page 85).

Ernest
Rutherford
(1871-1937)

Autunite, an ore from which uranium can be extracted

Rutherford was appointed a professor at McGill University in Montreal, and later returned to Britain as director of the Manchester physics laboratory. He and his team carried out important experiments into the structure of the atom, using particles called

Apparatus used by Rutherford for scattering alpha particles

alpha particles, which are emitted by radioactive substances.

From his experiments, Rutherford built up a detailed picture of the atom. He concluded that most atomic matter was concentrated into a tiny nucleus in the middle, with much lighter particles called electrons orbiting it, like planets around the sun. In 1908 Rutherford was awarded the Nobel Prize for Chemistry, and in 1919 he was appointed director of the Cavendish Laboratory, where he inspired much further research into atomic structure.

A new model of the atom

Niels Bohr grew up in Copenhagen, Denmark, the son of a professor of physiology. He was awarded a doctorate from Copenhagen University and in 1911 moved to Manchester to work with Rutherford. By 1913 he had devised a radical new model of the structure of the atom. It combined Rutherford's ideas with those of quantum mechanics. Bohr's model has now been superseded, but it is still a useful aid to understanding

This diagram is based on Bohr's work into the structure of the atom. He showed that electrons move around the nucleus in defined energy levels, sometimes called shells.

the way atoms behaved.

In 1913 Bohr returned to Copenhagen as professor of physics and helped develop new theories of quantum mechanics. He drew up models of the structure of the nucleus and discussed the energy changes involved in nuclear fission. He won the Nobel Prize for Physics in 1922.

Niels Bohr
(1885-1962)

Bohr was a committed anti-fascist and, when the Germans invaded Denmark in 1940, he refused to participate in atomic research for the Nazis. In 1943, in danger of arrest, he escaped by boat to Sweden and then on to the United States.

Shells

Electron

Nucleus

The origin of the universe

For thousands of years people have been seeking answers to questions about the origin of the universe. For a long time many people thought that the universe had always existed in its present form, and that it would always remain the same. But ideas on the nature of the universe have altered as scientific understanding has increased. Evidence gathered over the centuries has shown that, rather than staying the same, the universe is always changing. The science of the universe is called cosmology. Cosmologists study the entire universe to find out how it began and how it has evolved.

View of the Andromeda Spiral

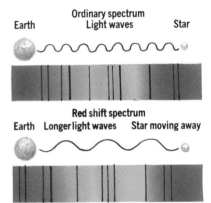

This bronze plate depicts the Chinese idea of the creation of the universe.

Galaxies beyond our own

Edwin Hubble was born and brought up in the USA and studied law at the University of Chicago. He first worked as a lawyer but then turned to astronomy. For the rest of his life he worked at Mount Wilson Observatory in California.

In 1923 Hubble examined a galaxy (a giant group of stars) called the Andromeda Spiral. At that time, most astronomers

The Mount Wilson Observatory

thought that our galaxy, known as the Milky Way, made up the entire universe. They believed that the spiral forms we now know to be other galaxies were only clouds of gases. But Hubble saw stars on the edge of the Andromeda Spiral and estimated that they lay well beyond the Milky Way. His work proved that the Andromeda Spiral was another galaxy and therefore that other galaxies existed apart from our own. Gradually he and others began to identify more galaxies.

This picture shows Edwin Hubble (1889-1953) at the controls of the Mount Wilson telescope.

The age of the universe

When examined closely, the light spectrum (see page 70) not only consists of the range of different shades, but also a series of lines. Astronomers noticed that when they examined light from stars, the shades and lines had moved toward the red end of the spectrum. This effect is known as "red shift". The reason for this is that when a source of light moves away from an observer, its

wavelength increases. The greater the speed at which the light source is moving away, the greater the red shift. Hubble realized that in order to produce the shift effect, the stars must be moving away from us. He also noticed that the fainter the galaxies were, the greater the red shift. This implied that the more distant the galaxies

Ordinary spectrum
Earth   Light waves   Star

Red shift spectrum
Earth Longer light waves   Star moving away

were, the faster they were moving. By 1929 he was able to measure the degree of red shift to calculate the speed of the galaxies and their distance from the earth. He found that the speed increases in proportion to the distance. This is known as Hubble's Law. His work provided the first evidence that the universe is expanding. This is the key to the Big Bang theory (see below). In addition, once astronomers were able to measure the speed at which galaxies are moving outward, they could calculate when the universe began. They now believe this happened between six and fifteen billion years ago.

Creation from explosion

Georges Lemaître was born in Belgium. He studied astronomy at the University of Louvain in Belgium and then trained as a priest. He moved to Cambridge University in England and was later appointed professor of astronomy at Louvain where he remained for the rest of his career.

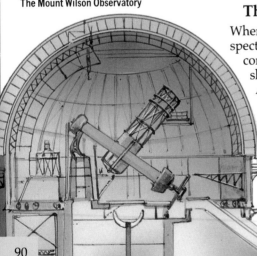

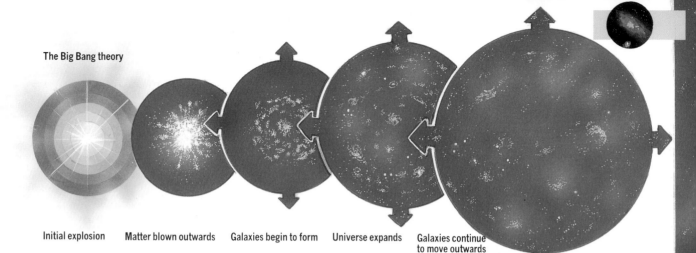

The Big Bang theory

Initial explosion   Matter blown outwards   Galaxies begin to form   Universe expands   Galaxies continue to move outwards

In 1927, using Einstein's General Theory of Relativity (see page 88), Lemaître proposed that the universe was still expanding. He claimed that at one time it must have been compressed into a tiny atom of energy and matter. He went on to suggest that the atom blew apart in a huge explosion, scattering hot gases in all directions This idea has become known as the Big Bang theory. At the time its true importance was not fully appreciated, but most scientists now see it as the best explanation of the origin of the universe.

Georges
Lemaître
(1894-1966)

As new discoveries in space have been made, the Big Bang theory has been refined and modified. In 1970 Roger Penrose (b.1931) and Stephen Hawking (b.1942) proved that if Einstein's General Theory of Relativity is correct, then it is possible that there was a definite beginning to the universe. At this point, called a singularity, space and time as we know them would not have existed. Moments after the explosion, the universe would have been an incredibly hot fireball. It expanded and cooled until, millions of years later, hydrogen and then other elements formed. Eventually, gravity drew atoms together and galaxies began to develop.

Another modification of the Big Bang theory, called the Oscillating Universe theory, states that the universe is alternately expanding and contracting. If this is true, when the limit of expansion is reached, the growth will stop and gravity will pull everything back together

The Oscillating Universe theory

Big Bang

Galaxies begin to form

Galaxies reach the limit of expansion

Galaxies fall back towards each other again

Big Bang

once more. The galaxies will be squeezed together so tightly that another cosmic explosion will set the whole process off again.

Staying the same

Hermann Bondi grew up in Vienna, Austria. He moved to England and studied at Cambridge University. In 1954 he became professor of mathematics at King's College,' London.

In 1948 Bondi proposed the Steady State theory, which says that new galaxies form at the middle of the expanding universe to replace those moving outward. As a result, he claimed, the universe would always look the same. However, later findings contradict this. For example, in 1964 two astronomers called Robert Wilson and Arno Penzias picked up faint radio noise from space. This is now thought to be the echo of the Big Bang.

Hermann Bondi
(b.1919)

Wilson (b.1936) and
Penzias (b.1933)

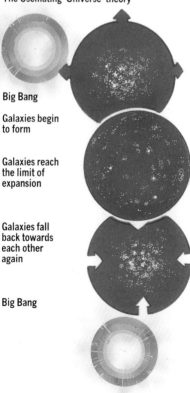

Women in science

Although many women throughout history have been involved in the development of science, their work has gained little recognition. For a number of reasons their achievements have often been ignored and their names left out of books. Women were unable to attend universities and were excluded from scientific societies and laboratories. Because they had little scientific education, many women could only serve as assistants to male scientists. The situation has improved slowly, but there are still far fewer women working in the sciences than there are men.

Early women scientists

Although there were women doctors in Ancient Egypt and Greece, there were very few opportunities for women to work in medicine and science in the ancient world. Accounts of the lives of successful women were invariably written by men who dismissed women scientists as immoral and dangerous. The first such scientist whose life is well-documented is Hypatia. Most of her writings have been lost, but there are a number of references to them by other scientists. Hypatia was born in Alexandria in Egypt, where she taught mathematics and philosophy. Her most important work was in algebra and geometry, but she was also interested in mechanics and technology. In

Tombstone of a woman doctor from the 1st century A.D.

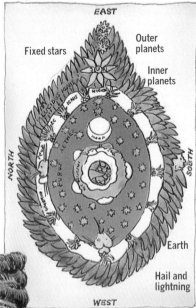

Hypatia of Alexandria (A.D.370-415), based on a classical statue

addition she designed several scientific instruments, including a plane astrolabe. This was used for measuring the positions of the stars, planets and the sun.

Abbess and physician

Hildegard of Bingen was the abbess of a convent in Germany. She was educated in a wide range of subjects, including music and medicine. She wrote many books on religion as well as a natural history encyclopaedia called *Liber simplicis medicinae* which described animals and minerals and as many as 230 plants and 60 trees. Hildegard devised a number of maps of the universe. In her first plan (shown below) of the universe, the earth lies in the middle surrounded by the stars and planets.

Hildegard of Bingen (1098-1179)

Hildegard's first plan of the universe

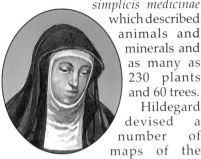

EAST

Fixed stars

Outer planets

Inner planets

NORTH

SOUTH

Earth

Hail and lightning

WEST

A forgotten mathematician

Anne, Countess of Conway (1631-79), a mathematician and philosopher, was born in London. Her brother, who acted as her tutor, supplied her with books and introduced her to the ideas of Descartes (see page 67). Her country house became a well-known meeting-place for scholars.

Ragley Hall, Lady Anne Conway's country house

Anne Conway's book, *The Principles of the most Ancient and Modern Philosophy*, was published eleven years after her death by a Dutch chemist called Francis van Helmont. It contained many of her scientific ideas and had a great influence on a German mathematician called Gottfried Leibniz (1646-1716). Although Leibniz acknowledged her importance, Conway's work was attributed to van Helmont and her name was soon forgotten.

A self-taught astronomer

Caroline Herschel (1750-1848) was born into a family of German musicians. In 1772 she moved to England to join her brother William, an astronomer. After teaching herself astronomy and mathematics with his help, she became his assistant. Later, in 1787, she became the first woman to be appointed assistant to the Court Astronomer.

This giant telescope, designed by Caroline's brother William, was built about 1780s.

Finding new comets

Herschel became recognized throughout Europe as a great astronomer. As well as her important collaborations with her brother, independently she discovered many new comets. She won a number of awards for her work, including the Gold Medal of the Royal Astronomical Society in 1828. Her success helped to open up astronomy to other women of her time.

Spreading scientific ideas

Mary Somerville made important contributions to science education. Born in Scotland, she became known as "the Queen of 19th-century science". Her first scientific paper, *On the Magnetizing Power of the More Refrangible Solar Rays*, had to be submitted to the Royal Society by her husband because women were banned from the organization. In 1831 she published *Mechanism of the Heavens*. As well as being her interpretation of the work of a French scientist called Pierre de Laplace (1749-1827), the book contained many original ideas of her own. For the rest of the century it was a standard text in the study of advanced mathematics.

Mary Somerville (1780-1872) and the title page of *Mechanism of the Heavens*

The first computer programmer

Ada, Countess of Lovelace, daughter of the poet Lord Byron, studied astronomy, Latin, music and mathematics. She worked with an English mathematician called Charles Babbage (1792-1871), as the designer of arithmetical operations for his calculating machines. As these machines are now often seen as the forerunners of computers, in a sense Lovelace was the first computer programmer. Her work for the machines and her ideas on their uses were published in 1843. But as it was considered unsuitable at that time for women to publish under their own names, she only signed the work with her initials. As a result, her work as a mathematician, like those of many other women scientists, has been largely forgotten.

Countess of Lovelace (1815-52)

Academic frustration

Sophia Krukovsky was a Russian mathematician who gained the very highest awards for her work but was continually blocked in her efforts to make a career in mathematics. After her marriage to a law student called Vladimir Kovalevsky, she moved with him to Heidelberg in Germany. As a woman, Krukovsky was not allowed to join the university there and had to study privately. In 1874 she was awarded a doctorate in mathematics from Göttingen University, but was unable to find an academic post.

Sophia Krukovsky (1850-91) and some of her mathematical calculations

In 1884 Krukovsky became the first woman professor at the new University of Stockholm, Sweden. In 1888 she was awarded the Prix Bordin, the highest prize of the French Académie des Sciences (part of the Institute de France; see page 69) for her work in mathematics. But still she was unable to secure a job in France. She decided to resign her post at Stockholm and to devote her time to research, but she became ill and died soon after.

The letter announcing Krukovsky's award of the Prix Bordin.

Key dates in scientific discovery

Dates B.C.

4241B.C. The first year in which events can be precisely dated. This is made possible by the Egyptian calendar.

c.2630B.C. Imhotep becomes medical adviser to Djoser, Pharaoh of Egypt.

c.1000B.C. First records of Chinese knowledge of astronomy.

c.700B.C. Original compilation of the *Ayurveda*, an ancient Indian medical text.

c.600B.C. Thales of Miletus tries to find rational explanations for natural phenomena.

551B.C. Birth of the Chinese philosopher Confucius.

c.500B.C. Pythagoras discusses the mystical importance of numbers and harmony in the universe.

c.450B.C. Birth of Hippocrates, later an influential doctor on the island of Cos.

399B.C. Death of Socrates, one of the most important Greek philosophers.

387B.C. The philosopher Plato establishes the Academy in Athens.

c.335B.C. Aristotle writes important scientific books on natural history and the structure of the universe.

287B.C. Birth of Archimedes, mathematician and inventor.

Dates A.D.

150 Ptolemy writes the *Almagest*, about the movements of the stars and planets.

161 Greek anatomist Galen moves to Rome, where he becomes a famous doctor.

c.600 Mayan civilization flourishes in Central America.

813 The school of astronomy is founded in Baghdad.

c.854 Birth of al-Razi (Rhazes), the greatest Arabic alchemist.

965 Birth of ibn al-Haytham (Alhazen), an Islamic physicist famous for his work on optics.

1253 Death of Robert Grosseteste, teacher of mathematics and science.

1264 Thomas Aquinas reconciles Christian thought with Aristotle's teachings.

1267 Roger Bacon challenges the authority of traditional Christian education.

1452 Birth of Leonardo da Vinci, inventor and artist.

1527 Paracelsus becomes professor of medicine at the university of Basle.

1543 Copernicus publishes his theory that the planets move around the sun, not round the earth.

Andreas Vesalius produces a new guide to human anatomy.

1551 Konrad von Gesner starts to publish his extensive study of the animal kingdom.

1574 Tycho Brahe sets up an astronomical observatory on the island of Hven.

1596 Birth of René Descartes, mathematician and philosopher.

1610 Galileo Galilei publishes *The Starry Messenger*, about his astronomical discoveries made with the use of the telescope.

1616 William Harvey lectures on the circulation of blood.

1618 Johannes Kepler publishes laws describing the planets' elliptical orbits round the sun.

1627 Publication of Francis Bacon's *New Atlantis*, with its influential ideas about the role of science in society.

1632 Galileo publishes *Dialogue Concerning the Two Chief World Systems*, which describes the earth's movement around the sun.

1642 Galileo dies.
Isaac Newton is born.

1644 Publication of Descartes' most important scientific work, *Principles of Philosophy*.

1661 Robert Boyle proposes that matter is made up of tiny corpuscles, in his book *The Sceptical Chymist*.

1662 The Royal Society is founded in London.

1665 Publication of Robert Hooke's *Micrographia*, which contains detailed drawings made with the assistance of microscopes.

1666 The Académie Royale des Sciences is founded in Paris.

1682 Edmond Halley charts and describes the orbit of a comet, which is later named after him.

1687 Publication of Isaac Newton's book *Principia*, in which he formulates his laws of universal gravity.

1703 Newton becomes president of the Royal Society, and retains this post until his death in 1727.

1704 Newton publishes his book *Opticks*, about lenses and light.
John Ray completes his classification of 17,000 plants.

1705 Francis Hauksbee produces flashes of electricity by rubbing a globe containing a vacuum.

1729 Stephen Gray conducts electricity over long distances.

1745 Invention of the Leiden jar, an instrument that stores electricity.

1748 Georges de Buffon completes his 36-volume survey of natural history.

1752 Benjamin Franklin shows that lightning is caused by electricity.

1753   Carl Linnaeus publishes his new binomial system for classifying plants.

1756   Joseph Black finds "fixed air" (carbon dioxide) can be produced by heating chemicals.

1774   Joseph Priestley isolates the gas we now know as oxygen, calling it "dephlogisticated air".

1775   Abraham Werner founds a mining school at Freiberg, and gradually develops the "Neptunist" theory of geological change.

1779   Antoine Lavoisier confirms the existence of "dephlogisticated air", and renames it oxygen.

1787   Caroline Herschel receives royal recognition for her contributions to astronomy.

1789   Publication of Lavoisier's *Methods of Chemical Nomenclature*, which lists 33 elements, and introduces the modern system of naming them.

1791   Luigi Galvani publishes the results of his electrical experiments on frogs.

1795   James Hutton's book *The Theory of the Earth* questions the biblical account of the creation. It suggests instead that geological change has taken place over millions of years.

1796   Edward Jenner vaccinates a child against smallpox.

1799   Alessandro Volta builds the first electric battery.

1808   John Dalton's book *A New System of Chemical Philosophy* contains important new ideas about atomic theory.

1809   Jean de Lamarck publishes his explanation of change in living beings, including his idea that acquired characteristics can be inherited.

1820   Hans Oersted shows that an electric current has a magnetic effect on a compass needle.

1824   Justus von Liebig sets up his research laboratory in Giessen, Germany.

1831   Charles Lyell is appointed professor of geology at King's College, London.
     Charles Darwin embarks on his voyage on HMS *Beagle*.
     Michael Faraday produces an electric current from a moving magnet.

1843   Ada Lovelace publishes her mathematical work.

1858   Darwin receives Alfred Wallace's manuscript about natural selection.

1859   Darwin publishes *On the Origin of the Species by Natural Selection*, which contains his theories of evolution.

1867   Joseph Lister describes his success in reducing infections by using antiseptics.

1868   Gregor Mendel finishes his research into pea plants, which forms the basis of modern genetic theory.

1869   Dmitri Mendeleev devises the Periodic Table of the Elements.

1871   Darwin publishes his second book on evolution, *The Descent of Man*.

1872   James Maxwell uses algebraic equations to quantify Faraday's electrical theories.

1882   Robert Koch discovers the cholera virus.

1885   Using vaccinations, Louis Pasteur saves the life of a boy bitten by a rabid dog.

1886   Heinrich Hertz begins research that demonstrates the existence of radio waves.

1888   Sophia Krukovsky wins the Prix Bordin.

1895   Wilhelm Röntgen discovers X-rays.

1896   Antoine Becquerel discovers that uranium is radioactive.

1900   Max Planck introduces the idea of "quantizing energy".

1905   Albert Einstein publishes three scientific papers, including the Special Theory of Relativity.

1910   Thomas Morgan's experiments with fruit flies confirm Mendel's ideas about heredity.

1911   Marie Curie receives the Nobel Prize for her work on radioactivity, becoming the first person to win the prize twice.
     Ernest Rutherford shows that atoms have a central nucleus.

1913   Niels Bohr proposes a new model of the hydrogen atom.

1915   Alfred Wegener publishes his theory of continental drift.

1919   Einstein publishes his paper on General Relativity.

1923   Edwin Hubble proves the existence of galaxies beside our own.

1927   Georges Lemaître proposes that the universe is continually expanding.

1928   Alexander Fleming notices that a growth, now called penicillin, kills bacteria.

1929   Hubble shows that the galaxies are moving away from each other. This forms the basis of the Big Bang theory.

1948   Hermann Bondi and Thomas Gold propose the Steady State theory of the universe.

1953   Francis Crick and James Watson discover the structure of the DNA molecule.

1963   Geological experiments confirm Wegener's ideas, and establish the theory of plate tectonics.

1964   Robert Wilson and Arno Penzias detect radio noise from space. This is thought to be the echo of the Big Bang.

F(K)
?=F(1)
:LET DF
JNS: MC
REPORT
ANAL
TH":PR
ER
(N):IF
ND N(5
78,1340
PRINT
;NS;"
"BANK
"OVER
T "BAN
ORDERS
STOCK L
";:LET
): ";:L
IRKUP
M
RINT "Y
PRINT
PRINT
SHOPS C
AS(=0
TAFF
AM(AS
PROFI
MU(=0
PEND O
AA(=0
ITEMS
AR(0
AO=0:6
PER I
AR)0
INT "Y
OTO 54
INT "D
"Y" TH
IV=SL
EM=AM
TO 600
INT(SL
NS=AS:
2)
T CS=1
ET CA=
LET CA
/4))
0000:L
000:IF
ET QF=
QF=0
IF VF(
CS+AF
T ES=)
ET ES=
D)=SC

The *Scientists* quiz

The answers to all the following questions can be found between pages 51 and 93 of this book. You will also find the answers upside down at the bottom of this page.

1. How did the Ancient Egyptians calculate when the River Nile would flood each year?
2. From what did the Mayans believe the world to be made?
3. Which Ancient Greek god was thought to cause earthquakes?
4. Name the two forces which Confucius believed were central to harmony in the Universe.
5. Name one of the two influential medical books written by Ibn Sina.
6. Name the four most important universities founded during the 12th-13th centuries.
7. What part of Tycho Brahe's body was cut off in a duel?
8. What two methods did Vesalius use to obtain specimens for his study of anatomy?
9. Identify these three scientists.

a)   b)   c)

10. Vesalius wrote one of the greatest scientific books ever published. What was its title?
11. What is the name given to the tiny blood vessels that connect veins and arteries?
12. Galileo was threatened with torture unless he denied which claim?
13. Name one of the founding members of the Royal Society.
14. What incident is said to have been the starting point for Isaac Newton's theory of gravitation?
15. Linaeus developed a method of classifying plants called "binomial nomenclature". What does it mean?
16. Can you identify the devices below and name their creators?

a)   b)   c)

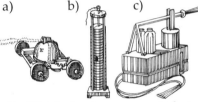

17. Which book proposed that species had developed over long periods of time?
18. Name the two different theories concerning the structure of the earth preferred by Werner and Hutton.
19. What is the name given to the supercontinent by Wegener?
20. What was the name of the ship on which Charles Darwin sailed to South America?
21. What is the modern name for the gas that Joseph Priestley called "dephlogisticated gas"?
22. What is the name given to Mendeleev's grouping of elements?
23. What is the name of the device Ewald von Kleist designed for storing static electricity?
24. What apparatus did Benjamin Franklin use to prove that lightning is a form of electricity?
25. Which measurement of electricity is named after an 18th century scientist?
26. Which process, discovered by Edward Jenner, is considered to be one of the most important advances ever made in medical science?
27. What is the name given to the process in which heat kills bacteria?
28. Who was the first person to receive two Nobel prizes?
29. On which plant did Mendel perform most of his experiments?
30. What was the equation Einstein used to express the relation between the mass and energy of moving objects?
31. Why did Niels Bohr go to live in the USA in 1943?
32. In 1927, Georges Lemaître proposed an idea that explained the origins of the Universe. What did this idea become known as?
33. Can you identify these scientific devices from the close-ups below?

a)   b)   c)

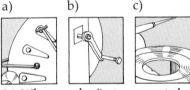

34. Who was the first woman to be appointed assistant to the Court Astronomer in 1787?
35. Why was Mary Somerville's first scientific paper submitted to the Royal Society by her husband?

EXPLORERS

Felicity Everett and Struan Reid

History consultant: Anne Millard
Designed by Russell Punter
Illustrated by Peter Dennis

Additional illustrations by Richard Draper,
Peter Goodwin & Ian Jackson

Managing editor: Anthony Marks
With thanks to Philip Roxbee Cox

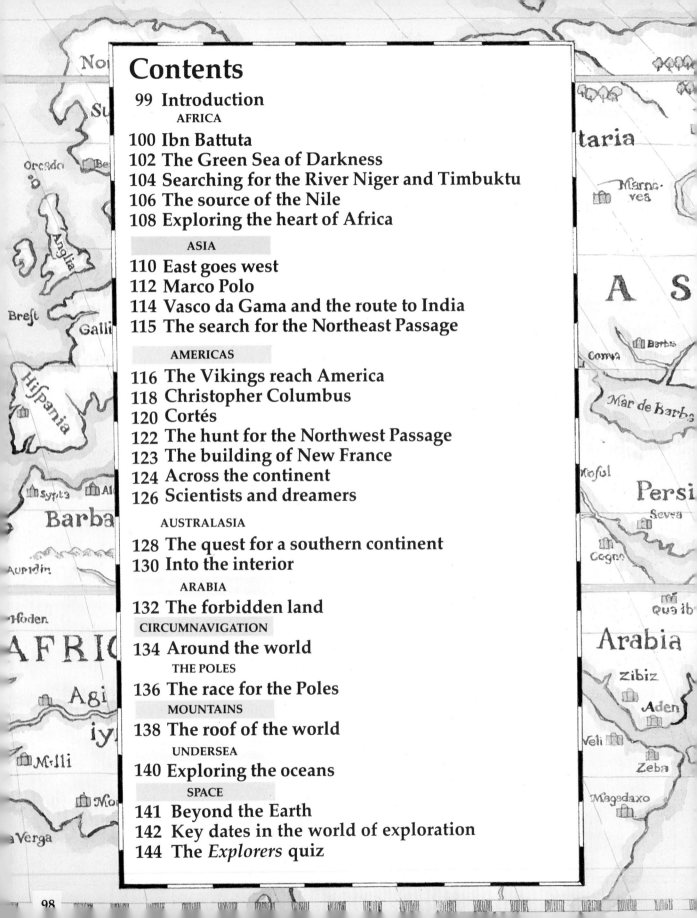

Contents

Introduction

This section of the book tells the stories of the lives of some of the world's greatest explorers. It is not a comprehensive history of exploration, but describes in detail the voyages of discovery that have had the most impact on the world.

What is an explorer?

Many of the explorers in this section of the book were not the first people to set foot in the lands they visisted, as the local inhabitants had been there for thousands of years. But they are thought of as explorers because they all changed the way people thought about the world. For example, Europeans returned from the Far East or America with important geographical information. Darwin's findings on the Galapagos Islands led him to challenge our basic ideas about the evolution of the planet.

Exploration is a way of learning about the world. As early travellers went further afield, they unravelled the mysteries of unknown continents. And even today, there are aspects of the Earth, and of space, that are still not fully understood. Each time scientists probe the frontiers of space, and when divers examine the sea bed, they continue to expand our knowledge with their explorations.

Why people explore

Throughout history, people have had an insatiable appetite for knowledge and adventure. But there have also been more specific reasons for exploration.

The competition for food forced our earliest ancestors in all directions in search of new places to live. Huge and powerful empires were built up through trade and

Mosaic of a Roman merchant ship.

conquest by the early civilizations - the Minoans, the Egyptians, the Phoenicians, the Greeks and the Romans.

Religion has always played an important part in the exploration of new lands. As early as the 5th century, Irish monks set out to convert the people of Wales, Cornwall and France to Christianity. But some later expeditions, though carried out

A 6th-century stone cross.

in the name of religion, were in fact accompanied by appalling savagery and destruction.

There were amateur explorers with a desire to see new places, like Ibn Battuta, Hsuan-tsang and Richard Burton. Others, such as Alexander Humboldt and Charles Darwin, led scientific expeditions which set out to learn as much as possible about the new lands.

How we know about exploration

Explorers, whether on land or on sea, have always kept records of the new lands and peoples they encountered, and some have used these to write books. The Greek explorer Diogenes' account of his journey inland from the east coast of Africa in the 1st century A D helped Ptolemy to draw his map of the world in the next century. In the 14th century, Ibn Battuta wrote down all he saw on his travels. Europeans

· Medieval map

soon developed a taste for the accounts of mystery and adventure. Mungo Park wrote a book about his travels in Africa which was a best-seller, and Stanley's latest reports from Africa were eagerly awaited.

Geographical arrangement

This section of the book is arranged into groups, according to region: Africa, Asia, the Americas, and Australasia. There are also individual pages on Arabia, the Poles, Mountains, Circumnavigation, Undersea and Space.

Each chapter is introduced with a small map showing the areas covered, and a chart giving the most important dates in the exploration of that region. There is also a more detailed date chart on pages 142-143 that shows all the events in this section of the book in one list.

Dates

Many of the dates are from the period before the birth of Christ. They are indicated by the letters BC. Early dates in the period after Christ's birth are indicated by the letters AD. Some of the dates begin with the abbreviation "c". This stands for *circa*, the Latin for "about" and is used when historians are unsure exactly when an event took place.

Maps

There are detailed maps on many pages. These show the routes taken by the explorers, and also many of the places they visited.

Ibn Battuta

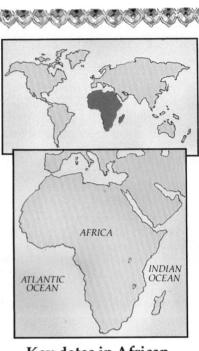

In the seventh century AD, the prophet Mohammed founded a new religion called Islam in Mecca, Arabia. Within a century of his death in 632 his followers, known as Muslims, had conquered a huge empire in the Middle East and North Africa.

Ibn Battuta was a rich Moroccan Muslim who in 1325 set out on a pilgrimage to Mecca. His adventures inspired him to travel further. He made daring journeys through parts of Africa, the Middle East and the Far East that before then were largely unknown to Europeans.

Ibn Battuta wrote detailed accounts of his travels. He used Arabic script, and probably had writing materials like these.

Key dates in African exploration

- ●c.600BC Pharaoh Necho II of Egypt sends out an expedition to explore the coasts of Africa.
- ●c.AD150 Ptolemy draws his map of the world.
- ●632 Death of the prophet Mohammed, founder of Islam.
- ●c.860 Chinese reach Somali.
- ●c.1060 Chinese reach Malindi.
- ●c.1187 Chinese reach Zanzibar and Madagascar.
- ●1304-77 Life of Ibn Battuta.
- ●1394 Birth of Prince Henry the Navigator.
- ●1405-33 Voyages of Cheng Ho.
- ●c.1420 Chinese ships possibly round Cape of Good Hope.
- ●1434 Gil Eannes rounds Cape Bojador.
- ●1487 Bartolemeu Dias rounds the Cape of Good Hope.
- ●1487 Pedro da Covilhã and Alfonso de Paiva set out.
- ●1497 Vasco da Gama sails round Africa on his way to India.
- ●1795 Mungo Park sails to Africa.
- ●1805 Park leaves on his second trip to Africa.
- ●1824 René Caillié sets out from France for Timbuktu.
- ●1851 David Livingstone, his family and Cotton Oswell cross the Kalahari Desert.
- ●1852-56 Livingstone becomes the first European to walk right across Africa.
- ●1856 Richard Burton and John Speke leave England in search of the source of the Nile.
- ●1858 Speke claims to have discovered the source of the Nile.
- ●1858 Livingstone sets out to explore Zambezi River.
- ●1860 Speke and James Grant leave on second journey to Africa.
- ●1871 Henry Stanley and Livingstone meet at Ujiji.
- ●1872 Livingstone starts out on his last journey, round the southern shores of Lake Tanganyika.
- ●1874 Stanley returns to Africa to map lakes Victoria and Tanganyika.
- ●1876-77 Stanley sails down the Lualaba and Congo rivers to the Atlantic.
- ●1887 Stanley goes in search of Emin Pasha in the Sudan.

Through the Middle East

Ibn Battuta crossed Egypt to the Red Sea, hoping to sail to Jeddah. Because of a tribal war, however, he had to abandon his plans and go back to Cairo. He travelled on to Jerusalem and Damascus, then made his way by land through Arabia to Mecca.

From Mecca he travelled north to Baghdad, and was horrified that the city had been destroyed by the Mongols (fierce Asian warriors). He visited Anatolia (now part of Turkey), then went back to Mecca where he studied law. His new profession enabled him to pay for more travelling, and he soon set off again.

Around the coast of Africa

Ibn Battuta next crossed the Red Sea to Aden. There he boarded a dhow (a type of ship) which was heading for Zaila in Somalia. In his journal, he described Zaila as the dirtiest place he had ever visited.

Dhows are still quite common on the coast of East Africa.

From Zaila Ibn Battuta sailed on down the coast to Mombasa and Kilwa. He was impressed by the fine wooden houses there, and intrigued by the dark skins of the Africans.

Further afield

To get back to Mecca Ibn Battuta sailed along the south coast of Arabia and into the Persian Gulf, then crossed the Arabian Peninsula. Before long, however, his curiosity made him impatient to travel again.

The Caucasus Mountains

This time he headed north to Syria, Kaffa (the Crimea), and the Caucasus Mountains. He later crossed Central Asia, through Afghanistan, to India. From India he travelled by sea to Canton in China, then began the return journey to Morocco (via Malaysia and India). He eventually reached Fez in 1349.

A caravan crossing the Sahara desert

Timbuktu as it might have looked in Ibn Battuta's time.

Across the Sahara

In 1352 Ibn Battuta set out again, this time to explore Africa. In many ways this was his most important expedition, for he was able to write about parts of the world that were unrecorded by other travellers at that time.

He crossed the Sahara Desert, heading for Mali. Conditions were harsh and bandits roamed the desert, so for protection he joined a caravan (a procession of traders and other travellers who used camels for transport).

First the caravan stopped in Taghaza, where Ibn Battuta noted that all the buildings were made of salt and camel skins. The travellers picked up supplies of water for the next ten days'

journey to Tasarahla.

Then came the trek to Walata, which was made very dangerous because of shifting sands. Progress was slow, and there was the risk the water would run out.

Into unknown territory

Despite these dangers Ibn Battuta crossed the Sahara safely. He reached Mali, then continued as far as the River Niger. This was very daring, as few travellers had

ventured that far into the African interior before. The territory was so forbidding (see pages 104-109) that it was not further explored for another 400 years.

For the return journey, he chose an equally challenging route. This time he visited Timbuktu, an ancient city famed for its wealth and splendour.

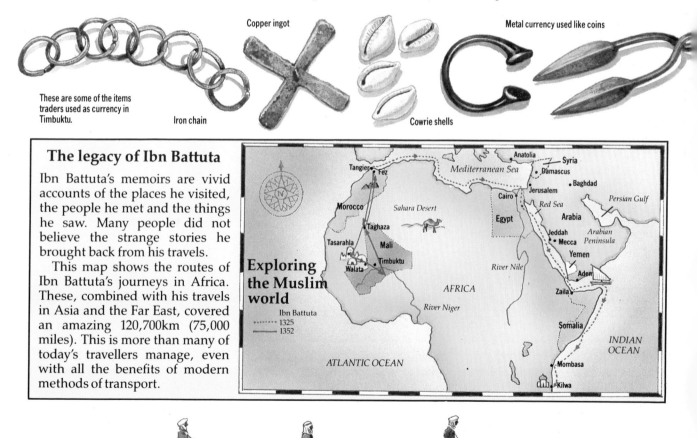

These are some of the items traders used as currency in Timbuktu.

Iron chain

Copper ingot

Cowrie shells

Metal currency used like coins

The legacy of Ibn Battuta

Ibn Battuta's memoirs are vivid accounts of the places he visited, the people he met and the things he saw. Many people did not believe the strange stories he brought back from his travels.

This map shows the routes of Ibn Battuta's journeys in Africa. These, combined with his travels in Asia and the Far East, covered an amazing 120,700km (75,000 miles). This is more than many of today's travellers manage, even with all the benefits of modern methods of transport.

Exploring the Muslim world

Ibn Battuta
•••••• 1325
——— 1352

Tangier • Fez
Anatolia
Mediterranean Sea
Syria
Damascus
Baghdad
Jerusalem
Cairo
Red Sea
Persian Gulf
Morocco
Sahara Desert
Egypt
Arabia
Taghaza
Jeddah
Mecca
Arabian Peninsula
Tasarahla
Mali
Yemen
Walata
Timbuktu
Aden
River Nile
AFRICA
Zaila
River Niger
Somalia
INDIAN OCEAN
ATLANTIC OCEAN
Mombasa
Kilwa

The Green Sea of Darkness

The first known journey round Africa took place about 600BC. Pharaoh Necho II of Egypt sent a sea captain to explore the coasts of Africa. The voyage was not repeated for almost two thousand years.

An Egyptian boat on a trading mission.

Europeans became interested in Africa during the Middle Ages. They acquired a taste for luxuries from the East such as spices, silks, sugar, pearls and precious stones. But the overland trade routes to the East were controlled by the Turks, who were at war with the Europeans. This made these goods very rare and expensive and the Europeans wanted to obtain them more cheaply. They became determined to find a sea route round Africa, avoiding the Turks, so that they could trade directly with India, China and the Spice Islands (now the Moluccas) in the Pacific Ocean.

The explorer who stayed at home

Prince Henry of Portugal was born in 1394 and later devoted his life to discovery. He was lured by the riches of the East and inspired by the stories of the Christian priest-king known as Prester John who was believed to live somewhere in Africa. Although the area opened up by his sailors was comparatively small, they took the first and most difficult steps into unknown lands.

Henry the Navigator (1394-1460)

In 1419 Henry was appointed Governor of the Algarve, in southern Portugal. On the wind-swept, rocky coast at Sagres, near the most southwesterly point of Europe (called by Europeans "the end of the world"), he built a palace, a church, a school to train navigators and pilots, an observatory and a shipyard. He recruited scholars, geographers, astronomers and mariners. He bullied and inspired his courtiers to lead expeditions that would open up new trade routes.

A barrier of fear

Henry sent out 14 expeditions over 12 years, but each one turned back at Cape Bojador on the west coast of Africa near the Canary Islands. This was as far south as the sailors dared go. They believed that at the Equator, in an area known as the "Green Sea of Darkness", the sun was so close to the Earth that people's skins were burned black, the sea boiled and there were whirlpools and thick green fogs where monsters lurked waiting to devour them.

The great breakthrough

Then, in 1434, one of Henry's courtiers called Gil Eannes managed to persuade his crew to carry on beyond the dreaded Cape. They survived to tell the tale, and from then on other Portuguese expeditions ventured further and further south.

None of Henry's ships had managed to sail round the southern tip of Africa by the time he died in 1460. But his inspiration paved the way for the journeys that would open up the world. Although he himself never sailed on any of the voyages he planned, he is always known as Henry the Navigator.

St Mary's rose, picked by Eannes from beyond Bojador.

This Portuguese ship was called a caravel. It was very sturdy and could travel long distances.

Round the Cape

In August 1487 King John II of Portugal sent out an expedition of three ships from Lisbon. It was led by Bartolemeu Dias, who was instructed to open the sea route round Africa's southern tip. King John believed that the way east would be clear once the Indian Ocean was reached.

John II
(reigned 1481-95)

Off Cape Volta the ships were caught in a terrible storm which lasted nearly two weeks. The terrified sailors were blown round the southern tip of Africa and into the Indian Ocean. They sailed north to the Great Fish River and then turned round for home.

On their way back to Portugal, Dias and his crew saw the Cape and realized their achievement.

A Portuguese ship rounding the Cape of Good Hope.

Dias named it "Cabo Tormentoso", the Cape of Storms. King John renamed it the Cape of Good Hope, for a sea route to the East had been found.

Two spies set out

Pedro da Covilhã was one of the King of Portugal's courtiers and an experienced spy. In May 1487, he and Alfonso de Paiva set out on a secret mission. Covilhã was to find out all he could about the route to India, while Paiva was to seek out Prester John's kingdom in Africa. First they travelled to Rhodes where they disguised themselves as Arab traders and joined a party of merchants travelling to Egypt. They sailed to Cairo where they boarded a boat travelling down the Red Sea to Suakin in the Sudan. Here they parted company.

Paiva set off in search of Prester John, while Covilhã sailed for southwest India. He noted every detail of his voyages, of the geography along the way, and of the fabulous cargoes of cinnamon, cloves, pepper, silks, rugs and precious stones. At Goa, superb Arab horses were sold to the Indian rulers.

A new adventure

From India Covilhã sailed to the Persian Gulf, then on down the east coast of Africa. Returning to Cairo in 1490 he learned that Paiva had died without finding Prester John. Covilhã himself took up the search for the elusive monarch, whose kingdom was by this time thought to be Abyssinia (now Ethiopia). He sent a report of his travels to the King of Portugal, then set off south. First of all he visited the holy city of Mecca (see page 100) dressed as a Muslim pilgrim.

The happy captive

Although Abyssinia was a Christian country, Covilhã was surprised and disappointed to find that it was not the fabulously rich kingdom he expected. (Prester John was never found, but stories of his empire persisted well into the 16th century.)

Perhaps because he had seen too much, Covilhã was forbidden to leave Abyssinia and spent the remaining 30 years of his life there. He was treated well in his new homeland, eventually marrying a rich local woman. From time to time he entertained ambassadors from Europe and he encouraged trade between Abyssinia and Portugal.

This is how 15th-century Europeans imagined Prester John.

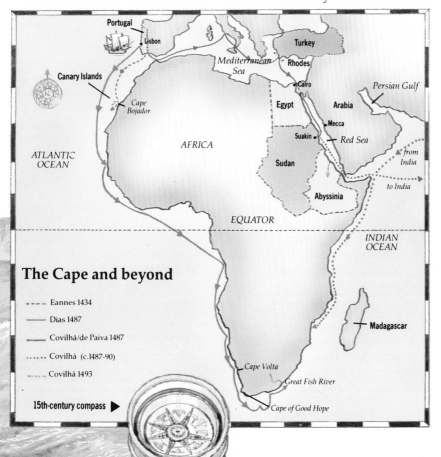

The Cape and beyond

- – – – – Eannes 1434
- ———— Dias 1487
- ———— Covilhã/de Paiva 1487
- · · · · · · Covilhã (c.1487-90)
- –·–·–·– Covilhã 1493

15th-century compass ▶

Searching for the River Niger and Timbuktu

The Romans were the first Europeans to explore the interior of Africa. After their conquest of Egypt and the north African coast during the 1st century BC, they sent various expeditions over the Atlas Mountains and into the Sahara Desert, usually in pursuit of nomadic tribes who had attacked their soldiers and then disappeared.

Scientific explorers

Europeans set up trading stations along the coastline of Africa from the 15th century, but the traders ventured only a little way inland. During the 18th century, however, a new spirit of scientific enquiry grew up. In 1788 the Association for Promoting the Discovery of the Interior Parts of Africa was founded. It aimed to find and plot the course of the mysterious River Niger and to find the legendary trading city of Timbuktu, famed for its riches and palaces. But the first expeditions were failures, with the explorers dying from terrible diseases and heat.

The adventurous doctor

In 1794 a young Scottish doctor called Mungo Park was chosen to lead an expedition to the source of the River Niger to find out whether it flowed into the sea or into a lake. Park left England by ship in May 1795, and arrived at Pisania in the Gambia two months later. He stayed there for some months studying the local language and eventually set off into the African interior in December.

Mungo Park (1771-1806)

Park would have carried a sextant similar to this, to calculate distances.

The Niger is sighted

At first all went well and Park was hospitably received. However, things started to go wrong when his guides became frightened and refused to go any further. Some of the local rulers robbed him of all his possessions until he had nothing left except the clothes he wore and his horse. Finally he was captured by horsemen and held prisoner.

Park was attacked and stripped of all his belongings.

Park was kept in terrible conditions in an isolated hut on the edge of the desert for four months. Late one night in June 1796 he managed to escape from his prison. But instead of heading back to the coast and safety he pressed on with his mission, travelling through the thick forests to avoid being seen. A month later he reached Segu and caught his first glimpse of the Niger. He was overjoyed and was able to confirm once and for all that the river flowed eastwards.

Park had managed to save the notes he had made throughout his adventures by carefully hiding them. After his return to Scotland, he used the notes to write a book called *Travels in the Interior Districts of Africa*. It quickly became a best-seller. But the lure of Africa proved too great and Park was eager to return and explore it further.

An illustration from Park's book, showing him knocking at the gates of a village to escape from a lion.

A doomed expedition

In January 1805 Park set sail for Pisania once more, this time to travel the whole length of the Niger. He went with a larger expedition of 30 soldiers and ten other Europeans. The expedition was doomed from the start. Park was impatient to leave, even though it was the rainy season. By the time they reached the Niger the river was swollen and 29 members of the team had died of exhaustion and disease.

Park was determined to carry on, for the river turned south towards the Atlantic. At Sansanding he found two old canoes and joined them together, intending to float down the Niger to the sea. But by now the party was reduced to just nine members. This exhausted group reached the rapids at Boussa, 805km (500 miles) from the mouth of the river. Here they were attacked by warriors of the local king. Park and his men drowned when their boat capsized.

Park and his team being attacked by African warriors.

Inspired by travel stories

At the beginning of the 1820's, the Geographical Society of Paris offered a prize of 10,000 francs to the first Frenchman to reach the city of Timbuktu and return. René Caillié, a young man from a poor family, heard of the competition and was determined to win the prize. He had wanted to become an explorer since reading *Robinson Crusoe* by Daniel Defoe. He began careful preparations for the journey and

René Caillié (1799-1838)

plotted his route. He worked hard and saved enough money to pay for everything himself, including equipment and helpers. In 1824 Caillié left France and sailed to Senegal on the west coast of Africa and remained there for three years, learning the Arabic language and finding out about the Muslim faith.

In April 1827 Caillié and his team of ten Africans joined a caravan and set off for the Rio Nuñez between Sierra Leone and Senegal. In June they reached Kouroussa on the Niger. They set off on the next leg of the journey, but soon afterwards Caillié fell ill with malaria and scurvy. Five months

Caillié in Arabic dress.

Caillié travelling through the African jungle.

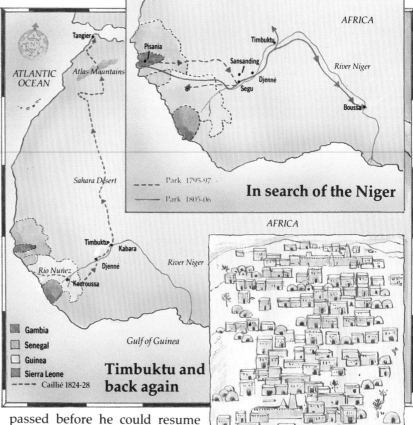

In search of the Niger

Timbuktu and back again

- Gambia
- Senegal
- Guinea
- Sierra Leone
- - - - Caillié 1824-28

Caillié's sketch of Timbuktu. The city was a pale shadow of the rich place it had once been.

passed before he could resume the journey. It was not until March 1828 that the little party reached Djenné, having walked nearly the entire distance of 1,610km (1,000 miles). From there they were able to sail down the Niger another 805km (500 miles) to Kabara, the port near Timbuktu.

Excitement and disappointment

They finally reached Timbuktu in April. For Caillié this moment, which he had looked forward to for years, was an anticlimax. The fabled city looked poor, neglected and drab. The trade in gold from Guinea had ceased many years before and the great trade caravans no longer visited it.

However, Caillié was welcomed by the inhabitants and stayed for two weeks. Then he joined a 1,000-strong camel caravan taking slaves and other goods across the Sahara. This return journey was hard and long, and he experienced such thirst that he could think only of water. When he reached Tangier, the officials there could not believe someone of his humble background could have travelled to Timbuktu and back. It was not until he was back in France that a panel of judges awarded him the prize.

105

The source of the Nile

The valley of the River Nile in Egypt is one of the most fertile areas in the world. Crops have been grown there since ancient times and the river has been a source of life to millions of people, many of whom have worshipped it as a god. But the origin of its waters remained a mystery for thousands of years. In the 5th century BC the Greek historian Herodotus wrote: "Of the sources of the Nile no-one can give any account." He believed that the river began at a fountain at the foot of some high mountains.

Over the centuries many expeditions tried to follow the river from Egypt to its source. One of the first of these was led by two Roman soldiers sent out by the Emperor Nero. But they had to abandon their journey when they reached a huge, impenetrable swamp known today as the Sudd. Later expeditions were defeated by the great distance, perilous swamps and stifling heat. In addition many explorers caught dreadful fevers.

In about AD150 a Greek geographer called Ptolemy drew a map of the world from various pieces of information. On it he showed two great lakes in Africa near a range of snow-capped mountains he called the Mountains of the Moon. He claimed that these lakes were the source of the Nile.

Ptolemy's map

The Nile

Burton & Speke 1857-59

Speke & Grant 1860-63

The rivals

By the middle of the 19th century no more was known about the source than in Ptolemy's days. In the 1840s German missionaries reported seeing two mountains, their tops covered with snow.

Richard Burton (1821-90)

John Speke (1827-64)

These were Mount Kilimanjaro and Mount Kenya. They also heard of the existence of two great lakes lying further inland. They were sure that these were the mountains and lakes on Ptolemy's map.

Many explorers and geographers wanted to be first to solve the mystery. In 1856 the Royal Geographical Society of London appointed Richard Burton as leader of a new expedi-tion, with John Speke as his deputy. They had travelled together before but they made an unusual pair. Burton was a flamboyant and brilliant scholar who spoke 29 languages and had written numerous books; Speke was a quiet and careful planner. But both men were ruthless and determined.

A view of the port at Zanzibar.

They sailed to Zanzibar, an important slave market off the east coast of Africa where they recruited the rest of their team. In June 1857 the expedition – consisting of about 130 porters, 30 donkeys and enough provisions to last two years – set off for the Sea of Ujiji (now called Lake Tanganyika). They believed this was one of Ptolemy's lakes and that it would prove to be the source of the Nile.

But after only two weeks both Burton and Speke were suffering from malaria. It took the expedition five months to make its way to Tabora, a large slave market lying between Zanzibar and the Sea of Ujiji. The two men were exhausted and had to rest for a month. Shortly after setting off again, however, they both became extremely ill. Burton's legs became paralyzed and Speke went deaf and blind. It was some time before they both recovered.

The expedition sets out for the Sea of Ujiji in 1857.

Some of the equipment carried by Speke and Burton.

Discovery and disappointment

Eventually, on 13 February 1858, they reached the Sea of Ujiji and spent three and a half months

Part of the team exploring the Sea of Ujiji.

exploring the area. But their hopes were dashed when they questioned some local people and discovered that although there was a great river at the northern end, it flowed into the lake, not out of it. This indicated that it came from elsewhere and was not the Nile.

Although the discovery of the lake was important, Burton and Speke were very disappointed that they had not found the source of the Nile and they returned to Tabora. Burton was pleased to be among the Arab slave dealers again as he had travelled in Arabia (see page 133) and spoke Arabic. But Speke knew little Arabic and felt excluded. As he was impatient to leave, the two men parted. Burton stayed to rest while Speke left to try and locate another great lake to the north, Lake N'yanza, which he had heard about but which no European had yet seen.

The start of a feud

After an easy journey of just 16 days, Speke reached Mwanza on the southern shores of the lake. The pale blue waters stretched out endlessly before him. He was certain that he had at last found the

Speke on the shores of Lake N'yanza (Lake Victoria).

source of the Nile. But he did not explore it thoroughly enough to prove his theory. He renamed his discovery Lake Victoria after Britain's queen, then hurried back to Burton to tell him the news. Burton is believed to have been furious. He may have been jealous of Speke's discovery, or angry that his partner had relied on guesswork and not collected enough evidence to back up his claim.

The two men decided to return to England and travelled as far as Zanzibar. Burton became too sick to continue. He and Speke parted, agreeing not to break the news of their discoveries until both were back home. Speke, however, rushed back, and by the time Burton returned he had already reported the expedition's findings and taken most of the credit for them. A bitter feud then broke out between the two men when Speke, rather than Burton, was appointed to lead a new expedition to Lake Victoria.

The second expedition

Speke and his second-in-command, James Grant, left for Africa in the spring of 1860. It was not until the end of 1861 that they reached the unknown territory of Karagwe at the southern end of Lake Victoria. In January 1862 they became the first Europeans to enter Uganda,

James Grant (1827-92)

where they met the young King Mutesa. They remained there until July, when they moved on. Grant soon fell seriously ill but, rather than wait for him to recover, Speke travelled on alone. On 21 July 1862 he arrived at Urondogani, where he stood alone on the banks of a river flowing north out of Lake Victoria. He was now certain that he was looking at the beginnings of the Nile and that Lake Victoria was the source. But once again he failed to explore thoroughly enough to prove beyond doubt that the river became the Nile.

A mysterious death

Speke and Grant returned triumphant to England, but there was still uncertainty about Speke's findings. To settle the dispute, a final public discussion with Burton was arranged, to take place before a panel of scholars. But in September 1864, the day before the meeting was due to take place, Speke died in a shooting accident. There were rumours of suicide - perhaps he did not dare to face the brilliant Burton. It was many years before Lake Victoria was finally proved to be the main source of the Nile by the explorer and journalist H.M. Stanley (see page 109).

Memorial to Speke in Kensington Gardens, London.

IN MEMORY OF
SPEKE
VICTORIA NYANZA
AND THE NILE
1864

Ugandan tribespeople entertain Speke and Grant.

Exploring the heart of Africa

A line of Africans being marched away to be sold into slavery.

David Livingstone came from a very poor Scottish family, and at the age of ten went to work in a cotton mill. However he was determined to study, and while he was working in the mill he also taught himself Greek, Latin and mathematics. This enabled him to go to Glasgow University. At the age of 25 he qualified as a doctor and in 1840 he was ordained a Christian missionary and sent to Cape Town in South Africa to do religious and social work.

In 1843 Livingstone founded his own mission at Kolobeng, south of the Kalahari Desert. Apart from his religious work, he was also fired by the idea of the eradication of slavery. Throughout his travels in Africa he was to be constantly reminded of this cruel trade in human life. He set about opening up the unknown central regions of Africa, so other Christian missionaries and Europeans could follow. He believed that this would lead to the collapse of the slave trade.

David Livingstone (1813-73)

◀ The Victoria Falls

Livingstone's travels

His first success in exploration, after two earlier failures, was to cross the wilderness of the Kalahari Desert in 1851 and reach Lake Ngami on the northern edge of the desert. His wife Mary and their children also accompanied him, as well as his great friend Cotton Oswell. They all nearly died when their guide lost his way and they ran out of food and water. In 1852 Livingstone's family returned to England while he stayed behind to devote his energies to African exploration.

Over the years 1852-56 Livingstone became the first European to walk right across Africa. He was also the first European to see the great waterfalls known locally as "the smoke that thunders", which he renamed the Victoria Falls. The news of these great exploits quickly reached Britain and when he returned to England he was welcomed as a national hero and introduced to Queen Victoria.

In 1858 he organized an expedition to the Zambezi River, hoping that the presence of Europeans there would help to end the slave trade.

The *Ma-Robert* on the Zambezi.

But when his paddle steamer (the *Ma-Robert*) could not cross the rapids on the river, Livingstone abandoned the expedition and returned to England. He was back in Africa again in April 1866 and disappeared for three years. This time he was trying to find the source of the Nile (see page 106). Heading towards Lake Nyasa (Lake Malawi), he entered the heart of slaving country. He set up a base at Ujiji on the shores of Lake Tanganyika but the supplies he was expecting to find had been stolen and there was little to eat.

H.M. Stanley

John Rowlands was the real name of H.M. Stanley. He was born in Wales in 1841 and spent most of his unhappy childhood in an orphanage. As soon as he could he ran away and worked as a cabin boy on a ship bound for North America. There, at the age of 19, he was adopted by a cotton merchant from New Orleans. In gratitude he became an American citizen and took the name of his benefactor, Henry Morton Stanley.

Henry Stanley (1841-1904)

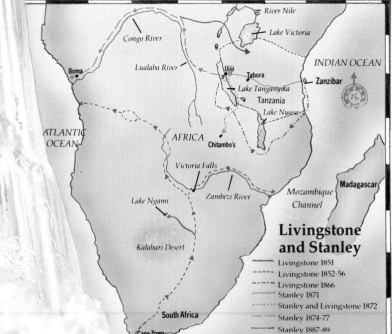

Livingstone and Stanley

- River Nile
- Lake Victoria
- Congo River
- Lualaba River
- Ujiji
- Tabora
- INDIAN OCEAN
- Zanzibar
- Lake Tanganyika
- Tanzania
- Lake Nyasa
- Boma
- ATLANTIC OCEAN
- AFRICA
- Chitambo's
- Victoria Falls
- Zambezi River
- Mozambique Channel
- Madagascar
- Lake Ngami
- Kalahari Desert
- South Africa
- Cape Town

Livingstone 1851
Livingstone 1852-56
Livingstone 1866
Stanley 1871
Stanley and Livingstone 1872
Stanley 1874-77
Stanley 1887-89

Stanley's boat, the *Lady Alice*, could be taken apart and carried overland.

Travelling down the Lualaba River in the *Lady Alice*.

A new life in America

The young Stanley led an adventurous life in his adopted country. During the American Civil War of 1861-65, he fought first on one side and then the other. He later spent some time in the navy. Eventually he drifted into journalism and became a foreign correspondent for the *New York Herald*.

The search for Livingstone

In 1869 the owner of the newspaper commissioned Stanley to find out the fate of Livingstone, who had not been heard of since travelling into the interior of Africa three years earlier. At the beginning of 1871 Stanley arrived in Zanzibar. He immediately set about organizing one of the most expensive expeditions ever mounted with 192 of the best porters and the finest supplies.

During the exhausting journey west, Stanley fell ill with malaria, his two European assistants died and

Stanley's hat and boots

the team was caught up in bloody battles between slave traders and African villagers. On 10 November 1871 they entered Ujiji. Stanley was led through the village by an excited crowd and, to his surprise and relief, he was introduced to the sick and frail Livingstone. Food and medicine soon restored Livingstone's strength and he and Stanley spent three weeks together exploring the northern end of Lake Tanganyika. At Tabora they parted company and Stanley returned to Zanzibar.

Stanley's meeting with Livingstone at Ujiji.

Livingstone's final journey

Before Stanley left Zanzibar for England, he sent new supplies to Livingstone. On 25 August 1872, Livingstone set out on his final journey, this time round the southern shores of Lake Tanganyika. Once more he caught a terrible fever, but at last he managed to reach a village in Ulala called Chitambo's. There he grew weaker and weaker and died eight months later. His heart was cut out by his faithful companions Chuma and Susi and buried under a tree. They then embalmed his body and carried it to Zanzibar, an eight-month journey of 1,609km (1,000 miles). From there it was shipped back to London and buried in Westminster Abbey. Livingstone is the only explorer to have received this honour.

Livingstone is carried dying into Chitambo's.

Stanley returns to Africa

Inspired by his travels with Livingstone, Stanley returned to Africa in 1874, leading a huge expedition to map Lake Victoria and Lake Tanganyika. While out in their boats they were attacked by tribesmen and hippopotamuses and drenched by storms. However, the journey did establish that Lake Victoria had only one major inlet and one major outlet – the Nile. Speke's guess (see page 107) had been proved correct.

In October 1876 the group left Lake Tanganyika on its most exciting journey. Stanley intended to travel down the Lualaba River, following it wherever it went. All the way they were attacked by warriors. They entered dark, forbidding rainforests, where cannibals lived among the damp, dripping trees. At one point they walked along a road flanked by 186 human skulls.

The Lualaba flows into the Congo River and they sailed on down it until they finally arrived at Boma on the Atlantic coast. The last of Africa's great rivers had been conquered. Of the original 356 members of the expedition only 114 remained. The rest had either died or deserted and all three of Stanley's English assistants had died along the way.

The last exploration

In 1887 Stanley travelled once more to Africa on his final journey through the continent. He went to southern Sudan to rescue a German explorer called Emin Pasha who had become cut off from the outside world. The team of 700 men had to hack through some of the world's densest jungle. This was the last major exploration in Africa. It was no longer the mysterious continent it had once been and already the European powers were beginning to divide it up into colonies.

Stanley attacked by tribesmen.

East goes west

The ancient civilization of China evolved in isolation from those in the West, protected behind the barrier of deserts and mountains of central Asia. It was not until the 2nd century BC that people from China ventured to make their first contacts with the kingdoms and empires of the West.

A Chinese official and his attendants.

Chang Ch'ien

During the 1st century BC, China's long borders were under attack from the Huns, fierce nomadic tribesmen from central Asia. The Emperor Wu Ti of China hoped to make an alliance with the Yuechi, a tribe who had been forced westwards by the Huns, against this threat. For this mission he chose an official called Chang Ch'ien.

Chang Ch'ien set off in 138BC on what turned out to be a very long journey. Almost immediately he was captured by the Huns and held prisoner. After ten years he eventually managed to escape and struggled to Heyuchi, the Yuechi capital lying close to the Khyber Pass .

But the Yuechi were not interested and Chang Ch'ien failed to win their support, so he set off on his return journey to China. This time he chose a roundabout route through Tibet to try to avoid the Huns. However, he fell into their hands once more. But he managed to escape and arrived back at Ch'ang-an, then the capital of China, after 12 years away and with just two of his original party of 100 men.

The Silk Road

Although Chang Ch'ien had failed in his mission, he learned a lot about the people and places he had seen along the way. This knowledge was used to open up the Silk Road, a trade route between China and the West. From about 105BC, long caravans of camels set out from China laden with bales of silk, spices, rare woods and resins, tortoiseshell, precious stones and pearls. They travelled through Asia to Antioch and then by ship to Rome.

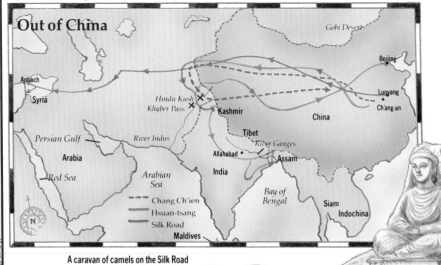

A caravan of camels on the Silk Road passes a statue of the Buddha at Luoyang, China.

Hsuan-tsang

One of the most adventurous travellers was a Buddhist monk called Hsuan-tsang. In AD629, against the emperor's strict instructions not to travel, he set out from China with the aim of learning more about his religion. His fortunes were to fluctuate from being honoured by kings to encounters with murderous brigands. His route to India, the birthplace of Buddhism, took him west through the Gobi Desert, along perilous roads and through dark gorges to Bactria, over the Hindu Kush and east into Kashmir. He remained study-ing for two years, visiting the libraries of monasteries in the Ganges valley.

Hsuan-tsang (c.602-664)

He visited Allahabad where he was captured by pirates and near-ly sacrificed. In Assam he joined the procession of King Harsha, in the company of 20,000 elephants and 30,000 boats. While crossing the River Indus he lost many of his rare manuscripts and his entire collection of flower seeds. He set off north across the mountains, this time accompanied by an elephant with a huge appetite which ate 40 bundles of hay and hundreds of buns every day.

Despite all the perils, Hsuan-tsang finally arrived back in China after an absence of 16 years. He entered Ch'ang-an with a chariot drawn by 20 horses piled with 700 religious books, and statues and relics of the Buddha. His expedi-tion was considered so important that, far from being reprimanded for disobeying the emperor's orders years before, he was show-ered with honours.

Cheng Ho

During the years following Hsuan-tsang's adventures, the Chinese established trade con-tacts with India. By the 8th cen-tury they had reached the Ara-bian peninsula and the east coast of Africa. Chinese coins and porcelain were exchanged for African gold, ivory, rhinoceros horns and precious woods and spices. In 1415 the Chinese emper-or was delighted when ambassa-dors from Malindi presented him with a giraffe.

In 1368 the Mongols, who had ruled China for 150 years, were driven out. At the beginning of the 15th century the new Emperor Cheng Tsu planned a huge prog-ramme of exploration abroad. The man put in charge was a high-ranking courtier called Cheng Ho. He was in command of more than 27,000 men and a fleet of 317 ships.

Between 1405 and 1433, Cheng Ho made seven great voyages visiting, among other places, In-dochina, Java, Sumatra, Siam (now Thailand), the Maldive Islands, Borneo, the Persian Gulf, Arabia and the east coast of Africa. Some of the ships were sent on surveying expeditions into the Pacific Ocean where they may even have reached the north-ern coast of Australia. Another group may also have rounded the Cape of Good Hope, for a Chinese map of about 1420 clearly shows part of Africa's west coast. This was 60 years before Bartolemeu Dias became the first European to round the Cape (see page 103).

Two years after Cheng Ho returned from his final expedition the last emperor of the Ming dynasty died. With him died the Chinese interest in exploration and a new foreign policy was adopted. They turned their backs on the outside world and stopped all exploration of the West.

15th-century Chinese map showing the Cape of Good Hope at the top.

The Chinese junk

15th-century Chinese ships, cal-led junks, were huge compared with European ones of the same period. Some of Cheng Ho's ships weighed more than ten times as much as Vasco da Gama's (see page 114).

Sea-going junks were de-signed with flat bottoms so that they could carry more cargo. There were special watertight compartments for the cargo.

Chinese junks were de-signed with three masts hun-dreds of years before Euro-pean three-masted ships. The sails were square and staggered so that they all caught the wind.

Marco Polo

In the 13th century, a warrior tribe from northeast Asia called the Mongols, led by Genghis Khan, conquered huge areas of land in China and the Middle East. They reached as far west as Poland and Hungary.

The Mongols were nomads (wandering people). They carried tents with them from place to place.

Hole for chimney

Felt covering

Wooden frame

At first, some European countries feared the Mongols would invade them too, leaving a trail of death and destruction. Once it became clear that this was not going to happen, however, Europe began to consider the Mongols as possible allies against their long-standing enemies, the Turks.

Ambassador priests

Several European countries sent ambassadors to the Mongol capital, Karakorum. In 1245 Pope Innocent IV sent a priest, Giovanni da Pian del Carpini, to meet the Great Khan (the Mongol leader). Later a monk, William of Rubrouck, made the same journey on behalf of the king of France. But both visits were diplomatic failures.

William of Rubrouck meeting the Great Khan

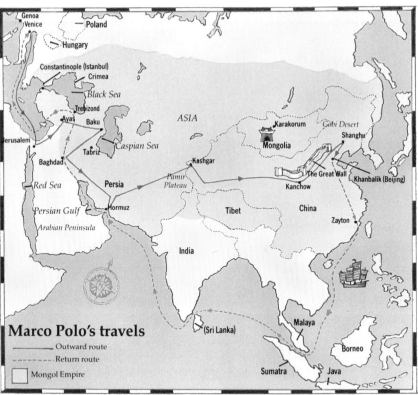

Marco Polo's travels

—— Outward route

---- Return route

☐ Mongol Empire

The triumph of trade

Carpini's route was later used by merchants. In the early 1260s the Venetian brothers Maffeo and Niccolo Polo, returning from a trade mission in the Crimea, found their way blocked by the Mongols. They made a lengthy detour, and on the way met a Mongol ambassador who invited them to China. They succeeded where the priests had not, and returned to Europe with a friendly letter for the Pope from Kublai Khan, the Mongol ruler in China.

Marco Polo's expedition

In 1271 the brothers set off for China again. This time they took with them Niccolo's son Marco, who was 15 years old. On the way they saw many amazing sights, such as a geyser pumping out hot oil, and large sheep with curly horns, each about 1.5m (4ft) in length. Marco noted many things, such as crafts and farming of the different areas, the people, and their religion and customs.

At Kublai Khan's court

Eventually, after three and a half years' travelling, the Polos reached Kublai Khan's court in Khanbalik (modern Beijing). They were again made welcome and Kublai Khan was particularly impressed by young Marco – so much so that he employed him as a representative of the imperial court. Marco went on many diplomatic missions, to such places as Malaya, Sumatra, Tibet and Sri Lanka, on behalf of Kublai Khan. He even recorded a journey to Burma and India.

Kublai Khan, the Mongol ruler of China, wearing Chinese imperial robes.

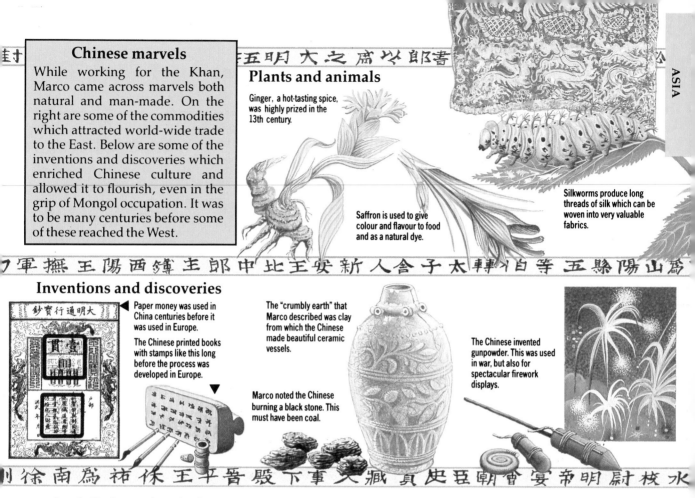

Chinese marvels

While working for the Khan, Marco came across marvels both natural and man-made. On the right are some of the commodities which attracted world-wide trade to the East. Below are some of the inventions and discoveries which enriched Chinese culture and allowed it to flourish, even in the grip of Mongol occupation. It was to be many centuries before some of these reached the West.

Plants and animals

Ginger, a hot-tasting spice, was highly prized in the 13th century.

Saffron is used to give colour and flavour to food and as a natural dye.

Silkworms produce long threads of silk which can be woven into very valuable fabrics.

Inventions and discoveries

Paper money was used in China centuries before it was used in Europe.

The Chinese printed books with stamps like this long before the process was developed in Europe.

The "crumbly earth" that Marco described was clay from which the Chinese made beautiful ceramic vessels.

Marco noted the Chinese burning a black stone. This must have been coal.

The Chinese invented gunpowder. This was used in war, but also for spectacular firework displays.

A final diplomatic mission

The Polos stayed in the service of Kublai Khan for 17 years. In 1292 they decided it was time to leave, but the Khan was reluctant to lose his loyal servants. A last diplomatic mission gave them an excuse: they were to return via Persia (now Iran), so that they could escort a Mongol princess to her husband-to-be, the Il-Khan Arghun. By the time they arrived, however, the Il-Khan had died. The Princess married his son instead.

The Polos sailed to Hormuz in Chinese boats called junks. From there they went by land to Trebizond and sailed back to Venice via

A Chinese town in the time of Marco Polo.

Constantinople. In all the journey took three years, and when they finally arrived back in Venice they had been away for 24 years. Marco was 39 when he returned. He married and became a merchant like his father and uncle.

Home to Venice

Settling in Venice again did not diminish Marco Polo's spirit of adventure. When Venice was at war with Genoa, he was taken prisoner while fighting for his city.

While in prison, Marco told his life story to his cell-mate, a writer called Rustichello. Rustichello later produced a book, *The Travels of Marco Polo*, which made his story famous all over the world.

Many of Marco's stories

seemed so far-fetched that people thought he had made them up. Some of his claims have never been verified. Although many merchants later followed the Polos' routes, they left no accounts of their travels to back up his claims. Marco's book inspired many later explorers, including Christopher Columbus (see page 118).

Marco Polo and Rustichello

The way east is closed

In 1368 the Chinese rebelled against the Mongols. They installed their own emperors who forbade visitors from Europe. Further west, some Mongols became Muslims and did not welcome Christians, so the land-route east from Europe was blocked again.

Vasco da Gama and the route to India

Having reached the Cape of Good Hope (see page 103), the Portuguese wanted to find a route around Africa to India. King Manuel I of Portugal chose a courtier called Vasco da Gama to lead an expedition to see if this route actually existed. Da Gama set sail in July 1497 with four ships and 170 men. Some of the men were convicts, recrutied to do the most dangerous tasks. The king ordered da Gama to investigate any opportunities for trade along the way.

Vasco da Gama
(1460-1524)

Into the unknown

The man who had first rounded the Cape of Good Hope, Bartolemeu Dias, accompanied the new expedition in his own ship as far as the Cape Verde Islands. From here, da Gama and his fleet took four months to reach the Cape. They then sailed up the eastern coast of Africa. From time to time they landed to take food and water on board, to make repairs, and to trade.

Scurvy strikes

Many of the crew fell ill with scurvy, a disease caused by a deficiency of vitamin C. Victims grew weak, developing fever and blisters, and rarely survived the illness. So many of his men died that da Gama had to burn one of his ships because there were not enough sailors left to form a crew to operate it.

Rival traders

Further up the coast, da Gama reached the ports of Kilwa and Mombasa. But trade in this area was controlled by Arab merchants. They were hostile to da Gama, fearing he would disrupt their trade agreements with the Africans.

Da Gama's ship being attacked.

Some African rulers were unimpressed with da Gama's goods and refused to trade. Others were more aggressive. In Mombasa armed men tried to capture the Portuguese, who only just managed to escape.

Monsoon winds to Calicut

In nearby Malindi, the locals were more sympathetic. Da Gama hired an experienced guide to steer his ships cross the Indian Ocean. Driven by a seasonal wind called the monsoon, they made the crossing in just 23 days. They reached Calicut in India after a total of ten months at sea.

A long way home

Da Gama was welcomed by the Indian princes, but his goods did not compare with their magnificent wealth. He could only buy small amounts of spices. Again, Arab merchants in the area were hostile. After only three months da Gama and his men left India for Portugal. The voyage was three months longer than the outward journey.

Da Gama returns

When he reached home, da Gama received a hero's welcome. He had only acquired a few samples of goods, but these proved to the king that there were good trading opportunities in India. Da Gama's voyage opened up the route for many later traders from Portugal.

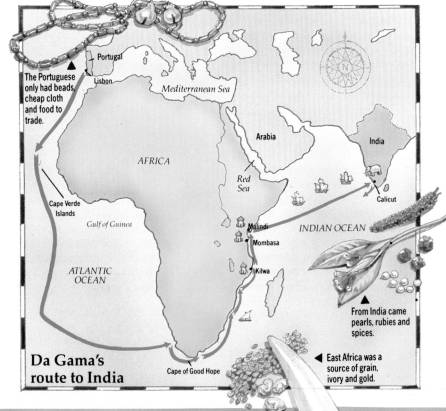

The Portuguese only had beads, cheap cloth and food to trade.

Portugal
Lisbon
Mediterranean Sea
Arabia
India
AFRICA
Red Sea
Calicut
Cape Verde Islands
Gulf of Guinea
Malindi
INDIAN OCEAN
Mombasa
ATLANTIC OCEAN
Kilwa
Cape of Good Hope

Da Gama's route to India

From India came pearls, rubies and spices.

◄ East Africa was a source of grain, ivory and gold.

The search for the Northeast Passage

To compete with Portugal for eastern trade, northern European countries needed another sea route to the East. There were many attempts to find a Northeast Passage round northern Asia into the Pacific Ocean, and on to China and India.

Willem Barents

Barents, a Dutchman, made several voyages to find a way through to the East. In 1594 he sailed round the tip of Norway

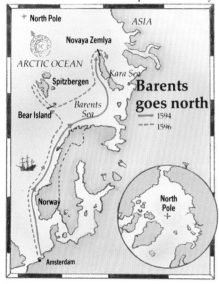

and reached the huge island of Novaya Zemlya. Here pack ice blocked his route and he had to turn back.

Trapped by ice

Barents sailed again in 1596. After reaching Spitzbergen he headed south and east to Novaya Zemlya once more. This time he sailed round its northernmost tip, but his ship became stuck in the ice. It was the beginning of the Arctic winter. Barents and his crew had no option but to build themselves a hut for shelter, and wait for warmer weather in the spring. Their ship was slowly crushed by the advancing ice, the timbers cracking.

A winter refuge

The hut was built from pieces of the wrecked ship. In 1871 a Norwegian fisherman found it, perfectly preserved by the ice.

Barents and his crew salvaged items which they could adapt for use on land. The crow's nest from the ship was put on top of the hut and used as a lookout tower.

The ship's bunks were taken ashore and used as beds.

The fisherman found books (including Barents' diary), a clock and cooking utensils.

A bath was adapted from a wooden barrel.

The front and side of the hut have been cut away in this picture to show the interior.

Surviving an Arctic winter

Barents and his men managed to survive the winter in their makeshift house. They killed bears and foxes for food, and burned polar bear fat and wood for light and heat. When the weather allowed, they played golf on the ice for exercise.

They suffered dreadfully from cold, hunger and scurvy. Even inside the hut the discomfort was hard to endure. The sheets froze on their beds and the smoke from the fire made it difficult to breathe.

When the Arctic spring came, and the ice began to melt, the expedition headed for home in the ship's two open boats. But for Barents, who was weakened by the rigours of the winter, the return journey proved too much. He had also fallen ill with scurvy and was so sickly he was unable to keep command of the boats. He grew weaker and weaker and died just five days after setting out for home, on Bear Island in the sea that is now named after him.

Polar bears often attacked the shelter.

Was there a way through?

Barents made great advances in Arctic exploration, but the Northeast Passage remained a mystery for centuries. Its existence was not proved until 1741, when a Dane, Vitus Bering, sailed through the narrow straits between Alaska and Asia which are now named after him. However the passage was far too dangerous and remote to be a good trade route.

The Vikings reach America

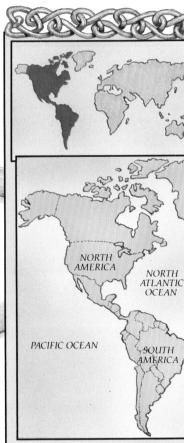

The Vikings were seafarers and warriors who had lived in Norway, Sweden and Denmark since ancient times. They began sailing west in the 9th century, searching for new territory. By about 860 some of them had reached Iceland and settled there. During their frequent journeys west, they became the first Europeans to discover America.

The Vikings were excellent metalworkers and used elaborately decorated swords like these.

Around 900, a ship commanded by a man called Gunnbjorn was sailing to Iceland from Norway. His ship was blown off course, and he saw a new land which he described to the settlers when he finally got to Iceland. His story inspired other Vikings to go in search of the new country.

Eric the Red

Eric the Red was a Norwegian who was banished from his country for three years for murder. He decided to use his period of exile to search for new lands to colonize, and set his sights in particular on the place that Gunnbjorn had spotted. After a hazardous voyage he arrived there but found that it had a hostile climate and landscape.

The Vikings' exploits were later recorded in long tales called sagas. This is a page from the saga about Eric the Red's discovery of Greenland.

Eric the Red wanted other Vikings to follow him there. He called the new country Greenland – not a very appropriate name for such unforgiving territory. By 986 he had convinced a group of colonists to settle there.

After a gruelling journey the expedition arrived in Greenland. It was summer, and conditions were favourable enough to establish farms. Settlements soon grew up, and the colonists were able to begin trading with Scandinavia.

Bjarni Herjolfsson

Soon another Norwegian, called Bjarni Herjolfsson, set out for Greenland, but went astray in fog and gales. He realized he had lost his way when land finally loomed out of the fog at him. It was not the harsh territory he had been told to expect when he reached Greenland. Instead it proved to be hilly and wooded.

In fact, the storms had blown Herjolfsson's ship far to the southwest of Greenland. We now know that the shoreline he saw was the northeastern coast of America. Instead of landing there, however, he turned back. When he finally reached Greenland, he reported his findings to the Viking colonists there.

A Viking warrior

A Viking ship

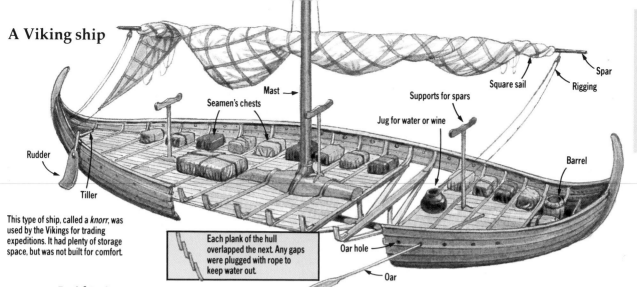

Rudder

Tiller

Seamen's chests

Mast

Supports for spars

Jug for water or wine

Square sail

Rigging

Spar

Barrel

Oar hole

Oar

This type of ship, called a *knorr*, was used by the Vikings for trading expeditions. It had plenty of storage space, but was not built for comfort.

Each plank of the hull overlapped the next. Any gaps were plugged with rope to keep water out.

Leif Ericsson

The first European actually to set foot on American soil was Eric the Red's son, Leif Ericsson. Around the year 1000 he and his men left Greenland and sailed southwest. They landed at three places on the eastern coast of America. Leif gave these names: Markland ("forest land"; now the region of Labrador); Heluland ("slab-land", after the rocky landscape; now Baffin Island); and Vinland ("vine-land"; experts are unsure, but Vinland was probably where either New England or Newfoundland is now).

According to the saga of his voyage, Ericsson found wild grapes on the American coast, and the biggest fish he had ever seen.

Defeated by the Skraelings

Ericsson's men spent the winter in Vinland, then returned to Greenland with the news of their discovery. Although Leif himself never returned to the new lands, his brother Thorwald set out in 1002 to set up a colony there. He and his men found Vinland, but they were not prepared for the hostility of the native American Indians (known by the

Vikings as Skraelings). Thorwald was killed in a fight, and his companions returned to Greenland discouraged.

Eric the Red's descendants made two more attempts to colonize Vinland. The first expedition included his daughter-in-law Gudrid and her second husband. They settled there and started a family, and succeeded in trading successfully with the Skraelings. But later relations between settlers and natives deteriorated. The Vikings had to give up their home and return to Greenland. They finally settled in Iceland.

This is what a Skraeling warrior might have looked like.

A second expedition was led by Eric the Red's daughter Freydis, but she too failed to establish good relations with the Indians. She also caused chaos among her own people, and murdered several of her fellow colonists.

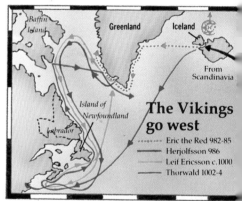

The Vikings go west

········· Eric the Red 982-85
———— Herjolfsson 986
———— Leif Ericsson c.1000
———— Thorwald 1002-4

The evidence

The theory that the Vikings had reached America was quite common for many years, but until the mid-1960s there was no reliable evidence. Doubts also arose when a map of the northeast coast, said to date from Viking times, turned out to be a fake. But in 1968 the remains of a Viking settlement were discovered in Newfoundland, proving that the Vikings had managed to reach America.

Fragments of Viking woodwork found at Newfoundland.

Christopher Columbus

Christopher Columbus is probably the most famous explorer of all. However his greatest discovery, the continent of America, was made by mistake.

Columbus (c.1451-1506) was given his own coat of arms in 1493, in honour of his discoveries.

Born in 1451 in Genoa, Italy, Columbus first went to sea as a young boy. He settled in Lisbon in 1479 and married the daughter of a Portuguese nobleman. From Lisbon he made various sea voyages, acquiring excellent skills as a navigator.

"Gold, God and Cathay"

Columbus's ambition was to sail to the Far East. His reasons are often summed up in the phrase "Gold, God and Cathay". The gold he had in mind was the fortune to be made bringing spices and silk home from China and Japan.

"God" refers to Columbus's wish to spread Christianity to non-Christian countries and to claim new lands in the name of God. This was a common motive among Europeans at that time. It was considered a worthy aim in itself, but

This Spanish gold cross symbolizes Columbus's motives for sailing to the Far East: spreading Christianity and making money.

Columbus hoped to find precious spices like cinnamon (left), nutmeg and peppercorns (below).

many explorers also saw another benefit. They thought that foreign trade would be easier with Christian countries.

"Cathay" was an ancient name for China. Columbus was obsessed with the Far East, and wanted to lead an expedition there.

Testing a theory

In the 15th century most people believed that the Earth was flat. Columbus, however, thought it was round. He hoped to prove this by sailing west to get to the Far East (see globe opposite), instead of taking the usual route from Europe, east round Africa.

Columbus took years to find money for his scheme, as few people believed it would work. Eventually, in 1492, Queen Isabella and King Ferdinand of Spain gave him the money he needed.

The voyage begins

Columbus left Spain on 3 August 1492 with three ships (see box). On 6 September they sailed from the Canary Islands out into open seas. At that time it was unusual to travel out of sight of the coast, and as days went by without a glimpse of land the crewmen became anxious. By the time they reached the strange, weed-infested Sargasso Sea, many of the men were desperate to turn back.

Many of Columbus's crew believed they were sailing into seas that were full of huge monsters.

Columbus persuaded them to go on by promising to give up if they did not sight land within a few days. But in his diary he recorded his intention to continue regardless of his men's desires.

Columbus's ships

These are the three ships that Spain provided for Columbus's voyage.

The Santa Maria

The *Santa Maria* was the fleet's largest ship, captained by Columbus himself.

The *Niña*

The *Niña* was smaller than the *Santa Maria*. The captain was Martín Alonzo Pinzón.

The *Pinta*

The *Pinta* was similar to the *Niña*. Pinzón's brother, Vicente Yanez Pinzón, was its captain.

Between them the ships carried 104 men and vast quantities of supplies, including live pigs and chickens, salted meat, flour, rice, wine and water. There was also equipment for repairing the ships.

Land ahoy!

On 12 October, the lookout on the *Pinta* saw land. It was what is now called Watling Island in the Bahamas, off the coast of America. Columbus, however, was convinced he had reached Cathay. As he had wildly under-estimated how long it would take him to reach the Far East, he was not at all surprised to find land when he did. He would not accept his mistake as long as he lived, and never realized the significance of his discovery.

Columbus's route would have worked if America had not been in his path.

Intended route
Actual route

Columbus named the island San Salvador. The inhabitants were friendly, and eager to trade. Columbus found little evidence of the riches of the East, but he was still certain that he was near his goal. Guided by the local people, he led the fleet onward in search of Cathay and its treasures.

He visited Cuba, then an island which he named La Española (now Hispaniola). He was then impatient to return to Spain to report his findings.

This woodcut, from the 1493 edition of Columbus's journals, shows some of the islands he visited.

The Allegory of Discovery

This Spanish gold shield, known as the Allegory of Discovery, was made in the 16th century. By this time the Spanish had understood the full importance of Columbus's achievements.

Neptune, the Greek god of the sea.

This figure represents Columbus.

The 'horn of plenty' – a symbol of the rich natural resources that explorers found on the American continent.

Disaster and triumph

On Christmas Day 1492, the *Santa Maria* was wrecked at La Española when it hit a reef. Columbus had to leave 43 men behind, as there was no room on the other ships. He was welcomed as a hero when he reached Spain. The islands he had found became known as "the Indies", as people thought they were off the coast of Asia in the Indian Ocean.

A second expedition

In 1493 Columbus led a new fleet to the Indies, but his visit was not a success. Firstly he found at La Española that the men he had left behind had been killed by the islanders. Then he formed a new settlement, but governed it badly, brutally mistreating the natives and Spaniards alike.

Columbus disgraced

News of Columbus's behaviour had reached Spain when he returned in 1496. Although the king and queen were angry, they let him go back to the Indies in 1498. But further unrest there alarmed Ferdinand and Isabella, and they appointed a new governor.

When Columbus reached Cuba having failed to calm a revolt on La Española, he was arrested by the governor and sent back to Spain in chains. Isabella later forgave him, but his pride was badly wounded. He claimed he had been misunderstood, and asked to be buried with the chains as a reminder of the way he had been treated.

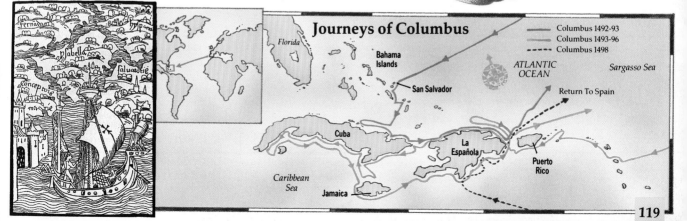

Journeys of Columbus

Florida
Bahama Islands
San Salvador
ATLANTIC OCEAN
Sargasso Sea
Return To Spain
Cuba
La Española
Puerto Rico
Caribbean Sea
Jamaica

Columbus 1492-93
Columbus 1493-96
Columbus 1498

Cortés

Columbus's death marks a turning point in the history of European exploration. Before that most explorers were professional navigators and seamen employed by monarchs. Though they wanted personal profit from their voyages, they had other, more long-term aims. These included finding trade routes for their patrons and taking Christianity to non-Christian countries. In the 16th century, new, more ruthless explorers became common. They are known as conquistadors, after the Spanish word for "conquerors".

Cortés
1485-1547

The conquistadors

At the turn of the century an Italian explorer, Amerigo Vespucci, sailed to the land Columbus had found and established that it was an entirely new continent. In 1507 this "New World", as it was known, was named America, after Vespucci.

The conquistadors were Spanish adventurers and soldiers. They believed America and its resources were there to be taken regardless of who lived there. In conquering the new lands many of them remorselessly wiped out whole civilizations.

Cortés sails to the New World

Hernándo Cortés was born in 1485 to a distinguished but poor Spanish family. He first studied law, but soon found he was more attracted to the excitement of a soldier's life. His first major expedition was with Diego Velazquez, a conquistador who set out in 1511 to seize Cuba. When Velazquez succeeded, Cortés did well out of the conquest. He was soon a rich and important man, and for a time he was even Mayor of Cuba's capital Santiago. Soon, however, rumours of an empire rich in gold on the American mainland aroused his curiosity, and he set off in search of it.

The Aztec empire

The Aztecs were American Indians who lived in what is now Mexico. Their civilization began in about 1325, when they arrived in the area from further north and began building their capital city Tenochtitlán. Aztec culture was highly sophisticated in many areas, especially science, art, architecture and agriculture. The Aztecs had their own mode of picture writing and a great many laws and elaborate religious rites and ceremonies. They were also highly skilled jewellers and weavers.

Sacrificial knives like this were used at the ceremonies.

Human sacrifices

One of the most shocking Aztec customs was the ritual of human sacrifice. The Aztecs believed their sun god, Huitzilpochtli, died each night, and would only be reborn the next day if he was nourished with a constant supply of human blood. Thousands of victims were brutally sacrificed each year. They were often slaves or prisoners of war, but sometimes Atzecs themselves. Many had their hearts cut out while they were still living.

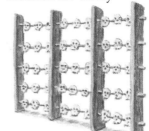

The heads of victims were kept on skull racks like this.

Towards Tenochtitlán

In 1519 Cortés left Santiago, intending to make his fortune by conquering the Aztecs. He sailed for the American mainland with

Shrine to the sun god

Sacrificial altar

This is what an Aztec temple might have looked like.

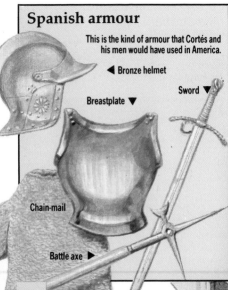

Spanish armour

This is the kind of armour that Cortés and his men would have used in America.

◄ Bronze helmet

Sword ▼

Breastplate ▼

Chain-mail

Battle axe ▶

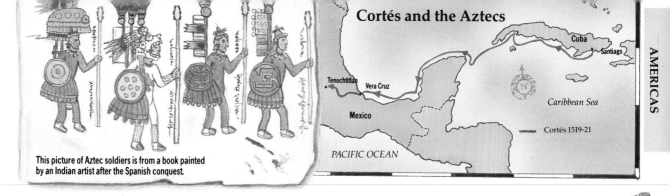

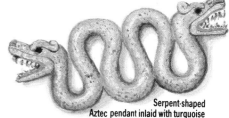

This picture of Aztec soldiers is from a book painted by an Indian artist after the Spanish conquest.

Cortés and the Aztecs

600 men, 16 horses and several cannons. After founding the city of Vera Cruz on the coast, he continued inland towards Tenochtitlán.

The Aztecs had recently conquered several rival tribes in the area and had made many enemies. Malinche, the daughter of one tribal chief, fell in love with Cortés and offered to accompany him on his journey as a guide and interpreter. (The Spaniards named her Dona Mariña.) Her services were crucial in gaining support from the other Indian tribes for his invasion of the Aztecs.

Mask of Quetzalcoatl (see below).

Warrior gods

The Aztecs were terrified by Cortés's cannons and horses. Some thought his arrival was the god Quetzalcoatl returning to Earth, as predicted in an Aztec myth. But their emperor Montezuma thought otherwise. Astrologers had spoken of an invasion and the downfall of the Aztec Empire, and he worried that the predictions were coming true. To put the Spaniards off their guard,

he treated them like the gods his people took them for, kissing the ground before their feet and giving them precious gifts.

Montezuma's downfall

Montezuma's attempt to pacify the Spaniards did him no good. Cortés took him prisoner and demanded a huge ransom of gold. The gold was paid, but Cortés cheated the Aztecs and kept Montezuma captive.

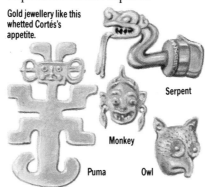

Gold jewellery like this whetted Cortés's appetite.

Serpent

Monkey

Puma   Owl

Then news reached Cortés that a rival in Vera Cruz had challenged his authority. He rushed to the coast to deal with the problem, and returned to find that one of his men had staged an unprovoked attack on an Aztec religious meeting and killed many of the participants.

The Aztecs were in uproar, so Cortés produced Montezuma, hoping to calm the rioters. But the former ruler had never been popular, and the sight of him enraged the crowds even more. They stoned him to death then turned on the Spaniards.

Cortés's men suffered heavy losses in the fighting and withdrew to

Serpent-shaped Aztec pendant inlaid with turquoise

the protection of friendly tribes nearby. Then in August 1521, Cortés besieged Tenochtitlán. Food and water were cut off for nearly three months. Countless Aztecs died. Some starved, but many caught smallpox which the Spanish had unknowingly brought with them from Europe.

An empire destroyed

After the fall of Tenochtitlán, the Aztec Empire was rapidly destroyed. The Indians had no immunity to European diseases, so millions of them died. In addition many conquistadors were brutal rulers. Within a few years of Montezuma's death, little of the Aztec world remained.

Aztec armour

The Aztecs had weapons and armour that terrified the Spanish.

Wooden club edged ▶ with sharpened flint.

Cane shield covered ▶ with painted animal hide.

◀ Padded cotton suit

121

The hunt for the Northwest Passage

Like the Spanish, the British and French were also keen to reach the riches of the East by sailing west. Rather than following the Spanish routes round South America (see pages 134-135), they sought a new route round North America. They were sure that they would find a channel through which their ships could sail. This was known as the Northwest Passage.

Frobisher meets the challenge

An English expedition to find the Northwest Passage was organized by the navigator Sir Humphrey Gilbert. Three ships set sail from London in 1576 under the command of a captain called Martin Frobisher.

Martin Frobisher (1535-94)

The coast of Greenland was blocked by ice and Frobisher's ship lost its mast in a gale. But he repaired the damage and continued with his journey. Believing he had found the approach to the Northwest Passage, he named it Frobisher's Strait, without realizing it was only an inlet (now Frobisher Bay) that led nowhere.

Encounter with the Inuit

While he was exploring the inlet, Frobisher was met by Inuit (the local inhabitants). They skimmed across the water in one-man canoes called kayaks and surrounded Frobisher's ship.

Kayaks are made from wooden frames covered with sealskins.

Wooden frame

When Frobisher first saw a kayak from a distance, he thought it was a seal or a large fish.

Sealskin covering

Paddle →

Kidnap

The Inuit seemed friendly and traded food and furs. But five of the crew were kidnapped when they left their ship. Frobisher captured an Inuit as a hostage against the return of his sailors, but they were never seen again. The Inuit was taken back to England, where he died of pneumonia.

The search for gold

One of the crew went ashore and brought back some black rocks streaked with glittering gold veins. When Frobisher returned to London experts declared that the rocks contained gold. On his next two voyages to the region in 1577 and 1578, Frobisher collected huge quantities of the rocks. When he returned home after the final journey, he was told that the rocks he had collected were worthless. They had been identified as iron pyrites, also known as "fool's gold".

Iron pyrites or "fool's gold".

The quest continues

The failure to find the elusive Northwest Passage did not discourage others from making the attempt. John Davis, who discovered the Davis Strait, made three voyages between 1585 and 1587.

In 1610 Henry Hudson sailed along the north coast of Canada in a ship called the *Discovery*. But his crew, convinced he had a secret hoard of food, cast him adrift with his son and a few loyal sailors. Hudson was lost forever in the bay that now bears his name.

In 1616 William Baffin and Robert Bylot sailed up the Davis Strait as far as Smith Sound, which would have taken them through to open sea, but the icy weather forced them to turn back. The Northwest Passage remained uncharted for centuries. It was finally navigated by Roald Amundsen (see pages 136-137).

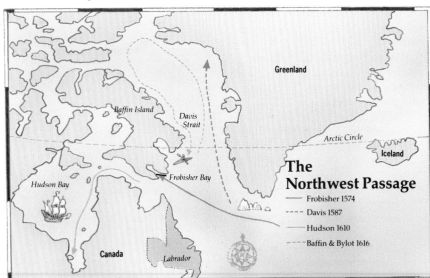

Greenland

Baffin Island

Davis Strait

Arctic Circle

Iceland

Hudson Bay

Frobisher Bay

Canada

Labrador

The Northwest Passage

— Frobisher 1574
---- Davis 1587
— Hudson 1610
---- Baffin & Bylot 1616

An Inuit hunting bow made out of walrus-tusk ivory.

Carvings of hunting scenes

The building of New France

Jacques Cartier
(1491-1557)

W hile the English were enduring the miseries of the freezing Arctic waters, the French were also trying to find a route through to the East. In 1534 King François I commissioned a sailor from St Malo called Jacques Cartier to find a way west to the Pacific and claim new lands for France.

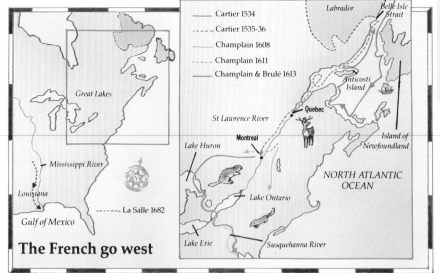

The French go west

Cartier 1534
Cartier 1535-36
Champlain 1608
Champlain 1611
Champlain & Brulé 1613

Missed opportunities

Cartier's expedition set out in two ships from St Malo in 1534. He headed for Newfoundland and then sailed through the Belle Isle Strait, noting that the rocky shores would be of no use to settlers. Rounding Anticosti Island, he sighted the mouth of the St Lawrence River. Mistaking it for a bay, he failed to investigate it and returned to France.

Help from the Indians

Cartier left on a second voyage in May 1535 and reached Belle Isle Strait at the end of July. He acquired two guides from the Huron tribe who led his party up the St Lawrence River. They passed the small native village of Stadacona (later Quebec), then pressed on upstream through the rapids to a town called Hochelaga where they met the Huron chief, Donnaconna. Cartier named a nearby hill Mont Réal (Mount Royal), which later became the site of the city of Montreal.

Cartier and his men spent a terrible winter at Stadacona, suffering from scurvy and extreme cold. On 6 May 1536 they finally sailed for home. On the way they

Cartier travelled by canoe with Indian guides up the St Lawrence River.

kidnapped Donnaconna to try to get him to reveal the whereabouts of gold mines. He was taken back to France, where he later died.

In the wake of Cartier

With wars raging in Europe, French kings lost interest in the New World for a time. However small groups of Frenchmen continued to follow Cartier's route up the St Lawrence and spread out along the many waterways. They learned how to survive in the wilderness, build birch-bark canoes and trap beavers and other animals for their fur. They established a trade network with the American Indians, which flourished rapidly. At the same time they were gradually building up an empire for France.

French explorers ▶ encountered many animals which they trapped for their fur and hide.

The French empire grows

Samuel de Champlain, the French Royal Geographer, founded Quebec in 1608 and Montreal in 1611, strengthening France's hold in North America. In 1613 he was joined by Etienne Brulé who later reached the Susquehanna River.

In 1678 King Louis XIV sent an explorer called Robert de La Salle to build a chain of trading forts across the continent. La Salle followed the Mississippi River, reaching the Gulf of Mexico in 1682. He named the lands he passed through Louisiana after the king.

Elk

Otter

Beaver

Marten

Across the continent

By the mid-18th century there were so many new immigrants entering North America from Europe that the original colonies in the Northeast were overcrowded. Expansion was difficult as the settlers were afraid to venture west into the unknown lands over the Appalachian Mountains.

In 1803 the United States government bought the state of Louisiana from France. This prompted Thomas Jefferson, the American president, to plan an expedition to explore the lands beyond the Mississippi. This was mainly to assess opportunities for trade with American Indians and Mexicans, but also to find a route to the Pacific Ocean.

The team departs

The leaders of the expedition were Captain Meriwether Lewis, the president's private secretary, and Lieutenant William Clark. Lewis chose all the equipment needed, while Clark recruited

William Clark
(1770-1838)

Meriwether Lewis
(1774-1809)

and trained the men. The team of 30 men was known as the Corps of Discovery and left St Louis in a blaze of publicity on 14 May 1804, sailing up the River Missouri. As well as the usual equipment such as rifles, medicines and food supplies, they carried with them many trinkets as presents for the Indians.

An air-gun used on the expedition

Clark's pocket compass

Entering new lands

The two leaders made many notes on the profusion of plants and animals they saw along the way. Lewis complained of the terrible weather and the swarms of mosquitoes that plagued them throughout the night and day.

Prairie dog

Lewis's woodpecker

Mountain flower

After eleven weeks they encountered the Oto, Missouri and Omaha tribes of Indians. They exchanged gifts and made peace and trade treaties with them. Then, moving deeper into the plains, they met about a thousand members of the Teton Sioux who made the team take part in a peace-pipe ceremony before allowing them to cross their lands.

Moving on

They reached an area now part of North Dakota where they set up camp and built a log fort. They spent the bitter winter there among the Mandan tribe. The team resumed its journey in the

A barge similar to the one used by Lewis and Clark

spring, travelling by barge up the Missouri. Gradually the currents ran stronger and the journey became more difficult, but by the end of May they were in sight of the majestic, snow-covered Rocky Mountains. Here they came across grizzly bears and were surprised by the power and ferocity of these huge animals that frequently attacked the party.

The explorers were often powerless when attacked by bears.

A way through the Rockies

Next, they had to find a way round the Great Falls on the Missouri as they could go no further. The task of moving the equipment round the falls took nearly a month and exhausted the men. By August they entered the lands of the Shoshoni Indians and here they encountered more difficulties, for they had underestimated the height of the Rockies. But they were helped by Sacagewea, the Shoshoni Indian wife of a Canadian interpreter in the party. She showed them the Lemhi Pass and guided them towards the Columbia River. They made contact with Sacagewea's people and were given new horses to continue their journey.

Sacagewea

Ocean in view!

The western face of the Rockies was very steep, criss-crossed by roaring waterfalls and slippery precipices. The going was tough,

Crossing the Rockies

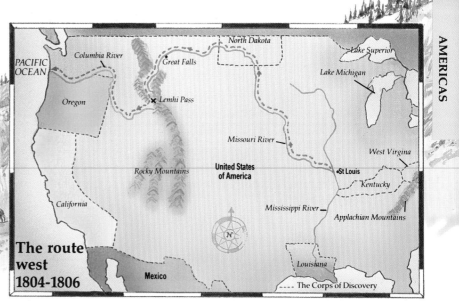

The route west 1804-1806

PACIFIC OCEAN

Columbia River

North Dakota

Great Falls

Lake Superior

Lake Michigan

Oregon

× Lemhi Pass

Missouri River

West Virgina

Rocky Mountains

United States of America

•St Louis

Kentucky

California

Mississippi River

Appalachian Mountains

Louisiana

Mexico

----- The Corps of Discovery

food was in short supply and the nights were bitterly cold. They passed through the lands of the Chinook, the Clatsops and the majestic Nez Percé tribe, and finally reached the Columbia River. They paddled towards the coast, and on 7 November heard the roar of the Pacific breakers and smelled the sea-salt in the air. They climbed to the top of the final hill and saw the ocean spread before them. At last they had reached their goal.

The journey home

Winter was now closing in, so they built a camp which they named Fort Clatsop. From there they could watch the Pacific to hail any passing ship that might carry them back east. But nothing appeared on the horizon, so the team packed up and on 23 March set off on their six-month return journey to St Louis. Although they now knew the way, it was as

exhausting as the outward trek. Also, conflict with the Blackfoot Indians caused difficulties which were to plague pioneers for many years. On 20 September 1806 they reached a French settlement where they saw the first Europeans for over two years.

A triumphant return

On 23 September 1806 they finally arrived back at St Louis after a journey of over 12,000km (7,456 miles) and an absence of two-and-a-half years. They had been gone for so long that many thought they must be dead. But Lewis and Clark had accomplished all they had set out to do. Most importantly, they had discovered a way to the West which gave access to the rest of the continent and the Pacific. They had also established good relations with many of the Indian tribes and opened up new trade routes.

The rush West

This mammoth expedition by the Corps of Discovery was followed by a new wave of explorers, mainly fur trappers known as "mountain men" who spilled over the mountains to make their fortunes. Further south, the Santa Fe, the Old Spanish, the Oregon and the Californian trade routes were established between the United States and Mexico.

Farmers and gold prospectors

Where the traders went, the farmers followed. In 1843 a group of settlers travelled west to Oregon in a thousand-strong wagon-train. When gold was discovered in California in 1849, a huge rush to the West began. Thousands of people left the East for the new lands, braving incredible hardship and the growing hostility of the Indians who realized that the settlers threatened their territory and way of life.

Mountain man in search of furs.

Gold nuggets from California.

A member of the party being attacked by Blackfoot Indians.

Scientists and dreamers

The first Europeans to explore and colonize South America in the 16th and 17th centuries were treasure hunters and missionaries. But during the 18th century many of the explorers were scientists. They were more interested in mapping the continent and in studying its geology and plant and animal life. The first such scientific expedition travelled to Peru in 1735.

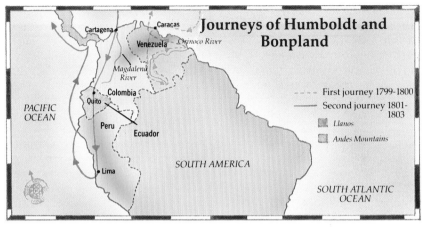

Journeys of Humboldt and Bonpland

Cartagena · Caracas · Venezuela · Orinoco River · Magdalena River · Colombia · Quito · PACIFIC OCEAN · Peru · Ecuador · Lima · SOUTH AMERICA · SOUTH ATLANTIC OCEAN

- - - First journey 1799-1800
—— Second journey 1801-1803
▨ Llanos
▨ Andes Mountains

Alexander von Humboldt

One of the greatest scientific explorers was a German called Alexander von Humboldt. As well as being a brilliant naturalist, he was an astronomer, biologist and geologist and also an expert linguist. In June 1797 Humboldt left his home in Berlin for Paris. In June 1799 he and a French doctor called Aimé Bonpland sailed from Europe to South America, reaching the north east coast near Caracas in present-day Venezuela the following month.

Alexander von Humboldt
(1769-1859)

Aimé Bonpland
(1773-1858)

One of their first projects was to explore the Orinoco River. But in order to reach it, they first had to cross the dry, baking and dusty plains called the *llanos* stretching to the south.

◀ The Incas were very skilled stonemasons. They cut the stones so accurately that they fitted perfectly.

All along the way they made detailed records of the many plants, animals and birds they saw and the country through which they passed – scorching deserts that parched their throats and dried up their skin. They travelled along winding rivers through hot steamy jungles, the silence pierced by the shrieks of parrots and monkeys, where they were plagued by swarms of blood-sucking insects.

Up mountains, down south

They made a second journey to South America in 1801 and reached Quito (one of the highest cities in the world) in January 1802, after an exhausting voyage along rivers and over mountains. Outside the city they climbed 5,878m (19,285ft) almost to the top of a volcanic peak called Chimborazo. Then they travelled south through lush forests and across the chilly slopes of the Andes Mountains until they reached Lima, Peru. Here they studied the archaeological remains of the Inca civilization. (The Incas flourished in Peru from the 13th century, but were wiped out by Spanish conquistadors (see page 120) in the 1530s.)

Humboldt also recorded the steady, cold current which flows along the Peruvian coast and is rich in stocks of fish. It was later named the Humboldt Current (now known as the Peru Current).

Back in Europe

Great crowds turned out to welcome the two explorers on their return to France in 1804. They had travelled 64,000km (40,000 miles) in South America and collected 30 chests of specimens and 60,000 plants, many of which were unknown before. Humboldt returned to Germany and spent the next 23 years preparing all their work for publication which eventually filled 29 volumes.

Bonpland identified thousands of plants for the first time.

Humboldt and Bonpland at the foot of Mount Chimborazo. ▼

Giant tortoise

Charles Darwin

Charles Darwin was an English naturalist and explorer. He joined a ship called the *Beagle* in December 1831 on a five-year expedition to map the coast of Chile. He made copious notes on all he saw, and although there was little room on the ship he built up a huge collection of rocks, fossils, plants, birds, animals and shells. The sights he saw and the observations he made would later lead him to challenge the traditional beliefs about how life on Earth began and evolved.

Charles Darwin
(1809-82)

The land of giants

The expedition reached Bahia in Brazil in the spring of 1832. Darwin was amazed by the number and dazzling colours of the flowers and birds he saw. The Beagle sailed south along the coast of Patagonia where the crew discovered the fossil remains of several extinct animals, including a giant sloth and armadillo.

This is how the giant sloth and the armadillo might have looked.

They travelled to the bleak and wind-swept lands of Tierra del Fuego, at the very tip of South America. Darwin made a journey inland to the plains of Argentina known as the *pampas*, living among the *gauchos* (cowboys).

Darwin on a plant-hunting expedition.

A world apart

In September 1835 the expedition reached the strange, remote Galapagos Islands, lying 965km (600 miles) off the coast of Ecuador in the Pacific Ocean. There Darwin saw birds, animals and plants that are found nowhere else on Earth. Cut off from the mainland they had developed in isolation from their relations in America. They were to play an important part in Darwin's theories on how animals and humans evolve (see below).

▶ These animals are only found on the Galapagos Islands.

Marine iguana

Galapagos finch

The Bible is questioned

The *Beagle* reached England in October 1836 and Darwin spent over 20 years writing up his findings. In 1859 he published *The Origin of Species*, which set out his theories on evolution. These turned the teachings of the Church upside down. One of Darwin's most revolutionary theories was that all living things had evolved over many millions of years. This caused uproar, because it questioned the biblical idea that the world was created in six days and had remained unchanged since then.

Percy Fawcett

Percy Fawcett was an army officer and surveyor with 20 years' experience of travel in South America. Inspired by the legend of El Dorado, "the golden man", he believed that somewhere deep in the Brazilian jungle lay the remains of a fabulous civilization. Near Salvador (Bahia) in 1921 he found remains which encouraged him and he intended to prove his theory by finding one of the lost cities, which he called "Z".

Percy Fawcett
(1867-1925)

An unsolved mystery

On 20 April 1925, Fawcett set off with his eldest son Jack and a school friend of Jack's called Raleigh Rimell. They followed piranha-infested rivers into the Mato Grosso region of Brazil, and were never seen again. Over the following years rumours of what had happened to them came out of the jungle. They were probably killed by Indians, but nothing could be proved and their disappearance remains as much a mystery as Fawcett's fabled city.

SOUTH AMERICA

Ecuador

Brazil

Galapagos Islands

Bahia (Salvador)

Mato Grosso

PACIFIC OCEAN

Chile

Darwin and Fawcett

Argentina

SOUTH ATLANTIC OCEAN

Pampas

Patagonia

Darwin 1831-1835
Fawcett 1925

Tierra del Fuego

Cape Horn

The quest for a southern continent

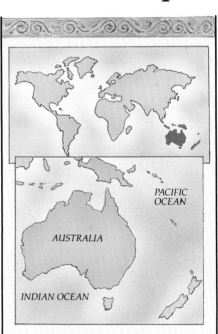

PACIFIC OCEAN

AUSTRALIA

INDIAN OCEAN

Key dates in Australasian exploration

- **1565** Andres de Urdaneta crosses the Pacific Ocean.
- **1606** Pedro Fernandes de Quiros reaches the New Hebrides Islands.
- **1606** Willem Jantszoon becomes the first European to reach Australia.
- **1642** Abel Tasman sights an island off the southern coast of Australia and names it Van Diemen's Land after Anthony van Diemen, Governor-General of the Dutch East Indies. It is now known as Tasmania.
- **1721** Jakob Roggeveen discovers Easter Island, on Easter Sunday.
- **1769** James Cook sails in the *Endeavour* to Tahiti and makes observations of Venus. He sails onto New Zealand where he discovers the east coast.
- **1770** Cook lands in Botany Bay, Australia.
- **1772** Cook's second voyage leaves Plymouth.
- **1774** Cook crosses Latitude 70° and the Antarctic Circle.
- **1776** Cook sets sail on his third voyage. Its main purpose was to find a route through the Northwest Passage from west to east.
- **1779** Cook sails to the Society Islands (Hawaiian Islands) where he is killed.
- **1785** Jean François de la Pérouse leaves France in search of the Solomon Islands.
- **1788** De la Pérouse lands at Port Jackson, New South Wales, Australia.
- **1795** Mathew Flinders and George Bass make the first inland expedition from the east coast of Australia.
- **1801-2** Flinders carries out a survey of nearly all of the Australian coastline.
- **1828** Charles Sturt and Hamilton Hume cross the Blue Mountains, Australia.
- **1860** Robert Burke leads expedition from Melbourne to cross Australia from south to north.
- **1861** John Stuart leads second, rival expedition north across Australia from Adelaide.
- **1861** Death of Charles Gray, William Wills and Burke.
- **1862** Stuart returns south, having completed his crossing of Australia.

I n 1565 a Spanish monk called Andres de Urdaneta made the first crossing of the Pacific. His account of the journey led many people to believe that a great southern continent lay somewhere to the west of the tip of South America. In 1606 Pedro Fernandes de Quiros, a Portuguese captain working for Spain, reached land he believed to be that continent. He named it "Austrialia" (after the King of Spain who was also Archduke of Austria), but it was in fact one of the islands now called the New Hebrides.

Discovery of a new continent

By the end of the 16th century, the Dutch were a powerful trading nation. In 1606 a Dutch captain from Amsterdam, Willem Jantszoon, became the first European to reach Australia. He sailed into the Gulf of Carpentaria on the northern coast. In 1642, another Dutchman, Abel Tasman, sighted the island that is now called Tasmania. He named it Van Diemen's Land after the governor of his employers, the Dutch East India Company. Tasman went on to discover New Zealand, then stopped at Tonga and Fiji. After this, Dutch interest in exploration dwindled. It was more than a hundred years before Australia was further explored.

Captain Cook

James Cook was born in Yorkshire, England. The son of a farm labourer, he received a very limited education at the local school. He began work when he was 12, first in a shop, then with a shipping company. In 1756 he joined the navy as a sailor.

Cook was a very tall man, with a strong character and great intelligence. He was a gifted navigator and astronomer and in 1768 was appointed a lieutenant and given command of his first ship, the *Endeavour*.

James Cook (1728-79)

The fight against disease

In the 18th century an average of 60 out of every 100 seamen died on long voyages, 50 of them from disease. Cook tried to reduce illness by introducing rigid rules. The men had to bathe every day. Their clothing and bedding were aired twice a week and the ship was regularly fumigated.

Cook took large quantities of fresh fruit on board ship. This was to prevent scurvy, a disease caused by a lack of vitamin C and one of the main causes of death among sailors. He also ensured that fresh meat and vegetables were obtained wherever possible. These measures improved the health of the sailors.

The *Endeavour* was built in Whitby, Yorkshire. It was originally designed to deliver coal to ports along the British coast.

Officer's cabin.

The great cabin was where the captain and his officers met to talk and eat.

The captain's private cabin, where he slept and worked.

Surgeon's cabin. Throughout the journey, sailors suffered from various illnesses and injuries.

Storerooms. The supplies of food for the long journey were kept here.

The men and the mission

In keeping with the scientific spirit of the times, Cook's first mission was to take his ship to Tahiti to observe the planet Venus as it passed between the Earth and the sun in 1769. Travelling with him on this voyage were a naturalist, a botanist and two artists. Cook carried with him a sealed envelope, to be opened after the observations had been recorded. It contained secret orders to seek out the fifth continent, to allow the scientists to study the plants, animals and native peoples, and to claim the land for Britain.

The expedition reached the island of Tahiti in April 1769. The scientists made their observations of Venus on 3 June and set sail again ten days later. Two of the islanders went with them as guides to help the expedition explore smaller islands nearby.

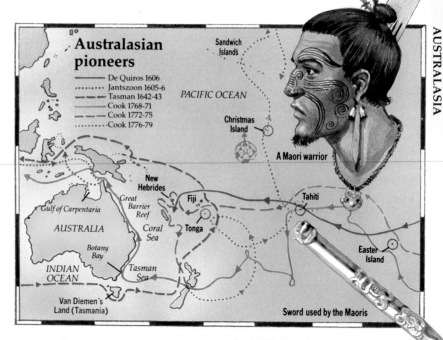

Australasian pioneers
— De Quiros 1606
···· Jantszoon 1605-6
— — Tasman 1642-43
— Cook 1768-71
— — Cook 1772-75
···· Cook 1776-79

PACIFIC OCEAN

Sandwich Islands
Christmas Island
A Maori warrior
New Hebrides
Great Barrier Reef
Gulf of Carpentaria
AUSTRALIA
Coral Sea
Fiji
Tonga
Tahiti
Easter Island
Botany Bay
INDIAN OCEAN
Tasman Sea
Van Diemen's Land (Tasmania)
Sword used by the Maoris

Breadfruit

Butterfly fish

The ships moved on to New Zealand, where they had a hostile reception from the Maoris. Fighting broke out and at one point the *Endeavour* was chased by about a hundred warriors in canoes.

Run aground

In April 1770 Cook landed at an inlet on the east coast of Australia. He named it Botany Bay after the many botanical specimens found there. Following the coast north, the ship was damaged when it ran into coral on the Great Barrier Reef. Once repairs were complete they set sail again and finally reached home in July 1771.

Cook's last voyages

Cook led two more expeditions, making further discoveries. The first set sail in two ships from Plymouth in July 1772. In January 1774 Cook and his crew crossed the Latitude 70°, the furthest south yet reached by Europeans, and visited Easter Island.

In 1779 Cook travelled to the Society Islands (now the Hawaiian Islands). At first the Hawaiians treated him like a god, but they soon grew tired of their visitors. Cook set sail but returned six days later when his ship, the *Resolution*, suffered storm damage. A fight broke out and Cook was stabbed to death.

Settlement of the continent

In January 1788, a French expedition under the command of a captain called Jean François de la Pérouse arrived in Australia. De la Pérouse intended to claim the country for the French, but he was too late. Only the day before, the British had established a colony there.

On Easter Island in the South Pacific Ocean there are giant stone heads, some 12m (40ft) tall.

Locker room. Sails were stored here, carefully folded.

Boatswain's quarters. Ropes, tackle, pulleys and various other pieces of equipment were kept here.

Storerooms. Powder and ammunition for the guns.

129

Into the interior

Australia's coastline was well-mapped by the end of the 18th century. For many years, however, the interior remained a mystery to all except the local inhabitants, the Aborigines. There were many theories about what lay on the other side of the Blue Mountains. Some believed the land there was rich, and fertile, but others thought it was desert or marshland.

Robert Burke
(1820-61)

William Wills
(1834-61)

Besides the glory of being first to cross the continent, there was a need to set up a telegraph line to link Australia to the rest of the world. The men who first ventured into the interior suffered dreadful hardships and some even lost their lives. The journey of Robert Burke and William Wills best illustrates the bravery, misery, bad judgement and terrible luck experienced by so many of these explorers.

In 1859 the government of South Australia offered a prize to the first person to cross the continent from south to north. Burke and Wills were appointed leader and surveyor of one of the most expensively equipped expeditions in Australia's history. But there was one fatal flaw. Neither Burke nor Wills had any knowledge of the outback or much experience of exploration.

Burke leading the expedition

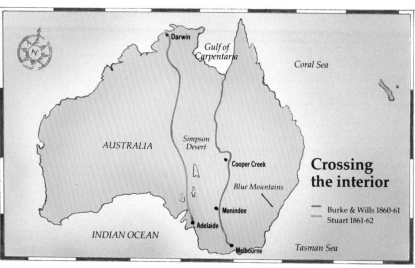

Crossing the interior

— Burke & Wills 1860-61
— Stuart 1861-62

The expedition sets out

The expedition left Melbourne in August 1860, cheered on its way by an enthusiastic crowd. Burke went first, followed by the other 15 members of his team and a long line consisting of 25 camels, 23 horses and wagons. After two months they had reached Menindee where they set up camp, but quarrels broke out among the men and Burke dismissed several of them. The expedition had now become very dispersed because of the varying speeds of parts of the team, with the wagons travelling long distances apart.

Hearing of a second, rival expedition, Burke became very impatient to move on. In scorching temperatures he, Wills and seven others set off for Cooper Creek, 645km (400 miles) northwest. The expedition was now divided into scattered groups. Once they arrived at Cooper Creek, Burke left one of the party, William Brahe, in charge of the remaining animals and provisions. Brahe was instructed to wait three months or until supplies ran out. Meanwhile Burke, Wills, Charles Gray and John King carried on to try and reach the Gulf of Carpentaria on the north coast.

Wildlife of the outback

The interior region of Australia is known as the outback. It contains many extraordinary plants and animals that are unknown elsewhere.

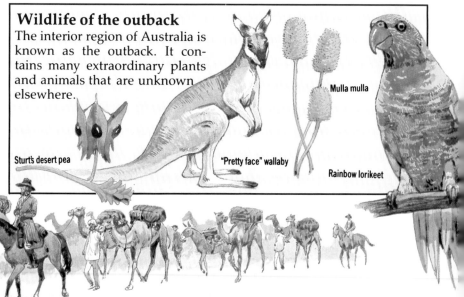

Sturt's desert pea

Mulla mulla

"Pretty face" wallaby

Rainbow lorikeet

Dead end

The weather suddenly changed and it rained endlessly for days. The ground became too waterlogged for the camels to move, so Burke and Wills went ahead on foot. By mid-February 1861 they were within sight of the shores of the gulf and could smell the sea. But their path was blocked by swamps of trees called mangroves and they decided to turn back.

The return journey

The journey south turned into a nightmare. Reunited with Gray and King, Burke and Wills headed back to Cooper Creek once more. Heavy rains fell for days on end, the men were soaked through to the skin and they became extremely feverish. The land turned into a quagmire of mud and slush. Food supplies were running so low that, one after another, the camels had to be shot for food and their baggage abandoned. Finally Gray, who seemed the strongest in the group, collapsed and died.

Aborigine

The deserted camp

Four days later, on 21 April, the three exhausted survivors staggered into Cooper Creek, hoping to find Brahe and the supplies waiting for them there. But instead they were horrified to find that the camp was deserted. They searched the place from top to bottom looking for supplies and eventually found a message left behind by Brahe. Believing they were dead, he had departed with the remaining animals for Menindee just seven hours before.

An Aboriginal bark painting

Instructions carved into a tree by Brahe.

Food and a message buried by Brahe.

Lost in the desert

Instead of trying to catch up with Brahe – unknown to them, he was only 23km (14 miles) away – Burke decided that they should return south by a shorter route towards Adelaide. They wandered in giant circles in the baking desert for weeks and ate the last of their camels. They were only saved from death because they were fed by some Aborigines who had been following them. The three exhausted men eventually found their way back to Cooper Creek.

To the Aborigines, the outback was a source of foods unknown to the explorers.

Witchetty grubs like this could be eaten raw.

The goanna (a type of lizard) could be captured and cooked.

By another incredible stroke of bad luck they had just missed Brahe once again. He had returned to Cooper Creek with a rescue party to look for them. But, seeing no sign that they had been anywhere near the camp, he moved on once more and headed back to Melbourne.

A tragic ending

Burke, Wills and King were only a few kilometres away, near to death. Their food had now completely run out and they began to slowly starve, growing weaker and weaker by the hour. King was the strongest and looked after the other two, doing as much as he could to help them. Wills was the first to die, followed by Burke some days later. King was now the only one left alive. Very weak himself, he staggered into the desert where he was looked after by some Aborigines living nearby. He was eventually found three months later by another search party from Melbourne. He was thin and burnt by the sun. Without the help of the Aborigines he would certainly have died. The remains of Burke and Wills were recovered and taken back to Melbourne for a state funeral.

Stuart wins the prize

Burke and Wills were the first to reach the north coast of Australia. But the first person to reach the coast and return alive was John McDouall Stuart. He was the leader of the rival expedition which left Adelaide in January 1861 in the race for the prize. This expedition arrived at the north coast seven months later. Burke, Wills and Stuart had proved that though much of the Australian interior was desert it was possible to travel across it.

John Stuart (1815-66)

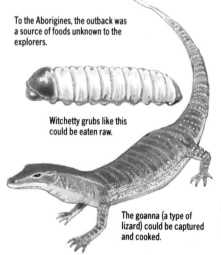

Burke, close to death, is looked after by King.

The forbidden land

AFRICA

Persian Gulf

Red Sea

Arabian Peninsula

INDIAN OCEAN

Key dates in Arabian exploration

● **c.1325** Ibn Battuta travels to Arabia.
● **1492** Pedro de Covilhã visits Mecca.
● **1503** Ludovico di Varthema visits Mecca.
● **1810** Johann Burckhardt visits Palmyra.
● **1812** Burckhardt enters Petra.
● **1813** Burckhardt rediscovers temple of Abu Simbel.
● **1814** Burckhardt visits Mecca.
● **1817** Burckhardt dies in Cairo.
● **1853** Richard Burton makes pilgrimage to Mecca.
● **1875** Charles Doughty reaches Palestine.
● **1876** Doughty explores northern Arabia.
● **1916** T.E. Lawrence (Lawrence of Arabia) explores Hejaz region in northern Arabia.
● **1930-31** Bertram Thomas crosses the Empty Quarter.
● **1932** Harry Philby crosses the Empty Quarter.

The Arabian Peninsula is surrounded on three sides by sea: the Persian Gulf, the Indian Ocean and the Red Sea. This made it a very important staging post on the trade routes from the Middle East, Africa, India and the Far East. Precious cargoes wound their way along the routes that criss-crossed the desert. Arabia also had valuable goods of its own to sell – incense, spices, drugs and perfumes, gold and precious stones. Because it was such a rich region, the Romans called it *Arabia Felix*, "Happy Arabia".

In contrast to the thin fertile strip along the south coast where rich kingdoms once flourished, further north the land rises steeply to a dry, barren region. Here nomadic tribes called Bedouin move flocks and herds between oases. In the centre of the peninsula are two fearsome deserts of shifting sand: to the north lies the Nefud while to the south lies the desolate Rub' al-Khali, the Empty Quarter.

A Bedouin encampment with tents made of goats' hair. ▼

An early adventurer

After the rise of Islam in the 7th century AD (see page 100), very few non-Muslims travelled in Arabia and the holy cities of Mecca and Medina were closed to all but Muslims. The first European to travel there after Covilhã's journey to Mecca in 1492 (see page 103) was a Venetian called Ludovico di Varthema. He arrived in Damascus in 1503 and set off disguised as a Muslim soldier in the pilgrim caravan to Mecca. He was the first non-Muslim to enter the Great Mosque and had many adventures before travelling on to India. He stayed there for some months before returning to Venice.

The rose-red city rediscovered

Johann Burckhardt was a Swiss scholar who had joined the Association for Promoting the Discovery of the Interior Parts of Africa (see page 104). He left for Africa via Syria, which he reached in 1809. He stayed in Aleppo for three years, learning Arabic and Islamic law.

The Khaznet Firaun (Pharaoh's Treasury) at the ▶ entrance into Petra.

On his way to Cairo in 1812, Burckhardt travelled through deserts and mountains to the remains of the fabulously rich city of Petra. This had been the capital of the merchant kingdom of the Nabataeans, who flourished from the 3rd to 1st centuries BC. Burckhardt was the first European to visit the city for over 1,500 years. He gazed on the Khaznet, a fantastic building carved from the pink-gold rock. Spellbound, he walked through the winding valley between elaborate tombs, temples and chapels, carved into the mountainsides and piled one above the other.

Johann Burckhardt (1784-1817)

Burckhardt reached Cairo and then travelled down the Nile Valley, stopping at the huge temple cut into the rock at Abu Simbel. He crossed the Red Sea to Jeddah and then visited Mecca, journeyed north through Arabia and arrived back in Cairo in 1815. Here he started to write up a report of his journeys. However, he died there two years later before he could continue his journey down into Africa.

El Haj Abdullah

In 1853 Richard Burton (see page 106) set sail from Suez in a pilgrim ship bound for Yenbo on the Red Sea coast. He went disguised as an Afghan doctor called El Haj Abdullah. The journey was chaotic, with fights breaking out among the pilgrims because of the lack of space. At the end of January they reached Medina where Burton stayed until August, writing an account of the city and its holy shrines.

Moving on, by the end of September he had arrived at the gates of Mecca. He prepared himself for entry into the city, shaving his head and donning the special white cotton pilgrim's robe. Inside the city, he took part in the holy ceremonies with hundreds of other pilgrims.

Burton had originally planned to cross the Arabian Peninsula from the west to the east coast. But, exhausted by the heat, he finally left Mecca at the end of the month and set sail for India.

Burton disguised as an Arab doctor.

A traveller's masterpiece

Charles Doughty (1843-1926)

Although Charles Doughty spent less than two years in just a small part of Arabia, he is now regarded as one of the greatest explorers of the region. During his travels he made no attempt to disguise the fact that he was a Christian European, even though it was still dangerous for non-Muslims to travel in Arabia.

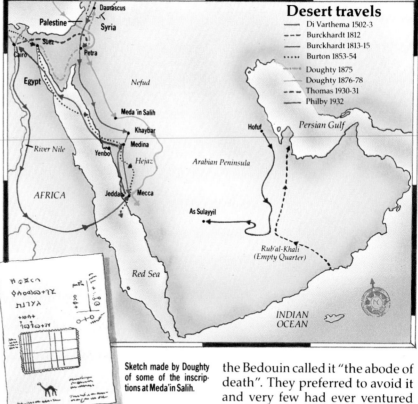

Desert travels

——	Di Varthema 1502-3
- - -	Burckhardt 1812
····	Burckhardt 1813-15
·····	Burton 1853-54
········	Doughty 1875
———	Doughty 1876-78
- - -	Thomas 1930-31
——	Philby 1932

Sketch made by Doughty of some of the inscriptions at Meda'in Salih.

In 1875 he sailed to Palestine and by November 1876 he was in northern Arabia, studying the monuments at Meda'in Salih. Like those at Petra, they were cut into the mountains and decorated with ancient inscriptions. He travelled along the edges of the Nefud Desert with his Bedouin companions, making careful observations of their customs and the countryside they crossed.

At times Doughty was thrown out of towns because he was a Christian, but on other occasions he was warmly welcomed. In 1878 he returned to England and spent the following ten years writing one of the greatest works of travel literature, entitled *Travels in Arabia Deserta*.

Crossing the Empty Quarter

There remained one last little-known area of Arabia, the treacherous Rub' al-Khali Desert or Empty Quarter. This desert is so vast and forbidding that even the Bedouin called it "the abode of death". They preferred to avoid it and very few had ever ventured inside the baking wilderness.

This great sea of sand was finally conquered in the winter of 1930-31 when Bertram Thomas, an Englishman who was acting as adviser to the Sultan of Muscat, crossed the desert from south to north. The following year another Englishman called Harry St John Philby crossed the desert from east to west, travelling 3,000km (1,864 miles) over the burning sand in just 90 days.

Philby in Arabic dress.

Philby and his travelling companions in the Empty Quarter.

Around the world

People still sail round the world as a test of skill and endurance. But the first people to circumnavigate the globe had very practical reasons for their travels: trade and colonization.

Key dates in circumnavigation

- **Sept. 1519** Magellan leaves Spain.
- **Oct. 1520** Magellan travels through Straits of Magellan.
- **March 1521** Death of Magellan.
- **Sept. 1522** Remaining crew return to Spain.
- **Dec. 1577** Drake sets sail round the world.
- **Nov. 1580** Drake returns to England.

Western Europe and West Africa are shown twice on the map below. This is so that the routes around the world described on these pages can be shown clearly.

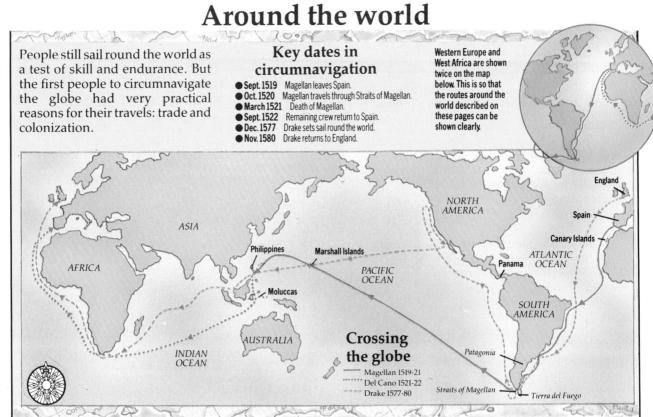

Crossing the globe

——— Magellan 1519-21
·········· Del Cano 1521-22
- - - - Drake 1577-80

Ferdinand Magellan (c.1480-1521)

The first circumnavigation of the globe was led by a Portuguese aristocrat called Ferdinand Magellan. He had already made several journeys to find trade routes for the Portuguese, but he quarrelled with the king and went to sea for the Spanish instead. The Spanish wanted to establish trade routes to the East and claim territory there, particularly the Moluccas (Spice Islands). Magellan believed he could reach the Moluccas by sailing west round the southern tip of America, instead of following the Portuguese sea routes to the East around Africa (see page 114). Only two months after Magellan's arrival at the Spanish court, the young King Charles of Spain (later Emperor Charles V) agreed to finance the scheme.

The fleet sets sail

In September 1519 Magellan left Spain with 260 men and five ships: the *Trinidad*, the *Vittoria*, the *Santiago*, the *Concepción*, and the *San Antonio*. They were carrying plenty of trading goods, but Magellan had underestimated the length of the voyage and did not take enough food and supplies. The fleet crossed the Atlantic, briefly stopping at the Canary Islands first. Then they sailed to Brazil and down the east coast of South America.

A mutiny and a shipwreck

Magellan encountered many problems. The weather was so bad that he decided to land for the winter on the coast of what is now

The Vittoria

Patagonia. Some of his men rebelled because of short rations and bitter cold, and he had to suppress the mutiny by executing the leaders. Later, the Santiago was shipwrecked.

The remaining ships finally found a route to the Pacific through a narrow sea passage now called the Straits of Magellan. From the ships, the crew saw fires that the natives had lit on the shore, so they named the area Tierra del Fuego ("land of fire"). Magellan's discovery of the straits named after him proved that there was another way to the East: to the south of the Americas.

Tierra del Fuego as it might have looked from the sea.

The starving sailors ate rats, animal hide and mouldy biscuits.

Disease, starvation, death

By this time conditions were worse. The *San Antonio's* crew deserted, sailing away with most of the fleet's food. Twenty men on the other ships starved to death as they crossed the Pacific.

After loading up with supplies at the Marshall Islands, the fleet continued to the Philippines. Here tragedy struck. Magellan became involved in a quarrel between local chiefs. He and 40 of his men were killed.

Magellan's successor

A captain called Sebastian del Cano took command of the 115 survivors. Without enough men to crew three ships, he abandoned the *Concepción*. The other ships sailed on, reached the Moluccas in November 1521, and bought the spices they set out for.

To improve the chance of getting at least some of the cargo home, the ships took two different routes back to Spain. The *Trinidad* went east towards the Spanish territory of Panama, but was seized by the Portuguese. Few of its crew survived.

A single ship returns

The *Vittoria* went westwards. It crossed Portuguese trade routes in the Indian Ocean and rounded the southern cape of Africa. It managed to avoid being captured, and reached Spain in 1522, having sailed round the globe in three years.

Francis Drake

The second great voyage of circumnavigation was led by an Englishman called Francis Drake. His voyage lasted from 1577 to 1580. At that time many people believed that Tierra del Fuego was part of a huge southern continent which they called Terra Australis. Others said the area was an island. Elizabeth I, the Queen of England, sent Drake to sail down the Straits of Magellan to find out which of these beliefs was true.

Francis Drake (c.1545-1596)

She also secretly expected him to bring back a good haul of treasure and spices. Both of them knew, however, that this would involve piracy and could damage relations between England and Spain. The expedition set sail in five ships: the *Pelican*, the *Marigold*, the *Elizabeth*, the *Swan* and the *Christopher*.

Drake plundered gold, silver, pearls and emeralds from Spanish ships.

Like Magellan, Drake suffered many hardships on his voyage. Storms, starvation and sickness provoked mutinies among his crew, but he pressed on through the straits. He did not find Terra Australis, but he did establish that Tierra del Fuego was an island. Drake returned to England on 3 November 1580. Queen Elizabeth visited him on board ship and knighted him.

Pigafetta's chronicle

Two pages from Antonio Pigafetta's account of Magellan's voyage.

This sand shark is probably the type Pigafetta saw.

One survivor of the voyage was an Italian sailor called Antonio Pigafetta. Most of our information about the journeys of Magellan and del Cano comes from his journal, which was published two years after his return. His account gives us many fascinating details of things he saw on his travels. These include man-eating sharks in the South Atlantic and a natural electrical phenomenon known as St Elmo's Fire. He recorded the terrible conditions the men endured, the cold and storms. He described the poor food and the stinking water they had to drink. He also wrote about the different people they encountered.

St Elmo's Fire made the ship's mast look as if it was burning.

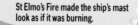

The race for the Poles

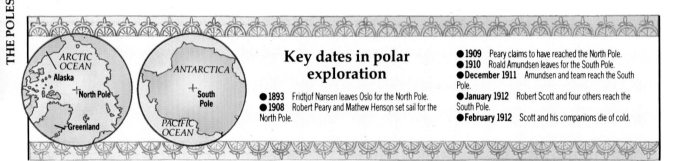

Key dates in polar exploration

- **1893** Fridtjof Nansen leaves Oslo for the North Pole.
- **1908** Robert Peary and Mathew Henson set sail for the North Pole.

- **1909** Peary claims to have reached the North Pole.
- **1910** Roald Amundsen leaves for the South Pole.
- **December 1911** Amundsen and team reach the South Pole.
- **January 1912** Robert Scott and four others reach the South Pole.
- **February 1912** Scott and his companions die of cold.

The North Pole lies in the Arctic Ocean and the South Pole in the continent of Antarctica. They are the most hostile extremities of the Earth. By the end of the 19th century much of the world had been explored but the frozen polar wastes remained largely unknown. A number of determined explorers, however, set their sights on becoming the first to reach the Poles. It was a dangerous race and many people died in the attempt to win it.

The great Norwegian

One of the greatest of the Arctic explorers was a Norwegian called Fridtjof Nansen. For his journey to the North Pole, Nansen planned to use the drift of the ice in the Arctic Ocean to carry his ship along, rather than try and force a way through it. He designed a ship called the *Fram* ("Forward") that could withstand the pressure of the ice and drift with it until the spring thaw.

Fridtjof Nansen (1861-1930)

Nansen and his crew of 13 set sail for the North Pole from Oslo in June 1893. In September the *Fram* became locked into the

Arctic ice. From then on the boat had to go wherever it was carried.

The movement of the ice was terribly slow. They drifted for months, but instead of being drawn across the North Pole they began to move west. So Nansen and one other team member set off for the Pole with dogs, sledges and two kayaks (canoes). 386km (240 miles) from the Pole they turned back as the ice was beginning to break up with the onset of spring.

By pure luck they were later discovered by an English team on Franz Josef Land and travelled back with them by ship to Norway. The *Fram* arrived safely back with the others a week later.

Peary's claim

In 1886, Robert Peary of the United States Navy made the first of many expeditions to the Arctic. On this and five later journeys he travelled to Greenland, each time edging closer to the North Pole.

In July 1908 Peary and his assistant Mathew Henson set sail for their goal in the *Roosevelt*. At Etah in Greenland they recruited 50 Inuit (the local inhabitants) and gathered 250 dogs. In February 1909 the expedition moved off, with teams of Inuit setting up bases, and Peary, Henson and the dogs following.

Peary and his team struggling over the ice and snow.

Gradually each team was sent back until only Peary, Henson and four Inuit, five sledges and 40 dogs were left. With the North Pole 214km (133 miles) away, this group set off on the final leg of the journey. It battled through blizzards, over ice ridges and perilous stretches of water.

On 5 April 1909 Peary recorded in his diary "The Pole at last!" believing he had finally reached his goal. However, experts raised doubts about whether he could have covered the distance so quickly. Despite recent attempts to prove that Peary did indeed reach the North Pole, the evidence remains questionable.

Seals at the North Pole.

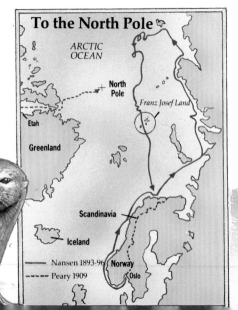

To the North Pole

Nansen 1893-96
Peary 1909

The *Fram* in the ice.

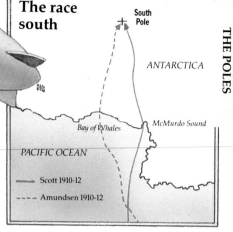

The triumph

In August 1910 a Norwegian explorer called Roald Amundsen set sail from Norway with eight others in Nansen's boat, the *Fram*. He originally planned to head for the North Pole, but hearing that Peary had reached it he decided to aim for the South Pole instead.

He was now entering a race against a British team that had already left for the South Pole led by Robert Scott, a captain in the Royal Navy. He sent Scott a telegram warning him that he now had competition. Although he had to contend with the same appalling conditions as Scott did, Amundsen's expedition was much more efficient. It had fewer men so it could travel faster. Amundsen's men also wore lighter but warmer Inuit-style clothing. They arrived at the Bay of Whales in January 1911 and set up camp at a point on the coast 97km (60 miles) nearer the Pole than Scott's camp. They struggled through blizzards with their dog sledges, and reached the South Pole on 14 December 1911. After remaining there for three days they headed back to their base camp, which they reached on 25 January 1912.

Roald Amundsen dressed in his special Antarctic clothing.

Amundsen and his team were able to travel more quickly because they were using light, fast husky dogs rather than heavy horses.

Later, in 1926, Amundsen became the first person to reach both Poles. He was a passenger on the airship *Norge* when it flew over the North Pole.

The *Norge*

The tragedy

Two months before Amundsen, on 1 June 1910, Robert Scott set sail for the South Pole in the *Terra Nova* with a team of 53 men. The expedition was carefully planned and lavishly equipped, but the choice of equipment was to lead to a tragic ending: scientific machinery was to slow the team down; their clothes would prove inadequate against the bitter cold; horses were brought along to pull the sledges, rather than the lighter and faster husky dogs used by Amundsen, which were better suited to the terrible environment.

After a slow journey through the pack ice, their ship finally reached McMurdo Sound where they established their base camp.

Adélie penguins at the South Pole.

In January 1912 Scott set out on the last stretch with Lawrence Oates, Edward Wilson, Edgar Evans and Henry "Birdie" Bowers. The progress of this smaller team became slower and slower and eventually the horses had to be shot because they got stuck in the snow. The men now had to haul the sledges along themselves. On 18 January the exhausted team finally reached the South Pole, only to find the Norwegian flag flying there already.

The race south

ANTARCTICA

South Pole

Bay of Whales

McMurdo Sound

PACIFIC OCEAN

——— Scott 1910-12

- - - - Amundsen 1910-12

Scott's team at the South Pole.

Disheartened, the men began the return journey to McMurdo Sound. But they were exhausted and frostbitten. With 692km (430 miles) to go, Evans collapsed and died. They eventually reached one of their depots, to find that the stored fuel oil had leaked away. There was now nothing to burn to keep them warm.

One night Oates, believing that he was holding up the team because he was so ill, walked out of their tent into the blizzard and was never seen again. His sacrifice was in vain for within two weeks the three remaining members were also dead. Their frozen bodies were found by a search party eight months later.

The roof of the world

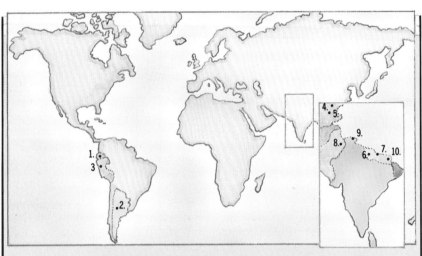

Key dates in mountain conquest

This chart lists ten of the world's highest mountains, in order of the date each one was first climbed. Each entry gives: the mountain's name and location; its height, the year of the expedition; the name and nationality of the expedition leader. The location of each peak is shown on the maps above.

1. Chimborazo, Ecuador; 6,267m (20,561ft). 1880, Whymper of Britain.
2. Aconcagua, Argentina; 6,960m (22,834ft). 1897, Zurbriggen of Switzerland.
3. Huascaran, Peru; 6,768m (22,205ft). 1908, Annie Peck of USA.
4. Lenin Peak, USSR; 7,134m (23,405ft). 1928, Soviet-German team led by Rickmers.
5. Communism Peak, USSR; 7,495m (24,590ft). 1933, Abalakov of USSR.
6. Annapurna, Nepal; 8,078m (26,504ft). 1950, French party led by Herzog.
7. Mount Everest, Nepal/Tibet; 8,848m (29,028ft). 1953, British party led by Hunt.
8. Nanga Parbat, Pakistan; 8,126m (26,660ft). 1953, Austro-German party led by Herrligkoffer.
9. K2 (Mount Godwin Austen), India; 8,611m (28,251ft). 1954, Desio, Lacedelli and Campagnoni of Italy.
10. Kangchenjunga, Nepal/Sikkim; 8,598m (28,208ft). 1955, Brown, Band, Streather and Hardie of Britain.

Since the very earliest times mountains have been regarded with awe and wonder. The peaks and summits were once believed to be the homes of gods and the cracks and crevasses the dwelling places of imps and demons. Howling winds echoed the eerie calls of the spirits and crashing avalanches warned people to keep away. Mountains such as Popocatepetl in Mexico and Mount Olympus in Greece have been worshipped as sacred places.

The earliest known climbs

For thousands of years people have feared mountains. It is only in the last 200 years that they have begun climbing them. Only a few genuine climbs are known to have been made in ancient times. In 350BC King Philip of Macedon climbed a mountain in the Balkans, and in about AD120 the Roman emperor Hadrian climbed Mount Etna to watch the sunrise.

Emperor Hadrian (AD76-138)

At the start of the Renaissance in Europe in the 14th century, people began to take a more scientific approach to their surroundings. Mountains were looked at in a different way, as places of interest rather than fear. The first known climb in the Alps took place on 26 April 1336 when the Italian poet Petrarch climbed Mont Ventoux (1,909m/6,263ft).

Petrarch (1304-74)

At first climbing was dangerous, for proper equipment was virtually non-existent. People simply wore warmer versions of everyday clothes. It was not possible to climb the highest peaks until suitable oxygen apparatus became available, because the higher a climber gets, the less oxygen there is in the air. This makes breathing very difficult. But as the years passed and experience increased, techniques were perfected and the equipment was improved. Mountaineers became able to climb higher and higher.

Modern mountaineering

Mountaineering as we know it today was developed by a Swiss scientist called Horace de Saussure. He was fascinated by the plants and rocks of the Alps, and in 1773 he made the first of many trips to the region. Gradually he became obsessed with the idea of climbing Mont Blanc, Europe's highest mountain at 4,807m (15,771ft), and offered a reward to the first person who could find a route to the top.

A plant from the Alps, Pygmy Ranunculus.

Early climbers caught in an avalanche.

Many attempts were made but they were repeatedly driven back by avalanches, steep walls of ice and deep crevasses. One local doctor called Michel Paccard tried a number of times. On 7 August 1786 he set out once more, with a deer-hunter called Jacques Balmat acting as his guide. They reached the top of the lower slopes and spent the night there. The following morning they continued their hazardous journey up slippery

Michel Paccard
Jacques Balmat

peaks, over jagged edges and wading through waist-deep snow drifts; they finally reached the summit the same evening.

The following year, Saussure himself fulfilled his ambition by climbing to the top of Mont Blanc. 18 others went with him and they opened bottles of wine at the top to celebrate the achievement.

Saussure's climbing shoes

A climbing expedition in the late 18th century. Their clothing was unsuitable for the terrain and cold.

The highest of all

No other mountain chain compares with the Himalayas. It contains the highest peaks in the world and stretches for thousands of miles across the length of northern India, and covers much of Sikkim, Nepal, Bhutan and southern Tibet.

In 1953 a British expedition led by John Hunt set off to climb Mount Everest, named after a British surveyor-general of India called Sir George Everest, but known locally as Chomolungma ("Mother Goddess of the World"). It is the world's highest mountain at 8,848m (29,028ft).

The climb to the final summit was made by the New Zealander Edmund Hillary and Tenzing Norgay of Nepal. On 29 May the weather cleared and they set off at 6:30am. On the way up their oxygen cylinders froze and there was a danger that they would not have enough oxygen. The going was extremely slow and they could only cover 0.3m (1ft) a minute.

The final obstacle was a sheer pinnacle of rock, 12m (40ft) high and covered with ice. Their route seemed to be blocked, but Hillary eventually found a way over it and edged himself up to the top. He then threw down a rope to Tenzing and at 11:30am on 29 May 1953, the two mountaineers stood alone at the top of the world.

The highest mountain in the world may have been conquered but many challenges still remain, including hundreds more peaks in the Himalayas and in other parts of the world. The urge to climb is as great as ever, spurred by the challenge, the thrill and glory of conquest and a deep respect for the mountains themselves.

Tenzing at the top of Everest

Hidden kingdoms of the Himalayas

After China broke off contacts with the West (see page 111) it once more became a land of mystery. But if China was remote, Tibet and Nepal, hidden away in the mountain fortress of the Himalayas, were even more inaccessible. In 1661 two Jesuit missionaries called John Grueber and Albert d'Orville became the first Europeans to reach Lhasa, the capital of Tibet. In 1811 a British official called Thomas Manning travelled in disguise to Lhasa, where he was received by the seven-year-old Dalai Lama (religious ruler) in the Potala Palace.

In the 1860s a French priest called Père (Father) David travelled extensively in Asia and China. He brought three animals to the attention of naturalists in the West: an unusual deer later named after him, a monkey named Roxellana's snub-nosed langur, and the giant panda.

Giant panda

Snub-nosed langur

Potala Palace, Lhasa

Père David's deer

Exploring the oceans

Key dates in undersea exploration

- **1690** Edmund Halley invents a method of pumping air down to diving machines.
- **1872** HMS *Challenger* starts its journey of exploration.
- **1930** William Beebe designs the bathysphere.
- **1943** Jacques Cousteau and Emile Gagnan design the aqualung.
- **1948** Auguste Piccard designs the bathyscape, *FNRS3*.
- **1950** *Challenger II* starts its journey of exploration.
- **1960** Jacques Piccard descends in the *Trieste*.

Nearly three quarters of the surface of the Earth is covered by water. For centuries people have been diving for precious underwater products such as pearls and natural sponges. But until the 20th century very little exploration had been made beneath the seas. This was because breathing apparatus was not available. Without it, divers could only stay below the water for as long as they could hold their breath.

Early diving devices

It is thought that in the 4th century BC Alexander the Great was lowered to the sea bed in a glass container to make observations. But he would probably have had to remain in shallow water because of the lack of air. It was not until 1690 that a method of pumping air down a pipe was invented, by an Englishman called Edmund Halley.

Halley's diving bell.

Going deeper

The deeper a diver goes in the sea, the greater the pressure of the water. In 1930 a North American called William Beebe designed the bathysphere, a spherical diving machine. Water exerts equal force all around a sphere, so it is able to withstand pressure at deep levels.

A modern bathy-sphere

In 1948 a Swiss scientist called Auguste Piccard designed a diving ship called a bathyscape. Known as *FNRS3*, it could dive and surface without having to be lowered and pulled up by a ship. On its first dive it reached a depth of 3,140m (10,300ft).

In 1960 Auguste's son Jacques Piccard descended nearly 11.25km (7 miles) in a craft called the *Trieste*. He reached the bottom

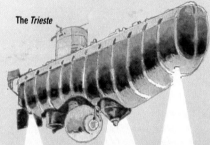

The *Trieste*

of the Mariana Trench in the Pacific Ocean. The journey down to the sea-floor took five hours.

Extra lungs

In 1943 two Frenchmen, Jacques Cousteau and Emile Gagnan, designed the first aqualung.

The aqualung consists of air cylinders containing compressed air and a mouth-piece. A "demand regulator" feeds the diver with exactly the amount of compressed air needed.

This invention opened a new period of underwater exploration and with its help many exciting discoveries have

Jacques Cousteau (1910-)

been made. Divers became able to descend to depths of 60m (200ft) without having to wear heavy protective suits and air cables. They were free to swim around and study underwater archaeology. They could photograph marine life, and also search for deposits of oil, tin, diamonds and other minerals.

A diver using an underwater "scooter".

The *Challenger* expeditions

In December 1872 a British ship, HMS *Challenger*, set sail under the command of George Nares. There were many leading scientists on board, led by a Scottish naturalist called Charles Thomson, and many cabins were converted into laboratories. It covered a distance of nearly 112,650km (70,000 miles) across the Atlantic, Indian and Pacific oceans. Measurements down to the sea bed were made to determine its contours, and currents and weather conditions were measured. The ship returned to England in May 1876, full of facts and figures and 4,417 species of fish and underwater plants.

In 1950 the *Challenger II* set out across the Atlantic, Indian and Pacific oceans and the Mediterranean Sea. The latest echo-sounding equipment was used to make accurate recordings of the ocean floors.

HMS *Challenger* setting out on its journey of three-and-a-half years.

Deep-sea red prawn

These types of fish are found at very

Beyond the Earth

Key dates in space exploration

- **1903** Konstantin Tsiolkovsky publishes theory of rocket propulsion, recommending the use of liquid fuels.
- **1926** Robert Goddard launches first liquid-fuel rocket.
- **1957** *Sputnik I* launched by the USSR.
- **1961** Yuri Gagarin becomes first person in space.
- **1969** Neil Armstrong and Edwin Aldrin become first people

on the Moon.
- **1971** *Salyut I*, the first space station, launched.
- **1977** Space Shuttle *Enterprise* makes first test flight.

Since the very earliest times the sun, the moon and the stars have always been objects of wonder and worship. Comets were believed to be warnings from the gods. Astronomy, the observation of the stars, is one of the oldest sciences. The ancient Egyptians were observing the planets thousands of years ago, and some people believe that Stonehenge in England, built in about 2500BC, was used as a giant observatory.

Early rockets

In order to travel in space, a rocket has to be powerful enough to break out of the pull of the Earth's gravity. In the 19th century a Russian scientist called Konstantin Tsiolkovsky made many experiments using liquid fuel. The first liquid-fuel rocket was launched in 1926 by an American called Robert Goddard. The flight lasted only 2.5 seconds but the break away from the Earth's atmosphere had been made. In October 1957 the Russians launched the first satellite into space, called *Sputnik I*.

Gird X, an early Russian rocket.

The first person in space

On 12 April 1961 a Russian astronaut called Yuri Gagarin became the first person to travel in space. His space-ship, *Vostok I*,

Vostok I

Yuri Gagarin (1934-68)

travelled at a speed of 8km (5 miles) a second, 160km (100 miles) above the Earth. Through his porthole, Gagarin

Telescopes

The first telescopes were invented in the 17th century. They enabled people to look at the moon and stars in more detail. The Italian scientist Galileo Galilei designed a stronger telescope. He was using it in 1610 when he discovered Jupiter's satellites, sunspots and mountains and craters on the Moon. Today, radio telescopes are used to detect radio waves coming from stars millions of light years away in space. These machines have discovered distant galaxies and strange objects like pulsating stars and black holes.

Galileo's telescope

The space telescope is designed to detect objects seven times further away than anything which can be seen from earth.

could see the world's surface laid out below him. *Vostok I* sped once round the Earth and after 108 minutes Gagarin returned, the cabin section of the spacecraft floating down on a parachute.

Exploring the moon

Tragically, Gagarin was killed in an air crash in 1968, before he could achieve his aim of being the first person on the moon. But his pioneering flights paved the way for Neil Armstrong and Edwin "Buzz" Aldrin of the United States to step out of their *Apollo* lunar module on to the surface of the moon on 21 July 1969. They took samples of rock and set up scientific equipment before returning to Earth.

One more manned lunar landing took place in 1969, two in 1971 and two in 1972. In 1970 and 1973 the Russians sent two unmanned vehicles called *lunokhods* to explore the surface of the moon.

The Apollo 11 lunar module on the moon.

Space stations and probes

During the 1970s giant space stations, such as the Russian *Salyut* and American *Skylab*, were launched into space. They were laboratories orbiting round Earth and manned by crews who stayed aboard for a number of weeks on end without returning to Earth. One of the main purposes of these stations was to study the effect on people of long periods in space.

The US Skylab space station

Today space probes are sent to the more distant planets in the solar system. They carry cameras to take photographs and equipment to measure the temperature, magnetic fields and radiation of the planets. *Mariner 10* took about 4,300 close-up photographs of Mercury during three visits from 1974.

In the future

By the early 21st century people may be living in bases on the Moon. But we have only just started the exploration of space. So far, unmanned spacecraft have landed on only two other planets in the solar system (Venus & Mars).

Key dates in world exploration

Dates BC

c.1492BC Queen Hatshepsut of Egypt sends out a trading expedition to the land of Punt.

c.600BC Pharaoh Necho II of Egypt sends out an expedition to explore the coasts of Africa.

c.450BC Herodotus draws a map of the world.

327-23BC Alexander the Great and his armies expand east from Persia.

c.300BC Building of the Great Wall of China begins.

138BC Chang Ch'ien leaves on a journey to Yuechi, China .

126BC Chang Ch'ien returns to China.

c.105BC Opening of the Silk Road, from China to the West.

Dates AD

AD150 Ptolemy draws his map of the world.

245 Chinese ambassadors travel to Funan (Cambodia).

304 Hsiung-nu (Huns) invade China.

629 Hsuan-tsang leaves China for India.

632 Death of the Prophet Mohammed, founder of Islam.

645 Hsuan-tsang returns to China.

c.860 Chinese reach Somali, Africa.
Vikings settle in Iceland.

c.900 Gunnbjorn sights Greenland.

c.986 Viking colony established on Greenland by Eric the Red. Bjarni Herjolfsson sights North America.

c.1000 Leif Ericsson lands on east coast of North America.

1002 Thorwald, brother of Leif, establishes a colony on the east coast.

1060 Chinese reach Malindi, Africa.

1162 Birth of Genghis Khan, later ruler of Mongols.

1187 Chinese reach Zanzibar and Madagascar, off the east coast of Africa.

1215 Genghis Khan captures Chung-tu (Beijing), capital of Chinese Chin empire, and establishes Mongol rule.

1240 Mongols capture Kiev, Russia.

1246 Giovanni da Pian del Carpini reaches the Mongol capital at Karakorum.

1253 William of Rubrouck sent to Karakorum.

1260 Kublai Khan proclaimed Great Khan.

1265 Niccolo and Maffeo Polo first reach the Chinese capital at Khanbalik (Beijing).

1269 Niccolo and Maffeo Polo return to Venice.

1271 Niccolo, Maffeo and Marco Polo leave Venice for China.

1292 The Polos leave China for home.

1325 Ibn Battuta travels to Arabia.

1368 The Mongols are driven out of China.

1394 Birth of Prince Henry of Portugal "the Navigator".

1405-33 Voyages of Cheng Ho in the Indian Ocean.

c.1420 The Chinese are believed to have rounded the Cape of Good Hope, Africa.

1434 Gil Eannes rounds Cape Bojador, West Africa.

1487 Bartolemeu Dias rounds the Cape of Good Hope. Pedro da Covilhã and Alfonso de Paiva set out from Portugal on their journeys East.

1492 Pedro da Covilhã visits Mecca.
Christopher Columbus leaves Spain for the East. He reaches and explores the "Indies".

1497 Vasco da Gama sails round Africa on his way to India.

1498 Da Gama visits Calicut.

1499 Da Gama returns to Portugal.

1503 Ludovico di Varthema visits Mecca.

1507 America is named after Amerigo Vespucci.

1511 Diego Velazquez and Hernándo Cortés sieze Cuba for Spain.

1519 Cortés sails to Mexico. Ferdinand Magellan begins his journey round the world.

1521 Siege of Tenochtitlán and fall of the Aztec empire.

1534 Jacques Cartier leaves France for North America.

1535 Cartier founds Montreal.

1569 Andres de Urdaneta crosses the Pacific.

1576 Martin Frobisher leaves England on his first voyage to find the Northwest Passage.

1577 Francis Drake sets sail round the world.

1585-87 John Davis makes three voyages to find the Northwest Passage.

1597 The Portuguese establish a trading station at Macao, China.

1606 Pedro Fernandes de Quiros reaches the New Hebrides Islands.
Willem Jantszoon becomes the first European to reach the shores of Australia.

1608 Samuel de Champlain founds Quebec.

1609 Henry Hudson sails along east coast of North America, in search of Northwest Passage.

1610 Hudson makes a second journey.

1642 Abel Tasman sights Van Diemen's Land (Tasmania). Tasman discovers the west coast of New Zealand.

1678-82 Robert de La Salle travels across North America.

1690 Edmund Halley invents a method of pumping air down to diving machines.

1700 William Dampier, an English pirate, discovers the north coast of New Guinea.

1721 Jakob Roggeveen discovers Easter Island.

1769 James Cook sails in the *Endeavour* to Tahiti and makes observations of Venus. Sails on to New Zealand.

1770 Cook lands in Botany Bay, Australia.

1772 Cook's second voyage leaves Plymouth.

1774 Cook crosses the Antarctic Circle.

1776 Cook sets sail on his third voyage, in search of the Northwest Passage.

1779 Cook sails to the Society Islands (Hawaiian Islands) where he is killed.

1785 François de la Pérouse leaves France in search of the Solomon Islands.

1788 De la Pérouse lands on the coast of New South Wales, Australia.

1795 Mungo Park sails to Africa.
Mathew Flinders and George Bass make the first inland expedition from the east coast of Australia.

1799 Alexander von Humboldt and Aimé Bonpland leave Europe for South America.

1801-2 Flinders carries out a survey of nearly all the coast of Australia.

1804 Meriwether Lewis and William Clark lead expedition across the United States.

1805 Park leaves on his second trip to Africa.

1810 Johann Burckhardt visits Palmyra, Syria.

1812 Burckhardt visits Petra, Palestine.

1813 Burckhardt rediscovers temple of Abu Simbel, Egypt.

1814 Burckhardt visits Mecca.

1817 Burckhardt dies in Cairo.

1824 René Caillié sets out from France for Timbuktu.

1828 Charles Sturt and Hamilton Hume cross the Blue Mountains, Australia.

1831 Charles Darwin leaves for South America in the *Beagle*.

1849 California Gold Rush.

1851 David Livingstone, his family and Cotton Oswell cross the Kalahari Desert, southern Africa.

1852-56 Livingstone becomes the first European to walk right across Africa.

1853 Richard Burton makes a pilgrimage to Mecca.

1856 Burton and John Speke leave England in search of the source of the Nile.

1858 Livingstone sets out to explore the Zambezi River.

1860 Robert Burke leads expedition from Melbourne to cross Australia from south to north.
Speke and James Grant leave on a second journey to Africa.

1861 John Stuart leads second, rival expedition to cross Australia, north from Adelaide.
Death of Charles Gray, William Wills and Burke.

1862 Stuart returns south, having completed crossing of Australia.

1871 Henry Morton Stanley and Livingstone meet at the village of Ujiji, Africa.

1872 Livingstone starts out on his final African jouney, round the southern shores of Lake Tanganyika.
HMS *Challenger* starts out on its journey of exploration in the Atlantic, Pacific and Indian oceans.

1874 Stanley returns to Africa to map lakes Victoria and Tanganyika.

1875 Charles Doughty reaches Palestine.

1876 Doughty explores in the Nefud, northern Arabia.

1876-77 Stanley sails down the Lualaba and Congo rivers to the Atlantic.

1880 Edward Whymper climbs Mt Chimborazo, Ecuador.

1887 Stanley leads expedition to Sudan to find Emin Pasha.

1893 Fridtjof Nansen sets sail from Oslo for the North Pole.

1897 Mathias Zurbriggen climbs Mt Aconcagua, Argentina.

1908 Robert Peary and Matthew Henson sail for the North Pole.
Annie Peck climbs to the top of Mt Huascaran, Peru.

1909 Peary claims to have reached the North Pole.

1910 Roald Amundsen and team leaves for the South Pole.

1911 Amundsen reaches the South Pole.

1912 Robert Scott and his team reach the South Pole.
Scott and team die of cold.

1916 T.E. Lawrence (Lawrence of Arabia) explores the Hejaz region in northern Arabia.

1925 Percy Fawcett disappears in the Brazilian jungle.

1926 Robert Goddard launches the first liquid-fuel rocket.

1930 William Beebe designs the bathysphere.

1930-31 Bertram Thomas crosses the Empty Quarter of Arabia.

1932 Harry Philby crosses the Empty Quarter.

1943 Jacques Cousteau and Emile Gagnan design the first aqualung.

1948 Auguste Piccard designs the bathyscape, *FNRS3*.

1950 *Challenger II* starts its journey of exploration.

1953 Edmund Hillary and Tenzing Norgay climb Mt Everest, Nepal/Tibet.

1957 *Sputnik I* launched by the USSR.

1960 Jacques Piccard descends to the bottom of the Pacific Ocean in the *Trieste*.

1961 Yuri Gagarin becomes the first person in space.

1969 Armstrong and Aldrin land on the Moon.

The *Explorers* quiz

The answers to all the following questions can be found between pages 99 and 141 of this book. You will also find the answers upside down at the bottom of this page.

AFRICA

1. How did Ibn Battuta protect himself from bandits in the Sahara Desert?
2. What was the name of the Christian priest-king for whom many explorers searched, but never found?
3. What was the prize offered by the Geographical Society of Paris to the first Frenchman to reach Timbuktu and return?
4. What happened to Livingstone's heart on his death?
5. Which lake was proved to be the source of the Nile?
6. Can you identify these countries by their shapes?

a)   b)   c)

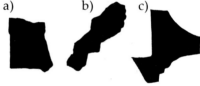

ASIA

7. What was the Silk Road?
8. How many elephants were there in the procession of King Harsha which was joined by Hsuan-tsang?
9. What causes scurvy, the disease which killed many early sailors?
10. How did Barents and his men exercise during the Arctic winter?
11. Who discovered the Northeast Passage?

THE AMERICAS

12. Why did Eric the Red choose the name Greenland for the country that he had discovered?
13. Who was the first European to set foot on American soil?
14. In the 15th century, what shape did most people believe the Earth to be?
15. Match the names of Columbus's three ships with the silhouettes below.

a)   b)   c)

16. Columbus reached America by mistake. Where was he originally heading on his journey?
17. After whom was America named?
18. How did the Aztec emperor Montezuma die?
19. What is another name for the iron pyrites rocks discovered by Frobisher?
20. What was the name given to the team of men led by Lewis and Clark?
21. What was the name given by Percy Fawcett to the lost city he hoped to find in the Brazilian jungle?

AUSTRALIA

22. What happened the day before a French expedition arrived in Australia to claim the country for France?
23. Where did Brahe leave his message for Burke and Wills?

ARABIA

24. The Romans called Arabia "Arabia Felix". What does it mean?
25. How did Richard Burton disguise himself on his journey from Suez to Mecca?

CIRCUMNAVIGATION

26. Name the five ships led by Magellan in his circumnavigation attempt.
27. What is the name of the natural electrical phenomenon recorded by Pigafetta?

THE POLES

28. What was the name of the ship used by both Nansen and Amundsen during their explorations?
29. Which member of Scott's team sacrificed his life because he believed he was holding up the expedition's progress?

MOUNTAINS

30. Can you identify these three explorers?

a)   b)   c)

31. What is the name of Europe's highest mountain?
32. Who were the first people to reach the summit of Mount Everest?

UNDER THE SEA

33. What is the name of the spherical diving machine designed by William Beebe?
34. Who designed the first aqualung?

SPACE

35. What was the name of the first satellite to be launched into space?
36. Who was the first person to travel in space?

Answers

1. He joined a caravan
2. Prester John
3. 10,000 francs
4. It was cut out and buried.
5. Lake Victoria
6. a) Egypt; b) Morocco; c) Mali
7. A trade route between China and the West
8. 20,000
9. A deficiency of Vitamin C.
10. They played golf on the ice.
11. Vitus Bering
12. He wanted other Vikings to follow him there and settle.
13. Leif Ericsson
14. Flat
15. a) *Niña*; b) *Santa María*; c) *Pinta*
16. The Far East
17. Amerigo Vespucci
18. He was stoned to death.
19. Fool's gold
20. The Corps of Discovery
21. Z
22. The British established a colony there.
23. In a bottle buried in the ground.
24. Happy Arabia
25. As an Afghan doctor
26. *Trinidad, Vittoria, Santiago, Concepción* and *San Antonio*
27. St. Elmo's fire
28. *Fram*
29. Lawrence Oates
30. a) Emperor Hadrian; b) Petrarch; c) Michel Paccard
31. Mount Blanc
32. Edmund Hillary and Tenzing Norgay
33. Bathysphere
34. Jacques Cousteau and Emile Gagnan
35. *Sputnik I*
36. Yuri Gagarin

144

KINGS & QUEENS

Philippa Wingate

History consultant: Dr Anne Millard

Designed by Russell Punter

Illustrated by Ross Watton, Peter Dennis,
Simon Roulstone and John Fox

Managing editor: Anthony Marks

Contents

Introduction

Amenhotep IV

Hippolyte

Shih Huang Ti

An Oba of Benin

Matilda

Henry VIII

What is a king or queen?

A king or a queen is the single ruler of a country or an independent state. Kings and queens are also known as monarchs, from the Greek for "single ruler".

Monarchs are given many different titles around the world. You will come across examples of many of them in this section of the book, including sultans and sultanas, rajas and ranis, tsars and tsarinas, pharaohs, khans, shahs and incas. Rulers who control lands so vast that they hold power over other monarchs are often given the title emperor or empress. Some kings and queens gain their title only because they are married to a ruling monarch.

Leadership, past and present

Since the earliest times, leaders have emerged among groups of people. At first they were chosen for their popularity, or their skill as warriors or hunters. Some ancient leaders were believed to have special powers that would bring their kingdoms good fortune. Later, in many countries, power was passed between the members of royal families, usually from father to son.

Today, many of the world's monarchies have disappeared. Most countries are ruled by presidents, elected heads of state who are voted into power for limited periods of time. Other countries are governed by dictators, who seize power and rule by military force.

A selection of monarchs are pictured on this page. You can find out about their lives and actions in this section of the book.

Montezuma

Elizabeth I

Louis XIV

Napoleon Bonaparte

Victoria

Elizabeth II

About Kings & Queens

This section of the book explores the lives of some of history's outstanding rulers. It examines how they worked and played, and how myths and mysteries grew up around them. It looks at the ceremonies and regalia which set monarchs apart from ordinary people. The people in this section are not arranged in historical order. They have been selected because their lives illustrate certain themes and topics.

Dates

Some of the dates mentioned in this part of the book are from the period before the birth of Christ. These dates are followed by the letters BC, which stand for "Before Christ". Dates in the BC period are counted backwards from the birth of Christ. For example, the period from 1-99BC is called the first century BC. Dates after the birth of Christ have no letters.

If historians are unsure exactly when an event occurred, the date is shown with a "c" in front of it. This stands for *circa*, which is the Latin for "about".

Acoronation is the ceremony at which the power and status of leadership is symbolically transferred to a new monarch. After the ceremony, the new ruler is set apart from ordinary people.

Choosing a monarch

When a monarch dies, a successor is immediately named. The rules of succession vary. In many societies, the monarch's eldest son inherits the throne. In some countries, a monarch chooses a successor from among all the adult male members of his family. In some places women are allowed to claim the crown if there are no suitable male heirs. Elsewhere, women are never allowed to rule in their own name.

Crowning a monarch

In most cultures the coronation ceremony includes some kind of religious blessing and the presentation of a crown to the new monarch.

The crowns of the Egyptian pharaohs

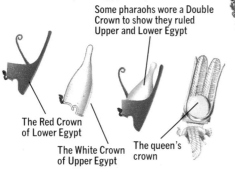

Some pharaohs wore a Double Crown to show they ruled Upper and Lower Egypt

The Red Crown of Lower Egypt

The White Crown of Upper Egypt

The queen's crown

Crowning an English monarch

The coronation ceremony of the kings and queens of England is one of the oldest state ceremonies in the world. Parts of it date back to the 8th century.

The pictures show stages of the coronation of Elizabeth II (b.1926), who was crowned Queen of Great Britain and Northern Ireland in 1953.

A selection of some of the surviving crowns from around the world.

(right) The Holy Roman Empire Crown was made for King Otto I of Germany in the 10th century.

(left) The Imperial Crown was made for Catherine the Great of Russia.

(right) This Kiani crown was made in 1789 for the coronation of Fath Ali, the Shah of Iran.

(left) This crown was made for Louis XVIII of France.

(right) The Emperor of Iran's crown was made in 1924 for the coronation of Reza Shah.

Enthroned

In early Germanic tribes, a new king was lifted up on a shield, supported by his warriors, so that he could be seen and acclaimed by his subjects. Ceremonies like this have now been replaced in many countries by a special chair or stool on which a monarch sits. The throne is usually placed on a mound or platform, so that the monarch is raised above the people.

A selection of famous thrones

This throne, found in the palace of Knossos, Crete, was probably used by the Minoan kings.

The throne of King Tutankhamun of Egypt is gold-plated and inlaid with semi-precious stones.

The Peacock Throne, used by the Shahs of Iran

The Coronation Chair, made in 1301 for Edward I of England.

Elizabeth II's coronation

The coach was built in 1761 for George III of England.

The coach is pulled by pairs of horses.

1. The procession – The queen arrives at Westminster Abbey in the state coach. She wears a robe of crimson velvet, trimmed with fur and bordered with gold lace and a diamond crown of precious stones.

2. The recognition – The archbishop introduces the queen to the people in the Abbey as the true monarch and they are asked to accept her.

Anointing the new leader

Today, many European Christian monarchs are anointed with holy oil during their coronation. They believe that this marks them as God's chosen representatives. The tradition was reintroduced by King Pepin of the Franks (c.715-68), who was the first king to be anointed with holy oil since the kings of ancient Israel. He felt he needed a special sign of divine approval for his reign.

This horn holds the oil used to anoint the new ruler of Sweden.

The oil is poured from this spout.

The gold horn is decorated with diamonds and rubies.

Regalia

Different cultures have various objects which are given to new monarchs at their coronation as symbols of their power. They are known as regalia, and include crowns, rods, staffs, scepters, orbs, rings, spurs and swords.

An African fly-whisk; a ceremonial sword of the ruler of the Akan (Africa); an Egyptian pharaoh's ceremonial crook

Stealing the crown jewels

During the reign of Charles II of England (1630-85), an Irish adventurer named Colonel Blood attempted to steal the crown jewels. Dressed as a clergyman, he visited the Jewel House in the Tower of London (see page 181) with a woman pretending to be his wife.

While looking at the regalia, the woman appeared to be taken ill. She was helped outside, giving Blood an opportunity to befriend the Jewel House keeper.

Blood stealing the crown jewels

One May morning, Blood returned with three men, and asked to see the regalia. The keeper took them into the Jewel House.

Blood beat the keeper over the head, seized the crown, sceptre and orb and, inexplicably, ran toward the farthest exit.

The thieves were stopped by the keeper's son. After a brief fight they were overpowered and arrested.

Blood was not punished. Charles II awarded him a pension and some land. Some people suspected the king had used Blood to steal the jewels, hoping to sell them to raise some much-needed money.

A new dragon king

In the fourth month of the Wood Tiger Year, at the Hour of the Serpent (June 2, 1974), Jigme Singye Wangchuck became King of Bhutan, known to its people as the Land of the Dragon. The coronation cost the country a fifth of its annual budget.

The king placed on his shoulders a shawl that belonged to his great-great grandfather, the first King of Bhutan. Only Bhutan's kings and spiritual leaders are allowed to touch it.

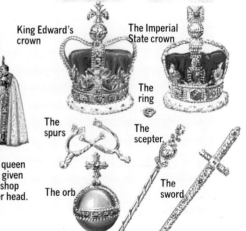

A dragon mask worn by a monk at the coronation

This diadem was worn by the queen before her coronation.

King Edward's crown

The Imperial State crown

The ring

The spurs

The scepter

The orb

The sword

3. The oath – The queen swears to maintain the laws and customs of the country and to defend the Church.

4. The anointing – The queen's robes are removed. Four knights hold a canopy over her. The archbishop uses holy oil to make the sign of a cross on her body.

5. The crowning – The queen is dressed in robes and given the regalia. The archbishop places the crown on her head.

Palaces

A palace is the home of the monarch and the royal family. Palaces are also used for state ceremonies, as meeting places for governments, and as holy places of religious worship. Here is a selection of some of the splendid palaces that have been built through the ages.

The hilltop palace of Masada

King Herod the Great (74-4 BC) built five great palaces. The most famous is Masada, a fortress-palace which stands on a rock 400m (1300ft) high above the Dead Sea.

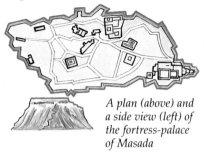

A plan (above) and a side view (left) of the fortress-palace of Masada

Masada was the scene of a tragic incident in 66. A group of Jews revolted against the Romans occupying Jerusalem. Some fled to Masada and resisted attack for three years. The Romans built a huge ramp to the top of the hill and thus were able to take the fortress. The Jews inside committed suicide rather than be taken captive.

Alhambra Palace, Spain

The Alhambra Palace, built on a hill above Granada in southern Spain, was the palace of Moorish kings. The Moors were Muslim warriors who invaded Spain from North Africa in the 8th century.

Pools of water cool the palace in the heat of summer.

The finest surviving example of Moorish architecture, the Alhambra was built in the 14th century by Yusuf I and Mohammed V. Its interiors are decorated with glazed tiles, geometric and floral patterns and scripts from the Koran.

Forbidden city

Some kings were considered too holy to be seen by ordinary people. They lived hidden behind palace walls. At different times, 24 emperors lived in the world's largest palace complex, the Forbidden City, in Beijing, China.

A Chinese illustration of part of the Forbidden City

Started in the 15th century during the reign of Emperor Yongle, the city took a million men 16 years to complete. It covers 72 hectares (177.9 acres) and has 8000 rooms, 17 palaces, halls, temples, libraries, courtyards and gardens.

The last Chinese emperor to live in the Forbidden City was Pu Yi (see page 177), who left the palace in 1924.

(see page 177)

The city is guarded by bronze lions.

A palace for the Sun King

The splendid Palace of Versailles, built outside Paris by Louis XIV (1638-1715), became the focus of French art and culture. Its design has been copied by other monarchs.

Louis was the most powerful of all the European kings at this time.

The picture below shows the Palace of Versailles and some of its main rooms.

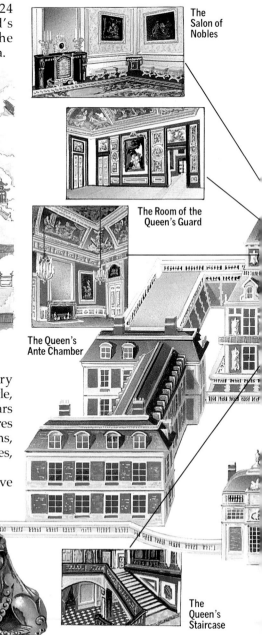

The Salon of Nobles

The Room of the Queen's Guard

The Queen's Ante Chamber

The Queen's Staircase

He reigned for 72 years, living a life of wealth and extravagance. He wanted to build a palace that reflected his glory. It took 47 years to complete Versailles, with its 1400 fountains and floors and walls of marble.

Louis XIV was known as the "Sun King"

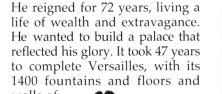

The Hall of Mirrors

Prinny and the Royal Pavilion

Palaces were often the product of a king's extravagant wishes. Prince George (1762-1830), who later became George IV of England, built the weird and wonderful Royal Pavilion.

Prinny, as he was known, loved Brighton, a small port on the south coast of England. He changed his villa there into a great palace

Prince George

called the Pavilion, which he filled with incredible furniture.

He threw extravagant parties there. At one meal, a stream with mossy banks, bridges and live goldfish, flowed down the middle of the table. When George became king in 1820, he was forced to abandon his palace and his carefree life and move back to London.

The Royal Pavilion at Brighton

Cutaway showing the banqueting hall

A dragon chandelier made of glass

Oriental-style decorations

Minarets and domes made the building look like an Eastern palace.

The facade of the Hall of Mirrors is 58m (63yds) long with 375 windows.

Over 1500 servants lived in the palace.

The kitchens were so far from the halls of State that meals were stone cold when they reached the king.

Louis XIV's bedroom

There were no toilets at the palace and only a few baths. Men and women covered themselves with perfume instead of bathing.

Room of the Bull's Eye

Home sweet home

Copy cat. The Maharajah of Kapurthala (1872-1949) built a copy of the palace of Versailles in the foothills of the Himalayas. He filled his palace with replica furniture, ornaments, a French chef and servants in 17th century costume.

A royal home. The largest residential palace belongs to the Sultan of Brunei. Completed in 1984, it cost approximately £300 million ($460 million) to build and has 1788 rooms, 257 toilets and a garage that can hold over 110 cars.

Fit for a king, a Rolls-Royce Corniche

People have always gathered around monarchs, attracted by their wealth and power. The home of a ruler is called a court, and the people who live there are called courtiers. Though courtiers live lives of luxury, they depend on the generosity of a monarch for their survival.

The role of a courtier

A variety of jobs were available at a royal court. But as the number of courtiers at some palaces grew, it was increasingly difficult to find them all roles. Louis XIV of France (1638-1715) had hundreds of courtiers and gave many of them meaningless tasks to perform.

Jobs at the court of Louis XIV

Many courtiers were required to help the king dress in the morning. The sole task of one man was to hold the royal coat.

The king's elaborate wig was curled and powdered by servants, but a courtier passed it to the king when he was dressing.

Another courtier attended every meal that the king ate so that he could pass him his napkin.

Sultan Abdul Aziz of Turkey (1830-76) had more than 5000 servants at his court. The only task of one man was to cut the Sultan's finger-nails when they grew too long.

Court rules

At most courts, there were strict rules outlining how courtiers should treat the royal family. At the court of the King of Siam, for instance, few people were allowed to touch the king and queen. So when a barge carrying Queen Sunanda (1860-81) overturned, the boatmen were not allowed to pull her out of the water. By the time someone of high enough rank to touch her arrived, she had drowned.

Following the fashion

Monarchs have often inspired fashions at court. Courtiers were able to flatter kings and queens by copying their appearance or style of dress.

As she grew older, Elizabeth I of England (1533-1603) wore thick white makeup on her face. Many of the women at the royal court followed her example. The white makeup contained lead, which eventually destroyed their skin.

This portrait of Elizabeth I shows many of the fashions she inspired.

Elizabeth wore thick white makeup.

The queen was famous for her red hair and high hair line.

Large ruff collars became very fashionable

During the 18th century, a hair-style known as the "pompadour" became very fashionable at the French court. It was inspired by a style worn by Louis XV's mistress, Madame de Pompadour, that became very exaggerated.

Constructing a "pompadour" hairstyle

Pads or cages were fixed on the top of the wearer's head.

The woman's hair, or false hair, was then smoothed over the cage. Sometimes it was covered in powder.

Hairstyles were decorated with ribbons, feathers, flowers and even fruit.

In 1778, there was a sea battle in which the ship *La Belle Poule* fought the English. French women wore model boats on their hair, with cannons, sails and flags.

A hairstyle inspired by La Belle Poule

Many women did not wash their hair for months, and they often found it full of lice or even mice.

Hairstyles reached great heights.

Courtly flattery

The position of a courtier was a vulnerable one, dependent on his or her popularity with the monarch. Some people were driven to great lengths of flattery to preserve their positions. In the 17th century, the Duc d'Antin supervised the building work at Versailles, near Paris. He deliberately had some of the statues in the palace gardens placed a little askew so that he could praise Louis XIV of France when he noticed the fault.

A statue from the gardens at Versailles

Maltreating the staff

Provoking the disapproval of a monarch could have terrible consequences for some courtiers. Empress Anna of Russia (1693-1740) forced three of her courtiers to live as hens for a week. Wearing feathers, they were put in "nesting boxes" in one of the main reception halls of the palace.

Empress Anna punishes Michael Golitsin

When a prince called Michael Golitsin offended Empress Anna, she forced him to marry an ugly servant girl.

On their wedding night, the couple were locked in a palace made of ice, with guards to prevent them escaping.

Miraculously, Golitsin and his wife both survived their ordeal and she later gave birth to twin sons.

Travel within kingdoms

It was important for monarchs to tour their realms, so that they could be seen and admired by their subjects. For some rulers, travel was an opportunity to find out what was happening in their kingdoms.

In the 3rd century BC, emperors of the Mauryan empire went on journeys in golden carriages. They were accompanied by noblemen, standard bearers, musicians blowing conch shells, horses and elephants decorated with plumes and pearls.

A selection of the types of transportation some monarchs have used.

This Egyptian chair was carried on the shoulders of four servants.

A chariot used by Emperor Wu-tsung of China in the 16th century

The Royal Yacht *Britannia*, used by Queen Elizabeth II of Great Britain and Northern Ireland

Courtly life

👑 **New goblets.** The court doctors of Ogadei Khan of the Mongols (a people from Central Asia) begged him to halve the number of goblets of wine he drank a day. The Khan readily agreed, but ordered his servants to bring his wine in new goblets that were twice the size of the old ones.

👑 **A funny profession.** Jesters were often employed to entertain the members of a court. The last jester in England was Muckle John, who worked at the court of King Charles I (1600-49).

👑 **A tragic tale.** Louis XIV's chef, Monsieur Vatel, found he was short of lobsters for a sauce. He was so terrified of offending the king that he committed suicide.

An elaborately carved wooden sled, found in the grave of a Viking queen

In some cultures monarchs have been closely associated with gods and goddesses. Some were thought to be deities or the children of deities, while others were thought to represent gods on earth.

Sacred kings

Many ancient societies believed that their monarchs had special powers to make crops grow and control the weather. Sometimes leaders were sacrificed to ensure the wealth and prosperity of their people. Other societies sacrificed a substitute human or animal instead of killing their leaders.

*Pharaoh
Ramses II*

The people of ancient Egypt held special ceremonies at which the powers of a monarch were symbolically renewed. Pharaoh Ramses II (c.1304-1237BC) celebrated 14 of these ceremonies, which were known as the *heb sed*.

Ramses II celebrating a heb sed

Ramses made offerings of food, wine and flowers to all the Egyptian gods and goddesses.

The pharaoh had to perform a ceremonial run to prove he was still fit and active enough to rule his country well.

After he had completed the run, Ramses attended a ceremony at which priests recrowned him as king.

God kings

Japanese emperors were believed to be directly descended from the sun goddess, Yamato. They held absolute political and religious power.

Emperor Hirohito (1901-89) lived as a god-king until 1946, when he had to give up most of his powers and renounce his claim to divinity.

Emperor Hirohito

The Oba of Benin

Rulers of Benin (a kingdom that is now part of Nigeria) were known as Obas. All-powerful, they could command anything and expected to be obeyed immediately. They were believed to be the earthly representatives of all Benin's gods, and they were considered godlike themselves. Anyone who insulted or resisted them was executed.

An Oba of Benin and two chieftains

A ceremonial hammer

The Oba wears an oversized necklace

An ornate kilt

Decorative anklets

The rulers of Tibet

The ruler of Tibet is known as the Dalai Lama. He is both a political and religious leader. The Tibetan people follow a religion called Buddhism, and they believe that the Dalai Lama's body contains the Buddhist spirit of compassion.

Approximately 3700m (about 12,000ft) above sea level, in the Himalaya mountains, stands the palace of Potala, the traditional residence of the Dalai Lama. A popular Tibetan belief is that the palace was built by the gods in just one night. In reality, the palace that can be seen today took many years to build. Work on it began during the reign of the fifth Dalai Lama, Lobsang Gyatso (1617-82).

The palace of Potala, residence of the Dalai Lamas of Tibet

The Potala was once described as "crowned with flames" because of its golden roofs.

The outer White Palace is so called because of its whitewashed walls.

In 1951, Tibet was occupied by the Chinese. In 1959, the 14th Dalai Lama Tenzin Gyatso (b.1935) fled to India with 80,000 followers. He continues to live in exile today.

*Dalai Lama
Tenzin Gyatso*

Choosing a Dalai Lama

Tibetans believe that when a Dalai Lama dies, the spirit of compassion leaves his body and enters the body of a child born at exactly the same moment.

Searching for the new Dalai Lama

The dying Dalai Lama gives his monks information about where to find the baby who will be the new Dalai Lama.

The monks, who are known as "lamas", travel throughout the mountains of Tibet looking for the special child.

There are tests which help the monks in their search. For example, the baby will recognize the belongings of the previous Dalai Lama.

The inner Red Palace contains a monastery, chapels, shrines, libraries, and golden pagodas containing the embalmed bodies of previous Dalai Lamas.

Ruling with divine approval

Emperors of China during the Sang Dynasty (17-11th century BC) claimed to be descended from Shang Di, the high god of Heaven. They used the title "Son of Heaven", and were considered responsible for bringing order and harmony to Earth.

The emperors were said to rule with the "Mandate of Heaven". This meant that the gods approved of the emperors and their actions.

A Chinese emperor in traditional robes

Divine right

In the 17th century, many European kings and queens believed they had been specially chosen by God. They claimed it was their "divine right" to rule, and that they were responsible to God alone for their actions. James I of England (1566-1625) and his son Charles I both firmly believed in the "Divine Right of Kings". They argued that nobody had the right to question their decisions or actions. This view was challenged by some of their subjects and finally provoked a civil war. This led to the execution of Charles I in 1649.

James I

Divine deeds

⚜ **Death wish.** In the 17th century, a sailor ran the King of Siam's barge onto a sand bank. The sailor was so horrified at having endangered his divine leader, that he insisted on being executed.

⚜ **Healing hands.** The French and English believed that victims of a skin disease called scrofula (known as the "King's Evil") could be cured by the touch of a monarch's hand. The last British monarch asked to perform this treatment was Queen Anne (1665-1714).

Queen Anne

Warrior kings

In the past, kings were expected to lead their armies into battle themselves. Many were barely competent military leaders, but some were inspired warriors who protected their realms from invasion and extended their frontiers to create vast empires.

A warrior pharaoh

The Egyptian pharaoh Tuthmosis III (15th century BC) was trained to be a soldier from a young age. He was an imaginative and resourceful leader, who led 17 military campaigns in the Middle East and Nubia. His success in battle helped create the greatest empire of the day.

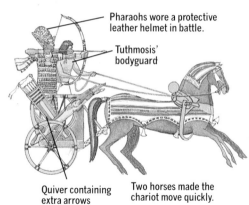

A contemporary picture of Tuthmosis III in his chariot

Pharaohs wore a protective leather helmet in battle.

Tuthmosis' bodyguard

Quiver containing extra arrows

Two horses made the chariot move quickly.

The mighty Khan

Temuchin (c.1162-1227) was the son of a minor chief of the Mongols, a people from Central Asia. As a young man he led a small group of followers on military raids. Success earned him the title Genghis Khan, meaning "Universal Leader".

He made the Mongols a formidable fighting force, conquering an empire that spread from northern China to the Black Sea and took two years to ride across.

A Persian miniature showing Genghis Khan on horseback

Alexander the Great

Alexander (356-323BC), King of Macedonia (now Greece), proved his ability on military expeditions while a teenager. He was a tactical genius, outclassing his enemies in battles, sieges and surprise attacks.

A mosaic depicting Alexander in battle

A map showing Alexander's empire

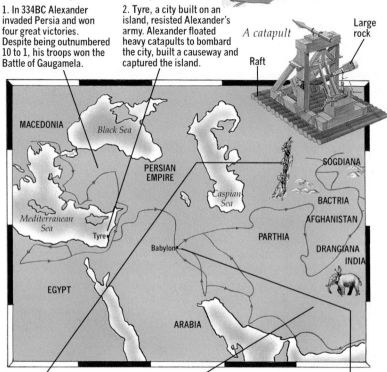

1. In 334BC Alexander invaded Persia and won four great victories. Despite being outnumbered 10 to 1, his troops won the Battle of Gaugamela.

2. Tyre, a city built on an island, resisted Alexander's army. Alexander floated heavy catapults to bombard the city, built a causeway and captured the island.

A catapult

Large rock

Raft

3. In 328BC Alexander came to the rock on which King Oxyartes had a fortress. Alexander's men drove iron pegs into the rock face. They attached rope ladders, climbed up and conquered the city.

4. When they reached India in 326BC, Alexander's men won a fierce battle against Rajah Porus. Porus gave him hundreds of elephants.

5. Exhausted, Alexander's troops refused to go on. Alexander was forced to march for home. Taken ill at a banquet in Babylon, he died in 323BC.

Akbar the Great

Akbar (1542-1605) was the greatest of a series of Indian emperors known as the Moguls. In the early years of his reign he crushed rebels within his own empire. Turning to foreign campaigns, he gradually conquered an empire covering most of northern India. The firmness and wisdom with which he governed his empire earned him the title "Guardian of Mankind."

Akbar (on the second elephant) pursuing his enemies

Frederick the Great

Frederick II of Prussia (1712-86) devoted himself to a military career. Victories against the French and the Austrians enabled him to double the size of his kingdom. His brilliant strategies and great courage earned him a reputation as a formidable military leader.

A Prussian infantryman

One of his great victories was at the Battle of Rossbach on November 5, 1757. In less than an hour 22,000 Prussians overcame 50,000 French and German troops. The Prussians took 6000 prisoners and 72 guns, losing only 300 men in the process. The picture below shows both armies engaged in battle.

A contemporary picture of Frederick's victory at the Battle of Rossbach

Zulu warrior

Shaka (c.1787-1828) was leader of the Zulu kingdom. He organized the army of 40,000 men into uniformed regiments called *impi*, and trained them rigorously. He managed to extend his kingdom over much of southern Africa.

Shaka introduced the stabbing spear

Shaka taught his men to use their shields and stabbing spears in a one-to-one attack.

A warrior hooked his shield around his opponent's, and pulled it out of the way.

This enabled him to use the stabbing spear to wound the unprotected man.

Fighting men

👑 **Attila the Hun.** Attila (c.406-453) was the king of an Asian tribe called the Huns. Known as the "Scourge of God", he mercilessly conquered many countries in Eastern Europe.

Attila the Hun

👑 **God's warrior.** Charlemagne, King of the Franks (747-814), led military campaigns to unite Western Europe under his control and spread Christianity.

Charlemagne

👑 **A great victory.** In 1415 Henry V of England (1387-1422) invaded France. Though outnumbered, his lightly armed archers managed to shoot the heavily armed French knights with ease, and so secure victory at the Battle of Agincourt.

A portrait of Henry V

The Prussian cavalry repeatedly charged the enemy until they broke and ran.

The Prussian infantry

Neumark

Brunsdorf

Frankeleben

Branderoda

The combined forces of the French and German army numbered 50,000 men (shown in red).

The 22,000 Prussians were outnumbered 2 to 1 by the French and German soldiers.

The town of Rossbach

Rossbach

The French and German cavalry retreated in disorder.

The Prussian artillery supported the cavalry.

Warrior queens

Traditionally, fighting was not considered a woman's role, and queens were only expected to make speeches to rally troops. Some female monarchs, however, led brave and ruthless military campaigns.

Vengeance for Queen Boudicca

Few military leaders have been able to challenge successfully the might of the Roman army, but Queen Boudicca inflicted major defeats on their ranks.

In 60, the Romans occupied much of Britain. They seized the land of King Prasutagus of the Iceni tribe. His queen, Boudicca (1st century), was captured and beaten in public and his daughters were humiliated.

The type of chariot used by Boudicca and the Iceni tribe

Many people wrongly believe that the wheels of Boudicca's chariot had blades attached to them.

Seeking her revenge, Boudicca launched a ferocious attack on Roman settlements at Colchester, St. Albans and London. Her army burned the towns to the ground, killing up to 70,000 Romans.

Eventually, the Romans rallied their forces and defeated Boudicca and her army, killing 80,000 Iceni warriors. Boudicca (and probably her daughters too) took poison rather than be captured.

Zenobia, queen of the East

Zenobia (3rd century), was a noble Arab lady. She was married to the king of the city of Palmyra, Syria (part of the Roman empire). She often joined her husband on military expeditions, riding or walking with his troops.

When Zenobia's husband was murdered in 267, she ruled until her son was old enough to inherit the throne himself. Zenobia infuriated the Romans, conquering their territory in Egypt, Syria and Asia Minor (now part of Turkey).

A fashionable costume at Zenobia's court

The Romans had taken control of Palmyra, but Zenobia announced that the city was independent of Rome. In retaliation, a Roman army, led by Emperor Aurelian, attacked the city. Zenobia and her bodyguards escaped on camels, but were arrested attempting to cross the River Euphrates to safety.

In Rome, Zenobia was paraded in Aurelian's victory celebration. Despite this humiliation, she survived. She married a Roman Senator and lived in luxury.

Aurelian's victory celebration in Rome

Elephants

Giraffes

Tigers

Gladiators

Elks

Ambassadors

Zenobia weighed down by chains made of solid gold.

Queen of the waves

In the 5th century BC, Queen Artemisia of Halicarnassus (now in Turkey) took five warships to join King Xerxes of Persia when he invaded Greece. During a naval battle off the coast of the island of Salamis, Artemisia was being pursued by her Greek enemies. She found her escape route blocked by the ship of one of her allies, so she decided to ram the ship to ensure her own escape.

Artemisia's ship ramming another Persian ship

A bronze ram sinks the ship.

People believed that these eyes scared enemies and helped the ship find its way.

The stern of the ship was decorated with a carved dragon's head.

Artemisia giving orders to her crew.

The ships shown in this picture are called triremes.

Two steering oars were used to control the ship's direction.

The oars were over 4m (14ft) long.

Platform for archers and spearmen

Spearman

Protected by a row of shields, a spearman fired at the enemy and tried to board their ship.

Experts think that the oarsmen sat three deep, but we do not know exactly how these ships were rowed.

Matilda, the queen who was never crowned

In 1120, the only son of King Henry I of England (1068-1135) drowned in a shipwreck. This left Henry's daughter Matilda (1102-67) as the only heir to the throne. The king made his nobles swear to support and follow Matilda when she was queen. But only three weeks after Henry died, his nephew Stephen seized the throne of England.

Matilda waged war on Stephen to win back the crown. She quickly proved to be a more able and ruthless leader than her opponent. For example, when Stephen's forces captured Matilda, the chivalrous king agreed to release her. But when she captured Stephen in a later battle, Matilda had him put in chains and humiliated. She declared herself "Lady of the English".

A contemporary picture of Matilda

Matilda went to London to be crowned, but she was very unpopular with many people. Her determination and courage were considered unnatural in a woman. On the eve of her coronation, the people of London rose up against her, and she was forced to flee to Normandy, France.

Stephen gradually regained power in England and so, despite her efforts, Matilda was never crowned Queen of England.

There are many stories of how Matilda avoided capture by Stephen's troops.

Once Matilda pretended to be dead and managed to get away from her enemies on a cart which carried coffins.

On another occasion she escaped a besieged castle during a blizzard by dressing in white and slipping past enemy soldiers.

During the blizzard Matilda was able to escape her pursuers by walking across the River Thames, which was frozen at the time.

👑 **Rest in peace.** One legend claims that Queen Boudicca is buried under platform eight of Kings Cross, a railway station in London.

👑 **Three golden flies.** While acting as regent for her son, Queen Ahhotep (16th century BC) led an army against rebels. She was later presented with three golden flies, Egypt's highest award for bravery.

Ahhotep's golden flies

👑 **Jinga the queen.** Some say Jinga Mbandi (c.1580-1663) killed her brother to become Queen of Matamba, West Africa. She negotiated independence for her kingdom with the Portuguese governor. When Portuguese troops drove her out, she trained soldiers herself and fought back repeatedly.

The Portuguese governor did not offer a chair, so Jinga sat on a servant.

👑 **Historical confusion.** Amanirenas, queen mother of the Kingdom of Meroë in Africa, led a successful attack on Roman garrisons in southern Egypt in 7BC. Roman historians called her Candace, which was not her name but her title.

👑 **The Rebel Rani.** In 1857 Lakshimbai, the Rani of the kingdom of Jhansi, joined rebel leaders in a revolt against the British who occupied India. She died fighting, but a British general admitted that she was a very brave and dangerous opponent.

The Rebel Rani wore jodhpurs and jewels in battle.

Many kings and queens commissioned buildings during their reigns. But some royal builders overshadowed the rest, erecting castles, great temples, vast fortifications and even entire cities.

The great pyramids

Several Egyptian pharaohs erected massive monuments called pyramids, to mark their future burial places. The largest is that of King Khufu who ruled in the 25th century BC.

Constructing Khufu's pyramid

2.3 million blocks were cut from quarries. Each weighed about 23,000kg (50,000lbs). They were floated across the River Nile.

Ramps made of rubble were used to raise the blocks above ground level. Wooden poles were used to lever them into position.

As the pyramid grew higher, the ramps were made longer. The pyramid was finally covered in white limestone to make it shiny.

Inside the pyramid

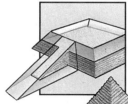

Air shaft

Burial chamber

Workmen's passages

Ramses' temple

Pharaoh Ramses II (c.1304-1237BC) undertook many massive building projects during his reign. Egyptian poets praised the beauty of Per-Ramses, the new city he built. He constructed a chain of fortresses to protect Egypt from the people of Libya, and built spectacular tombs and temples. His most famous building is the great temple at Abu Simbel.

Vast statues of Ramses II sit outside the temple of Abu Simbel.

Building the city of Babylon

Babylon, the capital city of Babylonia (now part of modern Iraq), was built by Nebuchadnezzar II in the 6th century BC.

A reconstruction of the city of Babylon

This temple platform, called a ziggurat, was built by Nebuchadnezzar for a god named Marduk.

It was the richest and most magnificent city of its time. Two massive walls 18m (60ft) high, stretching for 13km (8 miles), enclosed the temples and palaces of the inner city. When the site was excavated in the 19th century, the only part of the city still standing was a gateway. This is known as the Ishtar Gate, after the goddess Ishtar to whom it is dedicated.

Nebuchadnezzar married a princess named Amytis. When she became homesick for the hills of her homeland, he built gardens to remind her of them. Now known as the "Hanging Gardens of Babylon", they were built on steep terraces to imitate hillsides. Machinery raised water to the gardens from a nearby river.

A statue of the goddess Ishtar

The walls of Nebuchadnezzar's throne room were 3m (10ft) thick to combat temperatures that reached 55°C (131°F).

The gardens were said to be one of the Seven Wonders of the Ancient World.

The Ishtar Gate, decorated with glazed blue tiles depicting bulls and dragons

The Great Wall of China

When Zheng (259-210BC) became king of the province of Qin he united China under his rule. He took the name Shih Huang Ti, which means "First Emperor of China". He wanted to construct a wall to protect China from its enemies. Slaves, prisoners and peasants were forced to work in harsh conditions to build the wall. Many thousands of them died.

Shih Huang Ti

The Great Wall is the largest man-made structure in the world, and can be seen by astronauts orbiting the Earth. But it did not serve its purpose and was penetrated by many different invaders. The Mongol leader Genghis Khan is believed to have bribed guards on the wall to allow his army into China.

This picture shows the Great Wall in the last stages of its construction.

The wall varies from 4.5-12m (15-39ft) thick and is up to 9.8m (32ft) high.

Towers were built at regular intervals. They housed 4-5 soldiers.

Existing earth walls were joined together, and strengthened with stones.

A map showing the extent of the Great Wall

MONGOLIA

TIBET

Great Wall

CHINA

INDIA

There are 2400km (1500 miles) of wall.

If workers died, their bodies were built into the wall.

Peter the Great

Tsar Peter the Great of Russia (1672-1725) wanted to build a new city, St. Petersburg, at the mouth of the River Neva. He wanted to make it as great as any city in Europe, so he visited Germany, England and Holland, and took architects, crafts-men and artists back to Russia.

As the site was wet and marshy, building the city was difficult. Timbers had to be driven into marshland, forests were cleared and hills flattened.

Peter the Great

Modern method. An estimated 4000 workers spent 40 years building the pyramid of King Khufu. In 1974, experts calculated that, with modern equipment, it would take 405 workmen only six years.

These hieroglyphs mean "Khufu"

Big thinker. Sultan Moulay Ismail of Morocco (1672-1727) built a royal city with walls 40km (25 miles) long, 50 palaces, and a stable which could accommodate 12,000 horses.

A city in the clouds. The city at Machu Picchu, probably built by Emperor Pachacuti of Peru (1438-71), stands an incredible 600m (2000ft) up on a peak in the Andes.

Machu Picchu

An obsessive builder

Ludwig II of Bavaria (1845-86) had a passion for building. During his reign, he spent vast sums from the treasury constructing two castles and three palaces, at a time when Bavaria was in financial difficulty. By 1886, Ludwig's obsession had brought his country massive debts.

Neuschwanstein castle was built by Christian Jank, a theatrical designer.

The castle was built on the top of a mountain.

Most of the castle was made of white limestone.

Red sandstone gatehouse

Monarchs have often surrounded themselves with very gifted people. While some rulers were talented in their own right, others became famous as patrons (people who finance and support craftsmen, artists, scholars and explorers).

Henry the Navigator

Prince Henry of Portugal (1394-1460) devoted his life to discovery. As Governor of the Algarve, in Portugal, he built a shipyard and a school to train navigators and pilots. He recruited many mariners, astronomers and geographers, and inspired his courtiers to lead expeditions to explore the west coast of Africa. Henry sent out 14 expeditions, but each one turned back

Henry the Navigator

before rounding Cape Bojador. The sailors believed that beyond this point lay the "Green Sea of Darkness", where the sun burned people's skins black, the sea boiled and there were whirlpools and thick green fogs where monsters lurked. It was not until 1434 that courtier Gil Eannes sailed beyond the Cape and survived to tell the tale.

A Portuguese ship, and a map of Eannes' route round the west coast of Africa

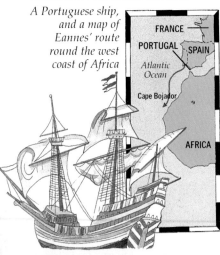

FRANCE
PORTUGAL SPAIN
Atlantic Ocean
Cape Bojador
AFRICA

Culture at court

Elizabeth I of England (1533-1603) spoke five languages, and had a passion for riding, music, dancing and poetry. When a diplomat from Scotland boasted to Elizabeth that Mary, Queen of Scots, was an accomplished musician, Elizabeth went to the virginal (a keyboard instrument) to prove that she too could play brilliantly.

Queen Elizabeth playing the lute

Elizabeth's court attracted many talented authors and artists. William Shakespeare (1564-1616) wrote his play *Twelfth Night* to be performed for the queen in 1599.

Shakespeare's plays were performed at The Globe

Portrait of a king

In 1632, Charles I of England (1600-49) invited the Flemish painter Anthony Van Dyck (1599-1641) to court. Van Dyck's portraits so impressed the king that he gave the artist a knighthood and a pension to encourage him to stay in England. The artist's style had a great influence on portrait painting in England for two centuries.

A portrait of Charles I by Van Dyck

The building had no roof. If it rained, plays were called off.

Galleries above the stage were used for balcony scenes.

The walls have been cut away to show wealthy guests and musicians sitting in wooden galleries.

It cost only a penny to stand in front of the stage and watch.

Pompadour porcelain

Madame de Pompadour (1721-64), mistress of Louis XV of France, passionately supported the arts. She encouraged writers, and persuaded Louis to patronize the finest artists, craftsmen and architects of his day.

The Sèvres porcelain factory owes its survival to La Pompadour. She asked the king to invest in the factory, and promote its products by making them fashionable at the Royal court.

Sèvres porcelain

Ludwig II and Wagner

The German composer Richard Wagner (1813-83) was in serious financial trouble when he was summoned to the court of King Ludwig II of Bavaria (1845-86). The king loved Wagner's music and promised to pay him a vast salary.

Wagner was quick to take advantage of the king's generosity. Once, when police arrived at Wagner's apartment to seize his possessions as security for his debts, Wagner sent a friend to the king's treasury and was able to pay the debt with 2400 florins.

The Swan King from a Wagner opera

Bavarian ministers hated Wagner, accusing him of meddling in politics. The final insult came when Wagner attacked the government in an article. Ludwig was forced to banish him from Bavaria.

Richard Wagner

Fabergé eggs

The customers of the craftsman Carl Fabergé (1846-1920) included many European monarchs and aristocrats. His greatest customer was Tsar Nicholas II of Russia.

In 1884, Fabergé was asked to make an Easter egg for the tsar's wife. Over the following years a total of 56 decorated eggs were delivered to the palace at Easter.

A selection of eggs made by Carl Fabergé

This egg is decorated with jewels. The picture of the tsar's children fits inside.

(left)This egg is a clock with a vase of lilies. The numbers on the clock are studded with diamonds and a golden arrow shows the time.

(below) These lilies of the valley are made from pearls and rose-diamonds, with gold and emerald leaves.

(below) This egg is decorated with imperial eagles and diamonds. A working model of the tsar's coronation coach fits inside.

👑 **A soldier's thoughts.** Emperor Marcus Aurelius (121-80) of Rome was constantly fighting to protect the frontiers of the Roman Empire, but he found time to study literature, philosophy and law. "Meditations", a record of his innermost thoughts, is still studied today.

A coin showing Marcus Aurelius

👑 **A royal composer.** Henry VIII of England (1491-1547) was an accomplished musician. He played the organ, virginal and the harp. Some people think he may have written the famous tune "Greensleeves".

A miniature showing Henry playing the harp.

👑 **Pen name for a queen.** Queen Elizabeth of Romania (1843-1916) published her poems and fairy stories using the pen name Carmen Sylva.

👑 **A late starter.** Charlemagne (747-814), King of the Franks, did not learn to write until he was an adult. However, he founded schools and gathered some of Europe's greatest scholars at his court.

Charlemagne encouraged very high standards in art, architecture and craftsmanship.

A bust of Emperor Charlemagne. His name means "Charles the Great".

Tragic monarchs

Assassination by enemies has always been one of the greatest hazards of leadership. Some monarchs were executed by rivals, while others perished at the hands of their own subjects.

The last Aztec emperor

The Aztecs were a race of people who inhabited Mexico from about 1325. In 1519, a group of Spanish adventurers, who are known as the conquistadors, landed on the coast of Mexico. They reached a city called Tenochtitlán, the capital of the Aztec empire. They were led there by a native woman known as Malinche, who had fallen in love with Hernando Cortés, the leader of the Spanish troops.

When the Spanish arrived, the Aztecs thought that they were gods and worshipped them. But Cortés ruthlessly imprisoned the Aztec king, Montezuma (1466-1519).

When a rebellion broke out among the Aztecs, Montezuma was brought out to calm his people. But he had never been a popular leader, and the crowd showered him with stones and arrows. He died from his injuries soon after.

Queen for 1000 days

Henry VIII of England (see page 168) desperately wanted a son to inherit his throne. When his second wife Anne Boleyn (c.1504-36) had a baby girl, he began to tire of her.

Anne was overjoyed when she became pregnant again. But she miscarried the baby, a boy, when shocked by stories suggesting the king had had a serious accident.

Henry believed that Anne had failed him, and put her on trial. Despite her innocence, she was found guilty of adultery and beheaded. Only 11 days later, Henry married Jane Seymour.

Anne Boleyn

A hired assassin

Philip II of Spain controlled the Netherlands. A devout Catholic, he persecuted Dutch Protestants until they revolted. They were led by William, Prince of Orange (1533-84). Philip offered a reward to anyone willing to murder the prince.

Prince William of Orange

Balthassar Gérards, a cabinet-maker's apprentice, boasted that he would kill William. In disguise, he went to the prince, who gave him a job. Gérards then bought a pair of pistols and killed William as he was about to dine. Gérards was executed, but Philip paid the reward to his family.

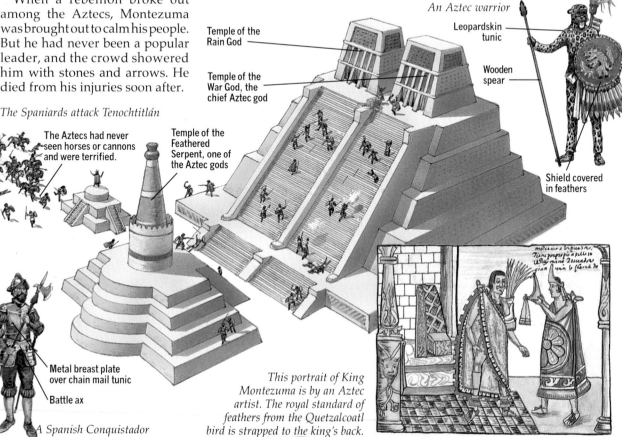

The Spaniards attack Tenochtitlán

The Aztecs had never seen horses or cannons and were terrified.

Temple of the Feathered Serpent, one of the Aztec gods

Temple of the Rain God

Temple of the War God, the chief Aztec god

An Aztec warrior

Leopardskin tunic

Wooden spear

Shield covered in feathers

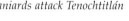

Metal breast plate over chain mail tunic

Battle ax

A Spanish Conquistador

This portrait of King Montezuma is by an Aztec artist. The royal standard of feathers from the Quetzalcoatl bird is strapped to the king's back.

164

Tried and executed

Charles I (1600-49) is the only English king to have been executed. During his reign, a war broke out between king and Parliament. Parliament wanted more say in matters of religion, finance and foreign policy, but Charles considered it his right to decide upon these matters.

In 1649 the king was captured, tried for treason and sentenced to death. The day of his execution was a cold one, so Charles wore two shirts. He did not want onlookers to think he was shivering with fear when he walked out to face the executioner's ax.

A contemporary picture showing the execution of Charles I of England

The queen of luxury

Marie Antoinette (1755-93) was the wife of Louis XVI of France (1754-93). She was notorious for her frivolity and extravagance. Living in luxury at the Palace of Versailles, she gave no thought to the suffering of the poor. Because of this, she became a focus for the French people's hatred of the monarchy.

When revolution broke out, Marie Antoinette and Louis tried to flee France, but they were intercepted, brought back to Paris and imprisoned. Louis was tried and executed in 1793 and Marie Antoinette followed him to the guillotine nine months later.

A sketch of Marie Antoinette on her way to the guillotine

How the guillotine was used

During the French Revolution, any man or woman suspected of being unpatriotic was sent to the guillotine. The prisoner was brought to the platform.

The prisoner was forced to lie on a wooden bench. The blade of the guillotine was raised, using a rope. When the rope was pulled, the blade fell, cutting the head off.

The head was caught in a basket. Sometimes it was lifted up to show the crowd.

The guillotine

The heavy blade fell quickly when the rope was pulled.

A rope was used to raise and lower the blade.

The prisoner's head was secured between these two pieces of wood.

Executing the Romanovs

Tsar Nicholas Romanov II of Russia (1868-1918) and his family lived in wealth and luxury until the Russian Revolution broke out in 1917 and he was forced to abdicate.

The Romanovs were imprisoned at a town called Yekaterinburg. On July 16, 1918, the tsar's supporters were nearing the town. The revolutionaries could not risk the tsar being rescued. In the middle of the night, the family were taken to a cellar and executed by a firing squad. Their bodies were taken away and disposed of.

Bones belonging to the tsar, his empress and three of their five children were found in 1991.

A photograph of the Romanov family

Tragic but true

♛ **A dish of mushrooms.** To ensure her son became the next emperor of Rome, Agrippina poisoned her husband, Emperor Claudius (10BC-54), with a dish of mushrooms. She also had his eldest son, Britannicus, murdered.

A bust of Claudius

♛ **A king's ransom.** The largest ransom ever was paid to Spanish adventurers by the Inca people of Peru in 1533. They filled a room with gold (the equivalent of $170 million) in return for the life of their leader Atahualpa. But the Spaniards still strangled Atahualpa.

King Atahualpa

Few kings and queens have resisted the luxuries that a life of great wealth and power can offer. But some rulers managed to live according to strict religious principles, piously devoting themselves to their chosen faiths.

Akhenaten

As a young man, Amenhotep IV (14th century BC) began to worship Aten, the sun god. When he became a pharaoh, he changed his name to Akhenaten, which means "living spirit of Aten".

Akhenaten banned the worship of all other gods and goddesses and built a city, called Akhetaten, as a tribute to Aten.

The king's subjects missed the old deities and soon went back to worshiping them when the king died. Later, they called him the "criminal of Akhetaten".

A statue of Akhenaten.

From slaughter to prayer

Asoka, king of the Mauryan empire in India, led his army to war in 273BC. Hundreds of thousands of men were slaughtered. The sight of the dead and dying appalled Asoka so much that he became a Buddhist. Buddhism is a religion which teaches its followers the importance of destroying greed, hatred and delusion.

Buddhism became the official religion throughout Asoka's empire. He sent out missionaries to spread its teachings. In Sri Lanka, they managed to convert the king and court.

One of many columns erected by King Asoka

Julian, the pious pagan

When the Roman emperor Constantine the Great died in 337, his three sons inherited the throne. All the male members of his family considered a threat to the throne were murdered. Constantine's nephew Julian (c.331-363) was spared because he was only a child. But he lost his father, brother, uncle and cousins. The tragedy turned Julian against Christianity, the faith in which he had been raised.

When he became emperor in 361, Julian devoted himself to the Roman gods and goddesses and rebuilt their temples.

Christianity was restored after Julian died and he became known as Julian the "Apostate" (someone who abandons one religion for another).

Emperor Julian dressed as a god

A selection of the Roman gods and goddesses that Julian worshiped.

Jupiter, king of the gods	Juno, goddess of women	Vesta, goddess of the home	Neptune, god of the sea	Dis, god of the underworld	Ceres, goddess of agriculture	Vulcan, god of craftsmen
Mars, god of war	Diana, goddess of hunting	Apollo, god of the sun	Minerva, goddess of wisdom	Mercury, Jupiter's messenger	Bacchus, god of wine	Venus, goddess of love

Saint Olaf

Viking warrior Olaf Haraldsson (c.995-1030) began sailing the Baltic Sea at the age of 12. He led many raids in Europe, and even pulled down London Bridge with grappling irons in 1010.

Olaf returned home to Norway, and was converted to Christianity. When he became king, he forced his subjects to become Christians, often offering death as their only alternative. Olaf was killed in battle, but people claimed to see miracles at his grave. Later he became Norway's first saint.

A manuscript illumination showing Olaf being killed at the Battle of Stiklestad.

Vladimir the saint

Ruler Vladimir (c.956-1015) killed one of his brothers in the struggle to become ruler of the kingdom of Kiev (now part of Russia). Once in power, he kept 800 concubines in his palace, and even encouraged human sacrifices.

A very shrewd politician, Vladimir won rich trading contacts with the city of Byzantium (now Istanbul) by becoming a Christian. He forced his subjects to undergo mass baptisms and built churches throughout Russia. Despite his often violent actions, Vladimir was later made a saint for converting so many people to Christianity.

Vladimir the saint

Priests were sent from Byzantium to baptize Vladimir's subjects.

Saint Clotilda

Clotilda was the niece of the King of Burgundy. In 493 she married Clovis, King of the Franks. Clotilda became famous for her great piety and her good works.

It is said that Clovis decided to become a Christian during a battle. While fighting, he began thinking of his wife and won a victory. Clotilda was later made a saint.

Statues of Clotilda and Clovis from the church of Notre Dame de Corbeil, France

Saint Louis, the crusader

Louis IX of France (1215-70) was a strong king and a deeply religious man. During an illness he vowed to join one of the Crusades, a series of military expeditions by European Christians to regain the Holy Land (Palestine) from the Turks.

Louis led the sixth Crusade (1248-54), but he was soon taken prisoner and was held until a large ransom was paid. In 1270 he set off again, but died of plague at Tunis in North Africa. He was declared a saint in 1297.

Louis IX of France

The side of this Crusade galleon has been cut away to show the stables inside

Saint Margaret. A young Anglo-Saxon princess named Margaret wanted to be a nun, but the Scottish king Malcolm III insisted that she marry him instead. Margaret encouraged her husband to build monasteries and to make changes in the Scottish Church. She was made a saint in 1251.

The Confessor. Edward, King of England (c.1003-66) was such a devoted Christian that he gained the name "the Confessor". He built Westminster Abbey, where he was buried in 1066.

Edward shown in the tapestry called the Bayeux Tapestry

A lookout stood in this crow's-nest.

The Crusaders' flag was decorated with a cross.

The main sails are folded away.

Cabin for the king

The horses were led up a ramp.

Stables

Crusaders waiting to board the vessel.

Since the earliest times, people at royal courts have plotted and schemed to achieve their political aims. Indeed, in his book *The Prince*, a 16th-century Italian statesman called Machiavelli advised rulers to be prepared to commit evil acts to secure power.

A harem conspiracy

Some societies have allowed kings to have many wives. This often led to intrigues, conspiracies and murders as wives competed with each other for supremacy.

At the court of Ramses III (1198-1167BC) one of his wives, Tiy, began plotting to ensure her son inherited the throne. 29 courtiers and several army officers helped her.

The conspiracy against Ramses III

The court conspirators made several attacks on the pharaoh. They attempted to hijack his royal barge.

They used witchcraft to try to harm Ramses III. Finally they openly attacked him, but were captured by the royal guard.

The conspirators were put on trial. Some were flogged or had their noses cut off, others were executed. Tiy and her son were allowed to commit suicide.

Herod, a family man

When the Romans gave the throne of Judea (now in Israel) to Herod the Great (74-4BC), it was unpopular with the Judeans. Herod often feared that people with a better claim to the throne would plot against him. In 29BC he married a Jewish princess called Mariamne. But he had her brother drowned and her grandfather strangled, believing that they wanted to seize his throne. When Mariamne showed anger at his deeds, Herod falsely charged her with adultery and she was executed.

Fiendish Fredegond

In the 6th century, King Chilperic of Neustria (which is now part of France) fell in love with a servant girl named Fredegond. She is believed to have strangled Chilperic's first wife so that she could marry the king herself.

When Fredegond had a son, she murdered Chilperic's other children in order to ensure that her son would inherit the crown.

King Chilperic of Neustria

The king refused to believe Fredegond was guilty, but in 584 he himself was killed, probably on the queen's orders. Fredegond ruled successfully on her son's behalf until her death in 597.

Vlad the Impaler

Vlad was a 15th century prince of Wallachia (in modern Romania). He became infamous for impaling enemy soldiers and many of his own citizens on sharpened sticks. As a result he became known as "Vlad the Impaler", and was feared and hated. During a war against Turkey, Vlad's men turned against him and killed him. The legend of Dracula the vampire is based on Vlad, whose father was named Vlad Drakul.

A modern image of Dracula

Henry VIII and his six wives

The lengths to which Henry VIII of England (1491-1547) went to get a male heir amazed Europe. In 1509, he married Catherine of Aragon. When all her sons died in infancy, Henry wanted his marriage declared invalid. The Pope refused, so Henry cut ties between England and the Catholic Church.

Catherine of Aragon

He then married Anne Boleyn, with whom he was already in love. But when she could not provide a son he had her executed for alleged infidelity.

Anne Boleyn

The king seemed to be genuinely fond of his third wife, Jane Seymour. But she died giving birth to a baby boy. The child was Henry's first male heir to survive infancy. His name was Edward and he was a weak, sickly child. He died at the age of 16 after he had reigned for only six years.

Jane Seymour

Henry VIII, as painted by Hans Holbein

The portrait was painted in 1537 when Henry was 28 years old and at the height of his power.

Henry is shown with extremely wide shoulders and his feet placed apart to emphasize his power and importance.

Henry's cloak is decorated with fur and gold thread.

The wealth of Henry's clothes and jewels were intended to reflect his success.

At the beginning of his reign Henry was tall and handsome, but he became grossly overweight and suffered with terrible ulcers on his bloated legs.

Henry divorced wife number four, Anne of Cleves, after only six months. At the age of 55 he fell in love with Catherine Howard, a teenager. But she was unfaithful to him and he had her executed.

Anne of Cleves (left)

Catherine Howard (right)

Henry's sixth wife, Catherine Parr, just managed to escape the executioner's blade. Henry died before he could sentence her to death.

Catherine Parr

Brotherly love

When the Sultan of the Ottoman Empire died, his son Mahomet III (1566-1603) was determined to get rid of rival claimants to his throne.

How Mahomet safeguarded his throne

Within hours of his father dying, Mahomet summoned his younger brothers. Led by the eldest who was eleven, the boys kissed Mahomet's hand.

Mahomet ordered guards to take the boys away into a room behind the throne room, where they were all strangled.

Mahomet also drowned seven ladies from his father's harem because they were pregnant and their children would have been potential rivals.

The diamond necklace affair

Jeanne de Motte was an ambitious countess who lived at the French royal court in the 18th century. She devised a plan to make her fortune. She knew that a man named Cardinal de Rohan desperately wanted to win the approval of the queen, Marie Antoinette. She pretended to Rohan that the queen had requested his help to buy a diamond necklace. But once Rohan had acquired the necklace, Jeanne stole it and gave it to her husband to sell.

When the craftsman who had made the necklace received no payment, he went to the queen. The queen refused to pay for something she had never even ordered.

Eventually the plot was revealed and Jeanne was imprisoned.

The necklace which caused a scandal

It contained 540 perfect diamonds.

It's scandalous!

A blind rage. An 18th century Shah of Persia had 20,000 people from the city of Kerman blinded when they refused to bow down to him. The Shah was assassinated in 1797.

No entry. The future George IV of England and his wife Caroline of Brunswick had a very unhappy marriage. Their relationship became so strained that when George was crowned, Caroline was actually turned away from the coronation ceremony.

Caroline of Brunswick

Royal marriages were usually arranged for political reasons rather than for love. Some monarchs struggled to be allowed to marry partners of their choice. Others made disastrous marriages and were forced to look for love elsewhere.

Antony and Cleopatra

Queen Cleopatra of Egypt (69-30BC) was said to be so beautiful that she brought chaos to the Roman Empire. She set out to win the love of a Roman general named Mark Antony. She sailed to meet him on a magnificent barge and entertained him with banquets and great luxury. Antony soon divorced his first wife and married Cleopatra.

Cleopatra (above) and Antony

Octavian, the brother of Mark Antony's first wife, declared war on Antony and Cleopatra. In 31BC the Egyptian fleet was defeated at Actium, off the coast of Africa. Antony committed suicide, by falling on his sword. Cleopatra is said to have held a snake to her breast and died from its venom.

This reconstruction shows Cleopatra arriving in a royal barge to meet Mark Antony.

Crowning the dead

In 1359, Dom Pedro (1334-69), son of Alfonso XI of Portugal, married Inez de Castro. The couple kept their marriage a secret because Alfonso disapproved of Inez. When he discovered the truth, he had Inez and her children murdered.

Pedro avenges his wife's death.

When Pedro became king, he tracked down his wife's murderers, had them brought back to Portugal and tortured them.

He ordered that Inez's body should be taken from her grave, dressed in coronation robes and crowned queen.

After the nobles had paid their humble respects to Inez's body, Pedro ordered her reburial.

The royal barge could travel under sail or powered by the oarsmen.

The barge docked on the banks of the River Nile.

The queen's royal cabin

Queen Cleopatra

Mark Antony

A captive bride

In 1523 Turkish raiders captured a red-headed Russian girl. They called her Khurren, meaning "Laughing One", but she is better known as Roxelana. She was presented as a slave to the Sultan of Turkey Süleyman the Magnificent (1494-1566).

Sultan Süleyman

Süleyman and his men riding into battle in a scene from a 16th century miniature

Süleyman was captivated by Roxelana's wit and intelligence. He released her from slavery and married her, becoming the first sultan to marry in 600 years.

Roxelana's influence over the Sultan was so great that some courtiers even believed she was a witch. She was determined that her son, Selim, should be the next Sultan. By convincing Süleyman that Mustafa, heir to the throne, was plotting against him, she provoked the boy's execution. When Roxelana died in 1558, she knew that her son would inherit the Turkish empire.

Roxelana

In love with an older woman

Aged 11, Prince Henri (1519-59) who later became Henri II of France, fell in love with Diane de Poitièrs (1499-1566), a woman of 31. Although he was married in 1533 to Catherine de Medici, he pursued Diane until she agreed to be his mistress.

Henri and Diane remained deeply in love until Henri died of wounds accidentally inflicted during a tournament. His widow, Catherine de Medici, ordered Diane to return all the jewels that Henri had given her. Diane retired to the country until she died.

Diane de Poitièrs

The chosen one of the palace

Shah Jahan (1592-1666), one of the most powerful emperors of India, met his future wife while she was selling gifts in a bazaar. Their wedding was celebrated with a great procession and fireworks. The shah remained devoted to his wife for 19 years.

She was given the name Mumtaz Mahal which means "the Chosen One of the Palace". When she died in childbirth in 1631, he was griefstricken. He decided to build her a tomb of white marble, to match her beauty. He called it the Taj Mahal.

Mumtaz Mahal

Shah Jahan planned to build his own tomb of black marble, joined to the Taj Mahal by a silver bridge. But his plan was wrecked when in 1658 he was deposed by his son. Shah Jahan died in prison and was buried beside his wife's

Shah Jahan

sarcophagus in an underground room in the Taj Mahal.

The Taj Mahal at Agra, India

The white marble of the Taj Mahal glows golden when the sun sets.

The Taj Mahal is hollow. It rests on a tower of bricks built above the ceiling of the tomb.

Sculptors carved hollows into the marble into which they slotted jewels.

The sarcophagi of Mumtaz Mahal and Shah Jahan.

Mumtaz is actually buried in an underground chamber.

Minarets

The tsar and tsarina

Martha Skavronskay (1684-1727), who later changed her name to Catherine, came from a peasant family in Lithuania. She worked for wealthy Russian families.

Tsar Peter of Russia (1672-1725) met Catherine and they quickly became close companions. They married in 1712 and had 12 children together.

The tsar changed the law so that Catherine could inherit the throne after he died.

Catherine I of Russia

A love story

👑 **A queen becomes king.** Experts think that when Pharaoh Akhenaten (14th century BC) realized that his wife Nefertiti could not give him a son, he married again. He tried to compensate Nefertiti by making her his co-ruler.

A bust of Nefertiti

👑 **Eleanor crosses.** When Eleanor of Castille (c.1245-90) died in Nottinghamshire, England, her husband Edward I of England (1239-1307) erected "Eleanor crosses" at every place her funeral procession stopped on its way to London.

Of 12 crosses, the Hardingstone is one of three that remain.

👑 **A divorced woman.** In 1937 Edward VIII of England gave up his throne to marry Mrs Simpson. As king, and head of the Church of England, he was not allowed to marry a divorced woman.

Edward and Mrs Simpson at their wedding in 1937

When kings and queens have complete control over the affairs of their countries, their decisions and judgment affect the lives of all their subjects. The consequences of a ruler afflicted by mental illness have often been catastrophic.

Caligula

Emperor Gaius of Rome (2-41) was known as Caligula because of the little soldier's boots, known as *caligae*, that he wore as a child.

A coin showing a bust of Caligula

After only a few months in power, Caligula suffered from an illness which left him deranged. He soon began to act very strangely.

Examples of Caligula's strange actions

Caligula believed that he was a living god. He became very arrogant and would not listen to advice.

He made his horse, Incitatus, a government official and built a marble stable with an ivory manger for him.

Caligula married several women in quick succession, and even had an affair with his own sister.

Preoccupied with fears of plots and treason, Caligula murdered many prominent Roman citizens. His extravagance emptied Rome's treasury. Eventually, senators and members of his own bodyguard conspired against him, and Caligula was stabbed to death.

The king who was made of glass

During his reign, Charles VI of France (1368-1422) suffered periods of madness. One of his delusions was that he was made of glass and would break if touched.

He first fell ill in 1392. While he was recovering, the Constable of France was assassinated. Charles took a force of soldiers to punish the murderer. While passing through a forest, a man appeared and told the king to turn back. Charles was terrified, and he thought he was under attack. Lashing out with his sword, he killed several of his own men and then collapsed.

Charles slowly recovered his senses, but after tragedy struck at a palace ball (see picture below) he suffered another bout of madness.

France floundered without strong leadership, and suffered terrible defeat in foreign wars.

Charles VI of France

Charles VI was left emotionally disturbed after he and his friends caught fire at a ball.

Charles and his friends went to the ball dressed as savages.

A spark from a flaming torch ignited one of the costumes. Soon all six men were ablaze and three of them died from their injuries.

Charles was saved by a duchess who smothered the flames with her skirts.

A king who lived up to his name

Ivan IV (1530-84) became Tsar of Russia at the age of three. His mother and her lover acted as his regents. Caught up in a power struggle between the crown and Russian nobles, Ivan and his brother were badly treated and often lacked food and clothing.

Ivan grew up suspicious and cruel, earning his title "Ivan the Terrible". As a teenager he had a young nobleman named Prince Andrei Shuisky thrown to the palace dogs, which tore him to pieces.

Ivan had a vast cathedral built. But it is said that he blinded the two architects so that they could never build anything more magnificent.

The cathedral built by Ivan the Terrible in Moscow

This type of pointed roof is called a tent roof.

The cathedral is known as "St. Basil the Blessed", because Ivan's friend and adviser, Basil, is buried in it.

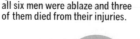

The proper name for the cathedral is the Cathedral of the Virgin of the Intercession by the Moat.

These domes were added in the 17th century. They are called "onion" domes, because of their shape.

The walls are made with brick and covered with blocks of stone.

The exterior of the cathedral was covered with bright tiling in the 17th century, giving it an oriental appearance.

Ivan set up a special body-guard called the *Oprichnina*, which tortured and killed his opponents. Ivan even took pleasure in assisting at many of the tortures and executions himself.

Ivan's savage temper was finally his downfall. In 1581, he argued with his eldest son. In a rage Ivan attacked him viciously and the prince died of his injuries. Ivan ended his life an embittered old man, leaving his throne to his second son Fedor, a sickly and incapable young man.

A woodcut showing Ivan the Terrible

The Cage

The Cage was introduced by Sultan Ahmet I of Turkey (1590-1617) as a method of avoiding wars of succession. When a new sultan came to the throne, all his brothers were locked up in a group of rooms known as the Cage. They were only released if they themselves were called upon to rule.

Many sultans emerged from the Cage completely insane.

When Osman II (1603-22) emerged from the Cage, he indulged his love of archery, using prisoners of war and his own servants as live targets.

Ibrahim the Mad, incarcerated for 22 years, had 280 of the ladies from his harem put in weighted sacks and drowned in the River Bosphorus.

One girl whose sack was not tied securely, swam to safety. When people heard her story, Ibrahim was deposed and murdered.

The Swan king

When Ludwig II (1845-86) became King of Bavaria his subjects thought him a handsome, capable leader. In reality, he was a sad and lonely young man. Increasingly detached from reality, he became obsessed with legends and fairy tales, particularly the story of the Swan King.

Ludwig's passion for building (see page 161) and for the composer.

This life-size swan vase was kept in Ludwig's bathroom.

Wagner (see page 163) drove Bavaria to bankruptcy. His ministers had him removed from office, declared him insane and imprisoned him in Berg Castle.

On June 12, 1886, the king and his doctor went walking in the castle grounds. When they did not return, a search party was organized. Both men were found drowned in the lake. Nobody knows if Ludwig's death was suicide or an accident. An examination found no water in his lungs, which would suggest that he did not drown.

Ludwig of Bavaria

Rational rulers?

👑 **Fire! Fire!** Emperor Nero of Rome (37-68) had his mother, his wife and many senators murdered. Some people believe that he started the fire which destroyed two thirds of Rome.

A statue of Nero

👑 **Juana the mad.** Juana (1479-1555), heiress to the Spanish throne, refused to allow her dead husband to be buried. Declared unfit to govern, she was locked up for 50 years, until her death.

Juana, known as "la loca" meaning "the mad"

👑 **The king is mad.** George III of England (1738-1820) suffered from periods of insanity. He foamed at the mouth, talked incessantly and he even thought an oak tree was Frederick of Prussia. Doctors now suggest that the king had porphyria, a disease which affects the brain.

George III of England

In the past, if a scandal occurred in royal circles it was covered up quickly and efficiently. Some events were so well disguised that historians still cannot penetrate the mystery that surrounds them.

Princes in the Tower

In 1674 the skeletons of two boys were found in the Tower of London. Historians believe that they could have belonged to King Edward V of England (1470-83), and his brother Richard, Duke of York.

After only two months on the throne Edward and Richard were imprisoned by their uncle, who became Richard III. The princes disappeared mysteriously. Nobody knows exactly what happened. They may have been murdered, but Edward was ill while staying in the Tower and could have died of natural causes. His brother might have been smuggled abroad.

The princes as painted by Millais (1829-96)

This plan shows the Tower of London as it was when the bones were found.

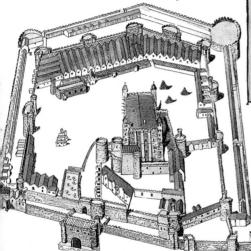

Murder at the Kirk o'Field

Soon after marrying her cousin Lord Darnley, Mary, Queen of Scots (1542-87) found that she had made a mistake. Darnley was a cruel man. He and his friends brutally murdered Mary's secretary, David Rizzio, in front of her.

When Darnley fell ill in 1567, Mary took him to a mansion in Edinburgh called the Kirk o'Field. She visited him every day, and sat for hours reading by his bedside.

On the evening of February 9,

Lord Darnley

the queen left her husband's room to attend a wedding celebration. At 2:00am the house in which Darnley slept was blown to pieces by gunpowder. His body was found in the garden. However, he had not been killed by the explosion. He had been strangled.

Three months later, Mary married the Earl of Bothwell, who is thought to have arranged Darnley's murder. Letters from Mary to Bothwell found in a casket proved that she knew of the plot in advance. Mary, however, insisted that the letters were all forgeries.

Mary Queen of Scots

A contemporary sketch of Darnley's murder at Kirk o'Field

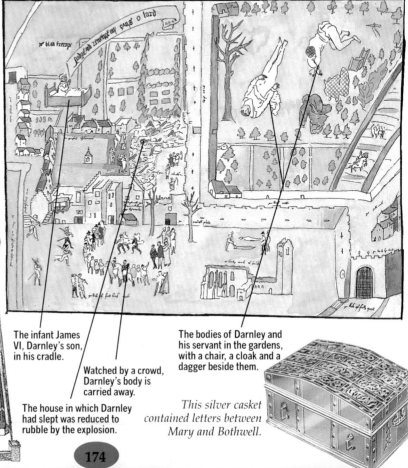

The infant James VI, Darnley's son, in his cradle.

Watched by a crowd, Darnley's body is carried away.

The house in which Darnley had slept was reduced to rubble by the explosion.

The bodies of Darnley and his servant in the gardens, with a chair, a cloak and a dagger beside them.

This silver casket contained letters between Mary and Bothwell.

Witchcraft at the French court

In 1667, the Chief of Police in Paris discovered that witchcraft was rife in the city. Courtiers were involved in devil worship, sacrifices, poisons and love potions.

Athénais de Montespan (1641-1707), the lover of Louis XIV, was said to have visited a witch and used black magic to seduce the king. 36 people were arrested. Louis ended his affair with Athénais. Fearing a scandal, he closed the police's investigation and destroyed the evidence.

This contemporary picture shows the trial of one of the suspected witches.

The death of a valet

In 1810, palace officials released a report of an attempt on the life of the Duke of Cumberland, the son of George III of England.

The duke's version of events that night

At 2:30am on May 31, the duke was attacked by his valet, Joseph Sellis, wielding a sword. The duke was badly wounded.

The duke called for help and managed to stagger into a room where Neale, one of his attendants, was sleeping.

After the attack, Sellis ran off to his own room, where he was later discovered dead. His throat had been cut.

A verdict of suicide was delivered at Sellis's inquest, despite several inconsistencies. First, the wound on the valet's throat was too deep to have been self-inflicted. Secondly, the cut was made by a right-handed person; Sellis was left-handed.

Many people thought that the duke himself had killed Sellis, but his own wounds were so severe that this is almost impossible. The truth remains a mystery.

Arsenic on St. Helena

The French emperor Napoleon (see page 179) died a prisoner on the island of St. Helena off the west coast of Africa. His death certificate says that he died of cancer, but the doctors who examined his body could not agree on the cause of death.

In the 1950s a Swedish dentist named Dr. Forshufvud, declared that Napoleon had been poisoned. While on St. Helena, the emperor had sent locks of his hair to people as souvenirs. Examining strands of this hair, Forshufvud found high levels of arsenic, a deadly poison.

This series of portraits of Napoleon show him getting increasingly fat, which supports the theory that he was poisoned.

1815

1817

1819

1820

The doctor suggested that Count Charles-Tristan de Montholon, stationed on the island, had stolen a large sum of money from the French army. Facing ruin and imprisonment if prosecuted, the Count may have accepted a pardon in return for poisoning Napoleon.

👑 **Poison at the palace.** During World War II, King Boris III of Bulgaria would not support Hitler, the German leader. After visiting Hitler, Boris fell ill and died in great pain. Was he poisoned? After the war Boris's coffin vanished mysteriously.

Adolf Hitler

Tragedy at Mayerling

On January 30, 1889 the bodies of Prince Rudolph, heir to the Austro-Hungarian Empire, and his lover Mary Vetsera were found in a royal hunting lodge at Mayerling. Revelations of a suicide pact between the lovers would have caused a scandal, so every effort was made to cover up what had happened that night.

The prince was buried with full ceremony, but Mary's body was dressed, propped up in a coach, and taken by her uncles to be buried in secret. Her mother was sent to Venice, to announce that Mary had died there.

Prince Rudolph's funeral procession outside the hunting lodge at Mayerling

Rudolph's coffin on a horse-drawn carriage

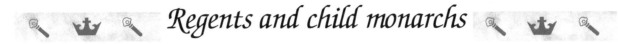

If a monarch dies leaving a child to inherit the throne, a person called a regent is appointed to run the kingdom. The regent remains in power until the child is old enough to rule. Some monarchs are best remembered for the events of their childhood, while there are regents who are more renowned than the monarchs they represented.

A gift for a young king

Pepi II (c.2262-2162BC) ruled Egypt from the age of six until he died aged 100, a record-breaking 94 years. There are many stories of the life of the child pharaoh. Once, a nobleman called Harkhuf sent news to Pepi that he had a "dancing dwarf" as a gift for the king. Historians think that on a trade expedition, Harkhuf had found a pygmy from West Africa.

Pepi wrote to Harkhuf giving him strict instructions to look after the pygmy carefully. Harkhuf was so proud of the letter that he had it recorded on the walls of his tomb.

An alabaster statue of King Pepi on his mother's knee

Because he is a king, the child is depicted as a miniature adult.

An ambitious stepmother

In c.1503BC, Queen Hatshepsut (1540-1481BC) became regent for her stepson, Tuthmosis III (see page 156). Within two years she seized power during a ceremony in a temple.

How Hatshepsut seized power

As a statue of a god was carried past Hatshepsut, it became so heavy that the priests carrying it sank to their knees.

Declaring this was a sign that the gods wanted her to rule, Hatshepsut pronounced herself "King" of Egypt.

She ruled well for 20 years, and is believed to have led successful military campaigns in Nubia and Syria.

After Hatshepsut died, her successor Tuthmosis III came to power. He could not bear to be reminded of the stepmother who had dominated him so completely. He gave orders for all her statues and inscriptions to be destroyed.

Archaeologists have only recently begun piecing together the surviving fragments of stone, in order to learn about Hatshepsut's great military achievements.

A statue of Hatshepsut, shown in men's clothing

Emperor Sheng Shen

Emperor Tai-tsung of China had many lovers, but preferred a woman called Wu Ze Tian (623-705). But Wu realized that the emperor would never marry her, so she married his son, who later became emperor. When her husband died, Wu acted as regent for one of her sons. But by 690, she was no longer content to be the power behind the throne. Wu gave herself the title Emperor Sheng Shen and seized the throne. Once in a position of power, she gave orders for many of the people who had opposed her to be tracked down and killed.

After an incredible 55 years in power, Wu was finally deposed during a coup led by her eldest son.

This figure shows the costume women wore at court.

A fine example

A more virtuous queen mother was Blanche of Castille (1188-1252) who became regent for her son Louis IX of France in 1226. She ruled France very successfully.

Blanche also managed to raise her family well. Louis became one of France's most respected kings. He asked his mother's advice for the rest of her life. When he left France to go on Crusades (see page 167), Blanche ruled in his absence.

Louis IX leaves for a Crusade

An unusual coronation

Henry III of England (1207-72) became king at the age of nine. Because his father had lost the real crown while crossing a muddy river, he was crowned with a chaplet (a kind of necklace) which belonged to his mother, Isabella.

This painting shows Henry being crowned at Gloucester Cathedral.

When Queen Isabella decided to return to her native France to remarry, a former warrior and loyal member of court named William Marshall was chosen to act as regent to the young king. Marshall, and the regents who succeeded him, ruled the country sensibly until Henry was old enough to govern himself.

A medieval picture showing William Marshall's formidable battle skills.

The last Chinese emperor

Leaders of the Chinese Revolution forced the emperor, Pu Yi (1906-67), to abdicate his throne when he was only four years old. The emperor continued to live in the ForbiddenCity (see page 150) until 1924, when he was forced to leave.

The communists who controlled China forced Pu Yi to live as an ordinary citizen and gave him the name Henry Pu Yi. He was imprisoned for 5 years and after his release he worked as a gardener and a librarian.

Pu Yi as a young child.

The Forbidden City, where Pu Yi lived until he was 18.

👑 **Respect.** In the kingdom of Benin, Africa, queen mothers continued to wield considerable power after their children were adults and ready to rule themselves.

The carved head of a queen mother of Benin

👑 **Permission granted.** Alice Botiller, nurse to Henry VI of England (1421-71), made the young king sign a charter which permitted her to scold him without fear of being punished.

The coat of arms of Henry VI of England

👑 **Royal prisoner.** Louis XVII (1785-95), heir to the throne of France, was thrown into prison after the execution of his parents, Louis XVI and Marie Antoinette (see page 165). Brutal treatment resulted in his death when he was only 10 years old.

The Emperor's Dragon Throne stands within the Hall of Supreme Harmony.

The Hall of Supreme Harmony was raised on a three-tiered terrace

A curved canal, called "Golden Stream"

A drum and bell were sounded whenever the emperor passed through the Meridian Gate, the Forbidden City's main entrance.

Many monarchs have occupied thrones to which they have little or no claim. The routes they have taken vary from marriage to conquest, rebellion, or election. Some "self-made" kings and queens have managed to pass their titles on to their children, while others have only remained in power for a short time.

Pepin the Short

In the 8th century, King Chilperic II ruled the Frankish empire, which covered much of central and eastern Europe. In 751, backed by a group of powerful nobles, Pepin the Short (c.715-68) deposed Chilperic II. He cut off Chilperic's hair and had him taken to live in a monastery. The Pope confirmed Pepin's succession to the throne, and went to France to carry out the coronation himself.

Pepin ruled bravely and well. The throne was inherited by his son Charlemagne who became one of the most powerful rulers of his time (see page 163).

Pepin the Short

Robert Bruce

When the direct line of the Scottish royal family died out in 1290, there were 13 people with a claim to the throne. Among them was Robert Bruce (1274-1329), who was determined to secure the throne for himself. It is even said that Bruce stabbed a man named

A picture of Robert Bruce

John Comyn, who was one of his 13 rivals for the throne.

Edward I of England saw the disputes over the Scottish throne as an opportunity to claim control of Scotland. Bruce was crowned King of Scotland in 1306, but he subsequently suffered two military defeats at the hands of Edward. In 1314, at the Battle of Bannockburn, Bruce returned to face and defeat an English army twice the size of his own. He ruled Scotland until he died of leprosy in 1329.

The seal of Robert Bruce

How to steal a throne

At the age of 16, Princess Sophia of Anhalt-Zerbst (1729-96) married Grand Duke Peter, heir to the Russian throne. She changed her name to Catherine. The marriage had been arranged by her mother, but it was not a happy one.

Peter became tsar in 1762, but he was neither a strong nor an efficient leader.

A brooch showing Catherine

Catherine and her lover, Gregory Orlov, joined the Russian army in a revolt against Peter.

The tsar was dethroned and murdered. Catherine became tsarina and was so successful that she earned herself the title "Catherine the Great". Her son Paul inherited the throne when she died.

A portrait of Catherine the Great

William conquers England

Edward of England (1003-66) promised his throne to William, Duke of Normandy (1027-87). But after Edward's death this promise was broken, so William decided to seize the crown for himself by force. The story of his invasion of England was recorded in the Bayeux Tapestry.

William of Normandy who became King of England

These extracts from the tapestry show William's quest for the crown.

Harold Godwinsson, Earl of Wessex, was forced to stay at William's court in Normandy after being shipwrecked. William forced Harold to swear to support his claim to the English throne.

Harold made the promise, but he did not realize that holy relics were hidden beneath the altar on which he had sworn. This made his promise a sacred oath.

A do-it-yourself emperor

During the French Revolution the king and queen were executed (see page 165). Following the revolution, France was thrown into a state of chaos. Napoleon Bonaparte (1769-1821), a brilliant general in the French army, saw an opportunity to seize power.

In 1799, he marched into the parliament building and dismissed its members. He set up a new government, called the Consulate. Declaring himself the First Consul, he became the French leader.

Napoleon was not satisfied as First Consul. In 1804 he had himself elected Emperor of France. In an elaborate ceremony at the Cathedral of Nôtre Dame, Paris, Napoleon took the imperial diadem from Pope Pius VII and placed it on his own head.

The imperial diadem

This painting, by the artist Jacques Louis David, shows the coronation of Napoleon.

Napoleon's mother

Napoleon, wearing the imperial diadem, crowns his wife.

Pope Pius VII

Napoleon's first wife, Josephine

Seizing power

⚜ **Elected king**. In 987 Hugh Capet (c.938-996) was elected King of France, by fellow noblemen, in place of the incompetent kings who had been in power before.

The coronation of Hugh Capet

⚜ **To the death**. When the King of Siam died in 1424, his two eldest sons decided to fight each other for the throne.

They fought on elephants, but both died, and their younger brother became king.

⚜ **A slave king**. In 1790, black slaves on the island of Haiti, in the Caribbean, revolted against their French rulers. Their leader, Toussaint L'Ouverture (1746-1803) was betrayed by the rebels, but one of his followers became Emperor of Haiti.

Toussaint l'Ouverture

When King Edward died in 1066, Harold broke his oath and accepted the crown. This gave William the excuse to invade England.

With a fleet of 700 ships, and an estimated 10,000 men, William attacked England later that year. His army was victorious at the Battle of Hastings.

In battle, Harold was killed, either by an arrow that pierced his eye or by a rider with a sword. William was crowned King of England.

Throughout history, monarchs have been challenged by people called pretenders, who claim that they themselves should be on the throne. Many pretenders were impostors, lured by the promise of great power and wealth. Others were provoked by the ambitious enemies of reigning monarchs. But a few pretenders may indeed have had an honest claim to the throne.

The changeling king

Shortly after the death of King Louis X of France in 1316, his wife gave birth to a son and heir, John I of France. However, the new baby king died when he was only a few days old, and was succeeded by his uncle, Philip. Stories began to spread that the baby king John had in fact been murdered by Philip's mother-in-law, an ambitious woman who wanted her daughter to become Queen of France.

In 1354, a merchant named Giovanni (the Italian version of the name John) from Sienna, Italy, was told an extraordinary tale, which suggested these stories might have been true.

The confession of Giovanni's mother

On her death bed, Giovanni's French mother confessed to him that he was not her son, but John I, the rightful King of France.

She told him that she had been the baby king's nurse. Fearing an attack on him, she placed her own baby son in the royal cradle.

The baby who had died in 1316 was her own son, but she had kept her secret and raised the king herself.

Many of the citizens of Sienna supported Giovanni's story, as did the King of Hungary. But the ruler of Naples refused to believe the story and threw Giovanni in jail, where he died in 1362. Even today nobody knows if Giovanni's dying mother was telling the truth.

Lambert Simnel

King Henry VII (1457-1509), had a rather weak claim to the English throne. This was exploited by his enemies. In 1487, they persuaded a young pretender named Lambert Simnel (c.1477-c.1534) to challenge Henry. Simnel said that he was Edward, the Earl of Warwick, the son of one of Richard III's brothers.

A portrait of Henry VII

The Earl of Warwick had been reported dead. In fact he was a prisoner in the Tower of London, where he had been since his childhood. To prove that Simnel's claims were false, Henry paraded Warwick through the streets of London.

Lambert Simnel was captured and punished. It was unusual for a pretender to survive at all, but he was sent to work in the royal kitchens, where he lived until the age of 57.

A prince returns from the grave

A more serious threat to Henry VII's throne was a young man who claimed to be Richard, Duke of York. Richard was the younger of the two princes in the Tower of London. He said that he had been rescued from the Tower and smuggled out of England. He was brought up under the name Perkin Warbeck in Flanders, an area of Europe now part of France.

Warbeck raised a small army and invaded England in 1498, but he soon faced defeat. Surrendering in return for a royal pardon, he was imprisoned in the Tower. After trying to escape and raise another rebellion, he was executed in 1499.

If Warbeck was an impostor, he was a very convincing one. He bore a striking resemblance to Edward IV, father of the princes.

A view of the Tower of London as it would have looked in the 16th century.

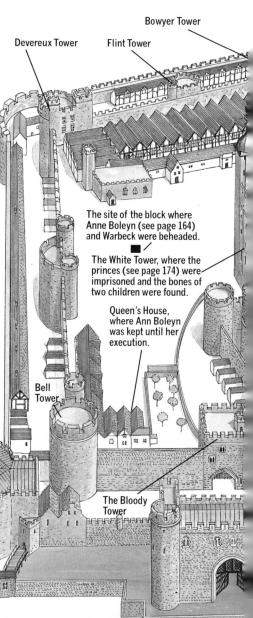

Bowyer Tower

Devereux Tower

Flint Tower

The site of the block where Anne Boleyn (see page 164) and Warbeck were beheaded.

The White Tower, where the princes (see page 174) were imprisoned and the bones of two children were found.

Queen's House, where Ann Boleyn was kept until her execution.

Bell Tower

The Bloody Tower

Margaret, Duchess of Burgundy was the sister of Edward IV, and the aunt of the two princes. She believed that Warbeck really was her nephew. Some historians think he may have been one of Edward IV's illegitimate sons. But with the deep mystery that surrounded the fate of the two young princes, it is just possible that Warbeck was telling the truth.

Edward IV

Brick Tower
Martin Tower
Brass Mount
Constable Tower
Broad Arrow Tower
Salt Tower
Lanthorn Tower
The Queen's Gallery
Jewel House (see page 149)
The Privy Garden
The moat

Prisoners, like Warbeck, were brought through Traitors' Gate.

The False Dimitri

In 1584, Ivan IV of Russia (see page 172) died and was succeeded by his son Fedor. Fedor was a weak leader and Russia was really controlled by a man named Godunov. When Fedor died, Godunov became tsar.

Ivan's youngest son, Dimitri (1583-91), the next heir to the throne, died at the age of nine in a bizarre accident involving a knife. Some people began to suspect that Godunov had murdered him; others thought he was still alive.

Godunov's royal seal

In 1603, Grigoriy Otrepieff, a monk, claimed that he was Dimitri. The False Dimitri, as he is known, invaded Russia and was crowned tsar, but soon became unpopular and was murdered in a revolt.

A second pretender appeared, also claiming to be Dimitri, but he did not look at all like his predecessor. He too was soon murdered.

Tsarevich Dimitri

Grigoriy Otrepieff

The last of the Romanovs

Most historians believe that Anastasia, daughter of Tsar Nicholas II of Russia, was executed with her family (see page 165). But the bones of two of the Romanov children have never been discovered.

In 1920 a young woman appeared in Berlin claiming to be Anastasia. She took the name Anna Anderson and spent 50 years trying to prove her royal identity. Many relatives of the Romanovs rejected her claims. Others believed her, because she knew detailed information about Anastasia and life at court.

After her death at the age of 82, Anna's true identity remained a mystery. But in 1994, tests on her body tissue showed that she could not have been the tsar's daughter.

The room in which the Romanovs were shot and (inset) Anna Anderson

Great pretenders

♛ **The Bonnie Pretender.** In 1745 Bonnie Prince Charlie invaded England, claiming the throne as the grandson of James II of Britain. When his army was defeated, a young woman called Flora MacDonald helped him escape to France by disguising him as a maid named Betty Burke.

Bonnie Prince Charlie

♛ **An unlikely story.** Louis XVII of France died in prison in 1795, but several people claimed to be him, including a watchmaker, and a man who was half Indian.

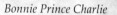

Many people have achieved great power and influence by becoming the trusted and valued friend of a monarch. But the sudden loss of royal friendship has often had disastrous or even fatal consequences.

A monument to friendship

Amenhotep, son of Hapu, was a talented official who rapidly rose through the ranks in the service of Amenhotep III of Egypt (c.1411-1375BC). The pharaoh paid many tributes to his chief minister, and he even put up statues of him in the temple of Karnak. When people came to the temple to pray to their god-king, they had to address the statue of his minister first, just as they had to do in matters of government. When minister Amenhotep died, his tomb was built in a style normally reserved for an Egyptian king. The Egyptian people worshipped him as a god of wisdom for several generations after his death.

A statue of minister Amenhotep

Plotting against the emperor

Roman emperor Tiberius (42BC-37) lived in constant fear of assassination. The only man he trusted was his friend Sejanus. Sejanus was a commander in the Praetorian Guard, which was the emperor's bodyguard.

Sejanus took advantage of Tiberius's fears. He managed to persuade the emperor to move to the island of Capri, convincing him he would be safe from assassins.

The uniform of a Praetorian guardsman

A helmet made of iron

A leather tunic with metal strips attached to it allowed freedom of movement.

A dagger hung from the left of the soldier's belt.

A groin-guard made of leather and metal.

A shield made of wood and leather with a metal rim. It was about 1.20m (4ft) by 0.7m (2.3ft), and curved.

Heavy sandals with metal studs

In this way Sejanus made sure that he was the only link of communication between Rome and the emperor.

Left in charge of Rome, Sejanus became increasingly powerful. Anyone who disagreed with him was executed or forced to commit suicide. Many of Tiberius's relatives were among Sejanus's victims.

Eventually Sejanus grew too ambitious for his own good. He devised a plan to marry Tiberius's niece, Livilla. Together they plotted to murder Tiberius and seize the throne. But Tiberius was warned of their scheme and Sejanus was executed.

A bust of Emperor Tiberius

Words spoken in anger

Thomas Becket (1118-70) was a close friend of Henry II of England (1133-89). The king made him Archbishop of Canterbury, expecting his support. But Becket took his role as a servant of the church very seriously, and soon the friends argued bitterly. They disagreed over whether churchmen should be tried in a royal court, or in a separate church court.

In a rage, Henry declared that he wanted to be rid of Thomas Becket. Overhearing these words, four knights rode to Canterbury Cathedral and killed Becket.

The murder of Becket as shown in a 15th-century illustration

Becket is shown with a halo as he was made a saint in 1173.

The knights are dressed in chain mail with tunics depicting their coats of arms.

The knights were named Reginald Fitzurse, Hugh de Merville, William de Tracy and Richard le Breton.

Friends and enemies

Queen Anne of England (1665-1714) was very fond of Sarah Jennings (1660-1722) her lady-in-waiting (a personal attendant). They had been friends since childhood. Anne even allowed Sarah to call her Mrs Morley so that the difference in their ranks would be forgotten.

Sarah's duties as lady-in-waiting and mistress of the robes

Sarah oversaw the ladies who dressed the queen, and kept a list of all the clothes in the royal wardrobe.

Sarah's main role was as companion to the queen. Here they are playing cards together.

Sarah ensured that all the queen's robes were clean and repaired, and ordered new materials if necessary.

Sarah's influence with the queen ensured the political success of her husband, the Duke of Marlborough, and his allies.

Sarah's position was a precarious one. Her fiery temper led her and Anne to quarrel. Anne transferred her friendship to a quieter lady-in-waiting named Abigail Marsham, Sarah's cousin. Sarah was dismissed from court and went abroad.

La Pompadour

Jeanne Poisson (1721-64) was determined to become the lover of Louis XV of France (1710-74). She came from a middle class background, which made it difficult to meet the king. But she caught his eye when she went to watch him hunt. Captivated by her beauty, Louis XV brought Jeanne to live at the palace at Versailles, where she became his "reigning mistress". He gave her the title Marquise de Pompadour.

Louis XV

La Pompadour, as she became known, dominated the French court for 20 years. She remained Louis' close friend until her death.

Jeanne's style of dress became very fashionable at court

Her hair was rolled back from her forehead and decorated. Later, this style became very exaggerated (see page 152).

Whalebones and canes were used to make her waist look tiny.

An opening in the front of the skirt showed a decorated petticoat.

The frilly sleeves of her under-dress

Buckled shoes

The mad monk

Tsar Nicholas II of Russia (1868-1918) discovered that his son and heir, Alexi, had a dangerous disease which prevented his blood from clotting. A tiny scratch could result in a sufferer bleeding to death.

Rasputin (c.1871-1916), a monk and healer, had a mysterious ability to reduce Alexi's suffering. He became a close friend of the tsar, advising him on policies, and choosing his ministers. Many people resented the monk's power and influence. In 1916 a group of nobles gave Rasputin cyanide, shot him and pushed his body under the ice of the frozen River Neva.

A cartoon showing Rasputin at court

Friends in high places

⚜ **Best friends.** Hugh le Despenser, friend of Edward II of England (1284-1327), was executed when the king was overthrown. Lady Diana Spencer, who is now the Princess of Wales, is his direct descendant.

Edward II of England

⚜ **An unlikely pair.** Queen Victoria and her servant, John Brown, remained close friends for 20 years. The queen allowed him to bully and protect her. When Brown died, Victoria erected memorials to him in many of her royal residences.

Many monarchs have had spectacular funerals and great monuments have been raised to preserve their memory. In many cultures, people believed that dead rulers would need riches and servants after death. Monarchs were often buried with all kinds of gifts and provisions for the next life.

Sumerian burials

In the 1920s, Sir Leonard Woolley, an archaeologist, uncovered tombs which dated from between c.2650-2500BC. They belonged to the rulers of the city of Ur in Mesopotamia (now part of Iraq). Each tomb included a chamber containing the royal body. Outside the chamber lay courtiers, guards and servants who had taken poison and died to be with their rulers.

The tomb of Queen Shudu-ad of Ur

Stone tomb chamber

Antechamber

Queen Shudu-ad

Gold, silver and copper bowls and a box inlaid with shell and lapis lazuli.

Wooden chest

Bowls

Gaming board

Wooden sledge

Five soldiers on guard

Two oxen to pull the sledge, and four grooms.

Ten handmaidens wearing headdresses and gold and silver trinkets.

Burying the pharaohs of Egypt

The Egyptians believed it was important to preserve a person's body for the next life. They preserved the bodies of dead pharaohs in a process called mummification (see below).

Once mummified, the rulers of the Old Kingdom (c.2649-2150BC) were buried in huge stone pyramids (see page 160), with piles of treasure for the next life. But robbers managed to plunder the tombs, so the bodies of later pharaohs were placed in chambers cut into cliffs near Luxor, where soldiers could guard them.

Mummifying a pharaoh's body

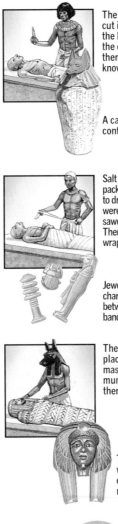

The embalmer made a cut in the left side of the body. He removed the organs and stored them in containers known as canopic jars.

A canopic jar containing organs

Salt called *natron* was packed around the body to dry it out. The insides were filled with linen or sawdust, resin and salt. Then the body was wrapped in bandages.

Jewels and lucky charms were placed between the layers of bandages.

The chief embalmer placed a portrait mask over the mummy's face. It was then put in a coffin.

The portrait mask was thought to enable the spirit to recognize its body.

Tutankhamun's tomb

The tomb of 18 year-old King Tutankhamun (14th century BC) lay undiscovered for 30 centuries. In 1922, men working for Howard Carter, an archaeologist, found steps leading to the door of the young king's tomb. It had been covered by rocks when the tomb of Ramesses VI was built.

Carter opening the tomb of Tutankhamun

Carter made a hole in the door of the tomb and peered inside. When he was asked if he could see anything, he said "Yes, wonderful things." Inside were the riches of a royal Egyptian burial, the only pharaoh's treasure ever to be recovered unplundered by robbers.

The four coffins of Tutankhamun

The funeral mask is a portrait of the young king.

This coffin is made of solid gold.

Mummified body

China's terracotta army

In 1974, farmers digging a well in Xian, China, found a huge underground complex. It was the tomb of Emperor Shih Huang Ti (see page 161), the largest tomb ever discovered. The burial chamber lies beneath modern villages and factories, making excavation work very slow. Ancient records say the tomb is protected by traps, such as crossbows set up to kill anyone who enters.

Outside the burial chamber, archaeologists have begun to uncover an army of 7500 pottery soldiers, horses and chariots. They had been put there to fight for the emperor in his next life.

A kneeling terracotta crossbow man

All the figures are life-sized.

Originally they were brightly painted.

A cross section of the pits in which the soldiers and horses stood

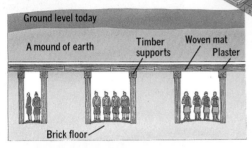

Ground level today

A mound of earth

Timber supports

Woven mat

Plaster

A mound of earth

Brick floor

The terracotta army of Shih Huang Ti

Each face is different, based on a particular soldier.

A squad of spear men

Four life-sized horses pulled each chariot

The outer coffins are made of wood covered with 22 carat gold and semi precious stones.

Burying a great queen

Queen Elizabeth I of England (1533-1603) died on March 24, 1603, at the age of 70. Her body was buried in Westminster Abbey a month later.

At Elizabeth's funeral, her coffin rested on a chariot pulled by four white horses. A wax effigy of the queen, clothed in royal robes, lay on top. The chariot was protected by a canopy carried by six knights.

This picture of Elizabeth's funeral procession was painted at the time of her death.

A wax effigy of Queen Elizabeth

Knights

The horse-drawn carriage was followed by a procession of mourners.

Fit for a king

👑 **Resting place.** The tomb of King Mausolus of Halicarnassus (now part of Turkey) was one of the most magnificent ever built. From his name comes the word mausoleum, meaning a building containing tombs.

During the 20th century, many monarchies have been overthrown, and the power of others has been restricted. But some countries are still ruled by powerful kings and queens.

Dictators and military leaders

Some monarchies have been destroyed in times of violence and revolution. The rulers that have replaced them have often ruled as strictly as any sovereign.

Mao Tse-tung (1893-1976) was the leader of the communists in China. He came to power after the years of unrest that followed the fall of the last Emperor of China (see page 177). He wielded great power over the country. His political ideas were written down in the "Little Red Book", which had to be carried by every citizen.

A picture of Mao Tse-tung

Mao Tse-tung was treated with great reverence. People were not allowed to throw away his picture. As newspapers were full of portraits of Mao, people saved every copy. Soon families had to move out of their houses which were full of newspapers. It was an offence to sit on a pile of newspapers containing Mao's picture.

Stamps commemorating China becoming a republic in 1949.

Presidents and heads of state

In some countries a monarch has been replaced by a leader elected by the people. These countries are called republics, and the title given to the leader is head of state or president. Many presidents are surrounded with the pomp and grandeur often associated with royalty and queens. For example, John F. Kennedy (1917-63) was one of the most popular presidents of the United States. He and his wife Jackie were seen by many people to be the ideal American family. During Kennedy's time in office the White House (the American presidential residence) was known as Camelot, after the court of the legendary King Arthur (see page 189).

The seal of the President of the United States of America

On November 22, 1963, John Kennedy was assassinated in Dallas, Texas. The event shocked the whole world.

President Kennedy and his wife Jackie, moments before he was shot and killed.

Constitutional monarchs

As countries have adopted democratic government (rule by the people), so the powers of monarchs have diminished. Today many kings and queens have little say in the running of their countries. They exist alongside governments that hold political power.

In many countries, royal power has been limited by a constitution. This is a set of guidelines outlining the powers and political principles according to which a country is governed.

Belgium, Sweden and the United Kingdom, whose flags are shown here, have constitutional monarchies.

A modern monarch

Elizabeth II, Queen of Great Britain and Northern Ireland is a modern, constitutional monarch. She has no role in governing the country. All political issues are decided by an institution which is called Parliament.

As queen, she is given information and advice on political issues by representatives of the government. But she has to remain free from ties to any political party.

Queen Elizabeth II's coat of arms

When laws have been passed by Parliament the queen gives them royal assent with the words "La reine le veut". This means it is the queen's wish that they become law.

Royal Duties

As a modern monarch, Queen Elizabeth II has a wide selection of duties to perform. She must lead formal ceremonies, such as the opening of Parliament. She is also head of the armed forces, and all soldiers have to swear loyalty to her.

Members of the royal family often visit foreign countries. This helps to maintain friendly relations between Great Britain and other nations, and encourages trade. The queen also supports many charities, using her name and influence to help them to raise money.

The queen can reward people whose actions have benefited the country. One of the top awards is a knighthood. The queen knights a person by touching them on their shoulders with a sword. This is called "dubbing".

Queen Elizabeth II travels by carriage to the official opening of Parliament.

Elizabeth II meets Jamaican women on a state visit.

Her Majesty Queen Elizabeth II, a state portrait by Sir James Gunn, painted in 1953

Still powerful

Today, there are a number of countries where the monarchs have retained substantial powers. For example, the leadership of King Fahd Ibn Abdulaziz (b.1921), who inherited the throne of Saudi Arabia in 1982, is of central importance to his kingdom.

King Fahd Ibn Abdulaziz

As head of Saudi Arabia's government as well as king, Fahd's decisions dictate policies both at home and in foreign affairs.

Return of the monarchy

There are some countries in which monarchies have been returned to power. In 1931, King Alfonso XIII of Spain was forced to leave the country when his subjects voted for Spain to become a republic. Later, Spain was ruled by Francisco Franco, a military dictator, who decided that the monarchy should be restored after his death. He named as his successor Alfonso's grandson, Juan Carlos, who became king in 1975.

A stamp showing King Juan Carlos

Teenager Grand Duke Georgy is the heir to the throne of Russia. He is a relative of Tsar Nicholas

Grand Duke Georgy

II of Russia, who was deposed by revolution in 1918 (see page 165).

Grand Duke Georgy has recently been granted Russian citizenship, and will receive his education at a Russian naval academy that was founded by his ancestor, Tsar Peter the Great. Maybe one day the Russian royal family will be restored as a constitutional monarchy.

Modern monarchs

Divine ancestors. Despite being a modern monarch, Elizabeth II can, in theory, trace her family tree back to Woden, an ancient father-god of Europe. She is descended from an Anglo-Saxon king named Cedric, who claimed to trace his family back to Woden.

Woden, or Odin as he is called in Scandinavia.

Mythical kings and queens

Before writing was widely used, stories of kings and queens were passed on by word of mouth. Often, as time passed, these stories were distorted and became extravagant tales of mythical figures. Historians often try to find out the facts which inspired the myths.

Gilgamesh

Legend tells of Gilgamesh, a king of Sumer (now Iraq), who set out on a quest looking for eternal life.

Gilgamesh's quest for eternal life

Gilgamesh went to the land of Dilmun. He met a man named Ut-napishtim, who told him that the secret of eternal life was a magic herb.

After many dangers, Gilgamesh found the herb, but it was eaten by a snake while he slept, depriving him of his goal.

Historians have found a king called Gilgamesh of Uruk, on an ancient list of Sumerian kings. The land of Dilmun has been identified as the island of Bahrain.

Amazon Queen

Hippolyte was the Queen of the Amazons, a band of women warriors described in Greek legends.

Amazons fighting Hercules

The Ancient Greeks believed that the Amazons lived on the coast of the Black Sea, in what is now Turkey. Later, they are said to have moved north, marrying Scythian horsemen. Their descendants were a people called the Sarmatians.

A statue of a Scythian archer

In the 1950s, archaeologists began to find graves of Sarmatian women containing weapons. This suggests the Amazons were not entirely mythical.

The palace at Knossos

According to Greek legend, the god Zeus fell in love with a princess called Europa. Assuming the shape of a bull, he swam to Crete with her on his back.

A picture of Europa and Zeus from an ancient vase

One of Europa's sons, Minos, became the King of Crete and lived in the palace of Knossos. Historians think that Minos was a title given to all the rulers of Crete, rather than one particular king.

Another legend tells of a Greek prince called Theseus who visited Crete. He killed a terrible monster, half human and half bull. It was called the Minotaur and lived in a maze called the Labyrinth.

To later generations, the ruins of Knossos may well have seemed like a maze, with its many rooms and corridors. The story of the Minotaur may have been inspired by a Cretan king wearing a bull's head mask during religious rituals.

This picture shows the palace of Knossos and some of its most famous artefacts.

This wall painting shows a young man in an elaborate headdress which suggests that he was a prince or a king.

Many bright wall paintings (like the one shown above) decorated the royal apartments

The palace was built and rebuilt several times between c.1900BC and 1450BC.

The queen's bathroom

Light entered the building through shafts

Experts think that over 30,000 people lived in the palace and surrounding area.

A fresco showing a bull-leaping ritual.
The figure on the right caught the leaper.

Archaeologists think that this is the throne of the kings of Crete.

The throne shown above was found in the throne room at Knossos.

The palace was decorated with images of a bull's horns.

The palace was built mainly of stone.

King Arthur

Arthur is a legendary king of Britain. He is said to have led a band of 1500 warriors, called the Knights of the Round Table, through many adventures.

King Arthur's name first appears in the 9th century writings of a monk named Nennius. The real Arthur is thought to have been a war-chief who fought the Saxons invading Britain around 500.

Arthur depicted as a medieval knight

Arthur presiding over his court, with his knights gathered at a round table

In the 12th century, monks at Glastonbury Abbey claimed to have uncovered the bodies of Arthur and his wife, Guinevere. It is uncertain whether they really did find the bones, or whether they hoped to raise money from pilgrims attracted by the find.

The elusive priest-king

The legend of Prester John began as early as the 12th century among Crusaders (see page 167). He was said to be a wealthy Christian priest-king who lived in the East.

In the 15th and 16th centuries people believed Prester John lived in Abyssinia (now Ethiopia). Many adventurers set off to find him, including Pedro da Covilhã, from the Portuguese court. Prester John was never found, but stories of him persisted into the 16th century.

An illustration of Prester John from a book of 1540

The buildings were arranged around a large courtyard which was used for religious ceremonies.

At its height the palace covered around 20,000 m² (215,000 ft²).

Store room

Food, oil and wine were stored in huge earthenware jugs that were taller than a fully grown man.

Fact or fiction?

The Golden mask. In 1876 Heinrich Schliemann excavated the city of Mycenae in Greece and found a body wearing a gold mask. He thought it was the face of King Agamemnon, a hero of Greek myths, but the mask belonged to a much earlier king.

The mask found by Schliemann

189

c.2649-2150BC Period of Old Kingdom in Egypt.

2262-2162BC Life of Pepi II, King of Egypt who reigned for 94 years.

c.2550BC The reign of Khufu of Egypt, buried in Egypt's largest pyramid.

17th-11th century BC The Sang Dynasty rules China.

16th century BC Queen Ahhotep acts as regent for her son.

1504-1450BC The life of Tuthmosis III of Egypt, a warrior king.

1503BC Queen Hatshepsut becomes regent for her stepson, Tuthmosis III.

c.1411-1375BC The life of Amenhotep III of Egypt, who befriends his chief minister.

14th century BC Akhenaten becomes Pharaoh of Egypt, and worships Aten the Sun god.

1361-1352BC The reign of Tutankhamun of Egypt, whose grave was uncovered in 1922.

1304-1237 BC Reign of Ramesses II of Egypt, a great builder.

1198-1167BC The reign of Ramesses III of Egypt, who suffers conspiracies at court.

7th century BC Amanirenas, queen mother of the Kingdom of Meroë in Africa, attacks Roman garrisons in southern Egypt.

5th century BC Queen Artemisia of Harlicarnassus fights at sea in Greece.

630-562BC The reign of Nebuchadnezzar II, who rebuilds the city of Babylon.

356-323 BC The life of Alexander the Great, King of Macedonia.

353BC Death of King Mausolus of Halicarnassus, who is buried in a great tomb.

273BC Asoka, King of the Mauryan empire in India, leads his army to war. Appalled by the slaughter, he becomes a Buddhist.

259-210BC The life of Zheng, who takes the title First Emperor of China.

69-30BC The life of Cleopatra of Egypt, who marries a Roman general called Antony.

37-4BC The reign of Herod the Great, King of Judea, who builds five palaces, including Masada.

1st century Queen Boudicca leads a rebellion against Roman forces in England.

14-37 The reign of Tiberius, Emperor of Rome, whose close friend is a man named Sejanus.

37-41 The reign of Caligula, Emperor of Rome, who suffered periods of madness.

51-54 The reign of Claudius, Emperor of Rome, who is poisoned by his wife.

54-68 The reign of Nero, Emperor of Rome, who is said to have set fire to Rome.

267 Queen Zenobia rules the city of Palmyra and fights the Romans.

361 Julian becomes Emperor of Rome and worships Roman gods.

c. 406-453 The life of Attila, King of an Asian tribe called the Huns.

c.500 A war-chief named Arthur fights the Saxons invading Britain.

584 King Chilperic of Neustria (now part of France) is murdered by his second wife Fredegond.

690 Wu Ze Tian seizes power and rules China.

751-68 The reign of Pepin the Short, King of the Franks.

771-814 The reign of Charlemagne, King of the Franks, a great patron of the arts.

c.956-1015 The life of Vladimir, ruler of the kingdom of Kiev.

987-996 The reign of Hugh Capet, King of France who replaces the Carolingian kings previously in power.

c.995-1030 The life of King Olaf Haraldsson of Norway, a Christian king. On one of his raids, Olaf pulls down London Bridge with grappling irons.

1066 William, Duke of Normandy, conquers England and becomes king.

1102-67 The life of Matilda, who, despite her efforts, is never crowned Queen of England.

1118-70 The life of Thomas Becket, Archbishop of Canterbury, close friend of Henry II of England and later a saint.

1216-72 The reign of Henry III of England, who becomes king at the age of nine.

1226 Blanche of Castille becomes regent for Louis IX of France.

1226-70 The reign of Louis IX of France, who joined the Crusades.

1272-1307 The reign of Edward I of England who marries Eleanor of Castile.

1306 The coronation of Robert I (1274-1329) of Scotland, known as Robert Bruce.

1359 Dom Pedro (1334-69), son of Alfonso XI of Portugal, marries Inez de Castro.

1362 A merchant called Giovanni is told by his dying mother that he is John I, rightful King of France.

1380-1422 Reign of Charles VI of France, who suffers from periods of madness.

1394-1460 The life of Prince Henry the Navigator, a Portuguese patron of explorers.

15th century The brutality of the prince of Wallachia (in modern Romania) gains him the name "Vlad the Impaler".

1413-22 The reign of Henry V of England, who invades France and wins the Battle of Agincourt.

1466-1519 The life of Montezuma, the last Aztec Emperor of Mexico.

1483 The reign of Edward V of England, one of the princes imprisoned in the Tower of London.

1485-1509 The reign of Henry VII of England, whose throne is claimed by two pretenders, Lambert Simnel and Perkin Warbeck.

1494-1566 The life of Süleyman the Magnificent, Sultan of Turkey, who marries a woman named Roxelana.

1509-47 The reign of Henry VIII of England, who marries six times.

1533 The largest ransom ever is paid for the life of Atahualpa, King of Peru.

1533 Henri, future Henri II of France, marries Catherine de Medici, but he is in love with Diane de Poitièrs, his mistress.

1530-84 The reign of Ivan IV, Tsar of Russia, known as Ivan the Terrible.

1533-84 The life of Prince William of Orange, killed by an assassin.

1542-87 The life of Mary, Queen of Scots, who marries her cousin Lord Darnley.

1542-1605 The life of Akbar the Great, one of the greatest Mogul emperors.

1558-1603 The reign of Elizabeth I of England, patron of the arts.

1566-1603 Life of Mahomet III, an Ottoman Sultan, who kills his brothers to ensure his throne.

1566-1625 The life of James I of England, who also rules Scotland.

1580-1663 The life of Jinga Mbandi, Queen of Matamba, West Africa, who gains independence for her kingdom.

1590-1617 The life of Sultan Ahmet I of Turkey, who introduces the Cage.

1592-1666 The life of Shah Jahan, one of the most powerful emperors of India.

1603 The False Dimitri invades Russia and is crowned tsar.

1617-82 The life of Lobsang Gyatso, the fifth ruler of Tibet, known as the Dalai Lama.

1625-49 The reign of Charles I, the only English king to be executed.

1638-1715 The life of Louis XIV of France, for whom the Palace of Versailles is built.

1660-85 The reign of Charles II of England, during which Colonel Blood attempts to steal the English crown jewels.

1665-1714 The life of Anne, Queen of England.

1682-1721 The reign of Peter the Great, Tsar of Russia, who builds the city of St. Petersburg.

1693-1740 The life of Anna of Russia, who treats her courtiers harshly.

1712-86 The life of Frederick the Great, King of Prussia, a formidable military leader.

1715-74 The reign of Louis XV of France, whose mistress is Madame de Pompadour.

1745 Bonnie Prince Charlie invades England, claiming the throne as the grandson of James II.

1746-1803 The life of Toussaint L'Ouverture, a revolutionary leader of the black slaves on the island of Haiti, in the Caribbean.

1760-1820 The reign of George III of England, who suffers from periods of madness.

1762-96 The reign of Catherine of Russia, known as "the Great".

1762-1830 The life of George IV of England, who builds the Royal Pavilion at Brighton and marries Caroline of Brunswick.

1774-93 The reign of Louis XVI of France, who dies with his wife Marie Antoinette at the guillotine.

1787-1828 The life of warrior Shaka, leader of the Zulu kingdom.

1804-15 The reign of Napoleon Bonaparte, First Consul and Emperor of France.

1810 The Duke of Cumberland, son of George III of England, is attacked by his valet.

1837-1901 The reign of Victoria, Queen of England.

1845-86 The life of Ludwig II of Bavaria, whose great passions are building and the music of a composer named Wagner.

1857 Lakshimbai, the Rani of the Kingdom of Jhansi, joins rebel leaders in a revolt against the British occupying India.

c.1871-1916 The life of Rasputin, friend and adviser to Tsar Nicholas II of Russia.

1889 Prince Rudolph, heir to the Austro-Hungarian Empire, is discovered dead at Mayerling.

1893-1976 The life of Mao Tse-tung, a Chinese leader.

1901-89 The life of Emperor Hirohito of Japan, who lives as god-king until 1946.

1918 Tsar Nicholas II of Russia is shot with his family at Yekaterinburg.

1920 Anna Anderson claims to be Anastasia, daughter of Tsar Nicholas II of Russia.

1924 Pu Yi, the last Chinese Emperor, leaves the Forbidden City.

1937 Edward VIII of England gives up his throne to marry Mrs Simpson, a divorcee.

1953 The coronation of Elizabeth II of Great Britain and Northern Ireland.

1959 Tenzin Gyatso, the 14th Dalai Lama of Tibet, flees to India.

1963 John F. Kennedy, President of the United States, is assassinated in Dallas, Texas.

1974 The coronation of Jigme Singe Wangchuck of Bhutan.

1975 King Juan Carlos is restored to the Spanish throne.

The Kings & Queens quiz

The answers to all the following questions can be found between pages 147 and 191 of this book. You will also find the answers upside down at the bottom of this page.

1. Which ruler had the shortest ever reign?
2. How many palaces did Herod the Great have built?
3. Who was the last Chinese emperor to live in the Forbidden City?
4. Why didn't anyone rescue Queen Sunanda when her barge overturned in 1881?
5. After whom was the French "pompadour" hairstyle named?
6. Ogadei Khan of the Mongols managed to halve the number of goblets of wine he drank each day while still drinking the same amount of wine. How?
7. Why did Louis XIV's chef, Monsieur Vatel, commit suicide?
8. Identify the following rulers:

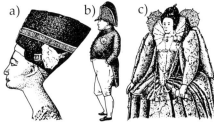

a) b) c)

9. From which goddess were Japanese emperors believed to be descended?
10. What is the name given to the ruler of Tibet?

11. How was Charles I of England executed?
12. Why was the skin disease scrofula known as the "King's Evil"?
13. Identify the shapes of these royal buildings:

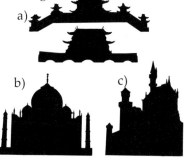

a)

b) c)

14. Which tribe did Boudicca lead into battle against the Romans?
15. What award for bravery was Queen Ahhotep given?
16. Which of the Seven Wonders of the Ancient World was created in Babylon?
17. Approximately how long is the Great Wall of China?
18. What was the name of the craftsman who made special eggs for Tsar Nicholas II of Russia?
19. Under what name did Queen Elizabeth of Romania publish her poems and fairy stories?
20. How was Marie Antoinette executed?
21. Upon which prince is the legend of Dracula based?
22. Who wrote a book called *The Prince*, advising rulers to be prepared to commit evil acts to secure power?

23. Name Henry VIII's six wives.
24. How is Queen Cleopatra of Egypt said to have died?
25. Why was Emperor Gaius of Rome known as Caligula?
26. Which king thought that he was made of glass?
27. What was the name of the bodyguard set up by "Ivan the Terrible"?
28. In the 17th century, who would have been locked up in the Cage in Turkey?
29. Anna Anderson spent 50 years trying to prove her royal identity. Who did she claim to be?
30. To which island did the Roman emperor Tiberius move in order to be safe from assassins?
31. Who stole the necklace shown here?

32. What is the name of the process that was used to preserve the bodies of Egyptian pharaohs after death?
33. Where was the terracotta army found?
34. What was Gilgamesh's quest?
35. What was the name of the band of warriors led by the legendary King Arthur?

FAMOUS WOMEN

Richard Dungworth and Philippa Wingate

Designed by Linda Penny

Illustrated by Nicholas Hewetson
Maps by Jeremy Gower

Managing designer: Russell Punter

Managing editors: Jane Chisholm and Anthony Marks
With thanks to Anna Claybourne and Rosie Heywood

CONTENTS

INTRODUCTION

Throughout history, remarkable women have become political leaders, record breakers and world-famous performers. Whether they were responsible for scientific breakthroughs or prison break-outs, these women achieved fame and recognition. This section of the book tells their stories.

Women and fame

Although women can be famous for all kinds of things, they are more likely to be well-known in certain fields. There are many famous female film stars and singers, for example, but fewer famous women politicians, doctors or artists.

Women who reach the top, like tennis champion Steffi Graf, are often paid less than male champions.

Some women, like the British politician Margaret Thatcher, are recognized for having succeeded in a man's world, doing a job traditionally associated with men.

It has always been hard for women to achieve success. This was especially true in the past. Women were traditionally expected to stay at home to bring up children and do housework.

This didn't leave them much time or opportunity to become great artists or athletes.

In many societies, women were "owned" or controlled by husbands, fathers or brothers. They didn't have their own money, which made it very difficult to start a business, travel, or create works of art.

Often the women who did succeed in their chosen field were born into well-off families. This gave them greater freedom from domestic chores to pursue their ambitions.

A 19th-century picture, showing a woman busy at her housework.

A few women chose to disguise themselves as men to escape the traditional female role and gain an education or social freedom. Miranda Stewart (see page 214), for example, spent her life dressed as a man so that she could be a doctor, at a time when women weren't allowed to study medicine.

The spread of fame

In the past, few individuals achieved long-lasting or widespread fame. Today, with mass media such as radio, television and the Internet, news travels across the world in seconds. This means that more women are enjoying greater fame than ever before.

Television creates its own "stars".

Women's rights

In many cultures, women still do not have equal rights. In parts of the world, such as Saudi Arabia and Kuwait, only men can vote. Even in the West, attitudes toward women's rights have changed slowly. In Switzerland, for example, women didn't have a vote until as recently as 1971. Many areas, such as politics, science and learning, are still dominated by men.

Toward the future

The 20th century has seen the growth of the feminist movement, whose followers believe in the social, economic and political equality of women. Women have fought to have the same rights as men and, as a result, things have changed. In many countries, women are allowed to work and have their own money. It is often illegal to discriminate against women in education or employment.

More and more women are rising to the top of their professions. The opportunity for women to gain fame and fortune is growing.

Today, a woman doctor is not an unusual sight.

THE FIRST GREAT WOMEN LEADERS

Since ancient times, there have been exceptional women who, despite the odds against them, have become great rulers. Their power and political skills made them great leaders.

Seizing the throne

Probably the first woman to wield real political power in ancient times was Queen Hatshepsut of Egypt (c.1540-1481BC). She began her career by acting as ruler for her young stepson. But instead of handing over power to him, she seized the throne herself during a religious ceremony.

The priests carried a statue of a god past Hatshepsut. It was so heavy that they sank to their knees.

Hatshepsut said that this was a sign that the gods wanted her to rule. She declared herself "king" of Egypt.

As ruler, she led successful military campaigns in Nubia and Syria, always dressing for battle in men's clothes.

When Hatshepsut died, her stepson finally became pharaoh. He hated Hatshepsut for depriving him of his position, and destroyed all the statues that had been made of her. Archeologists have only recently begun piecing together fragments of stone and finding out more about her achievements. It seems that her reign was very successful. As well as fighting battles, she encouraged trade and exploration, and built great works of architecture.

Nefertiti

Queen Nefertiti (14th century BC) had such a powerful influence over her husband, Akhenaten, that she may have become joint ruler of Egypt.

A stone bust of Nefertiti

Akhenaten showed his love and respect for Nefertiti by giving her a second name, which was Neferneferuaten. Usually, only kings were allowed to have two names.

In the 14th year of his reign, Akhenaten declared that someone called Smenkhkare was to become his co-ruler. The pharaoh gave his new co-ruler Nefertiti's name, Neferneferuaten.

Very little is known about Smenkhkare. Some historians think the mysterious co-ruler was actually Nefertiti herself. They think Akhenaten believed that his wife would never give birth to a son and heir, so he married his eldest daughter instead. In order to compensate Nefertiti for marrying someone else, he may have made her a "king".

A courageous empress

Theodora (c.497-548) rose from a poor background to become the co-ruler of a vast empire. She was born in Constantinople (now called Istanbul), where her father worked in a circus, taming bears. Theodora, who was famous for her beauty, worked as a dancer and mime artist. Later, she turned to religion and educated herself. While working as a wool spinner, she met Justinian, her future husband.

The palace of the Empress Theodora and Emperor Justinian in Constantinople

The Emperor and Empress were joint rulers and so each had a throne.

We know what kind of clothes were worn at the palace from a church mosaic.

These men have come to arrange a trading agreement.

Justinian was the nephew of the Emperor of the Eastern Roman Empire. He fell madly in love with Theodora and married her. In 527, they were crowned Emperor and Empress. They ruled the Empire from their beautiful palace in Constantinople.

Theodora had a great influence on her husband's policies and actions. She used her power to help women and the poor, and Justinian listened closely to her advice.

In 532, riots broke out in the city. Justinian prepared to flee the palace to save his life, but Theodora persuaded him to stay and fight. This proved to be wise advice. Justinian defeated the rioters and he and Theodora stayed in the palace. He survived to rule for over thirty years.

Armed guards protected the palace from attack.

Uniting force

During the 15th century, Queen Isabella (1451-1504) ruled Castile, one of the kingdoms which made up the country now known as Spain. She was a very ambitious queen. Her aim was to unite all the kingdoms and rule over them herself.

Queen Isabella and King Ferdinand

Isabella's first step towards this goal was in 1469, when she married Ferdinand, the heir to Aragon, another of the kingdoms.

The final kingdom to conquer was Granada in the south of Spain. Since the 8th century, it had been occupied by the Moors who were Muslims from northwest Africa. Isabella led an army against the Moors herself, and managed to drive them out of Spain. She also forcibly expelled all the Jews who lived in an area of southern Spain called Andalusia. By 1492, Isabella had succeeded in uniting Spain under her control.

During her reign, Isabella extended her empire overseas too. She gave Christopher Columbus, a Portuguese explorer, the money he needed to fund three ships to sail west in search of the Far East. In fact, Columbus ended up in the Bahamas, off the coast of America, by mistake. He became the first European to set foot there.

Columbus' route from Europe to America is shown in blue. His intended route is shown in red.

Columbus's ship, the *Santa Maria*

A great Czarina

A German princess named Princess Sophia of Anhalt-Zerbst (1729-96) married Grand Duke Peter, heir to the Russian throne, when she was 16 years old. She changed her name to Catherine and converted to Russian Orthodoxy, the official religion in Russia.

The marriage was not a happy one. Peter was mentally and physically weak. He spent much of his time playing with toy soldiers. When he became Czar in 1762, Catherine controlled the country. After only six months, she forced Peter off the throne. He was later murdered in prison.

A portrait of Catherine the Great

Catherine ruled Russia for 34 years until her death. During her reign, she encouraged education, art, science and religious tolerance. Although she sympathized with the plight of the poor, she did very little to help them. She ruled the country with a firm hand, putting down any rebellions mercilessly.

Her strength meant that her policies abroad were very successful. During her reign, she expanded Russia's territory, taking land from both Poland and Turkey.

MODERN LEADERS

During the first half of the 20th century, the efforts of women's rights campaigners, and the important role of women in both World Wars, has improved the political status of women in many societies. Some have even been chosen to lead their countries.

Golda Meir

Golda Meir (1898-1978) was born in Kiev, Russia, in a part of the city where Jewish families were forced to live. When she was eight years old, her family emigrated to the United States of America.

Golda trained as a teacher, but became active in Zionism, a political movement that wanted a homeland for Jews in Palestine. After she married, she went to live in Palestine.

She joined the Labour party and took part in creating the independent state of Israel in 1948.

The Israeli flag

Golda Meir held posts of increasing responsibility in the *Knesset*, the Israeli parliament. In 1969, when the Israeli prime minister Eshkol died, Golda took his place. During her five years in power, she campaigned for peace in the Middle East and security for Jews.

In 1973, a crisis known as the Yom Kippur War broke out against Egypt and Syria. Golda Meir helped to negotiate a ceasefire before she retired from politics in 1974.

An Israeli F4E fighter aircraft

Indira Gandhi

Indira Gandhi (1917-84) was the daughter of India's first prime minister, Nehru. At the age of 21, she became a member of the Congress party, and took a series of increasingly important jobs. In 1966, Prime Minister Lal Shastri died and Mrs. Gandhi, as she is now known, took his place.

Although she was an able politician, Mrs. Gandhi failed to deal with some of the enormous problems facing India at that time. Religious differences between groups of Muslims, Hindus and Sikhs led to fighting. The country suffered severe economic troubles, which were increased by a war with Pakistan. When rioting broke out, Mrs. Gandhi acted ruthlessly to regain control. She imprisoned thousands of her opponents, censored the press, and began to rule India as a dictator.

Indira Gandhi

These failures, along with accusations that she had cheated, caused Mrs. Gandhi to lose an important election in 1977. But she was determined to regain political power, and embarked on a campaign that covered 63,000 km (40,000 miles) in 63 days. She spoke publicly to over 240 million Indians.

She was re-elected Prime Minister in 1980, but she remained unpopular with many people. In 1984, Mrs. Gandhi was assassinated. The killers were her own Sikh bodyguards.

Evita

The popularity of Eva Perón (1919-52) played an enormous part in the political success of her husband, Juan, who become the president of Argentina in 1946.

Before she married, Eva was a well-known singer and actress in Argentina.

A poster for a show starring Eva Perón, before she gave up her acting career.

She was a brilliant speaker, and won the trust of the people, who affectionately called her "Evita". She founded hospitals, schools, parks and swimming pools, and attempted to improve conditions for workers.

When she died from cancer aged only 33, thousands of mourners filed past her coffin.

After his wife's death, Juan Perón's popularity fell sharply, and three years later he was ousted from power. He eventually remarried and was re-elected in Argentina many years later.

Eva Perón making one of her many charismatic public speeches

The Iron Lady

Margaret Thatcher was born in England in 1925. She abandoned an early career as a research chemist to become a politician. She joined the Conservative party, and became a member of the British Parliament in 1959.

The Conservative party symbol

In 1975, she became leader of the Conservative party, and in 1979 was elected Britain's first woman prime minister. She also became the first prime minister in the 20th century to win three consecutive elections. Margaret Thatcher was renowned for her tough style of leadership, which earned her the title "the Iron Lady".

The nickname reflected the way she dominated other members of her government, as well as her hard line on foreign policy.

In 1982, Britain's success against Argentina in the Falklands War increased Margaret Thatcher's popularity. But she was also seen as a heartless leader who didn't care about the poor, and was criticized for not supporting other women in her government.

In 1990, many Conservatives began to fear that she wouldn't win a fourth election. She had introduced the "Poll Tax", a method of taxing people, which had made her very unpopular. Eventually members of her own party forced her to resign as prime minister.

This is a view of the interior of the House of Commons, where the British Parliament meets.

The two leading parties sit on opposite sides of the House.

The leaders of the parties sit on the "front benches".

Front benches

Margaret Thatcher

Cory Aquino

In 1983, Senator Benigno Aquino was shot dead in Manila in the Philippines, the victim of a political conspiracy. The Philippines were ruled by President Marcos, a corrupt dictator who used the strength of the state army to maintain power.

Marcos's wife, Imelda, owned thousands of pairs of shoes. They became a symbol of the President's corruption.

Many Filipina people turned to Aquino's wife, Corazon Aquino (b.1933), known as Cory. They begged her to stand against Marcos in the 1986 election. The election was almost sabotaged by Marcos's supporters, but Cory was declared the winner. Some soldiers rebelled against Marcos, forcing him and his wife Imelda to flee the country, and Cory became president.

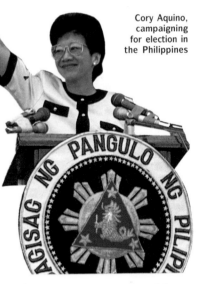

Cory Aquino, campaigning for election in the Philippines

She faced enormous problems. The luxurious lifestyle enjoyed by the Marcos family had plunged the country into debt. The political system was corrupt, and many of the people suffered terrible poverty.

Cory attempted to bring a new honesty and morality to Filipina politics. She survived several attempted uprisings, but didn't run for re-election in 1992.

FEMALE FIGHTERS

In many of the wars which have dominated history, women have taken up arms to defend their homelands and beliefs. Often they have had to disguise themselves as men to go to war.

Warrior queen

Boudicca, queen of a 1st-century British tribe called the Iceni, was one of the few leaders to defeat the mighty Roman army. When Roman troops raided Iceni territory in 60AD, they flogged Boudicca and abused her daughters. Enraged by this mistreatment, Queen Boudicca rallied her tribe for a ferocious military campaign.

Boudicca and her Iceni warriors attacked the Roman colonies of Camulodunum, Verulamium and Londinium (now the cities of Colchester, St. Albans and London). They killed 70,000 Romans.

The Roman governor of Britain gathered together an army of highly trained men. They overwhelmed the Iceni in a bloody battle. Facing defeat, Boudicca is said to have taken poison in order to avoid being captured.

One legend claims Boudicca's body is buried under platform eight of King's Cross, a railway station in London.

Far-eastern fighter

Hua Mu-lan (c.400) was the daughter of a 5th-century Chinese general. She became a fighter to protect her father. When he was called to war in his old age, Mu-lan feared for his safety. She insisted that she should go in his place, challenging him to a sword-fight, on the condition that he would allow her to go if she won.

Mu-lan won the duel, proving her sword skills. Then she disguised herself as a man, and went on to spend the next 12 years fighting battles for her country.

A Chinese painting of Hua Mu-lan

Legend says that Mu-lan's courage was so admired, and her male disguise so convincing, that one Commander-in-Chief offered her his daughter in marriage.

After her career as a soldier, Mu-lan returned home and gave up fighting. She lived the rest of her life at home, as a woman.

Iceni warriors leaving the settlement of Verulamium, having defeated the Roman army

The wooden Roman settlements were easily set alight.

Iceni warriors had padded tunics and oval shields.

Roman soldiers wore helmets and metal and leather tunics.

Boudicca, standing in an Iceni chariot, looks back on the ruins of the settlement.

God's soldier

In the early 15th century, a peasant girl from the French village of Domrémy began to hear voices. Jeanne d'Arc (c.1412-31) believed that the voices belonged to three Christian saints. They told her to overthrow the English army that had captured the Paris region of France. She was to ensure that Charles the Dauphin, the heir to the throne, was crowned as king of France.

Jeanne's religious conviction and great confidence inspired other French people to fight the English. She gathered an army and led them to victory in a battle for the city of Orléans.

The city of Orléans was protected by high stone walls.

Jeanne leads the Dauphin's army to defeat the city of Orléans.

Jeanne dressed for battle in men's clothing.

After capturing Orléans, Jeanne's army advanced to the city of Rheims, where the Dauphin was crowned.

Jeanne's sword broke while she was fighting the English near Paris. Her followers saw this as a sign of bad luck.

The English captured Jeanne and accused her of using witch-craft. She was burned at the stake in 1431.

After her death, Jeanne became a national heroine. She was eventually made a saint in 1920.

African Queen

Jinga Mbandi (c.1580-1663) was the sister of the ruler of the West African kingdom of Ndongo. She attempted to negotiate her country's independence from the Portuguese settlers who were trading in slaves there. During the negotiations with the Portuguese governor, Jinga sat on one of her servants because she wasn't offered a chair.

When her brother died, Jinga became queen. Soon after, the Portuguese drove her out of Ndongo. Jinga trained soldiers herself and fought back repeatedly.

Jinga Mbandi sitting on a servant

Soldiering on

In the 17th century, men were often seized and forceably recruited into the English army. Richard Welsh was a typical victim. His wife was less typical. Christian Welsh (1667-1739), best known as Kit Cavanagh, set out to find her husband.

Richard was made helplessly drunk, kidnapped and sent to fight French forces in the Netherlands.

Determined to rejoin her husband, Christian cut her hair, wore men's clothes and joined the army.

She spent 13 years as a soldier before finding her husband, and fought bravely in several major European battles.

Christian's true identity was only discovered by surgeons operating on a head wound she had received in combat. Even after this, she decided to stay in the army and worked as a cook. She died in a hospital for old soldiers in 1739.

REFORMERS

Many women have taken action against the injustices they have witnessed around them. They have fought, sometimes quite literally, for safety and equality for all.

New look Newgate

In 1813, having heard many stories of the appalling conditions in English prisons, Elizabeth Fry (1780-1845) visited Newgate, the largest and most notorious of London's jails. She was horrified by what she found.

Over 300 women were locked up, along with their children, in one cramped cell. Those convicted of serious crimes were held with others who were awaiting trial for minor crimes. The women were clothed in filthy rags, and had no proper beds, toilets, or washing facilities. Many of them drank heavily to try to forget the squalor.

Elizabeth began to pay regular visits to the women of Newgate.

Elizabeth Fry

She won their trust by bringing them fresh clothes and talking kindly to them. She persuaded them to work together toward an improved standard of living. In an empty cell, Elizabeth set up a school for the prisoners' children. She chose well-behaved inmates to keep order. She made a deal with the women that if they stopped gambling and drinking, she would find them paid work.

Elizabeth's ideas improved living conditions and prisoner discipline in Newgate to such an extent, that it was not long before other prison authorities copied her approach. She toured Europe giving lectures to promote her ideas about prison reform.

Soujourner Truth

Many women were involved in the struggle to abolish slavery in the USA. Isabella Van Wagener (1797-1883), an African-American woman, was born into slavery but gained her freedom in 1828, with the abolition of slavery in her home state of New York.

Isabella believed that God wanted her to fight for the abolition of slavery throughout the USA. She took the name "Sojourner Truth", which means "one who works for truth", and toured the country. Her powerful speeches drew large crowds, and helped bring about the end of American slavery.

Sojourner Truth

Before Elizabeth Fry's reforms, conditions in the cells were cramped and filthy.

Newgate Prison, with the women's wing on the right-hand side.

The women were able to earn a little money by sewing.

Elizabeth read aloud to the women to entertain and educate them.

Temperance tantrums

People who campaign against the abuse of alcohol are known as temperance workers. The most formidable was an American named Carry Nation (1846-1911). She was briefly married to an alcoholic doctor and this inspired her lifelong opposition to drink.

Carry led other temperance workers in "saloon-smashing" expeditions, when they wrecked the interiors of drinking establishments with hatchets. Despite being repeatedly imprisoned for breach of the peace, she continued to use "hatchetation" to oppose the sale of alcohol.

Carry funded her campaign and paid her many fines, by lecturing, appearing on stage, and selling souvenir hatchets.

In 1920, nine years after Carry's death, a ban on alcohol, known as Prohibition, was imposed throughout the USA. However, the ban proved too hard to enforce, and was lifted in 1933.

This cartoon shows Carry Nation wielding a hatchet. Besides alcohol, she opposed corsets, short skirts, tobacco and foreign food.

Working for peace

During her lifetime, Jane Addams (1860-1935) was called both "the greatest American who ever lived" and "the most dangerous woman in the country". She devoted her life to campaigning for justice and peace for all.

In her youth, Jane trained as a doctor. When poor health forced her to give up medical school, she remained determined to help people. She witnessed the terrible conditions suffered by families

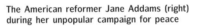

The American reformer Jane Addams (right) during her unpopular campaign for peace

who lived in the slums of Chicago. She opened Hull House, a settlement that offered help to poor immigrants. The idea caught on quickly, and local clubs were set up offering medical care, child care, and classes in English and fine arts. By 1893, there were forty clubs helping over 2000 women and girls a week.

Jane Addams lost her popularity, however, after campaigning for peace during World War I. She believed that fighting was wrong, an attitude many Americans considered very unpatriotic.

Despite violent opposition, Jane stuck to her beliefs. She set up a Woman's Peace Party in the USA and was the first President of the Women's International League for Peace and Freedom. After the fighting was over, she helped send food to Europeans who had been left poor, hungry and devastated by the war.

The Montessori Method

Maria Montessori (1870-1952) changed the way that young children all over the world were educated. After becoming the first woman in Italy to qualify as a doctor, Maria began working in a clinic in Rome with mentally handicapped children. She

Maria Montessori

realized that the oppressive style of education typical in her day wasn't very effective.

She believed that using bright, attractive teaching materials, and "fun" exercises would greatly improve the children's progress.

The Italian government asked Maria to set up a *Casa dei Bambini*, or "Children's House", in a poor area of Rome. She produced impressive results by using equipment and techniques which encouraged her pupils' natural tendency to learn by play. Her success led to the adoption of the "Montessori Method" of education in children's schools around the world.

Children learning through play and fun exercises, according to the Montessori Method.

REVOLUTIONARIES

There have been women who lacked political power, yet inspired revolutionary movements. Their words and ideas challenged the injustice and inequality they found in the governments of their day.

Revolution and Roland

The French Revolution of 1789 was an uprising against the privileges enjoyed by the aristocrats who dominated the country. Several people were responsible for developing the ideas of equality and liberty that led to the revolution. One was a woman named Manon Roland (1754-93).

Manon believed that French citizens of all classes should be treated equally. She hoped that revolution would end the unfairness in society.

Manon became well-known for organizing gatherings of famous political thinkers. Her ideas inspired people to overthrow the ruling classes.

Manon Roland

When revolution came, King Louis XVI and many aristocrats were executed by guillotine. A group of extreme anti-royalists called the Jacobins seized power. They hated Manon because she had been against the King's execution. Despite supporting the revolution, Manon was sent to the guillotine.

Crowds gather to watch an execution.

Voice of the people

Alexandra Kollontai (1872-1952) witnessed the terrible conditions suffered by workers and decided to devote her life to bringing about a revolution in her native Russia.

In 1896, Alexandra visited a textile factory in Finland. She was shocked by the workers' terrible conditions and long hours.

Back home in Russia, she saw the Czar's troops killing hundreds of workers who were peacefully demonstrating.

Alexandra made speeches calling for fair conditions for workers and freedom for women. But the secret police were watching her.

Alexandra was continually harassed for her political activities, so she fled abroad in 1908. She didn't return until 1917, after revolution had broken out and the Czar had been deposed.

In Russia's new government, she became Commissar for Public Welfare. But her outspoken views made her unpopular and she was sent abroad to help foreign trade. Finally, in Sweden, she became the first ever female ambassador.

The guillotine was a machine for beheading people.

This blade was released to kill the prisoner.

The victim's neck was held in a small hole and a blade fell on it from above.

The people cheered as members of the aristocracy were beheaded.

Red Rosa

Polish-born Rosa Luxemburg (1870-1919) was a devoted believer in the ideals of communism, which aims for a society without classes and with common ownership of property. After she had moved to Germany in 1898, Rosa began to organize many revolts and strikes, urging workers to challenge their bosses.

Rosa Luxemburg

Rosa was jailed repeatedly for her beliefs. She was even given the nickname "Red Rosa", because red was associated with communism.

In 1914, she set up an anti-war organization known as the Spartacus League. The League campaigned for an end to international wars, encouraging the German people to overthrow their government instead.

In January 1919, members of the League attempted an uprising. When it failed, Rosa went into hiding. She was found by soldiers, beaten and shot. However, her political writings continued to be very influential long after her death.

During her many prison sentences, Rosa was able to develop and write about her political ideas.

Freedom fighter

At the beginning of the 20th century, Ireland was governed by the British Parliament, based in London. Many Irish people wanted their country to have its own government. They were known as Republicans. Constance Markiewiecz (1876-1927) was one of their most famous and popular leaders.

Constance Markiewiecz

In 1916, Constance took part in the Easter Rising, in which Republican and British forces clashed at St. Stephen's Green in Dublin, the Irish capital. She marched at the head of a column of 120 Irish soldiers. Together, they fought for three days before being forced to surrender.

Constance leads the Republican soldiers to St. Stephen's Green.

Constance was sent to prison in England for her part in the Easter Rising. She was so popular, however, that in 1918 the people of Dublin elected her as their Member of Parliament. This made her the first woman ever to be elected. Constance refused to take up her seat, however, because she was opposed to British rule in Ireland.

Under house arrest

In 1988, a young woman named Aung San Suu Kyi (b.1945) became aware of the injustices being committed by the military leaders of Myanmar (formerly Burma). She decided to fight for the people's right to choose their own government, forming a political party called the National League for Democracy.

Suu Kyi showed great courage in her political activities. Once, soldiers threatened to shoot her for walking down a road. When she refused to stop, they aimed their guns, but two officers stopped them from firing.

For six years, Suu Kyi was under house arrest, unable to leave her house, or see her family who lived in Britain. Sometimes she didn't even have enough to eat. In 1990, her party won an election, although the authorities ignored the result, and in 1991 she was awarded a Nobel peace prize.

Suu Kyi was released from house arrest in July 1995 and began to campaign again. Despite regaining her freedom, she remains under surveillance and as yet, the Government has refused to hold meetings with her and her supporters.

Suu Kyi speaking to her supporters in 1995

WOMEN HELPING WOMEN

Throughout history, women have lacked rights and have been treated as inferior to men. While many women have put up with this, some have protested against unfair treatment and urged others to do the same. This kind of protest became the basis for modern feminism.

Speaking out

One of the first marches for women's rights was led by a Roman woman named Hortensia. In 43BC, a civil war was raging throughout the Roman Empire. Mark Antony, the leader of one of the factions, decided to raise funds for the war by taxing 1,400 wealthy women. The women refused to pay for a war which involved Romans fighting each other.

Mark Antony's head on a coin

They wanted the chance for their political opinions to be heard by the government, so they marched to the Forum, a meeting place in Rome, to put their case. Hortensia was their spokeswoman. She succeeded in persuading the Roman governors to reduce the number of women taxed to 400.

Hortensia meets the governors of Rome at the steps of the Forum.

Suffragettes

In most countries, women were denied suffrage – the right to vote in political elections – until the 20th century. In Britain, Emmeline Pankhurst (1857-1928) and her daughter, Christabel (1880-1958), were among the first to fight for votes for women. They were known as suffragettes.

At first, Emmeline organized peaceful marches, demonstrations and appeals to Members of Parliament. When this didn't work, she and her followers turned to more extreme methods.

Some suffragettes chained themselves to the railings outside the Prime Minister's residence.

Some broke windows in Parliament and shouted at Members from boats on the River Thames.

A suffragette named Emily Davison threw herself under the King's racehorse in the 1913 Derby and was killed.

Emmeline and her fellow suffragettes were often arrested. In prison, they went on hunger strike. This seriously damaged Emmeline's health.

The symbol of the Women's Social and Political Union, founded by the Pankhursts in 1903

Emmeline Pankhurst being arrested

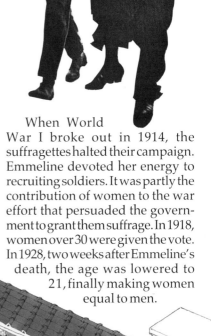

When World War I broke out in 1914, the suffragettes halted their campaign. Emmeline devoted her energy to recruiting soldiers. It was partly the contribution of women to the war effort that persuaded the government to grant them suffrage. In 1918, women over 30 were given the vote. In 1928, two weeks after Emmeline's death, the age was lowered to 21, finally making women equal to men.

The protestors gathered in the square.

Hortensia

Woman's army

As a child, Ch'iu Chin (1879-1907) realized that women in China were dependent on the men in their families and had very little freedom. Even the law said women were inferior to men. Blaming the Manchus, who had ruled for over 300 years, Chin decided to spend her life fighting for women's rights.

In 1904, Chin left her famly to study politics in Japan. It was an extreme step for a Chinese woman to take at this time.

By wearing men's clothes and learning to ride and use a sword, she encouraged women to behave as they pleased.

As part of her revolutionary plan to overthrow the Manchus, Chin learned how to fight and make bombs.

When she returned to China, Chin taught at a college. She set up a newspaper for women, and organized her students into a women's army. Government troops searched the college and found stashes of ammunition and weapons. Chin was arrested in 1907 and beheaded immediately.

Four years later, there was a revolution in China. The new rulers had a different attitude toward women. They praised Chin for the part she had played in preparing women for revolution.

Ch'iu Chin's photograph shown on a poster

Gaining control

While she was nursing in New York, Margaret Sanger (1883-1966) saw many of the difficulties facing women with large families. Many women endured poor conditions and ill-health. Her own mother had died at the age of 49, leaving 11 children.

Margaret encouraged women to limit the size of their families by using contraception – ways to prevent pregnancy. She came up with the name "birth control" to describe this process.

In a pamphlet called *Family Limitation,* she gave advice on how to use contraception. At that time, spreading information about birth control was illegal. When she opened a birth control clinic, Margaret was sent to prison.

She started the American Birth Control League, striving to gain political support for her views.

Margaret Sanger (left) outside the court where she was tried

Gradually, the law and public opinion began to change, and the number of birth control clinics grew. In 1937, the law finally allowed doctors to prescribe contraceptives.

Modern forms of contraception

Strong words

The French novelist and philosopher Simone de Beauvoir (1908-86) was a hugely influential feminist.

In 1949, she set out her ideas in a book called *The Second Sex.* Controversially, she argued that motherhood, marriage and social conditioning imprisoned women. The book became an international bestseller and a focus for the women's movement.

Simone believed that it was time for women to choose their own roles in society, which included deciding whether they wanted to have children. She argued that contraception should be easily available, and spoke in support of abortion. In 1974, she became president of the League for the Rights of Women and campaigned for help for battered wives, working women and single parents.

Simone de Beauvoir

With her lifelong companion, the philosopher Jean-Paul Sartre, Simone helped to set up a political newspaper, *Les Temps Modernes* ("Modern Times"). She was photographed around the world, meeting leaders who supported her political beliefs.

Although Simone's views were controversial, she was recognized in France as a heroine. In 1986, French radio interrupted broadcasts to announce her death.

ROBBERS AND ROGUES

Women are not generally known for breaking the law. Even today, male criminals vastly outnumber female ones. A few notorious women, however, are remembered for their crimes.

Moll Cutpurse

Mary Frith (c.1590-1659) was a pickpocket who chose her victims on the streets of London. In her day, people often carried their money in purses tied around their waists. Thieves would secretly cut the ties to steal the purses. Frith was so good at this that she gained the nickname "Moll Cutpurse".

Later, Moll found that she could make even more money buying stolen goods from other thieves, and then selling them for a higher price.

She sold her booty in a "second-hand" shop. The shop was visited both by robbers and by their victims, who came to buy back their stolen possessions. Moll became so well-known that, by the time she was 26, she was made the subject of a successful play, entitled *The Roaring Girle*.

A drawing of Moll from a poster advertising The Roaring Girle

The Bandit Queen

In the 19th century, the cowboy towns of the American "Wild West" produced several women bank robbers, swindlers, and cattle thieves. The most famous of these was the outlaw known as Belle Starr (1848-89) who became the subject of many stories and legends.

Belle Starr

She eloped with another outlaw, Jim Reed. In Texas, they took part in a famous stagecoach hold-up. But Reed was killed in a gun-fight a year later.

In 1880, Belle got married again, to the outlaw Sam Starr. They settled in Oklahoma together to pursue a life of crime.

Belle lived in a cabin she called Younger's Bend. It became a popular hideout for outlaws such as Jesse James.

She led a gang of outlaws that met at Younger's Bend to plan robberies. The newspapers called Belle "The Bandit Queen".

She masterminded several raids to steal horses. But thanks to her legal skills, Belle only went to prison once for her crimes.

The U.S. government offered thousands of dollars for Belle's capture, but she still survived longer than many of her fellow outlaws. In 1889, she was captured and stories circulated that her own son shot her dead in an ambush at Younger's Bend.

A poster issued by the United States government for the capture of Belle Starr

REWARD $10,000 IN GOLD COIN will be paid by the U.S. Government for the apprehension DEAD OR ALIVE of SAM and BELLE STARR Wanted for Robbery, Murder, Treason and other acts against the peace and dignity of the U.S. THOMAS CRA...

Mata Hari

Margarete Zelle (1876-1917) moved from the Netherlands to live in Java, in the East Indies, when she was 19 years old. There she learned the skills of exotic eastern-style dancing. With her new talent, she decided to go to France to become a dancer.

She gave herself the stage name "Mata Hari", which means "child of the dawn" in Javanese. She became well-known for her sensational performances in Paris.

Many important men sent her gifts, and before long she was a very wealthy woman. In 1914, however, World War I broke out and Mata Hari embarked on a new profession as a spy.

Mata Hari in an exotic dancing costume

In 1917, the French government accused her of coaxing military secrets from her lovers and sending the information to their German enemies. Mata Hari insisted that she had been spying for the French, but nobody believed her. She was executed by a firing squad. Some people still believe that she was innocent.

Mata Hari awaits execution by a firing squad in 1917.

Bonnie and Clyde

The American waitress Bonnie Parker (1911-34) and her lover Clyde Barrow were infamous criminals. At first they only committed petty crimes, such as burglary and theft, but they went on to bank robbery and murder.

At one point Barrow was sent to prison for two years. Bonnie managed to get a pistol smuggled into jail for him. He used it to escape.

Barrow was recaptured and was transferred to a much tougher jail, known by its prisoners as "Burning Hell".

As soon as Barrow was released, he and Bonnie started to gather other criminals together to form the "Barrow Gang".

Working with the Barrow Gang, they stole guns from a government weaponry, and used them in a series of robberies and killings.

Bonnie and Clyde fooling around with a machine gun

Bonnie and Clyde became famous throughout America. In 1934, they died in a hail of bullets as they drove into a police ambush.

Bonnie and Clyde were ambushed by police while driving a gang car.

The Beautiful Robber

Phoolan Devi (b.1963) is known throughout northern India as "The Beautiful Robber". When she was only 16, Phoolan ran away from her bullying husband and joined a gang of bandits. The gang's leader, Vikram Mallah, taught Phoolan how to use weapons and camouflage.

In 1980, two members of the gang, the Singh brothers, shot Mallah dead and took Phoolan prisoner. They beat and abused her for three weeks, until she managed to escape.

Phoolan soon took over the leadership of another gang of bandits. She led her gang in a revenge attack against the Singhs' home village, killing 24 of the Singhs' relatives and friends.

Thousands of policemen pursued Phoolan for over two years, before she finally gave herself up.

Phoolan held by police after giving herself up

Since her arrest, Phoolan Devi has become better known for her political opinions than for her crimes. When she was released in 1994, she began a political campaign to seek election.

Bullet holes in the side of the car after the ambush.

BRAVE AND BOLD WOMEN

Many women have shown remarkable courage in the face of adversity, often putting their own lives at risk to save others. Their heroic deeds have ensured their lasting fame.

Black Moses

In the mid-19th century, slavery was outlawed in the northern American states, but in the South it was still permitted. Black slaves in the South tried to escape to freedom in the North by following a route known as the "Underground Railroad".

There were some people along this route who disagreed with slavery. They provided the escaping slaves with food, clothing and shelter. The Railroad had "conductors", who guided escapees on their journey to the northern states and Canada where they would be safe from recapture. The most famous conductor was a woman named Harriet Tubman (c.1820-1913).

Slaves wore tags like this to show who they were.

Harriet had escaped from slavery herself and she repeatedly risked recapture by leading slaves to freedom. Among the 300 people she helped were several members of her family. Angry slave-owners offered huge rewards for her capture.

Harriet was given the nickname "Black Moses", after Moses in the Bible, who led his people, the Israelites, to the safety of the Promised Land.

$1200 TO 1250 DOLLARS! FOR NEGROES!!
NEGROES.
WM. E. TALBOTT

In this poster of 1853, a trader offers $1,200 or more for black slaves, who were at that time known as "negroes".

The rebellious Rani

British forces spent much of the 19th century trying to force the people of India to accept British rule. In an uprising known as the Indian Mutiny, several Indian states raised armies against the British. A woman named Lakshmi Bai (1835-57) became famous for her heroism during the Mutiny.

Lakshmi was married to the ruler, or *Raja*, of the Indian state of Jhansi, and took the title of *Rani*.

When the Raja died, Britain declared that Jhansi couldn't remain an independent state, but had to accept British rule.

This picture of Lakshmi Bai, the Rani of Jhansi, was painted in 1890.

Lakshmi protested to the British, but to no avail. So, at the outbreak of the Mutiny, she led Indian troops into battle. She fought courageously, wearing a soldier's uniform, wielding a two-handed sword, and holding the reins of her horse in her teeth, but was cut down by a British cavalryman.

Talking fingers

A less dramatic, but no less heroic, story is that of an American woman named Helen Keller (1880-1968), who showed great courage in overcoming severe disabilities. As a baby, she suffered from a disease called scarlet fever which left her totally blind and profoundly deaf. Helen's parents found an extraordinary teacher named Anne Sullivan to help Helen.

Harriet Tubman, who was nicknamed "Black Moses" for helping slaves escape.

This map of the United States of America shows the states in which slavery was still permitted in 1844.

States where slavery was permitted

Helen Keller "listened" to the radio by touching its case with her fingers to feel the vibrations.

Anne, who was partially sighted herself, proved to be a wonderful teacher. Under her guidance, Helen learned to read Braille and communicate using special finger movements to spell words into another person's palm. She could understand speech by placing her fingertips on a speaker's lips while they spoke.

Helen attended college and gained a degree with distinction. She was accompanied at all times by her teacher. In later life, she gave lectures on how disabilities such as hers could be overcome. Her relentless campaigning in aid of the American Foundation for the Blind raised over two million dollars. Her work promoted public awareness of the challenges faced by blind and deaf people all around the world.

This Braille watch has raised bumps which enable blind people to tell the time.

Against all odds

In the 1930s, an English woman named Gladys Aylward (1902-70) was working as a missionary in northern China. When Japanese soldiers invaded the region, Aylward went to work as a governess at a home for war orphans. She devoted herself to helping the Chinese army by spying for them. When the Japanese realized what she was doing, they came after her.

As Gladys fled from the Japanese soldiers across a graveyard, one of them shot her in the back. Fortunately, she was protected by her traditional, thickly padded Chinese coat.

Gladys Aylward's passport

Although the bullet knocked her over, it didn't seriously injure her. Quickly, she wriggled out of her coat and hid in a ditch. The soldiers shot at the coat again, thinking Gladys was still wearing it. Finally they went, presuming that she was dead.

Gladys decided that she must evacuate the war orphans in her school, and take them to the safety of Sian, in western China. She and over a hundred children set off on a two-month trek that took them over the mountains and across the Yellow River. They were helped by a group of Chinese soldiers, who gave them much-needed food and transportation. On one stretch of the journey, the children had to hide in coal wagons to avoid the Japanese troops. Against all odds, Gladys and her group finally reached Sian unharmed.

Gladys Aylward led her band of children to safety across many miles of Chinese countryside.

Secret agent

During World War II, some French citizens secretly gathered to oppose the German invaders. They formed the Resistance Movement. Violette Szabo was one of many British agents sent to help them. She was dropped into France by parachute in June 1944.

Violette parachuting into enemy territory

Violette sacrificed her life when she and a Resistance leader named Anastasie were ambushed by Germans.

As the two women fled through a cornfield, Violette stumbled and sprained her ankle. She couldn't go any farther.

Insisting that Anastasie went on, Violette crawled to the edge of the field, stood up, and opened fire on the soldiers.

She held their attention until Anastasie could escape. Finally, she ran out of ammunition and was captured.

Just two months before the war ended, Violette Szabo was shot. After her death, she was awarded medals for the incredible bravery she had shown.

NOTORIOUS WOMEN

The despicable deeds of certain women have ensured their lasting infamy. Some women are deservedly notorious for their crimes; in other cases their evil deeds have been exaggerated.

Popes and poison

Lucrezia Borgia (1480-1519) belonged to an Italian family that was renowned for merciless political scheming. Her father's ruthless plotting led him to become Pope Alexander VI.

By the time she was in her early 20s, Lucrezia had been married three times. Many people believed that she was also involved in a number of scandalous love affairs.

Rings containing capsules of poison

She was even said to be a witch, who had killed many people using special rings containing poisoned capsules. According to the stories, she slipped these capsules secretly into her victims' drinks.

After her marriage to the Duke of Ferrara, Lucrezia established her court as a place where many poets, writers, musicians and painters would gather.

Lucrezia Borgia probably didn't deserve her bad reputation. It is likely that she was accused of these crimes because of the unpopularity of several other members of her family. Despite this, however, she continued to have a reputation as a villainess.

Lucrezia Borgia was used as a model for the figure of Saint Catherine in this painting.

Bloody Mary

Mary Tudor (1516-1558), the daughter of Henry VIII and Katherine of Aragon, became Queen Mary I of England in 1553.

At this time, the country was divided between Catholics and Protestant members of the Anglican Church, set up by Henry VIII as the official Church of England.

Mary was a very devout Catholic, and several Protestant noblemen wanted to keep her out of power. Before Mary could take the throne, they crowned a 16-year-old named Lady Jane Grey, the great-granddaughter of Henry VII. After only nine days, Mary Tudor sent her troops to arrest Jane, and took the throne for herself.

Jane and her husband were beheaded on Tower Green in the Tower of London.

Queen Mary I of England

This scene shows Protestants being burned at the stake.

This marked the beginning of Mary's reign of terror. She planned to crush any rebellions, wipe out Protestantism, and restore Catholicism as the state religion in England. On her instructions, many Protestants were put on trial, including Thomas Cranmer, the Archbishop of Canterbury. They were accused of being heretics, because they refused to follow Catholicism. Those who were found guilty were burned at the stake.

Over 300 people were put to death during the five years of Mary's reign. For her cruelty and willingness to execute people, she was given the title "Bloody Mary".

The Tower of London, site of many executions

Each prisoner was tied to a pole, or stake.

Firewood around each prisoner was set alight.

The crowds jeered at the prisoners.

Mounted guards watched over the burnings.

Rat poison

At the age of 22, a Scottish woman named Madeleine Smith (1835-1928) agreed to marry William Kinnoch, a wealthy local businessman. But Madeleine was already secretly engaged to another man.

Madeleine's fiancé was a warehouse clerk named Pierre Emile L'Angelier. L'Angelier tried desperately to prevent her from marrying Kinnoch. He even threatened to show her father the passionate love letters that he had received from her.

Madeleine Smith

One of the letters sent by Madeleine to L'Angelier, which he used to blackmail her.

Pierre Emile L'Angelier

On several occasions, L'Angelier demanded that Madeleine meet him, and tried to persuade her to marry him instead of Kinnoch. After one of these meetings, in March 1857, L'Angelier died suddenly and painfully. When tests on his body showed that he had been poisoned by repeated doses of a deadly chemical called arsenic, Madeleine became the prime murder suspect.

She had an obvious motive for wanting to kill L'Angelier quickly, so that she could marry her wealthier suitor. The police also discovered that she had bought arsenic from a local chemist's shop three times shortly before the murder. But Madeleine claimed that she had used the arsenic to poison some rats that were infesting her house.

She was brilliantly defended by a top lawyer in what became one of the 19th century's most sensational trials. She eventually walked free after the jury returned a verdict of "not proven".

Nursery crimes

In 1892, Lizzie Borden (1860-1927) was accused of a double murder. The victims were her father and stepmother, killed with an axe at their home in Fall River, Massachusetts. The only other people in the house at the time were Lizzie and an Irish maid.

Almost a year after the murders, Lizzie Borden was put on trial. There was a lot of very strong evidence against her.

She had often argued with her father over his meanness, and had argued bitterly with her stepmother.

The axe was found in the Bordens' cellar, and Lizzie had been seen burning a dress, which may have been bloodstained.

Nevertheless, Lizzie was found not guilty because there was not enough evidence to convict her. Despite the hostility of the townspeople, she lived in Fall River for the rest of her life.

Today, children in America still sing a nursery rhyme that tells the story of Lizzie Borden's terrible crime. The words of the rhyme are shown below.

Lizzie Borden took an axe, Gave her mother forty whacks; When she saw what she had done She gave her father forty-one.

Terror tactics

In May 1970, Ulrike Meinhof (1934-76) helped Andreas Baader, a West German terrorist, to escape from prison. Baader had been arrested for setting fire to department stores in protest against German industrialists, government policies and American forces in Germany. When Ulrike, who was a journalist, interviewed Baader in prison, he convinced her that violent action was necessary to bring about political change.

She became a leader of a group called the *Röte Armee Fraktion* (Red Army Faction), which became known as the Baader-Meinhof gang. They robbed banks, planted bombs, and carried out political assassinations in an attempt to damage the government.

The Red Army Faction symbol

Ulrike Meinhof was finally arrested in June 1972 and sentenced to eight years in prison. On 9 May 1976, however, she committed suicide in her cell at Stammheim high-security prison.

Ulrike's arrest

CAREGIVERS

Looking after the sick has traditionally been seen as a woman's job, and millions of unknown women have spent their lives as carers. Few, however, have gained fame for their dedication and determination.

Medicine man

One of the most unusual medical careers was that of Dr. James Barry (c.1795-1865). Dr. Barry was an English woman named Miranda Stewart.

Miranda Stewart

In the early 19th century, women weren't allowed to study medicine. But by dressing as a man and using a false name, Miranda gained a place at medical school. In 1812, she became a fully qualified doctor, and by 1858, she was Inspector General of Hospitals.

Miranda had a long career. Her true identity was only discovered in 1865, when her body was examined after her death.

A selection of surgical tools

The Lady of the Lamp

In 1854, Turkish, French and British soldiers joined forces to fight the Russian army. The war was fought in an area near the Black Sea known as the Crimea. As the number of wounded men increased, nurses were desperately needed.

A map of the Crimea and the Black Sea, showing Scutari

Florence Nightingale (1820-1910) came from a wealthy English family. She was much admired in London for her nursing work. Sidney Herbert, the Secretary of State for War, asked Florence to gather a team of nurses and set sail for the Crimea.

When she arrived in Turkey, Florence was appalled by the conditions in Scutari Barrack Hospital. She worked 20-hour shifts, converting the filthy, rat-infested wards into a cleaner, brighter, more efficient hospital.

Inside the Barrack Hospital in Scutari

Florence's work at the hospital reduced the patient death rate from 42 per cent to just over 2 per cent.

Her patients adored her. They called her "the lady of the lamp" because of her habit of roaming the wards at night with a lantern, checking on their comfort and welfare.

By the time Florence returned to England, she was a national heroine.

She went on to write about the importance of diet and sanitation for good health. She also began raising money, which she used to found a nursing college, the Nightingale Training School for Nurses, in London.

Florence Nightingale's lamp

In 1907, Florence Nightingale became the first woman to be awarded the Order of Merit, which is given to British citizens in recognition of a great contribution to society.

Florence insisted that her patients get as much fresh air as possible.

Fresh dressings and utensils were kept on high shelves, away from rats and lice.

The hospital was kept as clean and hygienic as possible.

Florence checking the patients on her rounds

A dedicated nurse

A Jamaican woman named Mary Seacole (1805-81) became a nurse in 1850, during an outbreak of a disease called cholera. A few years later, she sailed to England to offer her services as a Crimean War nurse, but was turned down because she was black.

Mary Seacole, depicted in an 1857 issue of *Punch*, a popular English magazine

Undeterred, Mary paid for her own passage to the Crimea, and spent the next three years working with Florence Nightingale, providing medical care for the war casualties.

When she returned to England, Mary was praised for her bravery by the same people who had previously rejected her help.

Soldiering on

When German forces invaded Belgium at the outbreak of World War I, a British nurse named Edith Cavell (1865-1915) was teaching at a nursing school in Brussels.

The school Edith worked at was turned into a Red Cross hospital for wounded soldiers.

This image is from a French memorial to Edith Cavell.

Despite the constant threat of being discovered by the German army, Edith and her staff assisted wounded British, French and Belgian soldiers. She helped them to reach Holland, where they could rejoin the Allied Army.

Under cover of darkness, the soldiers would be secretly smuggled into the Red Cross hospital.

Edith carefully disguised them as hospital patients and treated those who were wounded.

By supplying them with false identification papers and civilian clothes, she helped over 200 soldiers to safety.

For her part in helping Allied soldiers to escape, Edith Cavell was arrested, put on trial and sentenced to death. She was shot at dawn by a German firing squad in 1915.

Mother Theresa

One woman who became internationally famous for caring for others is Agnes Bojaxhiu (1910-1997), known as Mother Theresa. At the age of 18, she left Yugoslavia and went to work in a convent in Calcutta, India. She took a new religious name, Sister Theresa.

Over the next 20 years, Sister Theresa worked as a teacher at the convent's school and at a school for poor children.

On September 10, 1946, a day known by her followers as "Inspiration Day", Sister Theresa heard a voice from God. It told her to help Calcutta's poor by living among them. So she moved into one of the city's worst slum areas and began teaching and nursing the poor and the sick. Her pupils and patients called her "Ma", or "Mother".

Mother Theresa was joined by other women who wanted to help the poor. As their numbers grew, they became known as the "Sisters of Charity". They set up their own hospital, Nirmal Hriday, which means "The Place of the Pure Heart".

In 1979, Mother Theresa was awarded the Nobel peace prize for the work she had done to set up Missionaries of Charity, a worldwide religious organization which cares for people anywhere in the world who are destitute or dying. She died in 1997 and was given a state funeral.

A Nobel peace prize medal

Mother Theresa worked and cared for the people of Calcutta, many of whom lived in great poverty.

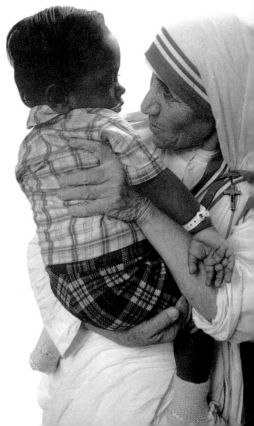

THE POWER BEHIND THE THRONE

Behind many of history's powerful men there have been powerful women. Among these are some women whose popularity or political skills have made them as famous, if not more famous, than their husbands.

The Old Buddha

At the age of 16, Tz'u-hsi (1835-1908) was taken into the Forbidden City in Beijing, to become one of the wives of Emperor Hsien-feng. She soon became the Emperor's close friend, and even advised him on State affairs.

The central area of the Forbidden City in Beijing, the largest palace in the world. It has 8,000 rooms.

The city is guarded by bronze lions like this one.

Tz'u-hsi sat on the Dragon throne in the Hall of Supreme Harmony.

A curved canal, called "Golden Stream"

The Hall of Supreme Harmony is raised on a three-tiered terrace.

A drum and bell were sounded whenever an emperor or empress passed through the Meridian Gate, the main entrance.

When the Emperor died in 1861, Tz'u-hsi claimed the throne for her son. Despite a law which forbade women to reign, she took political control herself. When her son died, she appointed her nephew as Emperor and continued to govern in his name.

Tz'u-Hsi was also known as the Old Buddha.

Throughout her reign, Tz'u-hsi fought hard to prevent modern ideas being introduced into China. However, she did abolish foot binding, an ancient tradition in which Chinese girls had their feet tightly bound to keep them small, which was considered attractive. Many women were crippled by this practice.

This woman's feet have been crippled by years of tight binding.

Tz'u-hsi ruled for over 50 years. She was a formidable figure to the last, and even organized the murder of her nephew, the Emperor, a day before she died.

First Lady of the World

The achievements of Eleanor Roosevelt (1884-1962) earned her the nickname "First Lady of the World". She was the wife of an American politician named Franklin D. Roosevelt. In 1921, he was disabled by a disease called polio. Eleanor took on his political work while he was ill. With her support, Roosevelt went on to become President of the United States in 1932.

President Roosevelt died in 1945. In the same year, a special council called the United Nations, or UN, was set up to promote international peace and cooperation. Eleanor Roosevelt was elected to be its American representative.

The UN symbol

Eleanor Roosevelt holding up a copy of the Declaration of Human Rights

In 1948, Eleanor led a committee which persuaded 48 countries to sign the Universal Declaration of Human Rights. This outlined the rights of all people to liberty and justice. For her commitment to human rights, the American public repeatedly voted her "Most Admired Woman of the Year".

Jackie Kennedy

The popularity and charm of Jackie Kennedy (1929-1994) contributed enormously to the success of her husband, John F. Kennedy, (Jack). He was President of the United States from 1960 until his assassination in Texas in 1963.

On November 22, the Kennedys were in Dallas, Texas, waving to the crowds from an open-top car, when Jack was shot.

Jackie panicked, and immediately tried to scramble out of the car to escape the assassin's bullets.

She insisted on wearing her bloodstained clothes at the ceremony to swear in a new president.

Jackie earned America's respect for her dignity as a widow. But she was criticized when she married a wealthy Greek ship owner named Aristotle Onassis. Some people thought she was being greedy and betraying her first husband's memory.

In her final years, Jackie worked for a publishing company in New York. She died of cancer in 1994 and was buried as a national heroine.

She who strives

Winnie Mandela (b.1934) worked hard to help her husband Nelson become president of South Africa in 1994. In 1964, Nelson had been sentenced to life imprisonment for leading a campaign of defiance against the South African government and its racist policies. Winnie campaigned tirelessly to keep her husband's name in the public eye during his long imprisonment.

Racial segregation, as shown by this sign, was supported by law in South Africa.

Winnie's African name is Nomzamo, which means "she who strives". This proved a fitting name, as she was often imprisoned, threatened and had her freedom restricted during her campaign.

Nelson was released in 1990. Later, he and Winnie divorced, because he didn't want to be associated with Winnie's controversial methods of political activity.

The Mandelas celebrating Nelson's release in 1990

Princess Diana

Diana, Princess of Wales (1961-1997) was one famous wife who overshadowed her husband in terms of popularity and star quality. In 1981, she married Charles, Prince of Wales, the heir to the British throne, and became one of the world's most recognized faces.

A sapphire pendant and ring that belonged to the Princess of Wales

She became a showpiece for British fashion, and the press photographed her wherever she went.

Her popularity increased as she gave her support to charities, which aimed to combat Aids, drug abuse and homelessness. She caused political controversy by demanding an end to the production of landmines.

Her marriage to Prince Charles was not a happy one, and it ended in divorce in 1996. Only a year later tragedy struck, when Diana died in a car crash in Paris. An estimated 2.5 billion people around the world watched the television broadcasts of her funeral procession.

Diana was famous for her fashionable style.

ADVENTURES OVERSEAS

Until the 19th century, it was very unusual for women to travel anywhere alone. A few women, however, set off on great explorations and became famous through written accounts of their adventures.

Hatshepsut

Egyptian Queen Hatshepsut was not an explorer herself, but sponsored a great expedition. In 1493 BC, she ordered a fleet of vessels to set sail for Punt, a land on the east coast of Africa (roughly where Somalia is today). The route had not been explored for over 200 years. The expedition's goal was to find myrrh trees, from which the Egyptians made incense to burn at religious ceremonies.

The adventures of the seamen were recorded on the walls of Hatshepsut's temple, Deir el-Bahari. Here they are shown with myrrh trees.

Even though the Egyptians had never attempted an expedition of this scale before, it was a great success and the ships came home laden with myrrh and ivory.

This is a reconstruction of one of the Egyptian trading galleys that Hatshepsut sent to the land of Punt.

Travel addict

After the death of her parents, an English woman named Mary Kingsley (1862-1900) set sail for West Africa. She intended to continue her father's scientific work there, but she quickly became addicted to travel.

Even in Africa, Mary wore a heavy skirt, a high-necked blouse, and took an umbrella.

In 1893, Mary sailed along the coast of West Africa in a cargo boat. She was fascinated by the many ports she visited. On her journeys, which took her along rivers and through swamps and thick jungles, she collected specimens of fish and beetles for the British Museum in London.

Specimens of beetles and freshwater fish taken from drawings made by Mary Kingsley

Mary explored alone, except for her native guides. She ate snakes and saw wild animals such as gorillas and elephants.

Once she was saved from death by her heavy skirts when she fell some distance onto a spike in a game pit.

In one hut belonging to a tribe of cannibals, she found a bag containing three big toes, four eyes and two ears.

When war broke out in South Africa, Mary worked in a hospital nursing soldiers. She died of a fever and was buried at sea.

Travels on a yak

The first expeditions Alexandra David-Neel (1868-1969) ever made were when she ran away from home several times as a child. On one occasion, she went from her home in France all the way to England.

In 1911, Alexandra set off on a short trip to India, but she ended up staying abroad for 14 years. Her travels took her through Burma, Japan, Korea, the Gobi Desert and Mongolia.

Alexandra was always accompanied by her adopted son, Yongden, who was a Buddhist priest. On one trip, they covered 3200km (2000 miles) to reach a monastery on the border of China and Tibet, where Alexandra studied Buddhism for three years.

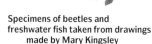

In Tibet, Alexandra sometimes rode a yak.

The Potala palace in Lhasa, Tibet

Alexandra's greatest journey, to Tibet, began when she was 54 years old. She crossed the country disguised as a Tibetan nun, to hide the fact that she was a foreigner. She dyed her hair black and darkened her face with cocoa. When she arrived in the capital, Lhasa, she was the first European woman ever to enter the city.

Desert adventure

As a result of her expeditions, Gertrude Bell (1868-1926), the daughter of a wealthy English family, became an expert mountaineer and a famous archeologist. In 1913, she set off for Arabia, the last great region of the world which had not been fully mapped.

Gertrude ignored warnings about dangerous desert conditions and set out for the city of Ha'il. While crossing the Syrian desert, her party was attacked by Arab horsemen. Gertrude remained calm and later described the attack as "a preposterous and provoking episode".

A map showing the route Gertrude Bell took to reach the city of Ha'il

When she reached Ha'il, Gertrude became only the second European woman to visit the mud-walled city. The ruler, Ibn Rashid, welcomed Gertrude, but then kept her in his palace, virtually as a prisoner. When she couldn't stand her confinement any longer, she announced in fluent Arabic that she was leaving. The Arab authorities were so stunned by this that they let her go.

This is a reconstruction of the attack on Gertrude Bell's group by a gang of Arab horsemen.

The men rode toward Gertrude, waving swords and rifles.

Gertrude was riding a camel, while her guides were on foot.

Ibn Rashid even gave Gertrude supplies and guides to help her on the difficult journey through the desert back to Damascus.

Gertrude Bell's account of her trip contributed enormously to Western knowledge of Arabian history, and the research she carried out on her travels helped geographers make more detailed maps of the Syrian desert.

Gertrude would have had an sextant like this to help her calculate distances.

Daring Dame

Dame Freya Stark (1893-1993) is probably the most famous female adventurer of the 20th century.

While working in Baghdad, she explored Iraq and Iran, including a remote set of mountains in Luristan.

Freya Stark, photographed in 1942

Freya wrote books about her travels and used the money she made from them to fund further trips and adventures. During World War II, Freya used her extensive knowledge of Arabia to help the British government with their military campaigns.

At the age of 76, Freya drove across Afghanistan in a jeep and camped at 2740m (9000ft) in the Himalayas, despite suffering from ill health. Aged 83, she sailed down the River Euphrates and at 86, she went pony-trekking in Nepal.

ALL AT SEA

There is an old superstition among sailors that women at sea bring bad luck. Despite this, many women have proved their seafaring skills. Some faced the sea alone; others managed to survive among hundreds of men aboard war and pirate ships.

Aboard a pirate ship

Anne Bonney left her home in Ireland for New Providence, one of a group of islands off the American coast now called the Bahamas. There she fell in love with John Rackham, a pirate captain also known as "Calico Jack".

Anne Bonney and Rackham's pirate flag

Mary Read

Anne helped Rackham steal the fastest ship in the local port. Together, they began a ten-year spree of piracy around the Caribbean.

Rackham often took sailors from other vessels to serve in his crew. Once, Anne found that a "young boy" who had been recruited in this way was actually a woman named Mary Read (1690-1720). Mary told Anne her story.

Mary Read began to dress like a man at an early age to increase her opportunities. She served as a cabin boy on a warship.

As an infantry soldier, she fought against Spain and France. She married a soldier who saw through her disguise.

When her husband died, Mary dressed as a man again and joined a ship. This ship was captured by John Rackham.

Anne Bonney and Mary Read became known all over the Caribbean as ferocious pirates. In 1720, Rackham's ship was finally captured by the British Navy off the coast of Jamaica. The two women fought fiercely with pistols, cutlasses and axes, even after the rest of the crew had surrendered.

Rackham and the crew were sentenced to death by hanging. Anne and Mary, however, couldn't be executed as they both claimed to be pregnant. They were released from their cells and disappeared. After that, nobody knows what happened to them. They were never heard of again.

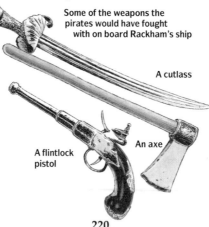
Some of the weapons the pirates would have fought with on board Rackham's ship

A cutlass

An axe

A flintlock pistol

Amazing Grace

On October 7, 1838, a steamship named the *Forfarshire* was dashed against rocks off the coast of Northumberland, England. From the nearby Longstone Lighthouse, Grace Darling (1815-42), the lighthouse keeper's daughter, spotted survivors in the water.

Grace and her father rowed to the rescue across rough seas. On their first trip they managed to pick up five survivors, two of whom helped them go back to the ship to rescue four more men.

The position of the wreck is marked with a cross. The route the Darlings rowed is shown in red.

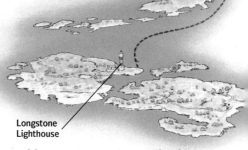
Longstone Lighthouse

Newspaper stories paid tribute to Grace Darling's heroism. Her part in the rescue was even recreated in a theatrical version of the wreck of the *Forfarshire*.

Unfortunately, the pressure of the publicity damaged Grace's health. Four years later she died, aged only 27.

A marble bust of Grace Darling

Over a period of 48 years, Ida Lewis (1842-1911), daughter of an American lighthouse keeper, rescued over a dozen sailors from shipwrecks around Lime Rock, off Newport, Rhode Island. Ida, however, enjoyed being a public heroine and she became the lighthouse keeper when her father retired.

Across the Channel

The first woman to swim the English Channel, the stretch of water between England and France, was a young American named Gertrude Ederle (b.1906). She was an international swimming champion who had won several Olympic medals and broken numerous world records.

To protect herself against the chilly waters of the Channel, Gertrude was smeared with grease.

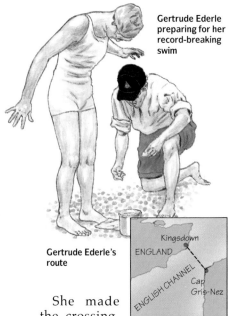

Gertrude Ederle preparing for her record-breaking swim

Gertrude Ederle's route

She made the crossing, from Cap Gris Nez in France

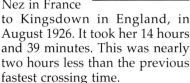

ENGLAND
Kingsdown
ENGLISH CHANNEL
Cap Gris-Nez
FRANCE

to Kingsdown in England, in August 1926. It took her 14 hours and 39 minutes. This was nearly two hours less than the previous fastest crossing time.

Since Gertrude Ederle's record-breaking swim, many other women have conquered the Channel, including a 12-year-old girl and a pair of twin sisters.

Solo achievement

In 1977, New Zealander Naomi James (b.1949) began her attempt to become the first woman to sail single-handed around the world. She set sail in her yacht, the *Express Crusader*, from the port of Dartmouth in England. Her kitten, Boris, was her only companion for the 48,000km (30,000 mile) journey.

Despite having very little sailing experience, Naomi managed to cope with a broken radio, a cracked mast, and several other near-disasters, before successfully completing the historic journey. Her voyage lasted 272 days and broke the record for the fastest ever round-the-world yacht trip.

In recognition of her achievement, Naomi James was made a Dame of the British Empire.

Naomi James on her boat, the *Express Crusader*.

This picture of the *Express Crusader* has been cut away to show the main living areas.

Life raft

Every available space is designed to be used. This is for food storage.

Sleeping bunk

The radio was Naomi's only link with the rest of the world.

All the navigation calculations were carried out on this table.

The wheel, used to steer the yacht

AVIATORS AND ASTRONAUTS

Since the 1780s, when hot-air balloons first carried human passengers, women have been proving themselves excellent aviators. The most famous female flyers have made solo trips, showing amazing stamina and determination.

Up, up and away

The first balloons were flown in France, and the first women to fly in them were four French aristocrats. In May 1784, the Comtesse de Montalembert went up in a balloon, accompanied by three friends. However, this was not a real "flight", as the balloon was tied to the ground by a rope.

Only a fortnight later, Madame Thible became the first woman to pilot an untethered balloon, soaring to a height of 2,789m (8,500ft). Thrilled by her experience, she burst into song in mid-flight.

Dolly Shepherd, an early British stuntwoman, parachuting from a balloon wearing gold-trimmed knickerbockers

Early aviators

In 1908, over a century after her four ballooning countrywomen had made history, Madame Thérèse Peltier became the first woman to fly solo in a powered aircraft. It was another Frenchwoman, Baronne Raymonde de Laroche, who became the first qualified female pilot in 1910.

Raymonde de Laroche was given pilot's license number 35.

Transatlantic triumph

Amelia Earhart (1898-1937), a social worker from Kansas, USA, was determined to become the first female pilot to fly across the Atlantic Ocean. She had already made the journey as a passenger, but she wanted to fly herself.

First, Amelia had extra fuel tanks, a new engine and navigational equipment added to her Vega aircraft.

She took off from Newfoundland on May 20, 1932. During the flight, she sipped tomato juice through a straw.

15 hours later, she landed safely in Ireland, in a field full of startled cows.

Amelia Earhart's famous transatlantic flight wasn't just the first by a female pilot. It was also quicker than any previous crossing. She went on to make many more adventurous long-distance flights.

In March 1937, she set out to fly around the world. But on the 2nd of July, toward the end of the trip, her plane ran out of fuel in the mid-Pacific. Amelia was never seen again.

This is a Lockheed Vega monoplane, similar to the one Amelia piloted on her record-breaking transatlantic flight.

Amy, Wonderful Amy

By spending most of the money that she earned on flying lessons, an English secretary named Amy Johnson (1903-41) fulfilled her ambition to become a qualified pilot and flight engineer. She then announced her intention to fly solo from England to Australia.

Amy took off from an airfield near London in her Gipsy Moth plane, *Jason*, on the morning of May 5, 1930. Over the next 19 days, she covered 16,000km (10,000 miles), landing to refuel at various airstrips on her flight path.

This is *Jason*, the bottle-green DH 60G Gipsy Moth plane in which Amy Johnson flew halfway across the world.

Amy had to repair *Jason*'s fragile structure several times during her historic journey.

In Burma, the broken wing of Amy's plane was patched using shirts donated by local people.

Extreme weather, desert sandstorms, choking fumes and only three hours sleep each night, all made Johnson's journey completely exhausting.

Unfortunately, a delay caused by a crash landing in Burma prevented Amy from reaching Australia in record time.

Amy Johnson in her protective flying clothes and helmet

Nevertheless, when she finally touched down at the airfield in Darwin, Australia, on May 24, 1930, Amy Johnson became the first woman to have flown solo across the world. She was an instant celebrity, and even featured in a popular song called *Amy, Wonderful Amy.*

Amy was killed 11 years later while flying for her country in World War II.

The cockpit where Amy sat was small, narrow and very cramped.

A songsheet for the song *Amy, Wonderful Amy*, written to commemorate Amy Johnson's flight

War in the air

As well as breaking records, female pilots have played important parts in wartime. During World War II, Hanna Reitsch, Germany's leading female aviator, became a top test pilot. She tried out many advanced fighter aircrafts, and became the first woman to fly a rocket-engined Messerschmitt Me 163. Adolf Hitler, the Nazi leader, awarded Hanna an Iron Cross medal for her bravery.

After the war it was claimed that Hitler had killed himself. But as his body couldn't be found, some people suspected that Hanna had flown him out of Berlin alive.

Hanna wearing her Iron Cross

Into the unknown

On June 16, 1963, a Russian textile worker named Valentina Tereshkova (b.1937) became the first woman in space. She was launched from Tyuratam Space Station in the tiny command module of a rocket called *Vostok 6*. Nearly three days later, Valentina landed safely back on Earth. She had orbited the planet 48 times, a distance of about 1,988,480km (1,242,800 miles).

Valentina in the command module of *Vostok 6*

This map shows the places where Amy Johnson landed during her flight. Some of them are listed below.

1 Croydon
2 Vienna
3 Istanbul
4 Baghdad
5 Karachi
6 Calcutta
7 Rangoon
8 Bangkok
9 Singapore
10 Port Darwin

Some of the things Amy took on board *Jason*.

LEADING LADIES

The ability to sing, dance and act has enabled many women to rise to fame. Performing is one area where leading ladies have succeeded in becoming the stars of the show.

Clara Schumann

From an early age, Clara Wieck (1819-96) displayed exceptional musical talent. She was performing professional piano recitals by the age of nine, and went on to become a composer of classical music and a great classical pianist.

At the age of 20, Clara married the composer Robert Schumann. She played many of his pieces and her tips and suggestions helped him achieve fame and recognition.

A piece of Robert Schumann's manuscript

After her husband's death in 1856, Clara became a successful music teacher. She helped many young musicians, including Johannes Brahms. She is said to have died while listening to her husband's piece *Intermezzi* being played by her grandson.

Clara Schumann at the piano

The divine Sarah

A French woman named Sarah Bernhardt (c.1844-1923) became one of the most famous stage actresses of the 19th century.

This picture shows Sarah Bernhardt in performance. She had a commanding stage presence.

Sarah toured the world, earning fame for her expressive acting and extravagant lifestyle. Her audiences never guessed that she suffered terribly from stage fright. She played hundreds of leading roles, including male ones, such as Hamlet.

Sarah became one of France's first film stars, but she always preferred the stage. She played many great roles in a theatre named after her, the Theatre-Sarah-Bernhardt in Paris.

Sarah worked right up to her death. She even went on stage with a wooden leg, after hers had been amputated.

Little Sure Shot

Annie Oakley (1860-1926), was the world's most famous trick shooter. As a child in her home state of Ohio, Annie helped her family pay their debts by shooting animals for sale at the market. By the age of 12, she had become a crack shot. She was later known as "Little Sure Shot".

In 1876, Annie married a marksman named Frank E. Butler, after beating him in a shooting match.

They developed a stage act in which Annie shot bullet holes through playing cards thrown in the air.

Annie's shooting skills impressed the crowds and earned her and her husband a living.

In 1885, Annie and Frank joined the Buffalo Bill Wild West Show and went touring all over the United States, along with several other performers. Annie soon had top billing in the show, and she soon became well-known throughout America. Later, Annie Oakley's life was turned into a musical called *Annie Get Your Gun*.

A poster advertising Annie and the Buffalo Bill Wild West Show

Dancing queen

The Russian dancer Anna Pavlova (1881-1931) was probably the most famous ballerina of all time.

When Anna was a girl, she was taken to see a famous ballet called *The Sleeping Beauty*. From that day, she decided that she wanted to be a ballet dancer.

A poster for one of Anna Pavlova's performances in England

Anna came from a poor family, and she had never been a healthy child. Nevertheless, she entered the Imperial Ballet School in St. Petersburg at the age of ten.

Three years later, she took part in the coronation celebrations of the new Czar. By the age of 25, she had become a *prima ballerina*, which means "leading ballerina".

Pavlova toured many countries with the Imperial Ballet. Later, she set up her own ballet company and gave over 3,000 performances.

Many people in remote parts of the world were introduced to classical ballet through Anna's dancing. Audiences adored her graceful interpretation of solo parts such as the heroine in *Giselle*. She was so popular that when she went to Denmark, ballet fans pulled her carriage through the streets themselves.

One of Anna Pavlova's most famous roles was in a ballet called *Les Sylphides*. A leading Russian choreographer (dance arranger) named Mikhail Fokine created a solo dance especially for Pavlova, called *The Dying Swan*.

Anna died of pneumonia at the age of 49. She was worn out by two and a half decades of touring the world. Today, Anna Pavlova's name is also famous because a kind of meringue pie was named after her - perhaps because the shape of the pie looked like her ballet skirts.

These pictures of Anna Pavlova show three different moments in the ballet *Coppélia*.

Anna Pavlova played the role of Swanhilda in *Coppélia*, a story about a doll who comes to life.

Maria Callas

Maria Callas (1923-77) became one of the most famous dramatic sopranos of the 20th century. She was born in New York of Greek parents, and went to Greece when she was 14 years old to study music at the Athens Conservatory.

La Scala opera house in Milan

In 1947, Maria was asked to sing in an opera called *La Giaconda*. She gave a magnificent performance which launched her career. Over the next twenty years, she sang in many of the greatest opera houses in the world.

Maria was particularly acclaimed for the combination of her amazing voice and brilliant acting ability. She dominated the world of opera in the 1950s and 1960s.

Maria Callas on stage

Maria's dramatic private life added to her fame. She had a relationship with Aristotle Onassis, one of the world's richest men.

After retiring from the stage, Maria trained opera singers in New York.

WOMEN AND WORDS

Throughout history, women have excelled at writing, becoming highly respected authors. This may be because they could write even when confined to their homes.

Sappho

The Greek poet Sappho lived on the island of Lesbos and wrote during the 6th century BC. Only 650 lines of her poetry, and only one complete poem, have survived.

Sappho led a group of women who gave worship to Aphrodite, the goddess of love. Many of her poems are about women and love.

Sappho shown on an ancient Greek vase

Little is known about Sappho's life, except what we know from her own poetry and from comic dramas written about her. She and her husband, Cercylas, had three sons and a daughter. One story about Sappho tells of her love for a man named Phaon, and how she committed suicide by throwing herself from a cliff.

Sappho's influence on other poets who copied her style shows that she was an important writer at a time when women rarely achieved recognition. She is best known for her lyric verse, a kind of songlike poetry.

Love letters

When she was widowed at the age of 25, Christine de Pisan (1364-1430) was left with her children, her mother and brothers to support. She became probably the first woman to earn her living through writing. At the court of Charles V of France she found many patrons (wealthy supporters) to pay for her writing.

Christine de Pisan

Christine produced a huge amount of work. She wrote about "courtly love", the medieval system in which men swore loyalty and devotion to the women they loved. She also wrote essays that encouraged women to educate themselves.

After a full career as a writer, Christine retired to a convent in 1418. She lived long enough however, to write a tribute to Jeanne d'Arc (see page 201) whom she saw as a model of feminine courage.

Many courtly love poems described tournaments at which knights jousted.

The women watch from their tent.

Knights fought on horseback, each carrying the banner of the lady he wanted to impress.

Pen names

In some countries, writing used to be considered an unsuitable profession for women. As a result, many female poets and novelists published their work under false male names, or "pen names".

The Brontës were three English sisters named Charlotte (1816-55), Emily (1818-48), and Anne (1820-49). They first found literary fame under the pen names of Currer, Ellis, and Acton Bell (keeping their real initials).

A portrait of Charlotte, the eldest of the Brontë sisters

Some female writers found it easier to live as a man as well. One French authoress named Amandine Aurore Lucie Dupin (1804-1876) published more than 40 novels under the pen name George Sand. She also frequently dressed in men's clothes, to enjoy the increased social freedom they allowed her.

A hidden talent

In the 1930s, the Nazis, a political party in power in Germany, began to terrorize the Jewish population. Otto Frank, a Jewish businessman, took his family to Amsterdam in the Netherlands to escape persecution. But in 1941, the Germans invaded the Netherlands, and the Frank family were in danger.

The Franks and another Jewish family called the van Daans went into hiding in a secret apartment at Otto's warehouse. For two years they avoided detection, relying on friends outside to bring them supplies and news.

A page from Anne's diary

Potatoes, cabbage and beans formed a large part of the Franks' diet while they were in hiding.

Throughout the ordeal, Otto's youngest daughter Anne (1929-45) kept a diary, recording the daily life of the family in hiding. She wrote it in the form of letters to an imaginary friend named "Kitty". The diary relates the difficulties the Frank family faced.

The building in this picture has been cut away to show the secret attic where the Franks and the van Daans lived in hiding.

A photo of Anne Frank

Dit is een foto, zoals ik me zou wensen, altijd zo te zijn. Dan had ik nog wel een kans om naar Holywood te komen.
Annefrank.
10 Oct. 1942

(translation)
"This is a photo as I would wish myself to look all the time. Then I would maybe have a chance to come to Hollywood."
Anne Frank, 10 Oct. 1942

Anne described how they were almost discovered when the building was sold and an architect came to look at it. Another time, the warehouse was searched by police after a burglary.

Tragically, the Franks were discovered by the Nazi police a few months before the end of the war, and were sent to concentration camps. Only Otto Frank survived. He published Anne's diary after the war. Its translation into more than 30 languages has made Anne Frank a worldwide symbol of wartime suffering and courage.

Anne wrote most of her diary in this attic room.

The beds were put away during the day to make space.

Secret entrance

The entrance to the attic was hidden behind furniture in the main part of the building.

The lower part of the building was a warehouse.

Maya Angelou

In 1970, Maya Angelou (b.1928) became the first African-American woman to have a non-fiction book in the bestseller lists. It was the first volume of her autobiography and was called *I Know Why the Caged Bird Sings*.

Maya Angelou

The book told of Maya's childhood in Arkansas in the 1930s. She grew up in a rural town called Stamps, where the black and white communities were strongly divided. At the age of eight, she was abused by her mother's boyfriend. When he was murdered, she blamed herself and didn't speak for five years.

Before turning to writing, Maya was an actress, a singer, a dancer and a cook. She also worked with civil rights leaders such as Martin Luther King and Malcolm X, who fought for equal rights for black people in America.

As well as her autobiographical books, Maya Angelou has published several volumes of poetry. She is one of America's leading poets, and was invited to read a poem at the 1993 ceremony at which Bill Clinton was made President of the USA.

CREATIVE GENIUS

There have been far fewer famous women artists than women writers. This may be because, in the past, the cost of being an artist was beyond many women. Now, however, the number of female visual artists is increasing.

An independent spirit

Today, the talents of the Italian-born figure painter Artemisia Gentileschi (1593-c.1651) are highly respected. From an early age, Artemisia was encouraged to paint by her father, who was himself a successful painter.

Artemisia is best known for her paintings of women in scenes from history, myths or the Bible. Her most famous work is called *Judith and Holofernes*. It shows the Jewish heroine Judith cutting off the head of Holofernes, who was an enemy of her people.

Artemisia became famous throughout Italy for her skill. She learned to stand up for herself and negotiated good prices for her paintings.

Some people think that Artemisia's determination to be a truly independent woman came from an incident that happened when she was only 18.

In 1612, Artemisia's father accused a man of raping his daughter and stealing some paintings.

The accused was a man named Tassi, Artemisia's painting teacher. She gave evidence against him, but he was set free.

After the trial, Artemisia went on painting. Her experience may have influenced her choice of subject matter.

Lights, camera, action!

Leni Riefenstahl was born in Berlin, Germany in 1902. She started her career as a dancer. After appearing in several films, Leni began to direct her own films and founded her own film company.

The dancer and film-maker Leni Riefenstahl

Leni Riefenstahl has been criticized for her association with Adolf Hitler, the leader of a political party called the Nazis who came to power in the 1930s. At Hitler's request, she wrote and produced a film called *Triumph of Will*, which shows a Nazi rally at Nuremberg. Technically it is a masterpiece, with its brilliant camera angles, moving shots and clever editing. But the film appears to glorify Hitler and his supporters.

Hitler provided money for Leni's film *Olympia*, a documentary about the 1936 Olympic Games in Berlin. When the film was finished, however, she refused an order from the Nazi party to remove scenes showing the black American athelete, Jesse Owens, who won four gold medals at the competition.

After World War II, Leni was put on a blacklist of artists who had been associated with the Nazis. She was refused work, and did not make another film until 1957.

Barbara Hepworth

Barbara Hepworth (1903-1975) knew she wanted to sculpt even when she was a child. She became one of the most influential sculptors of the 20th century.

Barbara studied art in London and Italy, and was one of the first great creators of abstract sculptures. Instead of portraying objects or people in a realistic fashion, her sculptures used lines, textures and shapes to convey emotions and moods.

Barbara worked in wood, metal and stone. She claimed that she always knew what the final shape of a sculpture would be before she began.

Orpheus (1956). The curving shapes of this sculpture are typical of Barbara's graceful style.

She often worked until her arms ached and her fingers were bruised and bleeding.

In 1939, Barbara moved to Cornwall, in southwest England, where she became influenced by the landscape, the sea and the sky and local ancient monuments.

Barbara Hepworth's most famous work was a large sculpture for the Dag Hammarskjöld memorial at the United Nations Building in New York. She was still working when she died, aged 72, in a fire in her studio in Cornwall in 1975.

Good vibrations

The British painter Bridget Riley (b.1931) became one of the world's leading abstract artists. She was fascinated by the patterns and vibrations she saw in nature. This led her to develop a new style of art known as Optical art, or Op art.

In the 1960s, Bridget painted striking black and white pictures which play tricks on the eye and appear to move and shimmer. Her style had an important influence on other artists and on the design world. Op art dresses with striking black and white patterns became very fashionable.

On a trip to Egypt in 1981, Bridget was inspired to use the shades chosen by ancient Egyptian artists, bringing a new intensity and light to her pictures.

A 1960s dress, showing the influence of the Op art style

Bridget Riley: *Fall (1963)*. Emulsion on board. 141 x 140.3cm (55.5 x 55.5in). Tate Gallery, London, England

A fairytale artist

Born in Portugal in 1935, Paula Rego became an internationally renowned painter, illustrator and printmaker.

At sixteen, she was sent to a school in England by her father, but left the school after a few months to attend art school in London.

Paula's early work in the 1960s consisted of collages, made by sticking pieces of paper together to make pictures.

Many of her pictures are based on the traditional fairy tales she heard as a child in Portugal. In her work, art is often used as another way to tell stories.

Like the fairy tales that inspired her paintings, her work can often be sinister and frightening. The idea for her picture *The Maids* is taken from a play by

Paula Rego's painting *The Maids*, based on a 20th-century play about a murder.

the 20th century French writer Jean Genet, in which a group of maids murder their mistress.

In 1990, Paula Rego became the first woman to be appointed an Associate Artist at the National Gallery in London. She began working from a studio in the gallery, and completed a large wall painting. The wall painting tells the stories of female saints and courageous women.

Little Miss Muffet, like many of Paula Rego's works, is based on a traditional tale.

SCIENTIFIC MINDS

Throughout history, women have been involved in the development of science and medicine, but their achievements have often gained little recognition. For centuries, women were unable to attend universities and were excluded from scientific societies and laboratories. Even today, there are far fewer women working in the sciences than men.

Tombstone of a woman doctor from the 1st century AD

Caroline compiled lists of the stars and comets they observed. She became the first woman to be appointed assistant to the Court Astronomer. As well as her work for her brother, Caroline discovered eight new comets herself. She won several awards for her findings and, in 1835, she and another scientist, Mary Somerville, became the first women to be awarded honorary memberships of the Royal Astronomical Society.

Caroline Herschel

Star gazer

In 1772, Caroline Herschel (1750-1848) left Germany and went to England to work with her brother William, an astronomer. She taught herself astronomy and mathematics so that she could assist her brother with his studies.

Together they built a giant telescope and used it to study the night sky.

The giant telescope built by Caroline and William Herschel

The telescope could be moved around on wheels.

The telescope tube was made of iron.

Winches were used to move the tube up or down.

An assistant sat in this hut to record observations.

Computer Countess

Ada, Countess of Lovelace (1815-52), was the daughter of Lord Byron, a well-known English poet. At the age of 18, she attended a lecture and saw an early calculating machine built by a famous mathematician named Charles Babbage.

Babbage's machine, known as the Analytical Engine

Ada was fascinated. She began to work with Babbage, using her exceptional mathematical ability to design arithmetical operations for the new machines. These calculating machines are now seen as the forerunners of modern computers. So, in a sense, Ada was the first ever computer programmer.

Babbage encouraged Ada to publish her work. She signed her work with only her initials, because it was considered unsuitable at that time for a woman to publish under her own name. As a result, her work as a mathematician, like that of many other women scientists, has largely been forgotten.

In addition to working with Babbage, Ada conducted several other mathematical investigations. She even spent time trying to develop a fool-proof gambling system. Her work was cut short when she died in 1852, at the age of only 37.

A portrait of Ada, Countess of Lovelace

Marie Curie

Polish-born Marie Sklodowska (1867-1934) was the first world-famous female scientist. She studied physics and chemistry at the Sorbonne in Paris. She worked long hours and could hardly afford to eat.

In 1895, she married Pierre Curie and together they began to research materials which gave out radiation. They discovered two new substances, which they called polonium and radium, that emitted high levels of radiation.

In 1903, the Curies won a Nobel prize for physics. Marie was the first woman to receive this award.

A medal showing a bust of Marie Curie

Three years later, Pierre Curie was killed in a road accident. Marie took over his position as professor in Paris, becoming the first woman professor in France. In 1911, she won a second Nobel prize, this time for chemistry.

Radium in small doses became very important in the treatment of cancer. But years of exposure to it had damaged Marie's own health. She died of a blood cancer in 1934.

Marie in the shed that was her laboratory

A model scientist

In 1951, English scientist Rosalind Franklin (1920-58) began studying a chemical called deoxyribonucleic acid (DNA). Scientists thought DNA acted as a chemical code of instructions that decided what characteristics an animal inherited from its parents.

Rosalind took part in a race between scientists to explain the structure of DNA. She and one of her colleagues, Maurice Wilkins, studied it using X-ray photographs.

They were beaten by two other scientists, Crick and Watson (both men), who built a model of a DNA molecule. Crick and Watson were accused of using the results of Rosalind Franklin's research to produce their model.

In 1962, Crick, Watson and Wilkins were jointly awarded the Nobel prize for medicine. Rosalind Franklin would have shared the prize, but she had died of cancer four years earlier, aged only 38.

The model of a DNA molecule looks a little like a twisted rope ladder.

Gene genius

When Barbara McClintock (b.1902) was a teenager, her parents discouraged her interest in science. They thought it was an unsuitable career for a girl. Eventually, however, she studied biology at Cornell University, USA.

Barbara McClintock

Barbara specialized in genetics, the science of heredity. She noticed that, in some cells, genes changed their position. This could cause other genes to stop functioning, with unexpected results. These genes were nick-named "jumping genes". In an African violet plant, for example, she observed that jumping genes caused pigment genes to stop working, causing a loss of pigment in some of the flower's petals.

This diagram shows how a gene "jumps".

1. This is a chunk of DNA called a transposon, containing one or more genes.

Transposon

2. The transposon moves position.

3. If a transposon lands in another gene, that gene may stop functioning.

Barbara McClintock's discovery wasn't taken seriously until the 1970s, when advances in molecular biology revealed that she had been right. In 1983, she received a Nobel prize for her work.

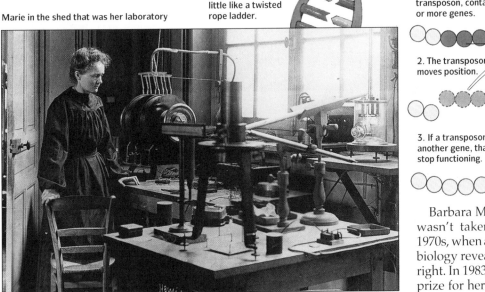

GREAT BUSINESSWOMEN

Big business has often excluded women from top jobs. Yet women have used new ideas, and their understanding of what other women want, to succeed in business.

Seeds of success

In the 18th century, one of the main industries in the southern states of America was growing, harvesting and processing cotton. Separating the seeds of a cotton plant from the fluffy part known as the boll, was a very slow process done by hand.

A head of cotton

In 1793, a man named Eli Whitney invented a machine known as the "cotton gin", which could separate the cotton from its seeds much faster than before. The idea was turned into a business success by Catherine Greene (1755-1814), the widow of a wealthy plantation owner.

A model of the cotton gin

This handle was turned.

Cotton bolls were fed onto wire brushes which separated the seeds.

Rows of brushes

Clean, fluffy cotton

Catherine realized that Eli Whitney's invention would revolutionize the cotton trade. She put her money into developing and publicizing the idea. The gin was so successful that it made her a vast fortune.

Fantastic wax

Swiss-born Philippe Curtius made his fortune sculpting portraits in wax. His wax museum in Paris, the *Cabinet de cire*, became a major public attraction.

Curtius taught his niece, Marie Tussaud (1761-1850), the skills of working with wax. She quickly became very good at making models, and her portraits of the famous people of her day helped to increase the museum's success. In 1774, Philippe Curtius died and Madame Tussaud, as Marie became known, inherited and took over the museum.

A wax model of Madame Tussaud making a head in her workroom

This self-portrait was the last model that Madame Tussaud ever made.

By 1802, Marie was having financial problems. She decided to seek her fortune overseas, and over the next 30 years, she toured the British Isles with her collection of life-size waxworks of rogues and heroes.

Marie was an excellent judge of what the public would pay to see, and continually added new models to her exhibition. Her waxworks were so successful in Britain that in 1835 she was able to set up a permanent exhibition, known as Madame Tussaud's, in London. Nearly 150 years after her death, the museum is still famous all over the world, and is one of London's main tourist attractions, with models of many modern celebrities.

A wax model of the Hollywood actor Mel Gibson, one of the modern exhibits at Madame Tussaud's

Champagne champion

When she was widowed at the age of 27, Nicole-Barbe Cliquot-Ponsardin (1777-1866) was determined to run her husband's wine-making business. Her father-in-law wanted to shut the company down, but Nicole-Barbe relaunched it with a new name, Veuve Cliquot and Company (*Veuve Cliquot* means "Widow Cliquot" in French).

Nicole-Barbe developed a way of removing unwanted waste from champagne, known as *la méthode champenoise*. It is still used today, over a century later.

A bottle is placed in a specially designed rack, which tips it gently so that the sediment sinks to the bottom.

The angle at which the bottle is tipped is slowly increased until the sediment rests on top of the cork.

The cork and the sediment are removed and a new cork is put in. None of the gas that makes the wine fizzy is lost.

Nicole-Barbe's business talents ensured that her firm's trade soared. She earned a personal fortune and a lasting reputation as a shrewd business woman.

Chanel

Gabrielle Chanel (1883-1971), known as Coco, was the daughter of a French peasant family. She was orphaned at a young age and began working with her sister, making hats.

The stylish Coco Chanel wearing one of her own designs

During World War I, Coco served as a nurse. But when the war was over, she borrowed money from an English lover and set up a dress shop in her hometown of Deauville.

The shop's popularity allowed Coco to transfer her business to Paris, where she opened another shop. Her designing talent sparked an international fashion revolution.

The secret of Coco's success was that she created clothes that were simple and comfortable, yet very elegant and glamorous. Designs such as the "little black dress" and the Chanel collarless suit soon became very popular.

This elegant suit was designed in the 1960s and is typical of the Chanel style.

Before long, Coco dominated the fashion trade. The success of her perfume, *Chanel No. 5*, made her a millionairess. She led a dazzling social life and was often written about in newspapers.

By 1938, however, new styles were competing with hers, and Coco decided to retire. But in 1954, she staged a successful comeback, quickly regaining her status in the fashion world. She relaunched her original designs, which soon proved to be as popular as ever.

A Chanel bracelet

Natural products

On her travels south of the equator, Anita Roddick (b.1942) noticed that many women cared for their skin and hair using traditional, natural methods. When she returned to England, she opened a small shop called The Body Shop, selling cosmetics based on natural ingredients.

Anita Roddick (left) working with the Ñahñu Indians

To keep costs down and reduce unnecessary waste, Anita packaged her cosmetic products in cheap plastic containers, and encouraged her customers to bring them back to be refilled.

Today there are over 1,400 branches of The Body Shop in 46 countries throughout the world. The company is committed to social and environmental change, trading with needy communities in developing and industrialized countries. In all of its products, it uses ingredients that have not been tested on animals. Through The Body Shop, Anita Roddick has become one of Britain's most successful businesswomen.

One of The Body Shop's 1,400 premises

THE BODY SHOP

SPORTING SUCCESS

The women of ancient Greece were not allowed to compete in the Olympic Games, which were held every four years in the city of Olympia. Instead, they set up their own sporting festival, the *Heraea*. Today, women not only take part in the Olympics, but also compete professionally in a wide range of sports, from diving to darts.

Statue of a woman runner

The ice queen

The first female sports celebrity was probably Sonja Henie (1912-69) who was born in Norway. She became the national women's skating champion at the age of 11. She went on to win a gold medal for figure-skating in three consecutive Winter Olympics, in 1928, 1932 and 1936.

Sonja Henie competing at the 1932 Olympics

After her third Olympic victory, Sonja decided to become a paid performer in ice shows. Later, she changed from a sporting career to acting stardom, and made 11 Hollywood films. She was the first to wear the short skating skirts which are still worn by skaters today.

A true talent

Probably the most versatile sportswoman of modern times was an American named Mildred Didrikson (1914-56). She excelled brilliantly in almost every sport she tried, from swimming, diving and skating, to tennis, baseball and billiards.

Babe, as she was known to her fans, began her sporting career at the age of 16, when she became a professional basketball player. At the same age, she won medals for swimming, and broke athletics records in every track and field event she entered.

During the 1932 Oympics in Los Angeles, Babe was cheered to victory by her home crowd. She won an incredible six medals, in events ranging from hurdling and high jumping to throwing the javelin. On one day, she broke four world records in only three hours.

In the 1940s, Babe went on to dominate yet another sport, becoming the world's top female golfer. In 1947, she won 17 successive golf tournaments.

Babe powering to victory in the women's 100m hurdles during the 1932 Olympic Games in Los Angeles

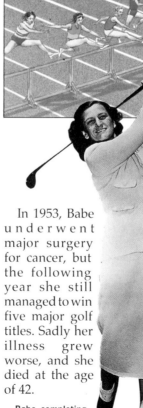

In 1953, Babe underwent major surgery for cancer, but the following year she still managed to win five major golf titles. Sadly her illness grew worse, and she died at the age of 42.

Babe completing a golfing swing

A controversial star

Australian-born Dawn Fraser (b.1937) was the first swimmer to win gold medals for the same event in three consecutive Olympics. The event was the 100m freestyle. During her career, she broke 27 world records. She estimated that she had swum a total of 16,000km (10,000 miles). Dawn became famous for her adventures both in and out of the pool.

Dawn was involved in a car crash. Tragically, her mother was killed and Dawn, who was driving, was badly injured.

In the 1960 Olympics, Dawn refused to swim in the medley relay, so she was dropped from the Australian team.

At the 1964 Games, Dawn stole a flag and a policeman's bike. She was banned from competing for ten years.

Perfect gymnasts

During the 1972 Munich Olympics, a tiny Soviet gymnast named Olga Korbut (b.1956) delighted crowds with her personality and performances. She won two individual gold medals and helped the Soviet squad win a gold team medal. Her trademark was a daring back flip in her beam routine.

Olga's dazzling displays had a huge effect on the worldwide popularity of gymnastics.

The gold medals won by Olga Korbut in the 1972 Games

Olga Korbut performing a back flip at the 1972 Olympics. The beam measures 10cm (4 inches) wide.

Olga swings her arms upward as she jumps.	She pulls her knees up to her chest to start turning.	She begins to untuck her legs to stop turning.	She lands firmly, with both feet on the beam.	She maintains her balance as she begins to stand.	She ends in a perfect finishing position.

Within months of Olga's success, many young people were inspired to take up the sport. Membership numbers of amateur clubs shot up worldwide.

In the 1976 Montreal Olympics, another young gymnast stole the limelight. Fourteen-year-old Nadia Comaneci (b.1961) of Romania became the first gymnast to achieve a perfect score of 10 out of 10. She received this score seven times, winning three individual gold medals and a team silver medal. Her most famous move was a dismount from the asymmetric bars, involving a twisting back flip.

Nadia performing her beam routine at the 1976 Olympic Games at Montreal, Canada

Number one

Martina Navratilova (b. 1956) was trained to be a world champion by her tennis-loving stepfather.

At the age of 19, Martina secretly left Czechoslovakia, after repeated arguments with the national tennis authorities, to live in America. In 1975, she became a professional player, and over the next two decades she won 167 titles and was ranked world number one for 332 weeks. By the end of 1994, she had won over $20 million in prize money.

Achievements during Martina's career

- She won 167 singles titles, more than any other player.

- She won 165 doubles titles.

- She won 19 titles at Wimbledon, having played there for 23 years.

- Between January and December 1984, she set the longest consecutive match winning streak, at 74 matches.

- She was ranked No.1 player in the world for 332 weeks.

- She was named Female Athlete of the Decade in the 1980s.

- In 1991, she became the oldest female finalist in U.S. Open history.

Martina Navratilova demonstrating the amazing strength and speed which made her a world champion

MEDIA STARS

Mass media, such as television, radio, film and the press, have been responsible for a greater, more widespread kind of fame. Some women have almost become famous for being famous.

A silent star

The first woman to dominate the movie world was American actress Mary Pickford (1893-1979). She began to act in touring shows at only five years old. She appeared in her first movie in 1909, when she was paid $5 a week to play a small role in *The Violin Maker of Cremona*.

Mary Pickford

Her acting ability and beauty soon brought her great success. She planned her movie career with care and determination. Her many successful films included *Rebecca of Sunnybrook Farm* (1917) and *Poor Little Rich Girl* (1917).

In 1916, she formed a film company which later became United Artists, one of the movie industry's leading companies. Mary was well-known for her tough business mind and became one of the richest self-made women in America, earning about $1,000,000 a year. Her vast fortune was estimated at $50 million. She worked hard however, often for more than 15 hours a day. She made over 200 silent movies and four "talkies". She decided to retire at the age of 40 years old, while she was at her peak of her profession.

In silent movies, the actors used gestures to show their feelings.

Cameras like these were used to shoot silent films.

Mary Pickford made over 200 silent movies.

Marilyn Monroe

The most famous Hollywood screen star and one of the most famous faces in history is American film star Marilyn Monroe (1926-1962).

Marilyn, whose real name was Norma Jean Baker, spent much of her childhood in foster homes, because her mother suffered from mental illness. In 1946, she became a photographer's model, but she dreamed of being a star and went to Hollywood.

After a series of small parts and a lot of publicity from the film studio she worked for, she starred in a film called *Niagara* (1952). She went on to make *How to Marry a Millionaire* (1953).

In January 1954, she married Joe di Maggio who was an American baseball star and national hero. Together they entertained American troops fighting in Korea.

In 1956, Marilyn married Arthur Miller, a famous playwright.

Marilyn often played the part of the "dumb blonde".

She went on to make some of her best films, including *Bus Stop* (1956), *The Prince and the Showgirl* (1957), and *Some Like It Hot* (1959), a comedy.

Marilyn's health, however, began to decline as she grew increasingly addicted to alcohol and sleeping pills. Tragically, she died of a drug overdose in 1962.

Marilyn singing to entertain US troops in Korea in 1954

In full voice

Lata Mangeshkar was born in Indore, central India, in 1929. Her father, a well known singer and actor, taught her to sing classical Indian music from an early age. He died when Lata was thirteen and, as the eldest of five children, she became responsible for supporting the family.

She became a "playback singer". This means she provided the singing voice of actresses in Indian musical fims. At first, her voice was considered "too thin" and the first song she recorded was cut from the movie. A year later, however, she proved her critics wrong and rose to the top of her profession.

In a career lasting for over 50 years, she sang in more than 1600 films. She appeared in *The Guinness Book of Records* for having recorded more songs than anyone else in the world.

Lata Mangeshkar has performed to audiences all over the world, and has received many awards both in India and abroad. In 1979, she was the first Asian to receive a platinum disc for her international record sales.

A poster for an Indian musical film

Madonna

Pop music has become a huge industry, with a great influence over the lives and ideas of young people. It is one area in which women's success has come close to that of men. Pop stars like Madonna are among the most famous people in the world.

Madonna performing in concert

Madonna, whose full name is Madonna Louise Ciccone, was born in the USA in 1958. She studied dance at the University of Michigan, but left her studies to seek fame and fortune in New York. She began her career working as a backing singer and club dancer, but was determined to become a superstar.

She certainly succeeded. Her first album, *Madonna,* included five hit singles. She has also starred in films, including *Desperately Seeking Susan* (1985) and *Dick Tracy* (1990).

In 1990, her controversial Blonde Ambition Tour cost 4.5 million dollars to produce. It quickly became notorious for its raunchy dance routines and outrageous costumes by the French designer Jean-Paul Gaultier.

Supermodels

The term 'supermodel' was invented by the media in the late 1980s. It was used to describe models who become celebrities in their own right, more famous than the fashion houses they represented. Supermodels such as American Cindy Crawford and German Claudia Schiffer became household names.

Many supermodels have used their fame to expand their careers beyond the fashion catwalks. They host television shows, promote beauty products and star in films.

A typical example is Naomi Campbell (b.1970), who was discovered by a model agency at the age of 15 when she was out shopping in London. As well as being a model, she has written a novel and released a record.

Naomi Campbell on the catwalk

Naomi is known as the supermodel who is most successful at selling outfits to an audience.

A LIST OF FEMALE FIRSTS

BC

2700BC
Probably the first recorded medical practitioner was a woman named Merit Ptah (Egyptian).

1503BC
The only recorded woman Pharaoh was Hatshepsut (Egyptian), who seized power from her stepson and ruled as a "king".

43BC
The first woman to lead a march for women's rights was a Greek woman named Hortensia who protested against unfair taxes on women.

AD

c.497
The first recorded female social reformer was Empress Theodora of Byzantium. She opened a home to rehabilitate prostitutes.

855
A woman may have been elected Pope. The story goes that her true sex was only discovered when she gave birth to a child in the middle of a procession through the streets of Rome.

c.1300
The first known sculptress was Sabina von Steinbach (German), who carved figures in the Cathedral at Strasbourg, France.

1766
The first woman to sail around the world was Jeanne Baret (French). She made the journey disguised as a man, on a ship called the *Etoile*.

1784
The first woman to fly in a tethered balloon was the Comtesse de Montalembert (French).

1784
The first woman to fly in an untethered balloon was Madame Thible (French).

1850
The first woman to become a model was Marie Worth (French), who wore dresses designed by her husband Charles Worth.

1867
The birth of Sarah Breedlove (American), the first self-made millionairess. Known as C.J. Walker, she made her fortune from "hair straightener".

1879
The first woman to plead before the American Supreme Court was Belva Lockwood (American).

1886
The birth of the first distinctive female Blues singer, Gertrude "Ma" Rainey (American).

1901
The first woman to pilot an airship solo was an actress named Aida d'Acosta (American).

1903
The first woman to receive a Nobel prize for physics was Marie Curie (Polish).

1905
The first woman to win a Nobel peace prize was Bertha von Suttner (Austrian). She is said to have persuaded Alfred Nobel to establish the peace prize.

1908
The first woman to set a world record for swimming was Martha Gerstung (German) for the 100m freestyle.

1909
The first woman to win a Nobel prize for literature was Selma Lagerlöf (Swedish), for her novel *Gösta Berlings*.

1909
The birth of Myra Logan (American), the first woman to operate on a human heart.

1917
The first woman to win a Pulitzer prize for biography was Laura Richards (American) for a book about her mother.

1919
The first woman pilot to fly across the Andes mountains in South America was Adrienne Bolland (French). She had to withstand severe cold and lack of oxygen.

1922
The first woman to win a Pulitzer prize for fiction was Willa Cather (American) for her novel entitled *One of Ours*.

1923
The first European woman to enter the city of Lhasa in Tibet was Alexandra David-Neel (French).

1926
The first woman to swim the English Channel was Gertrude Ederle (American).

1927
The first woman to appear in a "talkie" scene of a full-length movie was Eugenie Besserer, an American actress. The film was *The Jazz Singer*.

1928
The first woman to fly across the Atlantic was Amelia Earhart (American).

1930

The first woman to fly solo from London to Australia was Amy Johnson (British).

1930

The first female flight attendant was a nurse named Ellen Church (American).

1935

The first woman to become a sea-captain was Anna Schetinina (Soviet).

1943

The first female ambassador was Alexandra Kollontai (Soviet) who took a post in Sweden.

1947

The first woman to hold the position of foreign minister was Ana Pauker of Romania.

1952

The first woman to sail across the Atlantic single-handed was Anne Davison (British).

1953

The first woman to break the sound barrier was aviator Jacqueline Cochrane (American).

1956

The first swimmer to win the same title in three successive Olympic Games was Dawn Fraser (Australian). She was also the first woman to swim the 100m in under one minute.

1960

The first woman prime minister was Sirimavo Bandaranaike (Sri Lankan), who succeeded her husband.

1963

The first woman in space was Valentina Tereshkova (Soviet), who stayed in orbit for three days.

1966

Scientist Lise Meitner (Austrian) was the first woman to win a Fermi award. Her work proved that an atom could be split to release energy.

1968

The first African-American woman elected to the American Congress was Shirley Chisholm.

1969

The first woman to walk across the North Polar ice-cap was Myrtle Simpson (British). Unfortunately she failed in an attempt to reach the North Pole.

1969

The first woman to sail single-handed across the Pacific Ocean from Yokohama, Japan to San Diego, USA, was Sharon Adams (American).

1971

The first woman to row across the Pacific Ocean in a rowing boat was Sylvia Cook (British).

1971

The first woman judge at the European Court of Human Rights was Helga Pederson (Danish).

1973

The first modern woman bull fighter was Angela Hernandez (Spanish).

1975

The first woman to reach the summit of Mount Everest was Junko Tabei (Japanese).

1975

The first woman to receive the American Institute of Chemists award, for her work in discovering an antibiotic that was effective against disease, was Rachel Brown (American)

1976

The first woman to achieve a perfect score (10 out of 10) in gymnastics was Nadia Comaneci (Romanian).

1977

The first woman to sail successfully around the world single-handed was yachtswoman Naomi James (New Zealander).

1978

The birth of Louise Brown (English) the world's first test-tube baby.

1980

The first woman to be elected head of state was Vigdís Finnbogadóttir (Icelandic) who became the President of Iceland.

1990

Benazir Bhutto, Prime Minister of Pakistan, became the first head of state to give birth to a child while in government.

1993

Toni Morrison became the first African-American woman to be awarded the Nobel prize for literature.

1994

The first woman to win the Palme D'Or (a French award for film-making) was Jane Campion (New Zealander), with her film *The Piano*.

THE *FAMOUS WOMEN* QUIZ

The answers to all the following questions can be found between pages 195 and 239 of this book. You will also find the answers upside down at the bottom of this page.

1. What was Jeanne d'Arc accused of that led her to be burned at the stake in 1431?

2. At which notorious jail did Elizabeth Fry bring about reform?

3. What did Carry Nation smash up in order to oppose the sale of alcohol?

4. Name the following famous women:

a) b) c)

5. What nickname was Rosa Luxemburg given because of her association with communism?

6. Which famous uprising did Constance Markiewiecz take part in at St. Stephen's Green in Dublin in 1916?

7. How was suffragette Emily Davison killed?

8. Who came up with the term "birth control" to describe ways of preventing pregancy?

9. What was the name of outlaw Belle Starr's hideout?

10. What dangerous career eventually led Margarete Zelle (Mata Hari) to be executed?

11. What was the name of the route which Harriet Tubman used to lead slaves from the South to the North of the USA?

12. How did Helen Keller "listen" to the radio?

13. Which women made their famous journeys using these vehicles:

b) a)

14. What was the name of the nine-days queen who was beheaded at Mary Tudor's command?

15. What was the name of the German terrorist group led by Ulrike Meinhof and Andreas Baader?

16. Why was Mary Seacole turned down when she offered her services as a Crimean War nurse?

17. Grace Darling helped to rescue the passengers of which ship on October 7, 1838?

18. Who was the first woman to swim the English Channel?

19. How long did it take Naomi Jamés to sail around the world single-handedly in 1977?

20. The first qualified female pilot held pilot's license number 35. What was her name?

21. What was the name of the song written to commemorate Amy Johnson's solo flight across the world?

22. Who was the first woman in space?

23. In what show did Annie Oakley perform her trick shooting act?

24. Which ballerina had a meringue pie named after her?

25. Where did the poet Sappho live and write?

26. What were the real names of Currer, Ellis and Acton Bell?

27. Anne Frank's famous diary was written in the form of letters to an imaginary friend. What was the friend's name?

28. Whose autobiography was called *I Know Why the Caged Bird Sings*?

29. Leni Riefenstahl was criticized for her association with which political party?

30. What style of art was developed by Bridget Riley?

31. What substance discovered by Pierre and Marie Curie was to become important in the treatment of cancer?

32. Who discovered "jumping genes"?

33. What was the name of the sporting festival set up by the women of ancient Greece?

34. Name the women associated with the following objects:

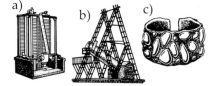

a) b) c)

INDEX

The *Inventors* picture quiz

This list reveals what the picture or cartoon beside the title of every chapter shows.

p.4 A primitive irrigation machine from Egypt called a shadoof

p.6 An Oriental clockmaker

p.8 Galileo's method of measuring the height of mountains on the moon

p.10 An idea for a steam turbine

p.12 A steam carriage

p.14 A railway policeman of 1844

p.16 Alexander the Great in a glass barrel

p.18 Icarus wearing wings

p.20 A vacuum cleaner operated using a foot pedal

p.22 Carlson's patent drawing for his photocopier

p.24 A toilet designed by John Harrington in 1596

p.26 A woodcut of a printer preparing type

p.28 Bell's first telephone

p.30 A 15th century box camera obscura

p.32 A portable radio set

p.34 An illustration showing an Edison phonograph recording a piano (1880)

p.36 An early firefighters' tower

p.38 A clockwork dental drill designed by Harrington

p.40 A hand gun of c.1400

p.42 A machine used to calculate the motion of the Sun and stars

p.44 A design for an aerial cycling machine of 1888

The publishers would like to thank the following organizations for permission to reproduce their material, or to use it as artist's reference:

Cover

Allsport; Eadward Muybridge Collection, Kingston Museum; Hulton Getty; Library of Congress, Washington, USA; Martin Breese/Retrograph Archive Ltd; Popperfoto.

Inventors

CNRI/Science Photo Library, 39; Duckworth, 44; Fox Talbot Museum, 1, 30; The Hulton Deutsch Collection, 15, 16, 19, 23, 25, 32, 41; Library of Congress, 31; Manchester University, 43; The Mansell Collection, 12; Eadward Muybridge Collection, Kingston Museum, 31; Royal Geographical Society, 7; Syndication International, 17. Elevator compartment illustration, p.24, by Peter Dennis.

Scientists

Science Museum Library, London; The Royal Society; The Ann Ronan Picture Library; Popperfoto; Mary Evans Picture Library; Bibliothèque Nationale, Paris; Dover Publications Inc. The three picture at the bottom of p.66 are based on drawings by Leonardo da Vinci in the Royal Collection, Windsor.

Explorers

Bibliothèque Nationale, Paris; The Genesis Space Photo Library; The Mansell Collection; Popperfoto.

Kings & Queens

The Ancient Art and Architecture Collection, 151, 162, 179; The Bridgeman Art Library, London, 174, 178; Express Newspapers plc, 187; The Hulton Deutsch Collection, London, 145, 154, 165, 173, 184; The Mansell Collection, London, 163, 177; The Office of Tibet, London, 154; Popperfoto, 171, 175, 181; Press Association, 187; Range Pictures Ltd, 186; The Royal Collection © Her Majesty Queen Elizabeth II, 187; Saudi Arabia Information Centre, 187; Times Books, 184

Famous Women

(l = left, r = right, t = top, b = bottom, tr = top right, bl = bottom left etc.) Allsport, 195(l), 234(l), 235(l); The Body Shop, UK, 233(tr, br), Ñahñu Indians/Antonio Vizcaino; The Brontë Society, 226; Camera Press, 229(l); Colorsport, 235(r); Corbis/Bettmann, 198(b), 207(t), 210, 231(l), 234(r), 236(tr,); Corbis/Bettmann/UPI, 199(b), 207(b), 209, 231(r), 236(br); Express Newspapers, 221; FDR Library, 205(t); Hulton Getty, 205, 206, 223(t), 236(l); Jane Addams Memorial Collection, Special Collections, The University Library, The University of Illinois at Chicago, 203(tl); Madame Tussaud's, London, 232; The Raymond Mander and Joe Mitchenson Theatre Collection, 225(l); The Maria Montessori Training Organization, AMI, London, England, 203(tr, b); Mary Evans Picture Library, 195(t), 223(b); Peter Newark's Western America, 224(b); Popperfoto, 216, 224(t), 227(b), 233(tl); Prudence Cumings Associates, 229 (t, br) *(The Maids /*Saatchi Collection)*; Punch, 215(l); Rex Features Ltd, 198(t), 199(r), 215(r), 217(r), 227(t), 233(bl), 237(t, br); Royal Geographical Society, London, 219, courtesy The Freya Stark Estate; Tate Galley, London, 228(r) *(Orpheus 1956* ©Alan Bowness, Hepworth Estate), 229(bl); Tony Stone Images, 195(r); Topham, 217(b), 228(l); Wallace Collection, London/Bridgeman Art Library, London, 197; Zoë Dominic, 225(r).

Every effort has been made to trace the copyright holders of material in this book. If any rights have been omitted, the publishers offer their apologies and will rectify this in any subsequent editions following notification.

First published in 1997 by Usborne Publishing Ltd, Usborne House, 83-85 Saffron Hill, London EC1N 8RT, England.

Copyright © 1997 Usborne Publishing Ltd.

The name Usborne and the device 🐝 are Trade Marks of Usborne Publishing Ltd.

First published in America in August 1997.
Printed in Spain.